AUSCHWITZ
1270 TO THE PRESENT

AUSCHWITZ
1270 TO THE PRESENT

*Debórah Dwork &
Robert Jan van Pelt*

W. W. NORTON & COMPANY

NEW YORK   LONDON

Dedication illustration: Bob Hanf and his score of Heine's poem "Ganz entsetzlich ungesund." Photo: Authors. Score: Music Library, The Hague Municipal Museum.

For information about permission to reproduce selections from this book, write to Permissions, W. W. Norton & Company, Inc., 500 Fifth Avenue, New York, NY 10110.

The text of this book is composed in Perpetua with display set in Michaelangelo

Composition by Crane Typesetting Service, Inc.

Manufacturing by The Courier Companies, Inc.

Book design by Chris Welch

Endpaper maps by Jacques Chazaud

Library of Congress Cataloging-in-Publication Data

Dwork, Debórah.

Auschwitz, 1270 to the present / by Debórah Dwork and Robert Jan van Pelt.

p.   cm.

Includes bibliographical references and index.

ISBN 0-393-03933-1

1. Oswiecim (Poland)—History.   2. Auschwitz (Poland : Concentration camp) I. Pelt, R.J. van (Robert Jan), 1955—   . II. Title.

D805.P7D89   1996

940.53'18—dc20   95-40275

W. W. Norton & Company, Inc., 500 Fifth Avenue, New York, N.Y. 10110

http://web.wwnorton.com

W. W. Norton & Company Ltd., 10 Coptic Street, London WC1A 1PU

1 2 3 4 5 6 7 8 9 0

This book is dedicated to our relatives who experienced a world in which exceptional evil became an unexceptional occurrence and common courtesy became an uncommon kindness.

In particular, we remember Bob Hanf, composer, painter, and poet. In hiding in Amsterdam since the spring of 1942, he was betrayed and arrested by the Security Police on 23 April 1944. He was kept at the SD offices at the Marnixstraat for four days and then brought to Westerbork, where he was incarcerated in block 67, the punishment barrack. While in Westerbork he managed to send two letters to his "aryan" brother-in-law. They revealed a remarkable detachment about his own fate. On 19 May, Bob, the other 207 members of the punishment squad, and 245 Gypsies were loaded into cattle cars and sent to the east. The transport arrived in Auschwitz on 21 May; 103 people were sent to the gas chambers immediately, and 100 women and 250 men, Bob among them, were admitted to the camp. The women were numbered A-5242 to A-5341, the men A-2846 to A-3095. According to the Information Service of the Red Cross, Bob Hanf lived until 30 September.

CONTENTS

Blueprints of Genocide follow page 320.

|

INTRODUCTION

"I WAS VERY ILL WITH PLEURISY AND TYPHUS," FRIEDA MENCO-BROMMET remembered. She was nineteen years old, Dutch, Jewish, and a prisoner in Auschwitz-Birkenau. "And then January came, January 18, 1945, and we heard shooting in the distance. The Germans came to our barrack and they said, 'Everyone march! If you don't get up, you will be shot.' So we had to go."

"I had no clothes; my mother fetched a few rags. She took me under her arm, dressed in those rags, and I fainted. I hadn't been on my feet for months. And people were walking over me." While the rest of the inmates marched on, Frieda's mother dragged her back. "We couldn't move. We stayed. And we were not shot."

Frieda, her mother, and other inmates too ill to move were about to be liberated by the Soviet army. "We were in no man's land for ten days, and my mother fed me with snow. Then the Russians came."[1]

Advance troops of Marshal Konev's First Ukrainian Front reached the town that the Germans knew as Auschwitz and the Poles as Oswiecim on Saturday, 27 January 1945. As the soldiers approached, they found a slave labor camp with 600 sick inmates. That same day the Red Army liberated 1,200 sick prisoners in a second, larger concentration camp in the Auschwitz suburb of Zasole, and 5,800 inmates (of whom Frieda and her mother were two) in an enormous compound in Birkenau, just west of the town. The SS, as Frieda said, had forced the rest of the camp, some 60,000 people, to march to the west in the middle of winter dressed, as was she, in rags.

They could have been better equipped. Between the blown-up remains of four crematoria, the Soviet liberators found a few barracks with 348,820 men's suits, 836,255 women's garments, 5,525 pairs of women's shoes, 38,000 pairs of men's shoes, 13,964 carpets, 69,848 dishes, huge quantities of toothbrushes, shaving brushes, glasses, and false teeth, and seven tons of hair. "Canada," as that section of the camp was called because of its material wealth, marked the last stage of a professionally managed process of expropriation that had begun in Germany in the late 1930s with the forced registration of Jewish-owned businesses, bank accounts, securities, insurance policies, trusts, real estate, and art collections and had ended in the early 1940s with the removal of the remaining possessions of gassed victims: clothes, shoes, glasses, the hair off their heads, and the gold caps and fillings from their teeth. Everyone in Germany knew about the first stages of dispossession; far from a secret, it was structured by law. And while few Germans may have known about the final plundering and the regular shipment of those goods to the Fatherland, a great many profited from it.

The Soviets carefully collected the remaining goods to serve as the most important exhibit in their case against monopoly capitalism. As they combed the site, they also discovered the files of the local SS-Central Building Adminis-tration, overlooked by the Germans when they dynamited the crematoria and destroyed incriminating evidence a few weeks earlier. The officers of the NKVD secured hundreds of boxes of material and handed half of them to Jan Sehn, the Polish judge commissioned to prepare the war crimes trial against the camp's SS men. They transported the rest to Moscow, where they were deposited in an archive controlled by the security police.

The Soviets used Birkenau as a prisoner-of-war camp for captured German soldiers. Within a year, the prisoners of war had been either released or transported to other camps in the Soviet Union, and the camp came under Polish government control. Needing shelter for construction workers employed in the rebuilding of ruined Warsaw, the government organized the removal of the portable horse stable barracks, which had been the last "home" of hundreds of thousands of Jews from all over Europe. The two remaining small brick ovens in each barrack, which could not be moved, left an eerie, desolate, and silent landscape of hundreds of chimneys.

THE CRUSHING NUMBER of murders, the overwhelming scale of the crime, as well as the vast, abandoned, and deserted site isolate "Auschwitz" from us. We think of it as a concentration camp enclosed on itself, separated from the rest of the world by "night" and "fog." This almost comfortable demonization relegates the camp and the events that transpired there to the realm of myth, distancing us from an all too concrete historical reality, suppressing the local, regional, and national context of the greatest catastrophe western civilization both permitted and endured, and obscuring the responsibility of the thousands of individuals who enacted this atrocity step by step. None of them was born to be a mass murderer, or an accomplice to mass murder. Each of them inched his way to iniquity.

Auschwitz, 1270 to the Present reestablishes Auschwitz as just another place which became what it did by ordinary people using standard procedures: requisition forms, transportation vouchers, planning permissions, bills of sale, bills of receipt. Tragically, these ordinary people had extraordinary ambitions: to recover the chimera they called Germany's lost past and to re-create an equally illusionary racially pure nation. Most histories of Auschwitz begin in 1940, but the men who established the concentration camp, like the great majority of their compatriots in the 1920s and 1930s, saw Auschwitz in a German history that had commenced seven centuries earlier. Founded by Germans in 1270, Auschwitz was lost to the Reich in 1457 and, as it went to Austria, almost returned in 1772. It would have had the history of any other border town, but for the late-nineteenth-century German obsession with what was called "the German East." Just as nineteenth-century European Americans were preoccupied with fulfilling their manifest destiny in the West, and Edwardian England was busy coloring the globe pink, the Germans turned to the East. The land beckoned and history called. While the prairies and plains betokened opportunity and promise for European Americans, what we now call Poland and nineteenth-century Germans called the German East signified a return to the pristine, lost past of the Teutonic Order and Frederick the Great, and heralded a paradise to be regained. "The German East is our nostalgia and our fulfillment," the minister of propaganda, Josef Goebbels, explained to Germany's young people, and for once he was correct.[2]

By the 1920s and 1930s the American frontier had become the stuff of Hollywood movies. For contemporary Germans, however, the promise of the German East, the call of their medieval and Prussian forebears, their entitlement to *Lebensraum,* or living space, the mission of forging a *Volk,* a nation of Germanic peoples, and their ideology of racial purity, which cast out everyone who was not physically perfect and genetically Germanic, was tangible and actual. It was the object of political rhetoric and the subject of military considerations. We may not take the Teutonic Order, Frederick the Great, *Lebensraum,* or the *Volk* seriously but, as we shall see, Adolf Hitler, Reichsführer-SS Heinrich Himmler, the commandant of Auschwitz, Rudolf Höss, and millions of Germans did. That history, and those objectives, informed their thinking and prompted their actions.

THE FUNDAMENTAL QUESTION of why Auschwitz was the site of a violent concentration camp designed to terrorize and incarcerate Poles, and why this camp became an extermination camp for Jews, is the focus of this book. The hundreds of architectural plans for the camp preserved in Auschwitz and Moscow, as well as blueprints and papers in the town, provincial, and federal German archives make it clear that, from the time the concentration camp was established in May 1940 until the Germans abandoned it in January 1945, the camp acquired a number of different functions. This consecutive evolution is captured in the designs and documents. A unique historical source, this material elucidates the possibilities considered and the options chosen, the ambitions as well as the outcome.

What we call Auschwitz was not a natural disaster. Human beings, mostly German and mostly male, transformed the site into a killing field incrementally. They developed the camp in stages, changing its role and adding operations. We shall examine this process, and through the oral histories of survivors as well as memoirs, depositions, and autobiographies we shall explore its impact on the daily lives of the camp inmates.

By the end of 1941, in the wake of Operation Barbarossa, the Judeocide was well under way in German-occupied Soviet territories. Gas vans were in operation near Chelmno, and stationary extermination camps at Belzec, Sobibor, and Treblinka were under construction. Auschwitz, however, did not yet figure as a possible center of genocide. The first transport of Jews was shipped to Birkenau in March 1942. These were trainloads of relatively young and able people, and everyone was put to work. When old people and children who were not fit for slave labor began to arrive in July, the SS introduced the system of selection on a platform adjacent to the Auschwitz station (the *Judenrampe*) and the immediate extermination of those who were deemed useless. By midsummer of 1942 Birkenau had become a killing site for all Jews except those granted a temporary stay of execution to allow them to carry on working in the camp or in German industries elsewhere. This was the last function of Auschwitz.

Korzenicz Flu.

Castrina Flu.

Kopcza wicze

Libias

Zabrea

Boissowy

Biasowicze

Obelna

Babicze

Bobrek

Gromiecz

PSCZINA

Wolia

Bizezicka

Brzo: zowka

Char mezij

OZW IECZIN

Dwory

Maruicze

Czwiklicz

Gora

Raisko

Podbo rze

Wlosie

Pize

Wislapolska

Brzescze

Przecze sin.

Poremba

Zawadka

Jawisso wicze

Skiedzi eu.

Grodziecz

Goczalkowicze

Rdzawa

Zebrac

Dam: ko wicze.

Polanck

Leki

Osick

Malecz

Gla.

Starawicz

Bielanj

Kanezuga

Sabrzeg

Besti wna.

Wilsano wicze

Sola Flu.

Nouawicz

Witkown ze.

Rud: zicza.

Lgotka

Checho wincze.

Kamoro wicze

Ianko wicze

Hekzato wicz

KENTI

Bol wic

Mlownic za

Mied zirecz

Masenicza

Mazanczo wicze

Biertolio wicze

Lipnik

Pizarzo wicze

Czamec

Piestreze

Rastropcza.

Stargbi elsko.

BIELSKON.

Halcz: now.

Buzikou

Kober nicze.

Porabka

Kowalie

Bielowicz ko.

Laza

Kamie mieza

Miklusso wicze

Kozi

Mied: zigorodhije.

Pogorz

Grodziecz

Iaworze

Bizczy

Wilko: wicze.

SKOCZOW.

Gorky

Buzcza Flu.

Lodwigo wicze.

Starzi swiecz.

Mermaː nicze.

ARS

Brenna

ZIWIECZ.

Mossczenicza

Mierodzim

Vstronie

Wissula Flu.

Sporys.

Kossoraba flu.

Sola flu.

Hunga

PART ONE

NOSTALGIA AND FULFILLMENT

CHAPTER 1

AN ORDINARY TOWN

Auschwitz used to be an ordinary town. Ordinary people lived there, and tourists visited to see the castle, the churches, the large medieval market square, and the synagogue. After a nice day that perhaps included a light lunch in Hotel Zator, they wrote postcards to family or friends while enjoying a cup of tea in Hotel Herz. In the early twentieth century there were cards for all tastes. One depicts a peacock with sights of the town on its spread tail. This relic of local pride is captioned with the cheerful words *Pozdrowienie z Oswiecima* and *Gruss aus Oswiecim*—"Greetings from Auschwitz."

In the late 1940s a very different postcard was sold in Auschwitz. The bird that had framed the earlier views had disappeared, as had the pictures of the medieval monuments and the bilingual greeting. Captioned in Polish, Russian, French, and English, the text reads, "Model of crematorium section." It depicts a plaster model of crematorium II, with plaster people descending a staircase into an already overcrowded underground space: the center of the "concentrational" city of silence.[1] For many people, it represents the more than one million human beings killed in the suburbs of the town of Auschwitz between May 1940 and February 1945. For others, it is the Holocaust of six million Jews. For Poles, it stands for the death of six million of their compatriots: three million gentile and three million Jewish Poles. For still others, it signifies evil.

Postcard. Oswiecim, ca. 1905. Towarzytwo Milosnikow Ziemi Oswiecomskiej. Depicted,
from left, *the old market square, a view of the town from the castle, the ruins
of the Dominican church, the castle, and the convent next to the new market.*

Most people who know of Auschwitz think of it as a concentrational city,
a place closed in upon itself, its victims, and its executioners. Its sole connection
to the outside world was the infrastructure of genocide Raul Hilberg has
described in his magisterial *The Destruction of the European Jews*—a technology
centered on the spatial-temporal-financial grid of the European railway system,
with its timetables and special group fares for transports of over 400 Jews.
For most of us, this necropolis of night and fog with its terminus that received
trains from all over Europe has very little connection to an ordinary town
named Oswiecim—the prewar Oswiecim and the Oswiecim of today. Now
a moderately prosperous city in south-central Poland, Oswiecim has become
one of the most important tourist sites in the country, but few if any of these
visitors pay much attention to the castle or other monuments. Too tense on
their way to the concentration camp museum, and too shocked afterwards,
they have no time for the town's other history. And so the camp remains
imprisoned in its own universe. There is no bridge to link the before of seven
centuries of ordinary history with the after of five years of extraordinary
suffering, the here of the town of Oswiecim and the there of the *Konzentrationslager*, concentration camp, at Auschwitz.

*Postcard. Oswiecim, 1952. Authors. Part of the plaster model of crematorium II as exhibited
in block 4 of the State Museum Auschwitz-Birkenau. A group of Jewish deportees
entering the underground undressing room, which led, via a vestibule, to the underground gas
chamber.*

This book examines that missing link. Our focus is the wartime history of
Auschwitz, when an ordinary town with an ordinary 700-year-old history
evolved into an extraordinary killing center with unique mechanisms for death.
Our aim is to reconstruct the historical and ideological context that shaped
the views of those who were interested in the history of Auschwitz and its
future: men like Heinrich Himmler, who wanted to mold the town and surrounding region, and the architect Hans Stosberg, whose job it was to design
German Auschwitz. Stosberg sent a New Year's greeting card to friends in
December 1941, and the four lines he wrote illuminate the mythology and
ideology that framed his vision. "In the year 1241 Silesian knights, saviors of
the Reich, warded off the Mongolian assault at Wahlstatt. In that same century
Auschwitz was founded as a German town. Six hundred years later [*sic*] the
Führer Adolf Hitler fends off the Bolshevik menace from Europe. This year,
1941, the construction of a new German city and the reconstruction of the
old Silesian market was planned and initiated."[2]

ZUM
JAHRESWECHSEL
1941-1942

WÜNSCHE ICH MEINEN GÖNNERN UND FREUNDEN
GESUNDHEIT UND GLÜCK
UND GUTES GELINGEN BEI JEDEM BEGINNEN

Hans Stosberg

DER SONDERBEAUFTRAGTE FÜR DEN
GENERALBEBAUUNGSPLAN DER STADT
AUSCHWITZ

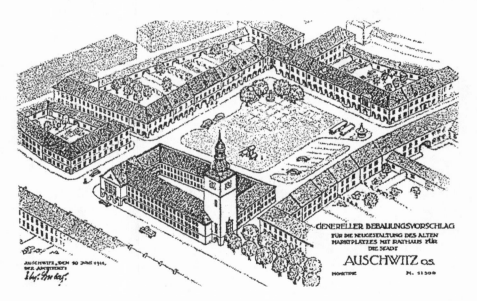

GENERELLER BEBAUUNGSVORSCHLAG
FÜR DIE NEUGESTALTUNG DES ALTEN
MARKTPLATZES MIT RATHAUS FÜR
DIE STADT
AUSCHWITZ O.S.

*Two sides of the double-folded New Year's card created and sent by the German architect
Hans Stosberg, December 1941. Provincial Archive, Katowice.* Front: *"For the
change of year 1941–1942 I wish all my patrons and friends health and happiness and
a good conclusion for every beginning."* The building with the tower is the new
town hall, which incorporates the terrace of houses on the north side of the Auschwitz Ring.

This idea of historical repetition originated in the early 1920s when, pariahs shunned by the Western world, Weimar Germans turned to the East, where they had achieved great victories during World War I and where, they believed, they had suffered grave injustice afterwards. The notion of repetition became even more powerful after the Polish campaign of 1939, when western Poland had been either annexed to the Reich or occupied. As Franz Lüdtke, the head of the main section responsible for the German East in the National Socialist Leadership Congress, explained in 1941, in the Middle Ages Polish kings, bishops, and landowners had competed to attract German immigrants. The newcomers had cleared the land, founded towns and villages, and brought their law and culture with them. In return, they had received an inalienable title to the soil which, seven centuries later, was still valid. National Socialist Germany had inherited their legacy and would complete what the medieval settlers had begun.[3]

The principle of repetition was transformed into a rhetoric of repetition, officially sanctified by Josef Goebbels's propaganda apparatus. In January 1941 Goebbels instructed the press to eschew the word "colonization" in their articles about the Germanization of the East, and to adopt a terminology that stressed the concepts of recovery, restoration, reclamation, and retrieval.[4] Conducted by Goebbels, the refrain was sung with different voices and in different settings, but it was always the same: the Germans had taken it upon themselves to complete the project of their ancestors. Their turn to the East was a return. An SS handbook repeating this theme delineated some of its consequences.

> Poland was defeated after an 18-day military campaign. This was the reward for centuries of German work on this eastern soil. What German diligence had created in the course of time returned to its original purpose, and once again became part of the German *Lebensraum*. The battle had to pull down much, had to break and destroy. The *reconstruction* will consolidate the gains of battle, and make it into an enduring part of the Greater German space. **For centuries the German East has been the German people's destiny**. **And in the centuries to come it will remain so**. . . .
>
> The *new ordering of the space of the East* not only affects the *German-Polish problem* and that caused by other ethnic minorities but, because in the East Jewry can be found in its most concentrated form, also raises the *Solution*

Illustrations of German castles in the East accompanying an article written by Reichsführer-SS *Heinrich Himmler in* Das Schwarze Korps *of 23 January 1941. Sterling Memorial Library, Yale University. These castles, symbols of German culture and monuments to the Germans' will to persist in the East, had preserved the legacy of the medieval German Push to the East. With great satisfaction Himmler noted that now the fields surrounding them once again had become German and that once again Germans had begun to build in a manner that honored the legacy of their forebears.*

to the Jewish Problem. **The Jews did not go to the East as colonizers, but as parasites. . . . Europe's East became a reservoir and launching pad of Jewry. New hordes of Jews repeatedly descended from the East on the world. The hordes of Jews who overflowed Germany and Austria after the World War also came from the East. . . .**

The problem of *fighting epidemics* in the East is closely connected with the solution to the Jewish Problem. Epidemics have always been more frequent and stronger in eastern Europe than in other areas of the continent. . . . These originated from the *ghettos.* To gain control over this curse we had to launch a total war in the East against epidemics. This involved inoculation and other sanitary measures. . . .

Jewry was one of the chief causes of the rotten situation in former Poland, and the cooperation of Jewry and Poles produced the notorious *"Polish State of Affairs."* During the Polish campaign even the simplest German soldier discovered for himself the nature of this Polish State of Affairs. *In the regained areas in the East a comprehensive reconstruction takes place which aims to overcome*

this Polish State of Affairs and to replace it with German order and German culture,
to lift up the suppressed and enslaved Germans from the East, and, finally, to link
this soil now and forever with the German nation.[5]

The relationship between the reconstruction of Poland as a land of German
destiny, the creation of a New Order, and the so-called Final Solution to the
Jewish Problem was clear and unequivocal: if Poland was to take its place in
the German living space as ''the German people's destiny,'' the Jews would
have to leave.

NATIONAL SOCIALIST HISTORIANS of medieval German settlement provided people like Stosberg, Lüdtke, Goebbels, and the hacks in the SS Education Department with the ammunition that transformed a not necessarily vicious thesis of
an ideological symmetry between the Middle Ages and the twentieth century
into a genocidal weapon. Historians played a major role in forging a seamless
unity between the immutable power of the past and the irresistible force of
ideology. This combative history began with an appropriately mythic Golden
Age, when the area occupied today by southern Sweden, Denmark, the Netherlands, Germany, and Poland was settled by Germanic tribes. For the National
Socialists, this millennium of Germanic settlement was a Nordic paradise of
blood and soil in which a racially pure people lived in harmony with the land
that Providence had given them. But then, as was inevitable, paradise was lost.
Hun raids forced these Germanic peoples to withdraw to the west. Slav tribes
followed in the wake of the Huns, and they eked out a marginal existence in
the vacated lands. According to the National Socialists, the cultural regression
of the area under the Slavs proved that the Germans were entitled to that
land—indeed, that they had never lost the title to the area between the Elbe
and the Vistula.[6]

Their interpretation of the subsequent history of the region substantiated
their own claims. To the National Socialists, the next seven hundred years
were a political and economic wasteland until Polish dukes in the thirteenth
century invited Germans to establish independent German towns within their
domains.[7] Realizing German immigration was key to the development of their
duchies, they competed to attract German clergymen who were comparatively
well educated and committed to a stable government, German knights whose
disciplined training compensated for the lack of mobilizable manpower, German craftsmen who brought better production techniques, German merchants
who exploited the economic potential of roads and waterways, and, most

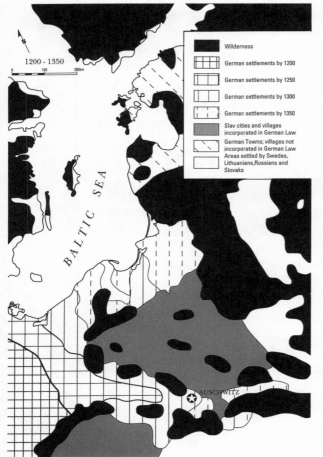

The eastern movement of German settlement between 1200 and 1350. By Robert Jan van Pelt and Don Bonner. In the north, the German Push to the East took two routes. One began in Brandenburg and went southeast along the Sudeten Mountains to Upper Silesia; the other also began in Brandenburg, and went northeast to the Lower Vistula and the land of the Teutonic Order (upper right). *Bohemia, sheltered by mountains, and Greater Poland, shielded by impassable marshes, successfully resisted Germanization. By the mid-fourteenth century, Silesia, Pomerania, and East Prussia were thoroughly Germanized; the eastern border of continuous German settlement had reached a line that roughly coincided with the eastern border of the German Reich in 1937. To the east of this line towns ruled by Polish nobility but dominated by German merchants and craftsmen, such as Cracow, Lublin, and Warsaw, were united with villages inhabited by Poles in* Weichbilder *(urban areas) structured by German law. To the north, in Livonia, towns ruled and inhabited by Germans, such as Riga, Reval (Talinn), and Narva, were not supported by a* Weichbild.

important of all, German Cistercian monks and German farmers whose agricultural knowledge was superior to that of their Polish counterparts. Hundreds of thousands of Germans moved to the East. In Silesia alone, 175,000 Germans settled between 1200 and 1335, where they established 1,200 villages, 130 towns, and twelve major monasteries. By the mid-fourteenth century, Silesia, Pomerania, and East Prussia were thoroughly Germanized; the eastern border of continuous German settlement had reached a line that roughly coincided with the eastern border of the German Reich in 1937. The systematic settlement of Germans led to their dominance over the area, which twentieth-century Germans applauded.

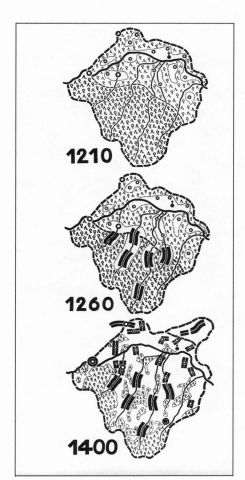

1210

1260

1400

Standardized development of Silesian territory. Trampler, Am Volksboden und Grenze (1935). Sterling Memorial Library, Yale University. German settlement followed a standard pattern. The first diagram depicts various Slav villages (circles) of about ten farms along streams and rivers. The forests on the higher grounds were not yet developed. The peasants lacked horse fodder and depended on a team of oxen to plow the land; this primitive technology could not cope with the heavy soil in the wood. Furthermore, they had no right to purchase the freehold on the land; it belonged to the local duke, who granted them use only. In exchange, they were obliged to perform various services. The second diagram shows the opening of the forests and the creation of the first German villages on the high grounds (two thick parallel lines). This move upland was organized by the locator *(settler)*, the medieval predecessor of the modern real-estate developer. The locator *was under contract with the local lord to develop unused land. He went to the more densely populated areas of western Germany and, offering peasants advantageous terms of settlement, encouraged them to return with him to Silesia. It was the* locator *who laid out the new village, and each farmer was given an equal amount of land. New surveying techniques allowed an area to be opened systematically by the establishment of villages as close as three or four miles from each other, with twenty to a hundred farms per village. Each village followed a standardized pattern peculiar to the region of settlement. In the southern part of Upper Silesia, for example, the so-called* Waldhufendorf, *or forest-farm village, prevailed. The* Waldhufendorf *sacrificed a sense of village community for economic rationality and the independence of each individual farmer.* Waldhufendörfer *stretched for miles along the road, with farms at both sides at regular three-hundred-foot intervals. The Germans' farming methods and equipment allowed them to move upland and produced a surplus for the first time. Towns were established with the new wealth. The third diagram depicts the establishment of a town along the main river, and the legal incorporation and Germanization of the remaining Polish villages in the river valley. Linked with five to fifteen surrounding villages in a social unit based on the exchange of goods and services, an economic unit arose that the Germans call* Weichbild, *or urban area. The formation of a* Weichbild *was the culmination of a social system of colonization that began with the* locator.

Wood engraving by Bodo Zimmermann depicting the Silesian landscape. Pudelko, Wir Schlesier! *(1937). Sterling Memorial Library, Yale University.*

There is no doubt that the Germans made a great contribution to the development of the area between the Oder and the Vistula, but National Socialists transformed a legitimate chronicle of past achievement into a pernicious caricature of German-Polish relations. To them every field, every farm, every village, and every town in Poland was the product of German toil. Ewald Liedecke, the chief planner of the newly (1939) created province of Danzig–West Prussia, dismissed the very possibility that anything the Poles had built was worth his attention. He declared unequivocally that every trace of culture within Poland was the result of German achievement: the remains of a German cottage testified to a higher culture than a newly built Polish government palace.[8] This sentiment was expressed even in the stamps issued in the occupied Polish territories. Portraying buildings such as the famous Cracow gate in Lublin, the town hall of Sandomierz, and the Wawel castle in Cracow, the architectural iconography was officially explained as a celebration

The German East, 1300. Map by Robert Jan van Pelt and Don Bonner. In the 1930s German scholars argued that the territorial expansion of Germany and of Poland had been in conflict since the Middle Ages. Germany sought to control all the lands along the southern and eastern Baltic coast. The maritime power of the Hanseatic League, which linked the towns of Lübeck, Danzig (Gdansk), Riga, Reval (Tallinn), and Narva, consolidated Germany's position. The Polish thrust proceeded from the Polish heartland along the Warta and middle and upper Vistula rivers and sought to gain access to the sea in Pomerania. When the Teutonic Order gained control over eastern Pomerania in the fourteenth century, it cut Poland's access to the Baltic. The conflict between Germany's determination to hold the whole of the eastern Baltic coast and Poland's need for secure access to the sea was to sour German-Polish relations in the fifteenth, eighteenth, and twentieth centuries, and it triggered the Second World War.

of "German sensibility, German power, German creativity, German will. [The depicted structures] prove that everything in this land that is beautiful and noble, powerful and enduring, meaningful and magnificent is of German origin and a symbol of the German hold over this space."[9]

Auschwitz was neither beautiful nor noble, meaningful or magnificent, but it was German, and it was relatively prosperous.[10] Established in 1270, it had become a midsize market town of 120 to 200 houses by 1300. It was the regional center of the eastern part of the duchy of Teschen, and the duke granted the town the right to become a lead and salt depot. With this economi-

Government General stamps, 1940. Authors. The Cracow Gate of Lublin and the Wawel Castle in Cracow. While the Germans were partly justified in claiming the Cracow Gate, their title to the Wawel was fictitious. The residence of Polish royalty, it did not belong to the German town of Cracow. The depicted Renaissance courtyard was built by an Italian architect.

cally important privilege, Auschwitz acquired local significance. The duke also granted the town the right to levy a toll on the two most traveled bridges over the Vistula and Sola Rivers. Located directly on one trade route (Vienna–Olmütz–Ostrau–Cracow) and slightly off another (Leipzig–Breslau–Oppeln–Cracow–Lemberg), Auschwitz was well placed to profit from the economic boom of the late thirteenth and early fourteenth centuries.

When the duchy of Teschen was divided in 1316 and the area east of the Biala River became the independent duchy of Auschwitz, the town of Auschwitz had 1,300 inhabitants, with another 700 in the immediately adjacent Polish villages of Babitz, Birkenau, Dwory, Harmese, and Rajsko. Neustadt, along the lower Skawa, was slightly larger, with a population of 1,400. The two small market towns upstream, Liebenwerde, along the upper Sola, and Frauenstadt, along the upper Skawa, were much smaller, with 400 and 285 inhabitants respectively. These towns comprised the four corners of German settlement; to the north and west were older Polish villages. However prosperous its towns, the new duchy was too small to maintain itself politically. A pawn in a power struggle between Poland, Bohemia, and Hungary, Auschwitz joined the Reich in 1327.

Paradoxically, the official absorption of the duchy into the Reich coincided with the decline of the German presence there. Arable land had begun to run out, and the duchy of Auschwitz ceased to be attractive to newcomers. The Black Death (1349) and a series of other epidemics led to a massive decrease in the population of Europe, and German emigration from the west to the east came to a complete halt.[11] Furthermore, throughout Europe the collapse

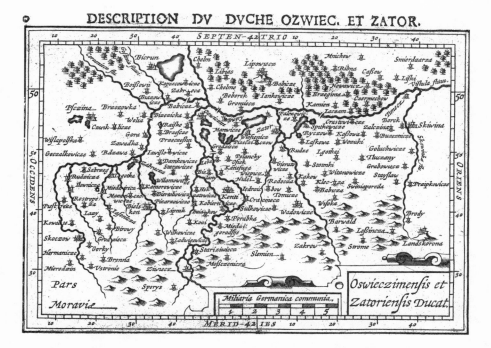

The duchy of Oswiecim and Zator, by Stanislas Porebski, Bertius, Tabularum geographicarum (1616). Around 1000 Auschwitz (center) and Silesia (left) were incorporated into the Polish state. The area was organized into castellanies ruled by local governors, or castellans, from strategically located strongholds. The castellany in Auschwitz counted some 3,000 inhabitants, who lived in small villages sprinkled along the Vistula (top). In 1241 a Mongol army passed through the castellany on its way west, leaving a trail of destruction. In response, the local duke initiated a development program in the sparsely populated castellany to attract German settlers. These new immigrants established two towns: Auschwitz (Ozwiczin), adjacent to the old castle along the Sola, and, upriver, Liebenwerde (Kenti). Each town was surrounded by dependent villages. The duchy of Oppeln was divided in 1282, and Auschwitz fell to Duke Miezko of Teschen. He continued to woo German settlers and granted them the right to establish the town of Neustadt (Zator) on the lower Skava River. Another town, Frauenstadt (Wadowicze), followed. By 1300 the four towns and their dependent villages occupied an area of 450 square miles. The duchy of Teschen was divided in 1316, and the eastern half became the duchy of Auschwitz. With 17,000 inhabitants the new duchy was economically viable, especially after a new wave of immigrants founded the market town of Saybusch (Ziwiecz) along the Sola, and nine villages. But the duchy was too small to maintain itself politically, and became part of the Holy Roman Empire. The eastern tip of the empire, the duchy of Auschwitz was separated from Poland on the north (Septentrio) by the Vistula (Vistula fluvius) and on the east (Oriens) by the Skavina (Skawinka flu). To the south (Meridies) the Beskid range of the Carpathians formed the border with the Slovak region of the kingdom of Hungary. To the west (Occidens) Auschwitz was bounded by two other Silesian duchies incorporated in the Reich. Across from the Biala and Vistula Rivers stretched Teschen (south) and Ratibor (north).

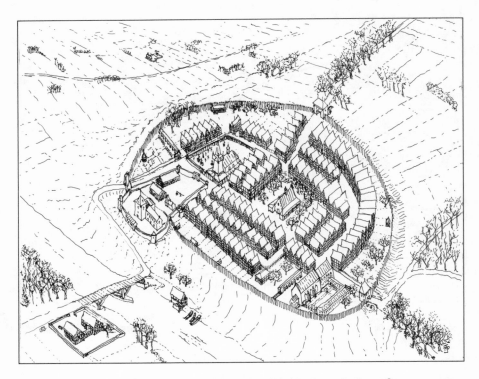

Bird's-eye view of Auschwitz, ca. 1350. Drawing by Philip Doele on the basis of reconstruction by Robert Jan van Pelt. Authors. Like all the settlements in the German East, the original plan of Auschwitz reflected an austerity comparable to the bold geometric layout of the Walfhufendorf. The town was based on a rational grid of main streets with a large, square market and town hall in the center. The wooden parish church is located north of the square. It was replaced by a stone church in the early fifteenth century. The castle of the duke of Auschwitz guards the bridge over the Sola. The large church near the southern gate is the Dominican church. The area between the castle, the square, the Dominican church, and the river became the Jewish neighborhood in the sixteenth century. By the nineteenth century it supported three synagogues.

of prices of agricultural products and a rise in urban wages initiated a protracted agricultural depression. Farmers left the countryside for the towns. In Upper Silesia, German farmers abandoned the homesteads their ancestors had carved out of the wilderness. Many returned to the west, where opportunities beckoned.

Poland, however, weathered the plague better than did other nations, and

*The Dominican church at Auschwitz, ca. 1940. Towarzytwo Milosnikow Ziemi
Oswiecomskiej. The first duke of Auschwitz invited Dominican preachers to come
to Auschwitz around 1320, and he and his wife sponsored the construction of their
large church in the southwest corner of the town. It became the burial place of the Auschwitz
dynasty (1316–1457). Destroyed by the Swedes in 1656, the church was rebuilt at
the beginning of this century by the Salesian fathers as the center of a mission
to provide wayward boys with education and apprenticeships.*

had a population surplus. As Germans left the villages, Polish peasants moved
in. The towns too were Polonized. In the duchy of Auschwitz the five erstwhile
German urban centers were known from then on by their Polish names:
Oswiecim (Auschwitz), Kety (Liebenwerde), Zator (Neustadt), Wadowice
(Frauenstadt), and Zywiec (Saybusch). But they did not prosper. Too small
to profit from the boom economy of the larger cities, these market towns
shared the economic decline of the countryside.

By the early 1400s criminals roamed the abandoned countryside. The duke
of Oswiecim did not have the resources to defend his interests and, placing
himself under the Polish King Jagiello's protection, he initiated Oswiecim's
political turn to the East. This move was consolidated by King Casimir IV of
Poland, who bought the rights to the duchy in 1457. Now separated from the

The German East, 1400. Map by Robert Jan van Pelt and Don Bonner. Having gained control of Pomerenia and Silesia, the Germans seemed to have a very strong position in the East. But the conversion of the Lithuanians (1386) obviated the need for the Teutonic Order as a crusading organization, and German knights ceased to join. The marriage of the Grand Duke Jagiello of Lithuania and Queen Jadwiga of Poland and the subsequent Polish-Lithuanian political union created a powerful state committed to acquiring access to the sea. In 1466 Poland-Lithuania annexed West Prussia and reduced East Prussia to a Polish fief; a century later it acquired most of the remaining lands of the order in Livonia.

other Upper Silesian duchies and from the Reich, Oswiecim drifted towards full integration into its neighbor. The increasingly loud Polish call for unity also encouraged the unification of Oswiecim with Poland, as did the acquisition of land and positions of power by Polish noblemen. The duchy was incorporated in the province of Cracow in 1564, completing the almost universal Polonification of this area.[12]

Oswiecim prospered during the first years of Polish rule, despite four large city fires which damaged most of the town and the castle. The duties on salt

Coats of arms of the duchy of Zator and the duchy of Oswiecim. Municipal Archive, Oswiecim. Both have the Silesian eagle, with a Z for Zator and an O for Oswiecim. On the death of Duke Casimir of Oswiecim (1433) his sons divided their father's realm into a duchy of Oswiecim and a duchy of Zator. It was reunited under the Polish crown as the duchy of Oswiecim and Zator in 1490.

and the bridge tolls over the Vistula and the Sola remained the major source of income. An important border crossing between Poland and Silesia, Oswiecim grew into a town of five hundred houses. Two hundred craftsmen made a living in the town, and the income derived from trade and industry generated enough money to build a new town hall on the Ring, restore the parish church and the Dominican church, and build a new synagogue. Jewish settlement had begun in the mid-fifteenth century, and by the time of Oswiecim's incorporation into Poland its Jewish population was so numerous that King Zygmunt II Augustus felt obliged to issue a decree to prevent further growth. Nevertheless, until 1941 Jews would form the majority of the population of Oswiecim.

The Jews had emigrated from western and central Europe at the invitation of the Polish kings, who hoped they would form an entrepreneurial middle class. Many Jews had come. The Crusades (1095–1215) had encouraged violent pogroms, and a small number had sought a new future in the East. The Black Death had led to new pogroms—350 Jewish communities were destroyed in Germany alone—and the rivulet had become a large stream. While the Jews enjoyed communal autonomy and the freedom to engage in

Tombstones of the Jewish cemetery, Oswiecim. Photo by Ryszard Kozlowski. Authors.

While the Jews enjoyed communal autonomy and the freedom to engage in all trade and industry throughout Poland, they could not participate in the political life of the towns, cities, or the nation. They were powerless in the ensuing struggles between the monarchy, the church, the nobility, and the town burghers, and their weak situation worsened as time progressed.

As it transpired, Poland too was weak, and her situation also worsened. Russian-Cossack forces laid waste to northeastern Poland in the mid-seventeenth century and, as the east of the country burned, the Swedish king grasped the opportunity to destroy Polish power in the Baltic. The Swedes invaded Poland and a garrison occupied Oswiecim on 30 October 1655. After an unsuccessful uprising by the local population, the Swedish soldiers burned the town.[13]

Oswiecim never recovered from the Swedes' punishment. At the end of the seventeenth century a little over three hundred people eked out a meager existence in the twenty or so habitable houses that remained. The cataclysmic impact of the war could not be overcome in Oswiecim, or indeed in the majority of Polish towns. Poland collapsed and in 1772 was partitioned by

Partition of Poland. Edwards,
The Polish Captivity *(1863).*
Sterling Memorial Library,
Yale University. Left to right:
Catherine the Great, Maria
Theresa, Stanislas Augustus
Poniatowski, and Frederick the
Great.

of its population were appropriated. In Lüdtke's opinion the neighboring powers were not at fault. "Poland, the oppressor of its citizens and peasants, the
promotor of Jews, the strangler of German civilization, the toy of the Jesuits,
the playground of self-seeking aristocratic factions, was condemned to destruction. . . . Poland was to blame for its own death."[14]

HISTORY PROVIDES THE raw material for nationalism, and German nationalists
like Franz Lüdtke interpreted the decline and ultimate disappearance of Poland
in the second half of the eighteenth century as not only a result of particular
circumstances but the reflection of an innate inability of the Poles to take
care of themselves. They were guilty of, as the nineteenth-century nationalist
historian Heinrich von Treitschke put it, "the wild doings which we colloqui-
ally call 'Polish inn-keeping.' "[15] Hitler used precisely this rhetoric to justify
the German occupation of Poland. In his Reichstag speech of 6 October 1939,

Hitler reminded his audience that in 1919 Poland had taken German lands developed over many centuries. In less than twenty years these fertile lands had been reduced to wasted prairies, and the main waterway, the Vistula, had become, depending on the season, either an unruly stream or a dried-up rivulet. Towns, villages, and roads had fallen into a state of disrepair. The situation in Poland had become a paradigm of "Polish inn-keeping."[16] In short, the country needed a firm German hand to set things right.

In the five years that followed, National Socialists proved conclusively that they had little in common with their ancestors six centuries earlier. If the medieval farmers and merchants had brought a measure of prosperity to the Polish lands, their descendants brought poverty: between 1939 and 1944 the real wages of the average Polish worker dropped to 8 percent of the prewar level. And while the early German settlers lived peaceably with their neighbors, the twentieth-century German invaders would not tolerate their existence. As an expensively produced, richly illustrated government-sponsored magazine about life in German-administered Poland boasted in 1944, "Millions of Jews

A *"Jewish house in Galicia."* Das Generalgouvernement *(1944). Authors.*

A "ghetto Jew." Das Generalgouvernement (1944). Authors. "Both politically and ethnically half-breeds, the cosmopolitan and nomadic Jews were able to persist in the diaspora only because they always received new blood from the Polish ghettos," the caption explains. "The Jewish type that personifies the 'Non-Human' developed in the Galician ghetto. The Polish Jew is the rubbish of humanity. He seeks to live a life with neither form nor culture, an amoral life driven by animal-like urges, a lawless and anarchic life that reflects the unbridled freedom of the instincts. He finds his best opportunities in chaos, in soulless matter, in the swamp."

lived amidst other ethnic groups in the territory of today's Government General. Here, in the breeding ground of modern World Jewry, the Jewish Problem reached its zenith. . . . We had a moral obligation to wipe out the breeding places of the most horrendous, the most inhuman, and the most beastly vice that, arising from Poland, infested the whole world. It was a task which, in its fulfillment, was meant to bring salvation to the whole of humanity."[17]

CHAPTER 2

THE PRUSSIAN CONNECTION

A FAMOUS NINETEENTH-CENTURY GERMAN HISTORIAN ONCE WROTE THAT history should record "how it actually happened." Shortly after the collapse of the Third Reich, a famous twentieth-century German historian wrote that in the face of the unprecedented atrocities committed by the self-declared Nation of Poets and Philosophers, the dictum should read, "How was it possible?"

No one after the war would have a one-word response, but many intellectuals in the prewar and war period believed that National Socialism, the militarism of Germany, her ruthlessness and violence, and the principle of absolute obedience to orders were the legacy of Prussia. Prussianism, the German-Jewish émigré writer Emil Ludwig declared in 1940, had hijacked the country of Goethe, Kant, and Beethoven. Prussianism was the root of Hitlerism, and the war against National Socialist Germany was a struggle against "Prussia."[1] Summarizing a whole literature on the issue, the Englishman Samuel Dickinson Stirk wrote that "without the 'Prussianization' of Germany . . . there would be no National Socialism; without Frederick the Great, Bismarck, Moltke, Hindenburg, and the other great Prussians there would be no Hitler."[2]

If to those who did not support the National Socialist cause Prussia embodied a threat, to Germans it represented self-defense. "The world is a universe

The original model of the Iron Cross. Arnold, 800 Jahre Deutscher Orden *(1990).*

Instituted in 1813 during the War of Liberation, the Iron Cross was patterned after the cross of the Teutonic Knights. The medal was the highest honor awarded in Prussia, but the material from which it was struck was the cheapest: the iron mined in Upper Silesia. This ascetism, called the Prussian style, became a source of pride. The National Socialists' adoption of the peasant's brown shirt as their uniform appealed to this sense of style.

of eternal war,'' the educator Julius Schmidhauser wrote in 1933. ''Prussian realism recognizes this constant state of war. And Prussian history proves it: conquest, retreat, conquest again. Prussia is the fruit of war, and it accepts the greatness and the guilt of being the seed of war. In a frightened world it says yes to war.''[3]

''Prussia'' is not responsible for Auschwitz, but its culture of unswerving devotion to the state, militarism, ruthlessness, violence, and absolute obedience to orders is part of the answer to the question ''How was Auschwitz possible?'' Furthermore, the political history of Prussia bridges the divide between the medieval Germans' Push to the East and the National Socialist revival of their ancestors' abandoned project six hundred years later. In the Germans' history of Auschwitz as a town built in 1270, lost in 1457, and reclaimed in 1939, ''Prussia'' is a fine but bright line of continuity.[4]

PRUSSIA WAS ONE of the results of the German Push to the East, first initiated in the tenth century by Emperor Otto I. It was centuries in the making. Indeed, progress was slow for two hundred years, until the German prince Albrecht the Bear conquered a poor, sandy, sparsely populated stretch of land between the Elbe and the Oder rivers and brought in German settlers and Cistercian monks to drain swamps, clear forests, and work the heavy and productive soil of the reclaimed areas with the Germans' silent weapon in their advance to the East: the horse-drawn iron plow. The colonists founded towns; Brandenburg was to give its name to the domain; centuries later Berlin was to become the symbol of all of Germany. Brandenburg was poor but, as later generations claimed proudly, under the leadership of the Hohenzollerns was destined to

A German history schoolbook illustration of the settlement of the lands between the Elbe and the Oder and Austria, by Anton Heinen. Die ewige Strasse II *(1943). Authors. The German Push to the East officially began in 937 when Emperor Otto organized the area east of the Elbe into a few marches. By 983 however the Germans were back where they started after a general uprising of the Slav Wends. After two centuries of much failure, German policy in East Elbia became more successful when Emperor Lothair urged German territorial princes to convert, conquer, and settle the Wendish lands (1130). The princes were allowed to keep whatever they gained. Energized by the prospect of limitless holdings in the East, the Wettins conquered the fertile hills of Saxony and the Schauenburg the heavy clay of Holstein. Henry the Lion defeated the Abrodites and Pomeranians along the Baltic shore, while the Ascanian Albrecht the Bear settled for Brandenburg. The Wends finally converted.*

starve its way to greatness. The Hohenzollerns were to rule Brandenburg from 1417 for a little over five hundred years, and they transformed the small, poor, and peripherally located province into the major European power of Prussia, which in turn became the foundation and core of the German Reich.

As the early colonists settled Brandenburg, a military organization founded in the Holy Land to care for sick and wounded crusaders began the conquest and conversion of what was then Prussia.[5] The Teutonic Order advanced systematically and adopted a harsh policy towards the heathen Prussians: those who opposed the order were slaughtered, and those who accepted it were moved from their ancestral grounds in a determined attempt to break their culture. A program of state-sponsored German immigration completed the Germanization of the country, and it was so successful that the territory resisted Polonification even after it was separated for over three hundred years from the other German lands.

The Teutonic Order also conquered Livonia (the medieval name for Estonia and Latvia). By 1400 it ruled a continuous domain that reached from the Oder to the Narva River. But the crusading spirit which had energized the only crusader state on European soil had been lost. German idealists of noble blood had ceased to join, and the organization was worn-out. In a final, futile attempt

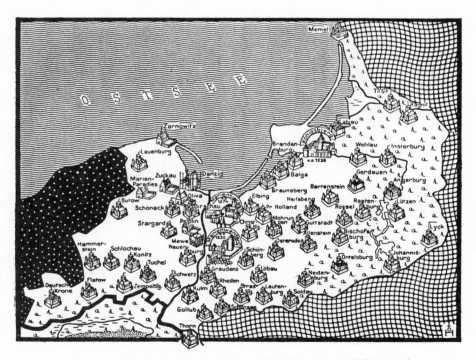

Medieval Prussia as "The Land of Castles." Franz, Wir Preussen! *(1936). Sterling Memorial Library, Yale University. The castles built by the Teutonic Order form a record of systematic German conquest.*

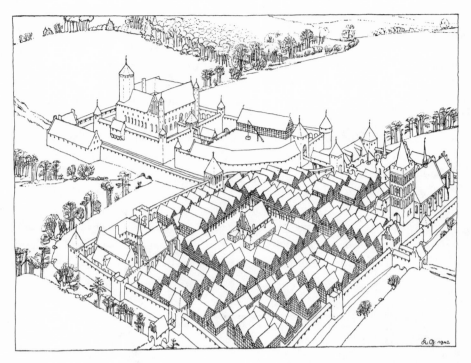

Bird's-eye view of a typical East Prussian town drawn by the prominent urban historian Karl
Gruber in 1942. Gruber, Die Gestalt der deutsche Stadt *(1952). Seeley G. Mudd Library, Yale*
University. The town is laid out on a regular grid, with a market and town hall in the center,
surrounded by the houses of the merchants who established the town. The parish
church and the convent of a mendicant order are located on the periphery. A standard-design
castle of the Teutonic Order guards the road into the wilderness.

to retain control of the Vistula delta, the Teutonic knights attacked the Polish-Lithuanian state and were crushed in a decisive battle near the village of Tannenberg in July 1410.

The Teutonic Order languished for another hundred years in East Prussia until, faced with the challenge of Lutheranism, its grand master accepted the Reformation, dissolved the organization, and became the first Duke of Prussia. This proved fortunate for the Brandenburg Hohenzollerns, to whom East Prussia was transferred almost a century later. An ambitious lot, they aspired to power and princely positions, and East Prussia helped them achieve their goals. The Hohenzollerns needed a sovereign territory outside the Reich where

*The Battle of Tannenberg, detail of King
Jagiello. Lithograph after the painting by
Jan Matejko (1878), National Museum,
Warsaw. Authors. In the first decade of the
fifteenth century the Teutonic Order imposed
increasingly higher taxes on the Prussian
cities and country. As the burghers of Danzig,
Elbing, Thorn, Kulm, and other towns and
the landed gentry began to consider the
possibility of less costly rule, Grandmaster
Ulrich von Jungingen decided on a preemptive
strike against the Polish-Lithuanian state.
The failure of his campaign led to King
Jagiello's invasion of Prussia and the decisive
battle near the village of Tannenberg on 15
July 1410. "The fatal Tannenberg
Business" (Carlyle) marked the end of the
medieval German Push to the East and the
beginning of Poland's tenure as a great power.*

they could indeed be sovereigns. The duchy of Prussia was outside the Reich,
and this geographical fact was at least promising.[6]

Frederick III of Brandenburg-Prussia exploited the possibilities of Prussia's
position when he obtained permission from the German emperor Leopold I
to call himself "King *in* Prussia." The new title energized the scattered domain
of the Hohenzollerns. As subjects of "King in Prussia," which very quickly
became in common parlance "King of Prussia," the good people of the collection of lands the Hohenzollerns had assembled over the years now began to
recognize themselves as somehow part of one Prussia under one king. This

The German East, 1700. Map by Robert Jan van Pelt and Don Bonner. On the map, Poland appeared to be a great power but, as an elective monarchy, was easily subject to influence from abroad. Each time a king was to be elected, Orthodox Russia, Catholic Austria, and Lutheran Sweden and Brandenburg-Prussia sought to influence results through Poland's Orthodox, Roman Catholic, and Lutheran populations. Compared with Poland, Brandenburg-Prussia was disadvantaged geographically, but politically it was united by a vigorous state authority and economically it was strengthened by systematic state-sponsored development.

grassroots sense of belonging and unity was the basis for political unification and military expansion to unite the scattered territories physically.

Frederick the Great realized the potential of the new dignity in a series of conquests and annexations. Immediately after his ascent to the throne in 1740 he occupied most of Silesia; Oswiecim, for example, remained Polish. With Lower Silesia, Frederick got a well-developed land settled by Germans. Upper Silesia, however, was poor and had become largely Polonified.[7] But while the situation on the ground was desperate, there was great promise below: minerals, metallic ores, and coal. Under government sponsorship, the Prussians began to develop

Upper Silesia's resources extensively. The energetic Count Frederick William von Reden headed the newly established Silesian Mining Authority. Its goal, he said, was "to make of this neglected corner a pearl in the Prussian crown, and to transform its inhabitants from poor, oppressed slaves into educated and happy human beings."[8] In 1796 the first coke-fired blast furnace began operation in Gleiwitz; this marked the beginning of the region's heavy industry.

Upper Silesia forged the weapons with which Prussia defeated Napoleon, and Upper Silesia mined the iron for Prussia's highest decoration of valor in battle—the first medal given to officers and men alike. In the early nineteenth century Upper Silesia's mines, forges, and foundries became forceful symbols of the Prussian resolve to defend, alone and without access to foreign resources, the principle of national liberty against foreign ambition.

While the government agencies developed Silesia's wealth, Frederick the

Front and back elevations of the Königshütte iron works in Upper Silesia, 1802. Hemigk,
Oberschlesische Landbaukunst *(1937). Sterling Memorial Library, Yale University.*
The Prussians' systematic development of Upper Silesia's resources began in 1769 with the adoption
of a unified legal code to regulate the developing mining industry, and reached its zenith
thirty-three years later with the state-sponsored construction of the Königshütte iron works which
secured, as one newspaper wrote, Upper Silesia's position as Germany's "England."

Engraved portrait of Frederick the Great, 1742. Authors.

The German East, 1775. Map by Robert Jan van Pelt and Don Bonner. By 1775 Prussia had become an important power. Through the conquest of Silesia (1740) Frederick the Great had prevented the creation of a continuous Saxon-Silesian-Polish territory. The first partition of Poland (1772) allowed him to unite West and East Prussia and, therefore, to upgrade his own royal dignity. So long as the Polish king had controlled West Prussia, Frederick had been merely King "in" Prussia. Now he was King "of" Prussia.

Great considered the annexation of West Prussia to consolidate his territory from Brandenburg-Silesia, the social and economic core of his country, to East Prussia, the territory that was the foundation of its legitimacy as an independent state. He joined forces with Russia and Austria, and his share of Poland's surrender of 28 percent of her territory and 38.6 percent of her population was the by then desolate West Prussia.

Frederick the Great's development of West Prussia, which involved the construction of roads and dikes, drainage of marshes, irrigation of fields, and the establishment of a total of 1,500 rationally designed colonist villages and hamlets populated by over 250,000 immigrants from other parts of Germany and 100,000 settlers from other parts of his kingdom, became the stuff of legend and the model of the National Socialist program for Poland.[9] "And then the king, in his usual grand way, brought culture to his country," the nineteenth-century writer Gustav Freytag rejoiced. "The very rottenness of

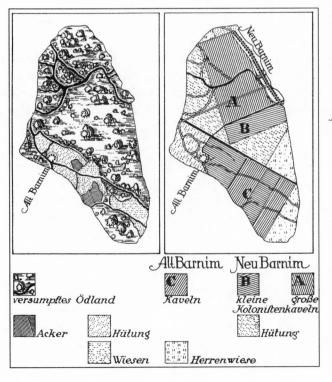

Map showing an example of Frederick the Great's development of West Prussia. Hoehm, Wir Brandenburger! (1935). Sterling Memorial Library, Yale University. Left: "before." Right: "after." Versumpftes Ödland =marshy wilderness; Acker = fields; Hütung = pasture; Wiesen = meadows; Kaveln = lots. Neu-Barnim shows the regular layout of the colonists' villages established during Frederick's reign. In the parts of Prussia he inherited, as well as in the acquired territories of Silesia and West Prussia, Frederick developed desolate regions. Himmler often invoked Frederick the Great's program as the precedent for his own reconstruction of the German East.

the country became an attraction for him, and henceforth West Prussia became what hitherto Silesia had been: his favorite child. . . . Everywhere there was digging, hammering, and building. Cities were peopled anew, street after street rose out of the heaps of ruins; new colonist villages were laid out and new modes of agriculture introduced."[10] There was something truly Faustian in Frederick's reconstruction of Silesia and West Prussia, "something enormous that appeared to his contemporaries almost supernatural and even at times inhuman. It was grand, but also terrible that during the whole operation he sought the success of the whole, and had no regard for the interests of the individual." Freytag observed that "in the marshes of the Netze Frederick counted the strokes of 10,000 spades but ignored the sufferings of the workers who lay sick with marsh fever in the hospitals he had built for them."[11]

Prussia had not only gained new territories; it had also acquired a Polish minority. By 1815 more than 800,000 Poles lived under Prussian rule.[12] At that time nationalism was not an issue in the area between the Oder and the Vistula. The region was politically, culturally, and ethnically mixed, and the designation "German" or "Polish" had very little meaning. Both the inhabitants of the area and the government in Berlin were cognizant that German and Polish history, culture, and politics coexisted in the eastern provinces.

The unification of Germany, which was completed in 1871, changed the official attitude towards the Polish minority. The eastern border of Prussia was now identified as the eastern border of the new German Reich, and Prussia ceased to occupy its ancient equivocal German-Polish position within Germany. The last trace of that German-Polish ambiguity disappeared as Prussia itself became the dominant force within the German Reich.

What had been a domain of encounter became a battlefield where the imperial and integral nationalism of the Germans faced the functional and emancipatory nationalism of the Poles.[13] German scholarship began to fix the area ideologically as a German East with no room for a Polish element, and the government initiated measures to combat Polish nationalism through a stiff program of Germanization.[14] Not surprisingly, the very policies that were designed to Germanize the Poles served as a catalyst to awaken Polish national identity. A national movement arose which sent its own Polish deputies to the Prussian Landtag and the German Reichstag, supported a flourishing Polish-language press, and created a network of social and economic organizations to aid the Prussian Poles. Finally, the general school strike of 1906–7 against the use of German as the exclusive language of instruction brought all Polish Prussians—children and parents, poor and rich, peasants and city dwellers—

*The German East, 1820. Map by Robert Jan van Pelt and Don Bonner. The Prussian government kept West Prussia, East Prussia, and Posen outside of Metternich's German Confederation (*Deutsche Bund*). This policy was especially welcome to the 800,000 Polish inhabitants of Posen, because it maintained and confirmed the dual German-Polish character of the Prussian state. When German liberals sought to unify Germany in 1848 by transforming the* Bund *into a union, the German inhabitants of Prussia's eastern provinces demanded and achieved inclusion of their lands. The Poles of Posen, who had been willing subjects of the Prussian crown, refused to become citizens of a German national state and revolted. German sentiment turned against the Poles, and an antagonism erupted that was to shape German-Polish relations in the century that followed.*

into open revolt against the government and sealed the schism between Germans and Poles.[15]

As Polish nationalism intensified, the Prussian Settlement Commission sent in more Germans. In the thirty years of its existence (1886–1916) the commission transplanted some 130,000 Germans. In absolute terms the commission is a testimony to the German power of organization, but the colonization did not stem a countervailing westward movement of Germans; over 1.5 million people migrated to the West between 1840 and 1910.[16] As the young Max Weber explained in the 1890s, the Prussian Junkers made the commission's task impossible. Owners of the vast agricultural estates in the East, they

Prussian policemen chase Polish children to school. Simplicissimus (1906). Sterling Memorial Library, Yale University. "You will learn German, you Polish gangs! After all we Prussians also had to learn it." The Prussians originally were heathens who were Germanized.

preferred to hire Polish laborers from Russian and Austrian Poland, as they were cheaper than Germans. The German laborers, in the meantime, were attracted by employment opportunities in Berlin, Hamburg, and the rapidly industrializing Prussian provinces of Rhineland and Westphalia.[17] Both Poles and Germans moved westward. In the first decade of the twentieth century, roughly half a million Polish seasonal workers flooded into East Elbia each year, and many stayed.

Neither the German public nor the government ever resolved the issue of the seasonal immigration of Polish workers, who were simultaneously seen as a cultural threat and an economic asset. There was much more consistent sentiment about Jewish immigration from the East. The events that triggered German concern about the so-called *Ostjuden* had little to do with Jewish

German colonist, statue adorning the cornice of the Prussian Settlement Commission, Posen. Threde and Nasaski, Posen und sein Preussische Streifen (1983). Sterling Memorial Library, Yale University.

emigration and everything to do with the severe depression after the economic boom following the German unification of 1871. With the increasingly popular view of the Jew as the symbol of the evils of capitalism, the 1879 collapse of the German stock market was widely blamed on Jewish machinations.

Russian Jews had begun to arrive in small groups in 1868 to escape the desolation wrought by cholera and famine.[18] The early trickle became a flood after the pogroms of 1881; 2.5 million Jews left Russia between 1868 and 1914, most of whom emigrated to the United States, Canada, and Argentina. For political, practical, and geographical reasons, Germany was the first stop on this westward migration. In the last decade of the nineteenth century, Germany, Russia, and Austria-Hungary established a large free-trade block which permitted Russian and Austrian citizens to cross the border to conduct their business.[19] Furthermore, German shipping companies, searching for an unexploited niche in the commercial shipping market, turned to the transportation of emigrants from central Europe to America via Hamburg and Bremen. Companies like Albert Ballin's Hamburg America Line began to recruit passengers actively in Russian and Austrian Poland. Immigration officials were obliged to allow Jewish migrants who held tickets for transatlantic passage on German ships to travel to the port cities.

The career of a typical eastern Jewish merchant. Simplicissimus *(1903).* Sterling Memorial Library, Yale University. From Moishe Pisch (piss), *the rag peddler in Congress Poland,* to Moritz Wasserstrahl (stream), *the women's fashions salesman in Posen, to Maurice Lafontaine* (fountain), *the art dealer in Berlin, the Jew became a threat to the German future. Nineteenth-century Germans believed that culture was the core of German identity. By trading works of culture, the Jew had bought the German soul.*

There was, however, a widely held suspicion that many Jews among the transmigrants preferred Germany to the United States, and that they disappeared into town life once they had crossed the border. The number of eastern Jews in certain cities began to rise significantly, or so it seemed from the very visible newly arrived *Schnorrer*, or panhandlers. Some 50 percent of the recent immigrants eked out an existence as small merchants and peddlers. Forced to make a living on the margins of the established economy, they sold cheap goods, and the German public soon came to identify the Russian Jew with shoddy merchandise. Another 35 percent of the eastern Jews found and held regular jobs as industrial laborers but, as they were at work, were not visible. The remaining 15 percent who had become beggars were all too noticeable. As far as the upright German citizens were concerned, these were the *Ostjuden*—work-shy parasites who deserved to be deported.[20]

This was not the only problem posed by East European Jews. According to the German public health officials, many *Ostjuden* were lice-ridden and in poor health when they arrived at the border, and immigration authorities established delousing procedures as early as 1882. Maryashe Antin, a twelve-year-old girl from Polotzk, described this process in a letter to her uncle, which she later

Maryashe Antin. Authors.

included in a memoir. It is both a blueprint for, and an eerie foreshadowing of, the "delousing" routine in Auschwitz sixty years later. The train stopped, and the passengers were told to get out, Maryashe explained. They were led into a large yard where many men and women dressed in white awaited them.

> This was . . . [a] scene of bewildering confusion, parents losing their children, and little ones crying; baggage being thrown together in one corner of the yard, heedless of contents, which suffered in consequence; those white-clad Germans shouting commands, always accompanied with "Quick! Quick!"—the confused passengers obeying all orders like meek children, only questioning now and then what was going to be done with them. . . . Our things were taken away, our friends separated from us; a man came to inspect us, as if to ascertain our full value; strange-looking people driving us about like dumb animals, helpless and unresisting; children we could not see crying in a way that suggested terrible things; ourselves driven into a little room where a great kettle was boiling on a little stove; our clothes taken off, our bodies rubbed with a slippery substance that might be any bad thing; a shower of warm water let down on us without warning; again driven to another little room where we sit, wrapped in woollen blankets till large, coarse bags are brought in, their contents turned out, and we see only a cloud of steam, and hear the women's orders to dress ourselves,—"Quick! Quick!"—or else we'll miss—something we cannot hear. We are forced to pick out our clothes from among all the others, with the steam blinding us; we choke, cough,

entreat the women to give us time; they persist, "Quick! Quick!—or we'll miss the train!"—Oh, so we really won't be murdered! They are only making us ready for the continuing of our journey, cleaning us of all suspicions of dangerous sickness. Thank God![21]

The deloused transmigrants were herded back to the railway cars and sent straight to the ports. To be on the safe side, public health workers disinfected the trains after unloading their human cargo. The step from the fear of lice as a hazard to the public health to the fear of the people infested with those lice was very small indeed. When a cholera epidemic broke out in Hamburg, the Jewish transmigrants were blamed and the shipping lines were obliged to create quarantine areas in the port to hold the Jews until their departure for America. Maryashe stayed in such a center. "This last place of detention turned out to be a prison. 'Quarantine' they called it, and there was a great deal of it—two weeks of it. Two weeks within high brick walls, several hundred of us herded in half a dozen compartments,—numbered compartments,—sleeping in rows, like sick people in a hospital." The daily routine was strikingly similar to that of the later concentration camps. "With roll-call morning and night, and short rations three times a day; with never a sign of the free world beyond our barred windows; with anxiety and longing and homesickness in our hearts."[22] The imprisonment of the Jews validated the identification of the people with infectious disease; it strengthened the association between Ostjuden and vermin, bacilli, and the plague.

Another group of Russian Jews, the so-called Luftmenschen, people who lived by their wits and appeared to trade in nothing, also roused suspicion.[23] These students, artists, and writers raised the specter not only of the "Jewification" of cultural life but also of political radicalism. After the unsuccessful Russian revolution of 1905 and the subsequent exile of many of the participants to Germany, Russian Jewish intellectuals came to be seen as bomb-throwing anarchists whose aim was to destroy the German social order. The Ostjude became a contradictory figure in the public mind: a corrupt, calculating, and opportunistic trader, a destitute, diseased, and backwards Schnorrer, and a radical revolutionary fighting for a Communist utopia. These contradictory characteristics were unified in the symbol of the parasite.

REMARKABLY ENOUGH, THE town of Oswiecim played a significant role as a border station where Galician Jews and Polish agricultural laborers converged

A 30-kreuzer coin struck in Vienna, 1776. Slawomir Staszak. Maria Theresa is depicted on one side. On the reverse is her title, ARCHID.AUS.DUX.OSW.ZAT.1776 (Archduke of Austria and Duke of Oswiecim and Zator, 1776), and a crowned shield with the coat of arms of Galicia (three crowns), Lodomeria (two chess fields) and Oswiecim and Zator (eagle), on which the shield of Austria is crowned by the German imperial crown. In the first partition of Poland Maria Theresa not only added the newly created title of king of Galicia and Lodomeria to the Habsburg family collection; she also revived the old title of duke of Oswiecim and Zator. Indeed, Oswiecim provided the Habsburgs with the strongest dynastic claim to the Polish territories ceded to Austria.

to cross into Germany. Oswiecim had fallen to Austria in the first partition of Poland and was incorporated into Galicia. For the next century the 2,000-inhabitant town was largely forgotten in the chanceries of Europe.[24]

Hampered by Austria's rigidly centralized system which stymied local enterprise and independent economic development, Galicia declined and became one of the poorest provinces of Europe.[25] Whatever local industry had existed was wiped out by the Vienna–Cracow railway line that passed through Oswiecim and brought better and cheaper goods produced in Austria's western provinces. The sole industries that survived were those connected to agriculture, such as flour mills, breweries, and alcohol distilleries. Oswiecim became a center of vodka, brandy, and other liquor production. The Jewish distiller Haberfeld became a major employer in town and quickly acquired a reputation for purity and quality throughout the empire.

While a liquor-producing town like Oswiecim profited from the link to the rest of the Austrian empire, Galicia's rural economy sank into misery. The large surplus rural population, unable to find employment in local industry, emigrated to the United States. Agents traveled all over Galicia to sell tickets. Oswiecim was well positioned to profit from this east–west migration. It enjoyed good rail connections via Cracow with the rest of Galicia and, with

Postcard. Oswiecim railroad station, ca. 1910. Towarzytwo Milosnikow Ziemi Oswiecomskiej.

the local Oswiecim–Kattowitz line, had a workable connection with the major railway corridor Kattowitz–Breslau–Berlin–Hamburg. Oswiecim quickly became one of the two chief crossing points for both gentile and Jewish Galician transmigrants into Germany, and this brought a lot of business to the town— most of which was illegal.

There was little coordination between the development of Germany's commercial shipping empire and its immigration policy as it applied to the admission of large groups of poor transmigrants into the country. While agents of the German shipping lines were trying to get people in, Prussian immigration officials at the border tried to keep them out. A largely illegal underground network arose to facilitate border crossings. The Prussian–Galician border became an almost lawless area, and the transmigrants, who depended on illegal operators to get into Germany, were easily blackmailed and plundered.

By the late 1880s Oswiecim had become the center of an enormous immigration racket, which involved the agents of the various German shipping lines from Hamburg and Bremen, the chief of Austrian customs, the chief of police of Oswiecim, the mayor of the town of Bielitz, the innkeepers of Hotel Zator and Hotel Herz, employees of the railways, and many less prominent local folk. Their task was to find people all over Galicia and convince them that Oswiecim was the best place to cross the Austrian-German border. Once in the town, prospective emigrants were forced to strip for "medical examinations" and their garments were taken away for "disinfection" to remove whatever money had been sewn into the clothes. One extraordinary scam, illustrating the emigrants' lack of sophistication, consisted of an offer, in exchange for a hefty sum of money, to telegraph the "Emperor" of America to ensure entry into the United States after their overseas journey. A mock telegraph apparatus was constructed out of an alarm clock, which had not yet made its way into the Galician villages of the late 1880s. The alarm bell, controlled by someone in an adjoining room, rang in a certain code to indicate the "Emperor's" affirmative answer. Such stratagems as these stripped the more unsuspecting transmigrants of their money, and many never made it into Germany. The racket finally was broken in 1889, and everyone involved was tried in Wadowitz; six hundred witnesses gave testimony, and hundreds submitted sworn statements. Relatively mild sentences ranging from four and a half years of forced labor for the shipping-line agents to four months for their helpers were imposed.[26]

By the time the trial ended, a new and more permanent kind of business opportunity had come to Oswiecim, and it was this business which created the physical foundations for the event that, within half a century, propelled

Postcard. The market at Oswiecim, ca. 1910. Towarzytwo Milosnikow Ziemi Oswiecomskiej.

The German East, 1900. Map by Robert Jan van Pelt and Dan Bonner. From 1618 to 1848 the eastern border of Prussia did not coincide with the eastern boundary of the German Reich or its successor the German Confederation. In this largely prenationalist era the designation "German" or "Polish" had very little meaning, and it is significant that the concept of a "German East" did not exist in this time. Increasing tensions between Germans and Poles in the wake of the 1848 revolution led to a gradual change in which the old "and-and" changed into Bismarck's "either-or." The Germans prevailed and in 1867 established the eastern border of the new North German Confederation (from which the German Reich arose four years later) at Prussia's eastern boundary. Now German scholarship began to fix the area ideologically as "The German East" (Der deutsche Osten) with no room for a Polish element, while Polish historians redefined the same region as "The Polish West" (Polski Zachod), from which Germans ought to be removed.

the town's name into the chronicles of world history. Oswiecim was perfectly situated to control the annual seasonal labor emigration. With the relaxation of immigration procedures between Germany, Austria, and Russia, seasonal labor emigration became a fixture of Galician life in the early 1890s. As we have seen, the flight of German agricultural workers to the West created a vacuum filled by Polish agricultural workers. The season began in March, and employers during the prior winter months tried desperately to arrange for the recruitment of agricultural laborers in Russian and Austrian Poland. As their agents were not allowed to enlist within Russian Poland, they conducted their business at border stations. German agents were, however, allowed to muster workers in Galicia, and every year hundreds of agents traveled to the region. It was not difficult for them to find workers; according to one estimate there was a labor reserve of 1.2 million men in Galicia.

By 1910 there was an annual seasonal emigration from Galicia of 315,000 persons. In the late winter thousands upon thousands of men camped in the small border towns of Oswiecim, Oderberg, and Myslowitz in the hope of finding a job.[27] At the outbreak of the Great War the Galician government regularized the situation at Oswiecim. It planned to build a migrant worker village, a government-controlled labor exchange, and a military control station in the suburb of Zasole to ensure that those wishing to leave had fulfilled or were exempt from service. The size of the problem was reflected in the physical structures the government erected: twenty-seven brick dormitories for 3,000 workers, ninety wooden barracks to house an additional 9,000 men, and buildings for infrastructural services to support the life of the temporary community, such as a chapel, theater, hospital, post office, telegraph station, police station, and so on. In 1914 Oswiecim itself had a population of a little over 10,000 people, of whom 5,000 were Jews. A special rail spur connected the suburb to the main line a mile to the west; special trains with workers could go from Zasole straight to Germany.[28]

At the beginning of 1918 the workers' cantonment was ready to receive its first migrants, but with the reconfiguration of the map of Europe, Oswiecim ceased to be a border town and there was no longer any need for the labor exchange. The settlement in Zasole remained empty until the newly established Polish army discovered that the brick barracks could house the twenty-first Artillery Regiment, which was to be stationed in the area. The ninety wooden barracks were soon used to shelter 4,000 Polish refugees from the former duchy of Teschen, which had been partitioned between Poland and Czechoslovakia after a plebiscite held on 7 and 8 March 1920.

Many journalists attended the vote in Teschen, one of whom was Ludwik Stasiaski. On his return to Cracow, he had to change trains in Oswiecim. Having a few hours on his hands, he strolled through the town and finished his tour with a visit to the synagogue and the Jewish quarter, with its "narrow streets and charming alleys." He found it enchanting. "Every gate of the Jewish quarter is a scene to be preserved forever. Dark vestibules, alleys, niches, ladders, nooks and crannies, blind windows, buttresses that fit without much logic to the architecture of the houses, and everywhere gates and portals." "All of this will disappear from the surface of the

Two refugees from Teschen standing in front of the wooden barracks that had been built as part of the labor exchange, ca. 1930. Auschwitz-Birkenau State Museum, neg. 8871.

Soldiers encamped in Zasole, 1935. Auschwitz-Birkenau State Museum, neg. 20012.

Oswiecim Jews on the Ring, 1930.
Behind the three men is the town
hall. Auschwitz-Birkenau State
Museum, neg. 20998/14.

earth," Stasiaski mused. "Every civilized person wishes to have such a
Jewish corner painted, but none wants to live in such a corner. And so
these courtyards, so very picturesque, will be swept away by modern utili-
tarianism and hygiene."[29]

THE EVENTS OF the next quarter of a century were to prove Stasiaski's offhand
remark prophetic. The Auschwitz ghetto was to disappear, and its liquidation
was to be justified by reasons of hygiene, although those who would resettle
the inhabitants and clear the area would be driven by an understanding of
hygiene rather different from what Stasiaski had in mind. To the German
population planner Fritz Arlt and the German architect Hans Stosberg, who
were to supervise the deportation of the Auschwitz Jews and the destruction
of the Auschwitz ghetto, measures to promote the cleanliness of the physical
environment were only part of a larger policy to ensure the racial hygiene of
the nation.

In Germany, their ideas had become respectable and were rooted in late-nineteenth-century neo-Darwinism and eugenics. The rhetoric of degeneration, criticism of the explosive growth of medical expenditure, and fear of the proletariat had converged into a call for "racial hygiene."[30] Its most important advocate, the physician Alfred Ploetz, argued that the primary and most important task of the physician was to prevent the wholesale degeneration of Germany into one large asylum. In this, the most crucial crisis that the German people had ever faced, the rights of the individual were of no consequence if they conflicted with the interests of the community.

Ploetz was supported by the respected and influential biologist Ernst Haeckel, who had been an early apostle of Darwinism among the Germans. Ignoring Darwin's injunction that civil society could not and should not be interpreted in terms of "selection" and "struggle for existence," Haeckel insisted that if selection determined the life of bacteria and bees, it also affected human beings: "artificial" selection should aid the process of natural selection. Indeed, Haeckel argued, if natural selection did not kill degenerates, human beings should step in. To illustrate what he had in mind, Haeckel adduced the example of Sparta. "A remarkable instance of artificial selection in man, on a great scale, is furnished by the ancient Spartans, among whom, in obedience to a special law, all newly-born children were subject to careful examination and selection. All those that were weak, sickly, or affected with any bodily infirmity, were killed. Only the perfectly healthy and strong children were allowed to live, and they alone afterwards propagated the race. By this means, the Spartan race was not only continually preserved in excellent strength and vigour, but the perfection of their bodies increased with every generation."[31] Haeckel lamented that any attempt to follow the Spartan example would be stopped by the same humanitarians who so easily accepted the destruction of thousands of young, vigorous men in war. In other words, if one accepted the selection of the physically fit and the rejection of the unfit at the recruiting office, then one should accept it in absolute terms at the crib.[32]

Inspired by Haeckel, Ploetz recommended the Spartan practice; he suggested that a commission of racial hygienists examine every young person who wished to marry and have children and grant permission for marriage and procreation. The commission was then to examine newborn babies and kill those it found unfit. "The parents," Ploetz observed, "will not permit rebellious feelings to overcome them but, having renewed their qualification to procreate, fresh and merry will attempt to do so a second time."[33]

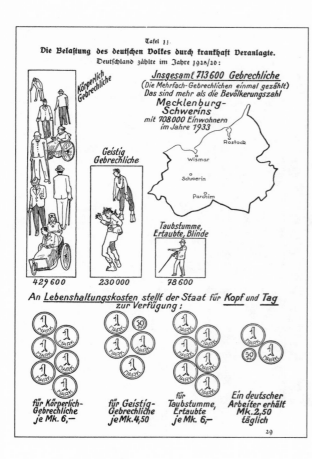

The burden of the unfit on German society. Helmut, Volk in Gefahr (1934). Seeley G. Mudd Library, Yale University. The caption reads, "713,600 [sic] people, more than the population of Mecklenburg-Schwerin, are either physically or mentally handicapped. The state pays six marks a day to care for each of the 429,600 physically handicapped and 78,600 blind, deaf, and deaf-mute people, and 4.50 marks for each of the 230,000 mentally handicapped people, while the average German worker earns 2.50 marks a day."

The judicial and medical establishment remained aloof from Haeckel and Ploetz until the carnage of the First World War, the subsequent revolution, and the economic difficulties of the postwar years led a few prominent lawyers and physicians to reconsider the merits of a radical shift in policy regarding the insane, the incurably sick, and the totally invalid. A catalyst in this change of opinion was the publication in 1920 of the very readable sixty-two-page *The Destruction of Life Unworthy of Life*, by Karl Binding, one of Germany's most eminent legal scholars, and the well-known neuropathologist Alfred Hoche. Reflecting on the war, which had wasted "the most valuable and self-sufficient lives full of energy and vigor," the authors compared it to the massive energy spent to sustain "worthless lives" in asylums. Now more than at any other time in Germany's history, the country needed every citizen to be 100 percent

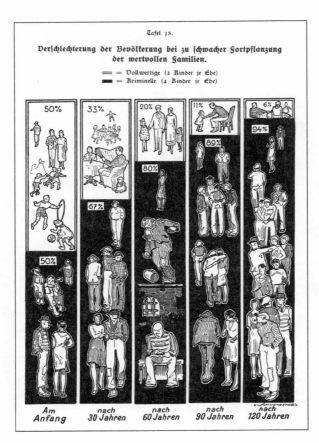

The long-term effect of the higher fertility of the criminal class based on the assumption that wholesomeness and criminality are inherited. Helmut, Volk in Gefahr (1934). Seeley G. Mudd Library, Yale University.

productive. "There is no place for those who can only manage 50 percent, 25 percent, or 12.5 percent of the normal contribution. The task which faces us as Germans will demand the highest mobilization of all possibilities for a long time to come."[34] It was time to bring an end to the practice of maintaining even the most socially worthless existence and to reconsider the merits of the "barbaric" practices of killing the unfit. And Hoche confidently predicted that "a new period" would come when "on the basis of a higher morality" an "exaggerated concept of humanity and an exaggerated view of the value of human life" would no longer hold.[35]

Binding and Hoche's ideas were echoed a few years later by no one less than Adolf Hitler. Sentenced to five years imprisonment for his role in an attempted coup d'état in Bavaria, Hitler settled into prison life comfortably and sat down to write his vision for Germany. He had no doubt that the state should adopt ruthless policies with regard to the unfit. "It is a half-measure to let incurably sick people steadily contaminate the remaining healthy ones," Hitler wrote in *Mein Kampf*.[36] Strict application of the laws of racial hygiene had allowed 6,000 Spartans "of high racial value" to rule 350,000 Helots. "This was the result of a systematic race preservation; thus Sparta must be regarded as the first folkish state. The exposure of sick, weak, deformed children, in short their destruction, was more decent and in truth a thousand times more humane than the wretched insanity of our day which preserves the most pathological subject, and indeed at any price, and yet takes the life of a hundred thousand healthy children in consequence of birth control or through abortions, in order subsequently to breed a race of degenerates burdened with illnesses."[37]

Not long after these words were written, the Prussian aristocrat Reich President Paul von Hindenburg appointed their author Reich Chancellor, and the German nation confirmed his choice in a national election.

CHAPTER 3

GERMANY'S TURN TO THE EAST

WHAT THE TEUTONIC ORDER, FREDERICK THE GREAT, AND THE PRUSSIAN Settlement Commission set out to do, the Great War accomplished irrevocably: it turned Germany to the East. And because of those earlier initiatives, because of the Push to the East in the 1300s, 1700s, and 1800s, the turn was popularly perceived as a return. The German army's success in East Prussia, precisely where the Teutonic Knights of yore had been defeated by their Polish adversaries, appeared to confirm the justice of their cause just a few weeks after the war began. Commanded by General Paul von Hindenburg and Lieutenant General Erich Ludendorff, the Germans smashed a massive Russian invasion.

The news of the victory was greeted with great jubilation in Germany. The hitherto unknown Hindenburg became a model of strength and his portrait an icon of adoration. The battle itself took on legendary proportions. Ludendorff called it the Battle of Tannenberg "in memory of that other battle long ago."[1] Half a millennium after their defeat by the Poles, the Germans recovered by routing the Russians. The campaign for the East had opened again. Inspired by this possibility, the twenty-seven-year-old volunteer Walter Flex wrote the instantly famous "Song of the Eastern Territories," in which the German East became the Holy German East—a sacred land open as the German heart, infinite as the German spirit, and strong as the courage of German men.[2]

*Members of Hitler Youth visiting the Marienburg study Hugo Vogel's painting of Hindenburg
in August 1914.* Neues Volk *(1934). Sterling Memorial Library, Yale University. Appointed
commander of the Eight Army after the Russian invasion had begun, Paul von Hindenburg
saw a steady stream of refugees on the run from the enemy (depicted in painting) on
his arrival at his headquarters at Marienburg. A few days later Hindenburg and his Chief of
staff, Erich Ludendorff, lured the Russians into a trap.*

The character of this Push to the East was quite different, however. It
embodied the worst of nineteenth-century imperialism flavored by anxiety
about Germany's strategic vulnerability. Many Germans believed that large-
scale annexations in the East, driving Russia back to its early-seventeenth-
century borders, were needed to secure the safety of the German heartland.
Farmers, businessmen, industrialists, and at least 1,347 German professors
urged the government to annex and settle Livonia and Lithuania.[3]

In late 1915 the German armies occupied Courland and Lithuania, and the
future of Livonia became a military priority. "It is up to Germany to continue
the comprehensive settlement policies of the Teutonic Order and to bring to
completion, after centuries of interruption, the work that it began," General
Ludendorff declared.[4] The general staff concurred; its proposals to the govern-

ment called for the transfer of Lithuania and Courland from Russia to Germany and the expropriation and deportation of Russian landowners.

THE GERMANS SAW themselves as the liberators of peoples suppressed by the czar. They envisioned a German-dominated commonwealth of autonomous nations of Poles, Lithuanians, Latvians, and Estonians. The problem was, Where did the Jews from this part of Europe belong? The Germans knew little about east European Jews, and they had no clue as to what to do with them. Until the outbreak of the war very few Germans visiting Russian Poland had ever ventured into the Jewish neighborhoods of Warsaw, Lublin, Vilna, or Lemberg. Now German soldiers patrolled these areas, and German administrators struggled with the endemic recurrent epidemics. They were not unsympathetic, but they were confounded by the poverty and misery of a world so close and yet utterly unknown to them. "We had no idea that something like that existed so close to our door," the editor of the respected *South German Monthly* wrote in a special issue of the magazine devoted to the *Ostjuden*, and his countrymen agreed.[5]

German soldiers enter a Galician town in 1915. Reventlow, Judas Kampf und Niederlage *(1937). Sterling Memorial Library, Yale University. Note the lack of tension, perhaps even the mutually good-humored reception.*

An eastern Jewish congregation, as drawn by Franz Kienmayer. Illustrierte Zeitung, no. 3920 (1918). Sterling Memorial Library, Yale University. Note the lack of negative caricature.

Apprehension followed in the wake of their surprise. The discovery of the ghettos intensified and gave new meaning to the hitherto marginal use by anti-Semites of a general terminology that associated Jews with vermin. If the reaction to the prewar immigration of the *Ostjuden* into Germany had focused on the threat that each individual posed to the collective health of the German nation, the descriptions of the ghettos suggested that the whole of Polish Jewry was one large diseased and alien entity. Many Germans feared that with no corner of Europe to call their own, the war would provoke massive migration of these Jews to the Reich. Individual measures had appeared sufficient before 1914, but it now seemed that radical measures were needed to address such a large-scale problem.[6]

Interest in the *Ostjuden* began to wane in 1917 when no such refugee horde materialized, and was overshadowed by the ethnic Germans in early 1918. Amid peace negotiations with the Bolsheviks in Brest Litovsk, the German army occupied the Ukraine, White Russia, and the rest of Livonia, and the German government began to plan the repatriation of most, if not all, of the two million ethnic Germans who lived in Russia to the conquered territories.

"The German Peace of the East." Allegorical depiction by Hugo Höppener of the new era of cooperation between Germans and the nations of eastern Europe in the wake of the Peace of Brest Litovsk (1918). Hermand, Der alte Traum vom neuen Reich *(1988). The Treaty of Brest Litovsk, concluded on 3 March 1918, confirmed the German perception that, however the war would end in the West, a new German millennium in the East had begun, a thousand years erected on the 700-year-old history of the German East. "Times are fulfilled," a magazine article celebrating the recovery of the Baltic provinces declared. "Signs and miracles appear in the heavens, in the east and everywhere else: The German Day has come! May all understand its meaning!"*

Throughout the late spring and summer of 1918 the prospects and problems of large-scale settlement in the East were discussed.[7] The clearer it became that the war was lost in the West, the more the Germans were convinced that it was in the East that the meaning of and the justification for the four-year suffering of the nation were to be found.[8]

These plans came to naught in November, when the Germans were forced to seek an armistice. "And so it had all been in vain," Adolf Hitler wrote in *Mein Kampf*. "In vain all the sacrifices and privations; in vain the hunger and thirst of months which were often endless; in vain the hours in which, with mortal fear clutching at our hearts, we nevertheless did our duty; and in vain the death of two millions who died." He called on their graves to open "and send the silent mud- and blood-covered heroes back as spirits of vengeance to the homeland which had cheated them with such mockery."[9]

The German generals articulated the same sentiment in another register. Unwilling to admit military failure, they repeatedly proclaimed that revolution on the home front and not defeat on the battlefield had caused the collapse. Germany would have remained unvanquished, Field Marshal von Hindenburg testified in a Reichstag inquiry, had it not been "for a secret intentional mutilation of the fleet and the army." Quoting the English general Sir John Frederick

Hitler (left) and his comrades at the western front, ca. 1918. Schultze-Pfaelzer, Hindenburg und Hitler zur Führung vereint *(1933). Authors. The caption reads, "The war volunteer became an old veteran, but he did not lose his enthusiasm, his sense of duty and loyalty, and his willingness to sacrifice himself. It earned him massive gas poisoning, which blinded him for some time."*

The "triumphant" return of the "undefeated" German army after the armistice, drawn "at the place and time" by Josef Correggio. Illustrierte Zeitung, *no. 3938 (1918). Sterling Memorial Library, Yale University. Without exception, artists' renditions of the army's return to Germany after 11 November 1918 suggest a victorious homecoming.*

Maurice, Hindenburg declared, "The German army was stabbed in the back."[10]

The Weimar Republic was not "Germany." The government that had signed the Versailles treaty was not "Germany." The millions of civilians who wanted if not to forget the war then at least go on with their peacetime lives were not "Germany." The "true" Germany was to be found not on a map or in civil society but within the soul of each German soldier, the veterans, conservatives, and nascent National Socialists blazed. This "Deeper Germany," or "Inner Reich," was unconquerable, even if the German Reich had been defeated and her soldiers had died. To the contrary: her size and actual existence were measured by the number of soldiers who had fallen on her behalf. In the trenches the soldiers had formed the real Germany; in their graves they embodied the eternal Germany.[11]

This heroic interpretation of Germany was coined during the war and it originally applied to all soldiers, but between 1918 and 1933 extremist groups antagonistic to the Weimar Republic successfully monopolized the idea and refashioned it: the true Germany resided in those who opposed the state that, by signing the Versailles treaty, had betrayed the sacrifice of two million soldiers. Many organizations declared themselves to be the ark of the True Germany, but only one was recognized by all the others as the legitimate heir of the Great War: the volunteers who had continued the war in Estonia and Latvia. In November 1918 the Allies insisted on German withdrawal from all occupied territories, but the English also made it clear to the German government that they were not keen on a Bolshevik reoccupation of Livonia. As the new Estonian and Latvian governments were unable to put armies in the field, the Germans, with the tacit approval of the English, sent a certain General Rüdiger von der Goltz to Livonia. He was to reorganize demobilized soldiers and local German residents into free corps to fight the Bolsheviks.[12]

The new German minister of defense, Gustav Noske, recalled a year later the particular genre of Baltic hysteria that took possession of Germany. "The propaganda drums were beaten. . . . Everyone who signed up for [service] imagined that he would stand on his own farm a year and a day later. And whatever the posters did not promise, the recruitment officers told the men orally." There were many volunteers, as "it was not easy to rebuild life in the defeated country. . . . A Baltic fever infected thousands, and was so strong that the stream of men did not cease even when it became clear that none of the dreams could be realized."[13]

Small troop of Baltic volunteers riding off into the sunrise to the east. Das Schwarze Korps *(1936). Sterling Memorial Library, Yale University. Illustration of Dwinger's novel the* Die letzte Reiter, *serialized in the SS magazine* Das Schwarze Korps *(6 February 1936 to 11 March 1937). No other novel received such exposure in the sole official SS periodical. With a 1936 circulation of 200,000,* Das Schwarze Korps *brought the story of the Baltic campaign to every member of the SS. Its editor, Gunther d'Alquen, praised the men "who took up arms with a clear sense of duty and without any commission or order, yes even against the instructions of their own government, to build a living wall against Bolshevism."*

The volunteers returned to the Reich, but they did so proudly, as they had fought while the representatives of the Weimar Republic had signed the peace treaty. They claimed that with the forced terms of Versailles, Germany had died in the German Reich. Versailles had reduced the German Reich to "an empty space on the map—a country which had no real existence," the free corps volunteer Ernst von Salomon complained. The men in the Baltic thus became "the last survivors of the German race."[14] It was an idea that did not die. Fifteen years later one of the protagonists in the most popular play of the day—and Hitler's favorite—Dwinger's *The Last Dream: A German Tragedy*, proclaimed to packed houses that Germany survived only in its Baltic volunteers. "We are the last in whom [Germany] still lives! . . . And if they think at home that the Great War has come to an end, we will say in one voice, 'It has only just begun!' "[15]

The Reich had ceased to be the fatherland. Livonia, a land colonized in the thirteenth century by German knights and protected in the twentieth century by German soldiers, was the true ancestral home. This was the message General von der Goltz brought to his adoring public. After his return to Germany from Livonia, Goltz went on a lecture circuit to propagate his mixture of anti-Bolshevism, colonization policy, and anti-Weimar sentiment. On 21 November 1921 he spoke in Munich, and a twenty-one-year-old student of agriculture, Heinrich Himmler, was in the audience. Himmler had been thinking about settlement in the East since the recruitment drives for the Baltic free corps had begun in early 1919 and, as an admirer of Goltz (whom he had not yet met), he had taken Russian lessons at the university to prepare for the reconstruction of post-Bolshevik Russia. By 1921 his initial enthusiasm had faded, but Goltz's lecture rekindled the old ideal. A meticulous diarist, Himmler noted that same evening, "I am more certain than ever before that when there is another campaign in the East I will join it. The East is what is most important to us. The West dies easily. We must fight and settle in the East."[16]

THE TRUE GERMANY was to be found in the soldiers who had refused to surrender, and her greatest enemies were those who were believed to have actively sabotaged that resistance to the treaty. Millions of Germans called on their government to refuse to sign. "All over Germany, in every region and every social circle, a storm of anger suddenly ignited over the enormous arrogance of the peace terms," a National Socialist study of the history of the German Jews reported. "Everyone was caught in this mood. But in that hour of destiny it was primarily the Jews who were already prepared to sabotage the will to

"The Mask Fell" by Alfred Sedelmann. Illustrierte Zeitung, no. 3960 (1918). Sterling Memorial Library, Yale University. Cartoon illustrating the Germans' perception of the Versailles peace treaty terms.

resist, and who thus broke the united front. In that hour they attacked the German nation in the back.''[17]

Once conservatives in general and National Socialists in particular had determined the line of a Jewish stab in the back, they found evidence for the deed everywhere they looked. From the Reichstag to the Prussian diet to the daily papers, it was the Jews who spoke in favor of the treaty and who urged the government to sign. And sign they did; they had no muscle to support defiant rhetoric. Nevertheless, according to right-wing Germans, the Jews had weakened the national resolve. ''We may, without any reservation, come to the historical judgment that without these Jewish writers and politicians the Reichstag would have decided differently, that is, against signing and in favor of rejection, and that no German government would have been willing to sign it.''[18]

Claiming to speak for the two million dead soldiers of the Great War, absorbing the legacy of the Baltic campaign, the anger about the Versailles treaty, and exploiting the death of sixteen men in the failed putsch of 9 November 1923, Adolf Hitler—one of the millions who had suffered in the trenches—successfully arrogated to himself and his movement the status of

"The Sacrificed, the Present, the Future." Die Brennessel *(1931). Sterling Memorial Library, Yale University. Cartoon showing Weimar Germans dancing around the golden calf and on the graves of the soldiers, while the sober National Socialists are the true heirs of the fallen war heroes.*

the True Germany. He and his followers, the incarnation of the nation, had remained loyal and true to Germany while their fellow countrymen, preferring to forget the four years of war, had given up and given in.[19]

Hitler, the man who had been most loyal to the country, stood at the center of the True Germany. Those who were most loyal to him formed the innermost circle around the core. Heinrich Himmler, known in party circles as *der treue Heinrich*, the loyal Heinrich, perceived this before anyone else, and used it almost flawlessly to bring a marginal party organization, the SS, and himself to prominence. Established in 1925, the original role of the SS, *Schutzstaffeln*, or Protection Squads, was to provide security for party meetings. At the 1926 Party rally in Weimar, Hitler entrusted the 200-strong SS with the Blood Flag, the standard stained with the blood of men shot in the melee of the putsch. The Blood Flag was the movement's holy relic, a symbol not of political miscalculation but of those who had fallen "with loyal faith in the resurrection of their people," as Hitler wrote in the dedication of his *Mein Kampf*.[20]

When the SS became the guardian of the Blood Flag it also became the steward of loyalty. Himmler, appointed by Hitler to lead the SS, appreciated

Hitler and the Blood Flag carried by an SS officer. Die Ewige Strasse V *(1943). Authors.*

the symbolism of the flag and understood the enormous potential of being identified with the virtue of loyalty.[21] He immediately orchestrated the presentation of the SS man as elect precisely because of his loyalty, limiting admission to the "best physically, the most dependable, and the most loyal men in the movement."[22] The SS were indoctrinated to owe unconditional loyalty to the person of Adolf Hitler, and their oath of allegiance proved it: "We swear to you, Adolf Hitler, as Führer and chancellor of the German Reich, our loyalty and bravery. We swear to you, and our superiors appointed by you, obedience to death. So help us God!"[23] Their motto was *"Meine Ehre heisst Treue,"* or My honor is loyalty. Loyalty was the center of their universe.

For Himmler loyalty transcended total obedience to commands given; it signified his duty to anticipate orders. Hitler was his liege, and loyalty to his liege meant total identification of his own aims with those of Hitler. The latter, his rock and his redeemer, did not need either to command or to review the loyal retainer's deeds. Himmler responded "with alacrity to every hint and signal from Hitler," the prominent Holocaust historian Christopher Browning has observed. "Himmler's stock rose precisely because he, more than any of his rivals, had the capacity to interpret Hitler's signals and ideological exhortations and to cast them into concrete programs."[24]

One such program was Himmler's racially perfect SS community. "It remains one of the greatest and most decisive achievements of the Reichsführer-SS," the official SS historian Gunther d'Alquen noted, "that he integrated and clearly applied, with both courage and logical consistency, the theoretical insights of the National Socialist ideology in this field to that which he had

Drawing by Wolfgang Willrich of an SS man. Odal (1936/37). Sterling Memorial Library, Yale University. An SS man not only had to be of good racial stock but also had to look the part. "I insist on a height of 1.70 meters," Himmler declared in January 1937. "I personally select a hundred or two a year and insist on photographs which reveal any Slav or Mongolian characteristics; I particularly want to avoid such types as the members of the 'Soldiers Councils' of 1918–19, people who looked somewhat comic in our German eyes and often gave the impression of being foreigners."

been entrusted to organize.''[25] The SS were selected according to racial criteria and they were obliged to contribute to the future of the race by producing many racially pure children. In his Marriage Order of 31 December 1931, Himmler required potential brides of SS men to be screened carefully; SS men needed his permission to marry. The SS took great pride in the Marriage Order, as it affirmed the loyalty of the individual to his leader. "This drastic order" proved "the self-confidence of this voluntary community," d'Alquen explained, as it meant the complete and to others "incomprehensible intrusion in the so-called personal freedom of the individual.''[26]

Himmler's SS selection procedures and Marriage Order translated Hitler's theories into practice. It was but one instance of his interpretation of the musings of Hitler the prophet and, after the latter's election, his anticipation of the wishes of Hitler the ruler. It was not a hardship; to a large degree, his agenda and Hitler's coincided. In the 1920s and 1930s, in no other domain was this so clear as in their shared belief in the regeneration of Germany in the East.

FACED WITH GEOGRAPHICAL, political, and economic collapse in the wake of defeat, many Germans believed that only the comprehensive reorganization of society would lead to recovery. They blamed the revolution of 1918, the political unrest of the years that followed, and the inflation of 1923 on the modernization of German society and the concomitant disintegration of traditional patterns of authority and loyalty. By the mid-1920s ordinary Germans in the urban areas had faced years of food scarcity, and sometimes even hunger. The metropolis, where the revolutionaries had clustered and the food lines had formed, became the symbol of all that was wrong with the country. The flight from the countryside swelling the city population was the cause of their problems, and it was a move from the rural East to the urban West. Anti-metropolitan sentiment began to merge with theories about the need to settle and strengthen the German East, and the Artaman Society unified these two ideas.

The society was founded in 1923 by Dr. Willibald Hentschell, whose ambition was to renew the German race by resettling urban young people in the countryside.[27] He urged German youngsters to become men, *Manen* in Old Middle German, of the fields, *Art*, or *Artamanen*. The young Heinrich Himmler joined the Artamans and quickly became the Artaman gauleiter, provincial leader, of Bavaria. In 1931 he was the official liaison between the Artamans and the National Socialists, who eventually absorbed the society in the Hitler Youth Land Service. Artaman ideals were to have a profound influence on Himmler's policies in Poland after 1939. And, as it was in the Artaman

Comparison of urban mortality and rural fecundity. Runge, Das Buch des deutschen Bauern *(1935). Seeley G. Mudd Library, Yale University.*

Society that he met the former Baltic volunteer Rudolf Höss, whom he later appointed commandant of Auschwitz, the theories of that organization provide an important context for the history of the concentration camp. Höss recalled the Artaman Society fondly as "a community of young patriotic people." United in their ambition to escape urban tensions, they sought "the natural way of life" in the country. "They hoped to return to the soil from which their ancestors had come forth, to the fountain of life of the German people, to the healthy farming community. This was also my way, my long-sought goal."[28]

The Artamans presented the East as the permanent solution to all that ailed Germany. "Germany's future, Germany's young power is in the East. Our destiny is not determined at the Rhine and the Ruhr, but at the Vistula and the Memel," they proclaimed.[29] As both the Vistula and the Memel flowed largely in the foreign territories of Poland and Lithuania, the Artaman ideology

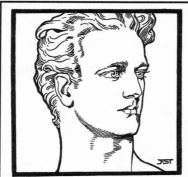

Artaman Poster. Odal, *vol. 11 (1942). Sterling Memorial Library, Yale University.*
"German Youth! The earth of the homeland calls you to voluntary labor service for the sake of People and Fatherland."

had an irredentist, if not belligerent, character. Nevertheless, that is precisely where long-range Artaman planning envisioned settlement. As the Artaman leader Wilhelm Kotzde put it, "Either we will go to the East, as our ancestors did once before in the twelfth century, or we will be erased as a people from world history."[30]

Walther Darré brought many Artaman ideas into theoretical focus and introduced them into mainline National Socialist thinking. A graduate of the German Colonial School at Witzenhausen, Darré had come to the conclusion by 1926 that the attempt to establish a colonial empire overseas had been a disastrous mistake.[31] Like many of his generation, Darré felt that Germany's failure before 1918 to reverse the Polonification of its eastern border region through policies of "inner colonization" had led to the loss of these lands to the new Polish republic. But his perspective was not limited to the pragmatics of power politics. He also trusted that such "inner colonization" would help to reverse the alienation of the German from his land. Darré believed that the Nordic race, which included the German people, was a peasant stock and that it was only as peasants that Germans would live in harmony with nature. In 1929 he published an impassioned plea for a return to the land.[32] Determined to live his doctrine, Darré joined an organization that appeared to provide the most promising means to achieve his own dream of a Nordic peasant state on German soil: Hitler's National Socialist movement.

From the moment that he became a member of the movement, Darré

Painting by Werner Peiner of the "German Earth," owned by Adolf Hitler. Reproduction. Authors.

wielded great influence on the formation of National Socialist agricultural policy, and in June 1930 he was appointed head of the party's Agricultural Organization. One of his allies was that other agriculturalist—the thirty-year-old Reichsführer-SS Heinrich Himmler. Darré's vision of a Nordic peasant state paralleled Himmler's, and he joined the SS to become Himmler's closest adviser on the rooting of a people, or *Volk*, in the earth; as they called it, blood and soil.

According to the National Socialists and their many fellow travelers, Germany did not have enough land to bring the population into harmony with the soil. The space the country needed was in the East. "The fate of Germany is rooted in the East. . . . National Socialism has once more turned the face of the whole people clearly and with conviction to the East, leaving behind us the pernicious influence of the dissolving and decomposing mental sphere of the West," Darré bubbled.[33] The East, however, was a land in trouble. "We look on with dumb resignation while formerly purely German cities—Reval, Riga, Warsaw, and so forth—are lost to our folk." Predicting that even Breslau, Berlin, Stettin, or Dresden could be lost to the Slavs, Darré foresaw great conflict. "Our people must prepare for the struggle and also for this, that in that battle there can be only one outcome for us: absolute victory! The idea of blood and soil gives us the moral right to take back as much eastern land *as is necessary to achieve harmony between the body of our people and geopolitical space.*''[34]

The Artaman perspective of the German East as paradise lost was supported by the scientific theory of geopolitics, according to which the East was the horizon of Germany's future. What the National Socialists admired and called geopolitics was based on the work of the brilliant German geographer Friedrich Ratzel, who in the late nineteenth century had explored the relationship between the political history of states and the geographical conditions of the ground they occupied. Ratzel was interested in the conditions that allow states to thrive. *Raum* (space) or, as he interpreted it, *Lebensraum* (living space) was essential. Ratzel's space was not so much a physical, geographical concept as a vision, a task, and a vocation. The prominent German cartographer Arthur Hillen-Ziegfeld expressed this idea succinctly in 1934. ''German living space is a challenge to our people. It is not an unchanging fact, but an eternal task.''[35] Geopolitics was therefore a science that concerned itself with spatial conditions and spatial requirements. With the questions ''Are the space needs of a state met? If not, how can they be brought into accord with geographical conditions?''[36] the German geopolitical scholar Otto Maull summarized the imperial scope of his discipline.

By the end of the 1930s living space had become, in the words of the German émigré Hans Weigert, ''the national obsession of the German people, strong enough to upset, in our day, the balance of the world.''[37] The popularity of the doctrine was undoubtedly the result of Hitler's enthusiasm for the geographer and retired major general Karl Haushofer, who had constructed a massive edifice of speculation on the foundations laid by Ratzel.[38] Hitler had come in contact with Haushofer through Rudolf Hess, who was an aide of the former and a student of the latter. Under the influence of Haushofer, Hitler devoted significant parts of *Mein Kampf* to geopolitical speculation. He proposed, for example, that ''for Germany . . . the only possibility for carrying out a healthy territorial policy lay in the acquisition of new land in Europe itself. . . . If land was desired in Europe, it could be obtained by and large only at the expense of Russia, and this meant that the new Reich must again set itself on the march along the road of the Teutonic Knights of old, to obtain by the German sword sod for the German plow and daily bread for the nation. . . . We take up where we broke off six hundred years ago . . . and turn our gaze toward the land in the east.'' This policy, he promised, would open ''a great and mighty future.''[39]

With such an endorsement, it is understandable that the medieval settlement of the East became a pivotal point in German historiography after 1933. "The German settlement of the East proved to be the central pillar in the total makeup of the German nation," the authors of a classic description of this Push to the East declared in 1937. "Its history mirrors, with penetrating clarity, German history in general. One must know it to understand the history of the German land and the German people and, consequently, for a correct and deep appreciation of the German character."[40] The central word was "settlement." According to the geopolitical doctrine of *Lebensraum*, the sole purpose of conquest was settlement. The powerful arrows on the geopolitical maps may suggest marching armies rather than plowing peasants, but to a German in the 1930s the identification of the German East with settlement was clear, and its historic place as the greatest feat in the nation's history was accepted without question.[41]

"BACK TO THE LAND" grassroots movements, geopoliticians, and revisionist historians transformed the three words *der deutsche Osten*, the German East, into a magic formula charged with passion and nostalgia. Versailles-engendered irredentism, however, colored the phrase with anxiety and resentment. Germany's territorial losses in the west, where it had been defeated in the field, paled in comparison with its losses in the east, where the country felt its army had won. The wholesale surrender of hitherto uncontested lands to a new nation, Poland, a nonparticipant in the war, that now profited from the defeat

A conservative party campaign poster calling on the electorate to save the East. The defenseless Teutonic Knight is held by a (French?) worker so that a Pole can strike him. Arnold, 800 Jahre Deutscher Orden *(1990).*

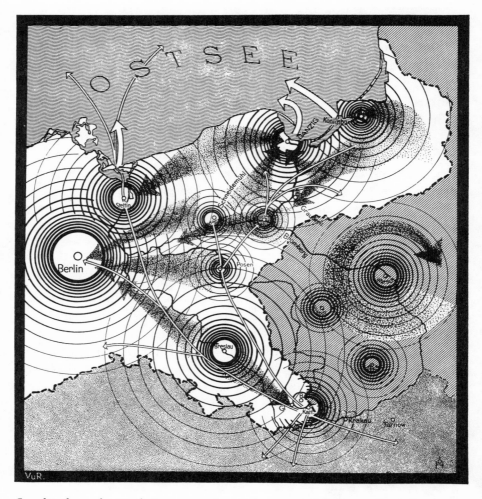

*Geopolitical map showing the interconnected economic structure of the German East before
1919. Heiss and Hillen Ziegfeld, eds., Deutschland und der Korridor (1933).
Sterling Memorial Library, Yale University. The depicted pair of maps by Arthur Hillen-
Ziegfeld show eastern Germany "before" and "after" Versailles. The first map,
"The Organic Economic Game until 1919," presents the region as an area with two well-
balanced and finely tuned economic systems: the German one, which operates on a
supraregional and even international level, and the Polish one, which is of only regional
significance. The most important economic centers are indicated, and concentric
circles show the regions immediately dependent on them. Thin arrows represent the export
of Upper Silesia's coal. Thick arrows show the movement of agricultural products,
suggesting a balance between agricultural production and consumption.*

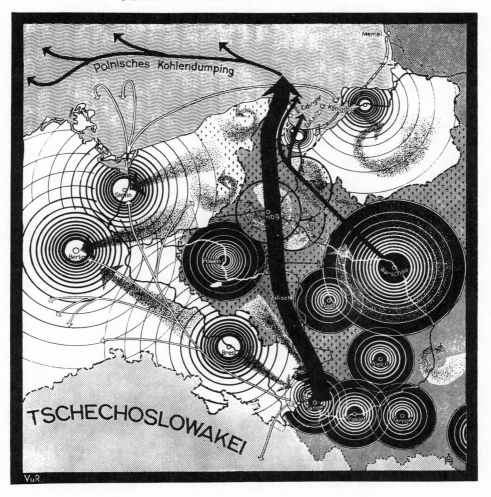

*Geopolitical map illustrating the disjointed economic structure of the German East after
1919. Heiss and Hillen Ziegfeld, eds.,* Deutschland und der Korridor
*(1933). Sterling Memorial Library, Yale University. "The Economic Chaos after 1919"
shows the disastrous results of Versailles. Previously the borders were permeable;
now they are sealed. Breslau has lost half of its economic province, and Danzig, enclosed
in its own little state, is reduced to a fraction of its original economic strength.
The enormous amount of coal the Poles export through the Corridor and the harbor of
Gdynia for lower prices (polnisches Kohlendumping) has closed German
exports through Stettin. Posen, Bromberg, and West Prussia have lost their places in the
"organic" economic system that existed before 1919 and have become part of
a wirtschaftliche Wüstungszone, economic destruction zone, symbolized by little
cemetery crosses.*

of the three powers that had ruled it before, was bitter indeed. Furthermore, the Germans had to transfer Pomerelia to Poland without a plebiscite to give the new state "free and secure access to the sea." The completely German port in that "Corridor," Danzig, became a "free city" in which Poland— and not Germany—enjoyed unrestricted use and service of all waterways, docks, basins, and wharves, and the control and administration of the Vistula, the whole railway system, and postal, telegraphic, and telephonic communication between Poland and the port.[42]

Of all the German territorial losses to Poland, none was so offensive as that of eastern Upper Silesia, the most important industrial region after the Ruhr. "Nowhere else was territory annexed in circumstances so cynical," a well-known historian of Germany, William Harbutt Dawson, observed in 1933. "It was no wonder, therefore, that in this part of Prussia I came into contact with German hostility to the Treaty in its most stubborn and combative form."[43] And he concluded, "Polish Upper Silesia is an irredenta which will figure as such on the map of Europe until it goes back where it rightly belongs."[44]

Many observers, like Dawson, credited the French in particular for the "piece of jugglery" partition of Upper Silesia subsequent to a general plebiscite on 20 March 1921. But a closer investigation reveals that local conditions were to blame for the failure of the referendum to appease either party. Despite the appearance of industrial strength, an urban social, technical, and educational infrastructure had not developed. Upper Silesia was one of the most densely populated areas of Germany, but its industrial face masked a rural heart.[45] There was no real industrial working class and no independent peasantry, just a large proletariat with a peasant-like mentality, robotmen as they were called (from the Polish robotnik, "[manual] worker"), who labored in the mines and factories during the day and worked meager farms in the early morning and evening. Neither industrial workers nor peasants, without trade unions or viable villages to support them, the robotmen fell into a social vacuum, helpless, neglected, and in many ways worse off than their serf ancestors.

In the days that followed the collapse of the German Reich and the Prussian monarchy, the robotmen looked to the new German Social Democrat government for help. But while the socialists could inspire them, they could not deliver improvements. The Polish nationalist Adalbert (Wojciech) Korfanty, one of the few Polish members in the German Reichstag since 1903, stepped into the vacuum and mobilized the robotmen for the Polish cause.[46]

Allied troops occupied Upper Silesia in February 1920 to establish conditions for the vote. The French general Le Rond, chairman of the occupation forces and of the plebiscite commission, was anything but impartial. Le Rond allowed Polish nationalists to organize militias and supported Korfanty secretly.[47] The Germans responded immediately. Volunteer units of demobilized soldiers hurried to the new battleground. After a first round of fighting the situation calmed down, and both sides continued the war through the marginally more peaceful means of propaganda, waging intensive campaigns to win the minds of the undecided.[48]

The plebiscite turnout was a remarkable 98 percent. Contrary to French and Polish expectations, 58 percent of the voters opted to remain part of Germany, while 42 percent chose Poland. The Germans interpreted the outcome as a victory and believed that Upper Silesia would remain within the Reich. The French, however, insisted that the result warranted partition. But where was the boundary to be drawn? The Poles had a majority in four of the seventeen voting districts, but these areas were not contiguous and not all of them bordered on Poland. Furthermore, all the cities had voted for Germany, while the four rural districts that had voted for Poland were without exception sparsely populated. Fighting flared up in this uncertainty in May. Directed by Korfanty, Polish units began to advance again.

This new attack galvanized the whole German nation. Among the young men who came forward to stop Korfanty was the Baltic volunteer Salomon.

Plebiscite poster. "The Polish wolf wants your home! Do not permit it!" Gauss, Das Buch vom deutschen Volkstum *(1935). Sterling Memorial Library, Yale University.*

"It was at six o'clock in the afternoon of May 4th that the newspapers ran the first news of the Polish uprising. I stood in the street and read about it, and decided that the time had come. So I went home, packed my rucksack, and hurried to catch the nine o'clock train." As the train continued to the east more and more volunteers boarded. "Everywhere, in every carriage, young men were sitting or standing. They were cheek by jowl with snoring commercial travellers and businessmen munching sandwiches; the railway officials kept a suspicious eye on them; they were dressed in worn field-grey and darned breeches like myself; their fair hair and arrogant faces gave them all a sort of family likeness, without one's being able to say exactly wherein the likeness lay. We recognized each other at once and saluted one another; we had come from all parts of the realm, scenting fighting and danger, without knowing of one another, without orders and with no definite goal, save only Upper Silesia." Veterans from the war and the free corps were not the only young men found on the train. Forestry students—"wearing green uniforms, hunting knives and cocked hats"—joined, as did high school students. "Student Associations arrived complete, Workers' Unions, soldiers, workmen and young business people. Balts, Swedes, Finns, men from Transylvania and the Tyrol, from East Prussia and the Saar district came, all young, all keen."[49]

These young men enjoyed broad public support. Germans felt that their country had surrendered enough with the transfer of Posen and West Prussia to Poland, and that they had shown themselves to be law-abiding with the plebiscite in Upper Silesia. The piecemeal liquidation of the country, which had begun in November 1918, had to end. At a large protest meeting on 22 May, the prominent Jewish industrialist, onetime leader of the German war economy, and soon-to-be minister of foreign affairs Walther Rathenau called for justice. Germany was a country of sixty million inhabitants, Rathenau reminded the audience, and was still conscious of its own strength and its rights. "We shall defend these rights by peaceful means; but no one shall deprive us of them. And if, owing to unfortunate circumstances, irresponsible persons should dare to separate this province from us, then it will be a sin, whose consequences will lie far more heavily on the nations than Alsace-Lorraine. A wound will have been made in Central Europe which will never close and which can only be healed by justice."[50] As Rathenau spoke, it seemed as if the German volunteer units were about to throw the Poles out of Upper Silesia. The Oberland Corps had conquered Annaberg, the center of the Polish lines. But it was unable to capitalize on its victory. The German government, which could not be seen to support irregular German units taking justice into their own hands, closed the province and interned all the volunteers it could find. Denied fresh reserves, the units at the front were forced to halt their advance. The Weimar Republic had betrayed the German land and people.

The League of Nations partitioned the province more or less along the front line. Hotly contested, the final boundary was carelessly or incompetently drawn. The eastern part of Upper Silesia went to Poland. It contained 85 percent of the Upper Silesian coal reserves and 75 percent of its industries.[51] A district that always had functioned as one economic unit and even individual establishments were severed. The network of narrow-gauge railways was destroyed by arbitrary cuts, and a town was denied its source of water. The partition was an infrastructural disaster. These problems were exacerbated by the peculiar social and demographic structure of Upper Silesia. As many of the robotmen lived on their farms in the rural German part of Upper Silesia far from the mines and industries where they worked during the day, and which ended up in Poland, they found themselves unemployed. The Poles quickly filled the vacancies with immigrants from other parts of Poland, and hastily erected, badly constructed settlements sprang up in the eastern part of Upper Silesia.

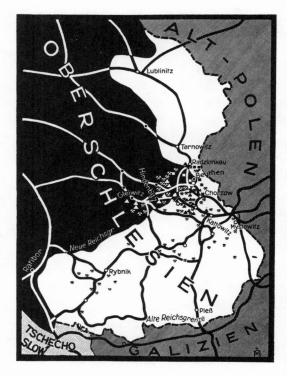

The partition of Upper Silesia. Heiss and Hillen-Ziegfeld, eds., Deutschland und der Korridor *(1933). Sterling Memorial Library, Yale University. The black area remained German; the white became Polish. Auschwitz is located in the gray "Galizien" district where the black railroad lines south of Myslowitz intersect.*

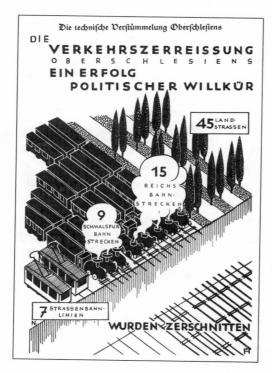

The destruction of the transportation infrastructure as a result of partition. Forty-five country roads, fifteen major railway lines, nine narrow-gauge lines, and seven streetcar lines were cut. Heiss and Hillen Ziegfeld, eds., Deutschland und der Korridor *(1933). Sterling Memorial Library, Yale University.*

The transfer of territory had a great impact also on the formerly Austrian part of Upper Silesia. Until 1919 Oswiecim had been separated from the industrial heart of Upper Silesia by an international border which now had been moved westward. Cities like Kattowitz (or, as it was now called, Katowice) were separated from their former sources of labor and supplies and they turned to the east; the northwestern part of the former duchy of Oswiecim and Zator was integrated rapidly into the industrial and social infrastructure of eastern Upper Silesia. Quick and largely uncoordinated development changed the physical and social landscape of the region. By the late 1920s many of the peasants in the area had become robotmen.

IN 1919 MAX WEBER predicted that if Germany had to give up large territories in the East "the world will witness the rise of a German irredentist movement, that will differ in its revolutionary means from the Italian, Serbian, or Irish only insofar as the will of seventy million will stand behind it."[52] Weber had seen the future correctly, as had William Harbutt Dawson. The Germans had resigned themselves to the conviction "that only another war will restore to them territories which

The German East, 1935. Map by Robert Jan van Pelt and Don Bonner. The Polish state included a substantial Lithuanian minority in the Vilna area, a White Russian minority in Polesia, a Ukrainian minority in Volhynia, and a German minority in Upper Silesia, Posen, and the so-called Corridor. The Germans used this lack of ethnic homogeneity to support their view of Poland as a thieving entity that had always sought to conquer more than it could develop. The Germans saw Poland as a monstrosity with no historical, ethnographic, geographic, or economic justification, a state that made sense only as a creation of the Allies' rage and vindictiveness at Versailles. In the 1930s, Germans had no doubt that, in time, Poland should go and that Germany's dismembered parts would be restored to her.

are still just as dear to them as Alsace and Lorraine are said to be to France,'' Dawson warned his fellow Englishmen. ''That is a dangerous frame of mind into which to drive a great nation.''[53] But that nation was already so driven. The German leadership as well as the general public felt that recovery of the German East was key to Germany's political, economic, cultural, and military reconstruction. They felt that the loss of Posen, Pomerelia, Danzig, and Upper Silesia was a disturbance of the natural order of things. The themes of German construction and Polish destruction, of German culture and Polish sloth, which in the mid-nineteenth century had been subjects of discussion, now became staples of popular resentment. The Polish campaign of 1939 was a long-awaited and warmly welcomed war.

CHAPTER 4

THE THIRD REICH

LOYALTY, OLD-FASHIONED PRUSSIANS LIKE FIELD MARSHAL PAUL VON Hindenburg believed, was bilateral: a soldier was loyal to his commander, and the commander was loyal to his men. In 1917 Hindenburg had promised land in the German East to the veterans under his command. Unable to honor his pledge in the years that followed, he nonetheless never forgot it. When a coalition of right-wing and conservative parties asked him to run for the presidency in 1925, Hindenburg agreed, but insisted that his vow of 1917 would be a plank in his electoral program.

Hindenburg at age eighty-four, 1932. Schultze-Pfaelzer,
Hindenburg und Hitler zur Führung vereint *(1933). Authors.*

After Hindenburg's election the government proposed to divide unviable estates in the eastern provinces into small holdings suitable for settlement by veterans. The Junkers objected: clearly this was the beginning of massive expropriations. They responded swiftly and successfully. The family property of the Hindenburgs, Neudeck, had passed into other hands, and the East Prussian Junkers raised the million marks needed to purchase the estate and restore the house. On the eve of his eightieth birthday they handed Hindenburg the title deeds to Neudeck. Now the man who had been born a Junker finally could live like one. It proved a very good investment: Hindenburg increasingly identified with their interests, and his support for the settlement of veterans waned.[1]

When the depression hit the German East, many Junkers faced bankruptcy. They converged on Neudeck, and in March 1930 Hindenburg wrote the Social Democratic chancellor, Hermann Müller, that the future of that region depended on immediate help for the estates, as these provided the economic base of the area.[2] Soon after Müller received the letter, his government fell, but the honorable and competent new centrist chancellor, Heinrich Brüning, took on "the recovery of eastern agriculture as the foundation of the national and political salvation of the German East."[3] The Brüning government issued an emergency decree to reschedule agricultural debts and to stimulate rural settlement over a period of

Neudeck. Schultze-Pfaelzer, Hindenburg und Hitler zur Führung vereint (1933). Authors. On Hindenburg's request, the main fireplace was marked with his motto: "Loyalty is the mark of honor."

five years. The latter made the Junkers nervous; settlement could only mean land reform. Many of them began to wonder whether, perhaps, the National Socialists would prove more accommodating to their interests.

The law passed, and the newly appointed Reich commissioner for aid in the East, Hans Schlange-Schöningen, began to draft legislation to permit the expropriation and division of nonviable estates.[4] Details of the proposals were leaked and again the government fell. In the election that followed in July 1932, the National Socialists won 230 of the 608 seats and became the largest party in the Reichstag. Overlooking Hitler, Hindenburg appointed Franz von Papen chancellor, but the new Reichstag did not confirm his choice. Hindenburg dissolved the Reichstag once more, setting elections for November 6. When all the votes were in, it seemed that the National Socialist tide had passed. Their share of the popular vote had dropped from 37.4 percent to 33.1 percent, and they won 196 of the 584 seats. Once again Hindenburg ignored Hitler and appointed General Kurt von Schleicher chancellor.

Although Schleicher was determined to stop Hitler, he failed utterly. As with Brüning, it was the issue of the German East which brought him down. In his radio address to the nation of 15 December, Schleicher called for "the more intensive use of our thinly populated East following the example of Frederick the Great's program of inner colonization." Massive settlement

Cartoon criticizing the aid to the East because it helped the Junkers. Die Brennessel *(1933). Sterling Memorial Library, Yale University. "Aid to the East. 'You cannot say that we big agriculturalists do not let the small farmers have their share!'"*

would secure the border ''because in the end it always has been people living on their own land who form the best border wall against the advance of alien nations.''[5] The Junkers interpreted Schleicher's program as a revival of Schöningen's proposals, and once again descended on Neudeck and told Hindenburg that Schleicher had to go. And once again, the eighty-five-year-old Reich president, who by then had slipped into senility, listened to his peers.

On 30 January 1933 Hindenburg asked Adolf Hitler to form a coalition government in which he would be chancellor and Papen vice chancellor. Papen and the other seven gentlemen in the cabinet were confident they could control the ill-bred chancellor and his two crude cohorts, Interior Minister Wilhelm Frick and Minister without Portfolio Hermann Göring, but the trio refused to play by the Junkers' rules. They needed a two-thirds majority in the Reichstag, and they began a campaign to ensure that by the time of the new elections on 5 March the majority of upright German citizens would understand that a fully National Socialist government was the only way to prevent Germany's descent into Bolshevik chaos.

The National Socialists' pièce de résistance was the Reichstag fire of 27 February 1933. Quickly and conveniently blamed on the Communists, it created the atmosphere of apprehension that encouraged Hindenburg to sign an

The Reichstag session of 23 March 1933. Schultze-Pfaelzer, Hindenburg und Hitler zur Führung vereint *(1933). Authors. Göring chaired the first session of the new Reichstag. There was only one point on the agenda: the adoption of the so-called Enabling Act to transfer legislative power to the executive. With only the 94 Social Democrats dissenting and the remaining 441 deputies voting in favor, the act passed easily and Germany accepted dictatorship.*

emergency decree "as a protection against Communist acts of violence endangering the state."[6] In the week between the fire and the election many political opponents were arrested, taken into so-called protective custody, and detained in hastily set-up *Schutzhaftlager*, protective custody camps or, as they were also called, *Konzentrationslager*, concentration camps. Remarkably, the National Socialists did not win a majority. But with eighty-one Communist deputies under arrest or in flight, and with the support of Nationalist and Catholic deputies, Hitler attained an effective majority to suspend the constitution. It was the end of the Weimar Republic.

HITLER'S FIRST MAJOR social program was the Law for the Prevention of Hereditarily Ill Offspring. Himmler had anticipated Hitler correctly: it was the Führer's wish to establish a racially pure, physically perfect people. The policies Himmler had set for the SS were now adapted and adopted for the nation. Ordering the sterilization of the mentally handicapped, schizophrenics, manic-depressives, hereditary epileptics, and the blind, deaf, or alcoholic, this edict was followed by the Law against Dangerous Habitual Criminals, which provided for the castration of serious moral offenders. Initial estimates suggested that some 400,000 people would be sterilized or castrated, but these measures did not go far enough for Hitler. As Himmler had foreseen, marriage itself was to be regulated: the Law to Preserve the Hereditary Soundness of the German People forbidding the marriage of people who had, or had been diagnosed as having, a dangerous contagious disease, a mental disorder, or various hereditary diseases, was passed in 1935.

The new laws and policies were not kept secret from the general public. To the contrary; using the educational curriculum of National Socialist organizations like the Hitler Youth, schoolbooks, articles, and films, the government rallied the population behind its increasingly ferocious and far-reaching racial hygiene policies. A Hitler Youth instruction book, *About the German Nation and Its Living Space*, for example, warned that the increase of the "less worthy" was six times that of healthy people. "Most of these congenitally diseased and less worthy persons are completely unsuited for life. They cannot take care of themselves, and must be maintained and cared for in institutions." Claiming that 1.2 billion marks was "lost" annually in this way, the authors asked, "How many gymnasia, swimming pools, homesteads, and kindergartens could have been built with this money?"[7] New schoolbooks introduced the economics of racial hygiene in math problems: "The construction of an asylum costs 6

Contrasting racial hygiene images in a National Socialist magazine. Neues Volk (1934). Sterling Memorial Library, Yale University. Left: asylum inmates. Right: grandmother with racially healthy grandchildren. "The blessing of the Law for the Prevention of Hereditarily Ill Offspring, which came in force on 1 January, will be obvious only when our mental institutions have to close their gates because there are no hereditarily ill offspring any more. Healthy, happy people in the New Germany! This is how it must be."

million marks. How many new houses at 15,000 marks apiece can be built for this sum?"[8]

Similar arguments were presented in films like *Victims of the Past* (1937). On Hitler's explicit instruction that everyone see this twenty-four-minute movie, it was shown as a trailer in all German cinemas during the Führer's birthday month of April.[9] "Hereditarily healthy people lived in narrow, dark alleys and half-collapsed tenements, while palaces for idiots and imbeciles were built," the narrator lamented, as scenes of squalid slums were followed by views of monumental asylums.[10] Sequence after sequence showing the life of

Racial hygiene image.
Neues Volk (1934).
Sterling Memorial Library,
Yale University. "This nurse,
a powerful, healthy man,
exists only to take care of this
crazy person who is a danger
to all. Shouldn't this picture
shame us?"

inmates unable to communicate or feed themselves and requiring the constant attention of ''racially valuable'' nurses were accompanied by dire warnings. The future of the nation was at risk. In the previous seventy years the German population had increased by 50 percent while the number of people with hereditary illnesses had risen 450 percent. ''If this development continues, fifty years from now one in five people will suffer from hereditary disease,'' the audience was told.[11] Reviewers praised the film for revealing the great threat the German people faced.

As the National Socialists prepared plans to empty the asylums, they enthusiastically filled the camps. Quickly recognized as proof of the regime's resolve to destroy the old social and political structures, the camps became a staple of German life. The concentration camps ''reeducated'' political enemies; the labor service camps awakened young people to the unity of the German nation, forged their consciousness of the *Volk* to which they belonged, and renewed the German race through working the soil. "Physical labor is the way to unify a nation at war with itself," Hitler declared in his May Day speech of 1933. "It is our firm intention that every German, whomever he may be, rich or poor, son of a professional man or of a factory worker, shall once in his life be a manual laborer, so that he may learn what manual labor is and that he may be able to command more easily because he himself has learned to obey."[12]

From its inception in 1933, labor service was compulsory for all university-bound men and this policy was extended to women a year later. A few months of hard work would prevent the academic elitism that plagued the German universities, and give students a healthy respect for the life of the German laborer.[13] In 1935 the service became obligatory for all young men and by the late 1930s had become the focus of the nation's sentiment and pride. The scope of its plans was enormous: the reclamation of marshes, the drainage and irrigation of underdeveloped soils, the concentration of fragmented farm

Labor Service men at work in the Emsland marshes. Erb, ed., Der Arbeitsdienst *(1935). Sterling Memorial Library, Yale University. "On many occasions everyone has to work together. Here a cart has to be put back on the rails." In his May Day speech of 1933, Hitler predicted that by working the land together, Germans would regain the self-confidence to overcome the defeat of 1918. "Germans! You are not second-rate, even if the world wishes to have it so a thousand times. You are not second-class and inferior. Awake to the realization of your own importance."*

properties, the protection of lowlands by dikes, and the reclamation of land from the sea were to affect one-fifth of Germany.[14] The *Arbeitsmänner* began "where Frederick the Great left off," they were reminded. They were to continue "the great settlement work, the internal colonization, which Frederick the Great carried out."[15]

Hitler's goal was to create a unified, healthy, racially pure National Socialist people. Marriage, medical care policies, school curricula, the national labor service, and youth organizations conduced towards that end. Theoretically, so did concentration camps. In the early days of National Socialist rule, ordinary people and ideologues alike believed that the newly established camps served a pedagogical rather than a punitive purpose. Hard labor and rigid discipline would return the errant sons to the National *Socialist* community. There was, in other words, no fundamental difference between the labor service camps and the concentration camps. They differed only in degree.

Many members of the party well remembered that the very men incarcer-

Roll call at Oranienburg concentration camp, 1934. Schäfer, Konzentrationslager Oranienburg *(1934). Seeley G. Mudd Library, Yale University. The legal origins of the camp system was Hindenburg's emergency decree "For the Protection of People and State" (28 February 1933), which promised protection against Communist acts of violence. It led to mass arrests of political opponents of the National Socialists and the creation of protective custody camps or concentration camps. The immediate purpose of these camps was to make the Communist threat visible to the general public.*

ated because they were Socialists or Communists had risked their lives for the Fatherland in the Great War. The National Socialist ideologue Gregor Strasser pounded that message home: in the trenches, all soldiers, rich or poor, had been equal in a true "community of need." After the war, this community had been abandoned. The poorer half of the nation "had been denied the most basic needs of life by the other half." The German workers' movement, he insisted, had been "nothing but the cry of millions of fellow German countrymen for acceptance into the nation on equal terms."[16]

The camp commandants themselves accepted this view. The commandant of Oranienburg, Werner Schäfer, for example, presented his institution as a hard school where duped and deceived Germans were reeducated against their will but for their own good. The goal was to attain political insight and a work ethic, he wrote in his 246-page rhetorical analysis, *Konzentrationslager Oranienburg* (1934).[17] His task, he said, was to knock sense into men who should know better than to be tools for the International Jew. He stressed that he taught by example and through work; the beating was purely metaphorical. "One should not underestimate the difficulty and value of such educational work. It is absolutely clear that the character of a great percentage of the German people has been damaged by the fourteen-year-period of want [1918–32] with its clash of opinions, its unemployment, and its pauperization." After that, the usual pedagogical tools were no longer useful; only "example and work" were salutary.[18]

Reformed ex-inmates thanked him for their conversion in the camp, and fathers asked him to reeducate their sons. One father was prepared to pay for his son's stay, and another offered a charitable contribution of five hundred marks for poor SA men. But camps like Oranienburg were not for such young men. "I believe that for such recalcitrant and perhaps licentious people the labor service is of greater value . . . than to undergo our educational effort, which is more appropriate for explicit asocials," Schäfer explained.[19]

In 1933 and 1934, National Socialists like Schäfer believed that, in their adherence to notions of international class solidarity, Communists and Social Democrats exhibited asocial behavior. Their (misguided) idealism, however, at least revealed a consciousness that could be reeducated. By contrast, the very existence of tramps, addicts, and beggars damaged the community of the nation. And while the incarceration of bourgeois Social Democrats may have been unsettling for the German middle class, that same bourgeoisie had no qualms about using the camps to clean up its cities. As early as July 1933 the

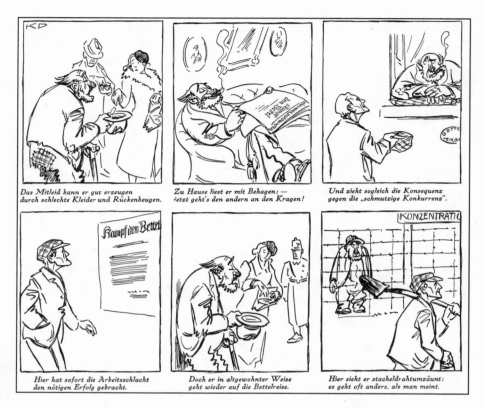

"Ballad of the Habitual Beggar." Die Brennessel *(1933). Sterling Memorial Library, Yale University. The "Jew" begs but lives well, and ends up in a concentration camp. The "German" initially is a beggar, but heeds the party's disapproval and goes to work. Rudolf Höss, later commandant of Auschwitz, joined the concentration camp system in 1934. Responsible for a barrack of asocials, he saw it as his main task to teach them the value of hard work, which would bring structure and endurance to an unstable life. Höss therefore adopted Theodor Eicke's motto* Arbeit macht frei *(Work will set you free) as his own and, six years later, nailed it above the gate of Auschwitz.*

German Society for Public and Private Welfare petitioned Rudolf Hess to take advantage of the camps to solve the problem of the vagrants and asocials who "pillaged" the welfare offices. Representatives of the three major German welfare organizations, religious leaders, and national, provincial, and local bureaucrats meeting a few months later agreed that concentration camps were the right place for asocials. As the conference wound up, the new chief of police of Bavaria, Heinrich Himmler, ordered the first dragnet operations to clean the province of the undesirables. It was the beginning of his political career, and the end of the line for many who were caught. Most of the prisoners were sent to the concentration camp in Dachau, which Himmler had established on 21 March of that year in a derelict munitions factory. The upright citizens of Bavaria were relieved; the sole dissenting voice came from the Chamber of Commerce. It feared that, as concentration camp workers were not paid, camp products would undercut the competition.[20]

The asocials were not the main target of police concern, however. For the first years of the Third Reich, while consolidating its power, the regime concentrated the limited (even in Germany) resources of the Kripo (*Kriminalpolizei*, or Criminal Police) and Gestapo (*Geheime Staatspolizei*, or Secret State Police) on political opponents. In the years that followed, the definition of asocials to be reeducated in the camps was altered and expanded to fit the government's changing needs and goals. For example, by 1938 the shortage of workers for the Reich had become so acute that Himmler, by then chief of the German police, detailed his subordinate Reinhard Heydrich, head of the SD (*Sicherheitsdienst*, or Security Service), to organize a comprehensive swoop of asocials because, as the latter announced, "the strict implementation of the Four-Year Plan demands the employment of every able-bodied person and does not allow asocial individuals to avoid work." Asocials were now defined as vagabonds, beggars, pimps (past, present, or even just suspected), and "persons with several convictions for creating disorders, doing bodily harm, causing brawls, breaking the peace, etc., who have thus demonstrated that they are not prepared to fit into the national community." Even more ominously, Heydrich also included "gypsies and persons travelling in gypsy fashion who have shown no desire for regular work or have violated the law" and "all male Jews with previous criminal records."[21] Ethnicity had become a salient factor.

While the Gestapo began its raids to cleanse the German streets of the so-called work-shy, Himmler founded DEST (*Deutsche Erd- und Steinwerke*, or German Earth and Stone Works) to exploit the incarcerated men. Utilizing their slave labor, the various branches of the company, such as the granite quarries of Mauthausen, the brickyards of Sachsenhausen, and the limestone quarries in Buchenwald, produced the building materials needed for the Führer's construction projects. The sale of these competitively priced products (labor costs were minimal) supported SS programs not funded by the state.

"Usefully Employed." Jewish slave labor from Mauthausen as depicted in an SS publication. Das Schwarze Korps *(1941). Sterling Memorial Library, Yale University. This is one of the few images of concentration camp inmates in contemporary German literature. The text reads, "The pictures on this page are not the result of years of intensive collection activity. Nor are they taken in a wax museum or a display case of freaks. They also are not pictures of Germany's now long past housecleaning of Jewish criminals. These illustrations merely depict Dutch labor leaders. Having committed terrible crimes, they are now employed in strict working conditions for the public good, and this time against their will. Not too long ago they must have thought that their 'future business' would be quite different."*

For Ulrich Greifelt, Himmler's liaison with the Four-Year Plan, the camps were "the ideal means . . . for achieving the productive deployment of the labor potential of criminal and political prisoners. . . . More than 10,000 of these asocial forces are currently undertaking a labor training cure in the concentration camps, which are admirably suited for this purpose."[22]

HIMMLER REALIZED THAT control over part of the economy was the key to permanent political power, and in the late 1930s the Four-Year Plan to make Germany self-sufficient controlled German production and consumption. As plenipotentiary for its implementation, Göring had become Germany's economic dictator. One of his responsibilities was the allocation of increasingly scarce labor to the various areas of economic activity. Göring favored the large industries and did not care about agriculture. Confronted with a new flight from the land, the Junkers began to hire migratory foreign labor, as they had done prior to 1914. While Göring did not care about migrant workers, this development disturbed Himmler. Both his suspicion of Göring's policy and his need to cooperate with him informed his decision to establish a special liaison bureau between the SS and the Four-Year Plan Office, and he appointed the forty-one-year-old Greifelt as director.

Himmler and Greifelt shared a vision. They saw that *Volksdeutsche*, ethnic Germans who lived outside the Reich and who did not have German citizenship, provided a huge labor reserve to work the estates, if they could be brought to Germany. Many of them lived in German enclaves dating from the Middle Ages; others, in the German villages in Galicia and Volhynia, traced their roots to settlement projects in the eighteenth and early nineteenth centuries. Once pillars of Hohenzollern, Habsburg, or Romanov power, after 1918 these scattered communities had become unpopular and unwelcome relics of collapsed regimes.

The plight and the future of the ethnic Germans had become central issues in Weimar culture. And awareness of their position quickly turned into an

Distribution of ethnic groups in Middle Europe. Haushofer and Fochler-Haube, eds., Welt in Gärung: *(1937). Sterling Memorial Library, Yale University. Key: white boxes = non-German minorities; and gray boxes = German area of settlement and ethnic German areas. In his 1927 study on borders, Haushofer wrote that ethnic German areas of settlement were of great geopolitical significance. "All these regions are biologically part of the Reich," Haushofer claimed, and one of the great tasks of geopolitics was "to keep that knowledge alive."*

Germany and German States

Germany	65,000,000	98.5%
Austria	6,500,000	95.5%
Switzerland	2,950,000	72.0%
Danzig	400,000	98.1%
Luxembourg	285,000	95.0%
Liechenstein	10,000	100.0%
Total:	**75,000,000**	

Non-German States In Europe

Czechoslovakia	3,265,000	23.3%	Yugoslavia	700,000	5.0%
Bohemia	2,300,000		Banat-Batshka	450,000	
Moravia	800,000		Croatia-Slavonia	160,000	
Slovakia	150,000		Slovenia	70,000	
Carpatho-Ruthenia	15,000		Bosnia	16,000	
France	1,700,000	4.0%	Hungary	600,000	7.5%
Alsace-Lorraine	1,580,000		Italy	250,000	n/a*
Soviet Union	1,240,000	0.8%	Belgium	150,000	1.8%
Volga Germans	392,000		Lithuania	120,000	5.6%
Ukraine	395,000		Holland	100,000	1.2%
Crimea	45,000		Latvia	70,000	3.7%
Caucasus	75,000		Denmark	60,000	1.7%
Siberia	120,000		Estonia	23,000	2.0%
Poland	1,150,000	3.6%	Other countries in Europe	60,000	
Posen-Pomerelia	350,000		**Total**	**10,300,000**	
East Upper Silesia	300,000		Africa	104,200	
Teschen	40,000		Asia	21,000	
Congress Poland	350,000		North America	8,500,000	
Galicia	60,000		South America	1,200,000	
Volhynia	50,000		Australia and New Zealand	77,000	
Romania	800,000	4.4%	**Total**	**95,000,000**	
Banat	300,000				
Transylvania	230,000				
Bessarabia	90,000				
Bukovina	80,000				
Dobrudja	14,000				

*Percentage not provided because Fascist Italy was a German ally, and the German government did not want to antagonize the Italians by playing up the importance of ethnic Germans.

Table 1. Distribution of Germans in Europe and the world. Gauss, ed., Das Buch vom deutschen Volkstum (1935).

exaggerated view of their contribution to Central and East European culture. Just as other European colonists had carried the "White Man's Burden" in the jungles and deserts, the Germans had fulfilled that destiny in the Baltic and the Crimea, in Galicia, Volhynia, Podolia, Bessarabia, Bukovina, Transylvania, and the Banat. By showing the Slavs, the Magyars, and the Romanians what diligence could achieve, they taught by example. In a fundamental sense, these ethnic Germans had continued the medieval task of the German settlers who had arrived in Poland as *Kulturträger*, bearers of culture.[23]

Before 1933 the National Socialists had presented their movement as the champion of the German people as a whole, both within and outside the boundaries of the German Reich. After taking control of the government, Hitler needed to consolidate his power within the Reich. He could not afford confrontations with neighboring states, and he therefore could not meddle openly in their internal affairs. So while he sought to bring the various German organizations involved with the ethnic Germans and their ethnic German communities under National Socialist control, he could not support the ethnic Germans publicly.[24]

Himmler's concern with ethnic German affairs was based on a number of considerations. First, he recognized the political value of responsibility for over ten million ethnic Germans. Just as the SD and the SS-run concentration camps strengthened his position, the ethnic Germans too could be a source of direct power. Furthermore, the ethnic Germans could provide the men for armed SS units, the later Waffen SS. Within the Reich, only the army had the right to recruit, and Himmler understood that if he wanted to build his own armed forces he needed to look elsewhere for young men. Finally, Himmler believed that major ethnic German communities, such as those in Livonia or Transylvania, had remained racially pure.[25]

Himmler's interests were respected. With the appointment of his aide Werner Lorenz as head of the newly established (January 1937) Vomi (*Volksdeutsche Mittelstelle*, or Ethnic German Liaison Office), and Hermann Behrends, head of Section II of the SD Main Office, the division that dealt with Jews, churches, Freemasons, and other perceived enemies of National Socialist Germany, as Lorenz's chief of staff, Himmler effectively took control of that organization.[26] Ultimately Vomi became an official part of the SS, formalizing the fact that from its very inception it had been Himmler's own instrument of foreign policy.

By 1938 Himmler had seen the pawn value of the ethnic Germans in his

German Balt. Paul, Grundzüge der Rassen- und Raumgeschichte des deutschen Volkes *(1935). Sterling Memorial Library, Yale University. National Socialists rated the German Balts as the elite of the ethnic Germans; these descendants of the Teutonic Knights were paradigms of the German* Herrenmensch, *or master race. Respectable scholars commended the Balts' unwillingness to intermarry with the indigenous populations as a unique example of German race consciousness. From the Balts twentieth-century Germans could get a sense of what their ancestors had been like. According to the then well-known anthropologist Gustav Paul, "in the Baltic, German culture developed to especially splendid heights supported by a class of aristocratic and bourgeois* Herrenmenschen. *It is well known to what extent they have influenced the science, scholarship, and art of the motherland, and to what infinite extent they have enriched it." One of the most attractive aspects of the Balts was that their isolation had allowed them to escape "the disastrous rule of the Enlightenment, of liberalism, of Marxism, and of industrialization, and with that the destruction of the organic order, the total interbreeding, and the purposeless, anemic intellectuality" that had ravaged the Reich.*

battles with Göring, and he had appointed Greifelt to sign them up as agricultural laborers in the East. Greifelt was stymied by the various national governments' policies which did not permit the recruitment of ethnic Germans exclusively. By then the labor shortage had increased to over 550,000 men, and Greifelt began to consider permanently resettling ethnic Germans in the Reich. "In these Germans who live outside the borders of the Reich we find the natural reserves we need to satisfy the Reich's requirements for labor in the near future," he told Himmler's staff in January 1939. "In his New Year's message of 1939 the Führer has said that the problem of labor must be solved. The repatriation of German labor and life power will be an important, albeit partial, solution to this task given to us by the Führer. The Reichsführer-SS has taken it upon himself to initiate and steer this repatriation."[27]

It was the fate of the ethnic German community in South Tyrol which focused Himmler's attention on the possibilities of repatriation. South Tyrol had belonged to Austria-Hungary before the First World War, but it had been given to Italy as a reward for joining the Allies in 1915, even though 80 percent of the 260,000 inhabitants were German. The Italians initiated an intensive program to introduce their language and culture, but the South Tyroleans did not appreciate this good fortune. In early 1939 Vomi received instructions to prepare for their comprehensive resettlement.

The operation was based on the principle that the community should be relocated as a whole. But where was an area to be found that could house 200,000 people? Himmler addressed this problem in a memorandum of May 1939. The required space had to be found in the East, he wrote. "It is to be preferred that this area will be inhabited by a non-German population, and will be emptied of all occupants. . . . I can imagine that such an area can be created in the Bohemian-Moravian space, preferably in northern Moravia . . . which has the advantage of ensuring that Moravia, which ought to become totally German again, will receive the valuable addition of 200,000 racially sound, very conscious and militant Germans."[28]

BY THE TIME Himmler suggested the deportation of part of the Moravian population, the Czech lands were already under German control. The occupation of Bohemia and Moravia on 15 March 1939 had led to a worsening of relations between Germany and England and France. The Allies had given in to Hitler's demands until then because, to them, the Anschluss of Austria and even the annexation of the Sudeten could be justified on the grounds of self-determination for the local populations. The German occupation of what had remained of Czechoslovakia after the secession of Slovakia could not be explained as a reunification of Germans with Germany, however. As suspicion increased in London and Paris, the German minister of foreign affairs, Joachim von Ribbentrop, demanded the return of Danzig to the Reich and the creation of an extraterritorial highway and railway connection between Germany and Danzig—East Prussia. On Sunday, 26 March, the Polish government politely but firmly rejected any such course of action. Five days later the British prime minister, Neville Chamberlain, rose in the House of Commons to announce that Britain and France "would lend the Polish Government all support in their power" if Poland were attacked.[29]

A war of nerves followed; German-Polish relations broke down completely and in August the Polish government began to mobilize its forces secretly. One of the officers called up for duty was the twenty-five-year-old diplomat Jan Kozielewski. A second lieutenant in the reserve, Kozielewski was ordered to report immediately to an artillery regiment stationed in Oswiecim. He did not take the mobilization very seriously. ''It might even turn out to be fun. I remembered that Oswiecim was situated in the middle of an expanse of fine, open country. I was an enthusiastic horseback rider and I relished the notion of galloping about in uniform on a superb army horse.''[30] Discussion of the political and military situation at first was taboo in the pleasant officers' mess in the camp. ''When we did, at length, launch upon a consideration of [the] present position and the possibilities that were in store for us, our opinions tended to confirm each other and finally congealed into a uniform optimism.'' They were confident that ''Germany was weak and Hitler was bluffing. When he saw that Poland was strong, united, and prepared, he would back down quickly and we should all go home. If not, the farcical little fanatic would be taught a severe lesson by Poland and, if necessary, by England and France.''[31]

On Thursday, 31 August 1939, the farcical little fanatic signed a directive. ''Now that all the political possibilities are exhausted for a peaceful resolution of a situation on the eastern frontier which is intolerable for germany, i have determined on a solution by force.''[32] That night the Germans staged an attack

The former labor exchange dormitories turned Polish army barracks at Zasole, late 1930s. Auschwitz-Birkenau State Museum, neg. 2100.

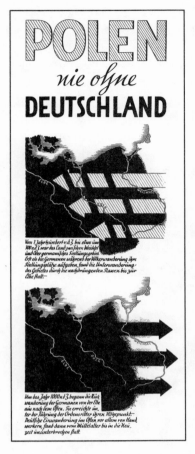

by SS men dressed in Polish uniforms on the German radio station in the Upper
Silesian city of Gleiwitz. In response to the "Polish attack" the German army
began to cross the border on 1 September at 5:45 A.M. A military base close
to the border, Oswiecim soon came under attack. According to Kozielewski,
the Luftwaffe came first and armored units followed shortly thereafter.

> The extent of the death, destruction and disorganization this combined
> fire caused in three short hours was incredible. By the time our wits were
> sufficiently collected even to survey the situation, it was apparent that we
> were in no position to offer any serious resistance. Nevertheless, a few

batteries, by some miracle, managed to hold together long enough to hurl some shots in the direction of the tanks. By noon, two batteries of our artillery had ceased to exist.

The barracks were almost completely in ruins and the railroad station had been leveled.[33]

In the years that followed, Jan Kozielewski (better known by his underground name, Jan Karski) proved an extremely courageous man; he was one of the first to give to the West eyewitness testimony of the destruction of Polish Jewry. But, writing in 1943, he creatively projected the ruined face of Poland onto a town and a military base that, because of the hasty Polish retreat,

"Difficult advance on Polish 'streets.'" Illustrierte Zeitung, *no. 4932 (1939). Sterling Memorial Library, Yale University. In his report on Himmler's repatriation of ethnic Germans,* Ruf des Reiches— Echo des Volkes *(1940), the well-known National Socialist writer Hanns Johst focused on the Poles' neglect of their roadways as a symbol of national character and culture. The poor condition of the Polish roads justified history's death sentence for the Polish state because the law of nature dictates that an organism with clogged arteries must die. If the Poles could not fill a few potholes, they certainly could not be trusted to run a whole country.*

suffered relatively little damage. After the battle the barracks at Zasole stood as solidly as they had before, intact and available for use by the Germans. And far from having been leveled, the railroad station quickly became a major point on the maps of the German Reich railways.

A week later, as Franz Lüdtke reminisced in 1941, "Poland had lost the land robbery of Versailles; in just one week the German soldier stood deep in the Polish land. The standards of our incomparable army fluttered in places where in early times German men had worked the fields, and where in the Middle Ages German burghers and farmers had built towns and villages."[34] On 17 September the Soviet army sealed the fate of Poland with an invasion from the east. Ratified on September 28, the fourth partition of Poland established a new border, running along the Bug River, between Germany and the Soviet Union.[35]

AS THE GERMANS marched into the newly conquered territory, they saw traces of their homeland everywhere. "Here, in the easternmost part of the Government General one expects, perhaps, a mass of wooden houses with a market full of Jews, but never an old town center that betrays its German builders so clearly," the National Socialist writer Hermann Seifert remarked in a popular book about the Jewish Question in occupied Poland. Standing in the middle of Lublin, "one believes oneself to be in the heart of the Reich."[36] But while the German settlers had cleared the land and established villages and towns, the Jewish immigrants were parasites who exploited the business opportunities generated by the Germans.[37] According to Seifert, they were able to do little else. Polish Jewry was a degenerated race, suffering from "inbreeding, dementia, inherited diseases, pests, dirt and vermin, no joy in giving birth, and so on." Paradoxically, their reduced vitality did not mean a dimunition "of the Jewish danger." Germans "should not forget that this East Jewry has been the source of the regeneration of World Jewry."[38]

How well the National Socialist propaganda had done its work can be measured from the reactions of German soldiers in 1939 as compared to their predecessors who had advanced into Russian Poland a quarter of a century earlier. Whereas the soldiers of 1915 had been a bit bewildered by the Jews and the Jewish ghettos, and had written sympathetically about the poverty of these "victims of the czar," the men marching into Poland in 1939 expressed only contempt and revulsion. Jews were the main culprits responsible for Poland's mess, and the chief obstacle to their mission to prepare the ground for the reconstruction of the German East. "I do not understand how this kind of people is biologically capable of remaining alive," a German soldier wrote in his diary on 11 November. "Figures that elsewhere can be seen only in hospitals walk around by the thousand. . . . In addition to the biological corruption is the filth, which cannot be described." Neither, evidently, could the Jewish physiognomy. "The primitive Jewish face, which has not yet been covered by a Western makeup, is unspeakably alien, and cannot be compared to anything. . . . Even the most impervious Asiatic face is an open book compared with the ghost that overtakes these Jewish faces."[39]

That soldier was speaking for many Germans in the fall of 1939—Polish Jewry was lice-ridden, diseased, and degenerate. The popular *Illustrierter Beobachter* magazine, for instance, ran an article on what the editors considered to be the most important ritual of Polish Jews: the daily search for lice.[40] German physicians eagerly pointed out that body lice were carriers of exanthematic typhus, and they claimed that the lack of cleanliness in Jewish neighborhoods was due to moral sloth, not poverty. A certain Dr. Erich Waizenegger observed in a book on the control of epidemics in the Government General that "the Jew totally lacks any concept of hygiene." The living quarters of Jews were "full of filth and rubbish," and they "very seldom changed" their "ragged and unbelievably dirty clothing and linen." Throughout the ghettos the Jewish population was "infested with lice" which, naturally, could but lead to "the spread of spotted typhus."[41]

The wretched conditions of eastern Jewry provided the Germans with the empirical evidence to "prove" their anti-Semitic ideology. The SS bi-weekly, *Das Schwarze Korps*, for instance, ran two articles graphically summarizing the alien character of the Jews. Immediately after the German occupation of Polish towns and villages "a swarming mass of peculiar and unbelievable figures erupted from the dark basements and filthy tenements." These ghettos were an "unfathomable reality. . . . Here was the breeding-ground of World Jewry." The association with vermin was emphasized once again.

> In an unbelievable environment of filth and sanitary pollution, in a bizarre labyrinth of alleys, multileveled basements and built-up courtyards, thronged an innumerable mass of Jews, which constantly multiplied despite poverty and typhus. Countless habitual criminals, murderers, swindlers, and pickpockets hid in these dark caves—types who, as we have already shown in one of our last issues, had to be taken from underground rats' nests by German cleaning crews at the risk of their own lives. This clearing work strained the nerves of the men of the SS and police who were responsible for this task. They had to fight their way through

strong-smelling clouds of stench, through muck, muck, and more muck, through vermin-infested and disgusting Jewish living spaces. Everyone who was there still shivers with horror when he remembers, and admits that he only recognized the true nature of Jewry through those experiences.[42]

The next issue, the editors of the SS biweekly promised, would discuss an exemplary solution "to the Jewish Problem: Productive Work!"[43]

A fortnight later readers of *Das Schwarze Korps* learned from an article mockingly entitled "Gruesome Exaction" that the German authorities had established the principle that "only he who works will eat." Referring to Hans Frank's decrees subjecting all Jews between fourteen and sixty-one years of age to forced labor, the authors marveled that Jews had to work, "truly and honestly work with their hands." Of course, Jews were rather useless as laborers: four Jewish workers accomplished less than one unskilled German. Nevertheless, "with the establishment of Jewish workshops and the comprehensive organization of Jewish labor" Himmler's agent in Lublin, Odilo Globocnik, had endeavored successfully "to solve the Jewish Question." His effort "transcends local significance, and perhaps offers a road to a generally applicable, positive order."[44]

German newspapers carried many gleeful and profusely illustrated articles about the new anti-Jewish measures introduced in the Government General. "The Jews Must Work!" ran the headline over a photograph of Jewish men carrying bricks in the weekly *Illustrierter Beobachter* of 12 October.[45] "It gives us particular pleasure to use the beloved gentlemen of Abraham's seed for carrying straw and setting up camps," one Dr. Emil Strodthoff wrote in the *Völkischer Beobachter* of 28 November. "We simply went through the streets, collecting them, and whoever, despite a friendly request, thought he had no time, was soon taught better."[46] The anti-Semitism was propaganda, but the news was not, as the press in neutral countries reported. "Untold thousands of Jews, who in former times belonged to the professions, are now compelled by the German authorities to do other kinds of work, such as building roads, clearing forests, etc.," the Zürich paper *Die Tat* announced in its issue of 1 January 1940.

In the district of Lublin, where as is known most of the Jews live, they now have begun to call upon Jews for reclamation work. Spread over wide areas, they are at work on the regulation of streams and rivers,

"Jews must work."
Illustrierter
Beobachter *(1939).*
Sterling Memorial
Library, Yale University.

building dikes and draining swamps. In the Lublin district, from 12,000 to 14,000 Jews were rounded up for this kind of work. They have been allocated to forty-five work centers. They live in thirty-four camps. Within the next few weeks other districts will follow the example of Lublin and, as the *Warschauer Zeitung* reports, the remaining Jews will be employed in this and similar work.[47]

Paradoxical as it may have seemed to some, Jewish forced labor was to make good the German promise to repair the Polish roads, straighten the riverbanks, and dig new canals.

ADOLF HITLER DID not mention the thousands of Jewish laborers in his speech to the Reichstag on 6 October. Reiterating the claim that the Poles were

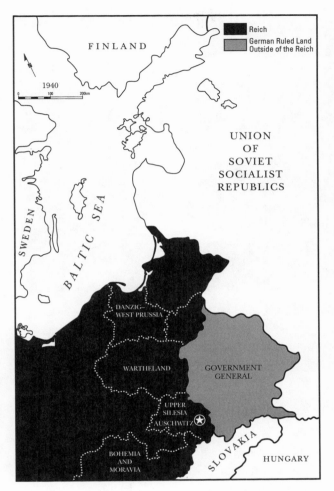

The German East, 1940. Map by Robert Jan van Pelt and Don Bonner. The German public was enthusiastic about the return of Danzig, West Prussia, Posen, and Polish Upper Silesia, but Silesia's governor Josef Wagner and his top civil servants opposed the annexation of Auschwitz and Eastern Upper Silesia to the Reich. Given the economic disparity between the area that had remained German after 1921, the land that had been Polish between 1921 and 1939, and the part that had not belonged to the Reich since 1457, they felt that the German government would do better to add the central and eastern regions to the Government General. In the end the Silesian bureaucrats were overruled by no one less than Hitler, but he accommodated them by granting Upper Silesia separate provincial status, and he appointed Wagner's deputy Fritz Bracht governor.

unable to husband the earth, he once again declared his resolve to bring order to Poland, and explained explicitly how this was to be done. It was Germany's most important task, he declared, "to establish a new order of ethnographic conditions, that is to say, resettlement of nationalities in such a manner that the process ultimately results in the obtaining of clearer dividing lines than is the case at present."[48]

Hitler also tendered a peace offer to England and France, but neither England nor France was interested. Faced with their rejection, Hitler proceeded to annex the western part of Poland, thus enlarging two extant provinces, East Prussia and Silesia, and creating two new ones, Danzig–West

*Jewish forced laborers in Auschwitz, 1940. Auschwitz-Birkenau State Museum, neg.
20829/19. Jews from the town of Auschwitz were drafted to repair the bridge
over the Sola, which had been destroyed in the first days of the war. After the SS took
the barracks at Zasole, Jewish forced laborers were dispatched to clean the
buildings and the site.*

Prussia and Wartheland. With these additions to the Reich, the potential space
for the South Tyrolean resettlement increased significantly. Hugo Hassinger,
geographer and *Lebensraum* specialist from Vienna, was commissioned to study
the possibilities. Only one seemed feasible: ''In the Beskid Mountains, in the
territory of the onetime German duchies of Teschen, Auschwitz, and Zator, the
old German colonist tradition can be resumed.''[49] Oswiecim was envisioned as
the political, economic, and cultural center of this New South Tyrol. Surveyors
were sent to make an inventory of the housing stock. One of them assayed
the former Polish military base; on his plan he noted that ''in normal conditions'' the twenty-two brick dormitories afforded space for 2,100 men, while
the twenty-two wooden stables could shelter 836 horses.[50] A new German
municipal government was appointed. To prepare the town for its pride of
place, these officials hastily renamed the town Auschwitz, and the old market,
which for centuries had been known as *Ring* to the Germans and *Rynek* to the
Poles, Adolf Hitler Platz.

Jews had no place in what had become another ordinary town of the Third Reich. Soon after the rechristening of the town and the market, the first 1,000 Jewish inhabitants of German Auschwitz were deported. A fourteen-year-old witness lost his grandparents. "It was the first really terrible ordeal the people suffered. Every family mourned, each home was filled with weeping. The rabbinate called a day of fasting, loud prayers rose from every *Shtibl* [prayer house], *Tilim* [psalms] were heard from every window."[51] God did not listen, or care, or act, or if He did nobody noticed. Jewish life in German Auschwitz became increasingly constricted and circumscribed. The synagogue was closed, and burned in early 1940. But the community saved the Torahs, and they were entrusted to individual families. In these homes, the Jews continued to gather and to pray.

The 1,000 deportees were sent to a newly established Jewish reservation south of Lublin. This new "homeland" for the Jews was the initiative of Adolf Eichmann, a member of Heydrich's Security Police who, at the time of the Polish campaign, headed the Office of Jewish Emigration for the Protectorate of Bohemia and Moravia. Eichmann had gained quite a reputation in post-Anschluss Vienna when he oversaw the emigration of 117,000 Austrian Jews in one year. In April 1939 he was moved to Prague, where he had less success; by then Czech Jews found it almost impossible to get visas. Fearing failure, Eichmann began to look for another solution. In late September he found a new "home" for Czech Jewry: the region surrounding the Polish town of Nisko. Eichmann and his immediate superior, Franz Stahlecker, visited the area. "We saw an enormous territory," Eichmann recalled in 1960, "river, villages, markets, small towns, and we said to ourselves: This is perfect, why not resettle the Poles, seeing that there's so much resettling being done in any case, and then move Jews into this big territory." Eichmann believed that a reservation for Jews "would take care of one point of the party program: solution of the Jewish problem."[52]

Eichmann explained his plan to Heydrich, who told Himmler, who told Hitler. With their approval, trains for Nisko left from Vienna, Ostrau, Kattowitz, and Auschwitz a few weeks later. There the deportees were left to fend for themselves. "What may prove to be the final act of the incredibly brutal and cruel tragedy which Adolf Hitler has inflicted on the Jews in his power is now going on," the American writer Oswald Garrison Villard wrote in the December issue of the *Spectator*. Almost two million Jews were to be brought to the 3,000-square-mile area. "This mass-migration by force has been begun now, in the dead of winter, and in a manner that cannot be interpreted as anything else than a determination to create, not a Jewish state, but a most horrible concentration camp, which can certainly become nothing else than a habitation of death.'' No preparations had been made in advance of the deportees' arrival. ''If they cannot find shelter in the deserted homes of the evacuated Polish peasantry, why, they can freeze to death, or build new homes, without means, without materials, without tools, without anything.''[53]

When Eichmann conceived the Nisko project, he had given no thought to the problem of how to get the Jews there. It quickly became clear, however, that he had to create holding pens where Jews from smaller communities could be assembled before being transported en masse to the East. The large industrial city of Lodz was one of his designated points of concentration. To control and confine the Nisko-bound Jews, the Lodz chief of police ordered the creation of a ghetto in February 1940. Incarcerating more than 160,000 people, it was closed on 30 April.

The Lodz ghetto had been conceived as a transit point on the way to Nisko, but by the time it had come into existence Eichmann's project had collapsed: scandalized by the ineptitude of its execution, the German military and civil authorities in the Government General had persuaded Göring, who was responsible for Jewish policy, to cancel it. A total of 95,000 Jews had been moved to Nisko. Many had died. None of the surviving deportees was allowed to return home.

The Germans did not want Jews in the German East and did not know what to do with them. After the Nisko fiasco, Heydrich and the German Foreign Office formulated the so-called Madagascar option, which envisioned the wholesale deportation of European Jewry to the French-ruled African island of Madagascar. As France did not cede Madagascar and England did not even consider permitting the transport of Europe's Jews to the island, Heydrich shelved the plan. Another solution to the ''problem'' of Polish Jewry had to be found.[54]

With the German military buildup for war with the Soviet Union, fears increased of epidemics among the more than a million German soldiers to be brought to the Government General. By the beginning of September 1940, German public health officials were vociferously insisting that the Jewish neighborhoods could become the cause of a massive typhus epidemic, and they urged the governor general to follow the example of Lodz. Frank took their advice, separating the gentile and Jewish populations through the creation of closed ghettos.[55] ''The German Army and population must at all costs be

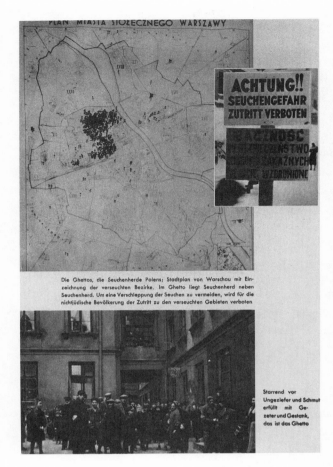

Die Ghettos, die Seuchenherde Polens; Stadtplan von Warschau mit Einzeichnung der verseuchten Bezirke. Im Ghetto liegt Seuchenherd neben Seuchenherd. Um eine Verschleppung der Seuchen zu vermeiden, wird für die nichtjüdische Bevölkerung der Zutritt zu den verseuchten Gebieten verboten

Starrend vor Ungeziefer und Schmutz erfüllt mit Gezeter und Gestank, das ist das Ghetto

Page from a German propaganda book. Gauweiler, Deutsches Vorfeld im Osten *(1941). Sterling Memorial Library, Yale University.* Map caption: *"The ghettos are the source of epidemics in Poland. A map of Warsaw with indications of the infected areas. In the ghetto one source of epidemics is next to another. To avoid the spread of epidemics, the non-Jewish population has been forbidden to enter the infected areas."* Lower caption: *"Bristling with vermin and filth, filled to the brim with scolding and stench: that is the ghetto."*

protected from the immune bacillus-carrier of the plagues—the Jew,'' his decree explained. In any case, the Jews had to be removed from society to permit the successful completion of ''the German work of reconstruction.''[56]

It took Frank little time to establish ghettos throughout the Government General. In Warsaw, the educator Chaim Kaplan recorded in his diary entry of 10 November that streets were cut off by walls. ''Before our eyes a dungeon is being built in which half a million men, women and children will be imprisoned, no one knows for how long.'' And he added, ''The *Judenrat* is building this great mass grave with its own funds.''[57] A week later the ghetto had been closed. ''We see ourselves penned in on all sides. We are segregated and separated from the world and the fullness thereof, driven out of the society of the human race.''[58]

He had few illusions: the Jews would molder and rot in the ghetto, he noted on 19 November, and a week later he wrote, "A community of half a million is doomed to die, and awaits execution of their sentence."[59]

Kaplan was right. With 400,000 people crammed onto 1,000 acres, without sufficient food, clean water, soap, or medicine, the only question that remained was whether death would come in the shape of starvation or disease. The same conditions applied in many ghettos of the German East. Sara Grossman, twenty-one years old and incarcerated in the Lodz ghetto, remembered it well.

Children where brought into the ghetto who couldn't walk for lack of nourishment. They just couldn't walk. This is how rampant hunger was. That is what malnutrition did to us. We were always on the lookout for some food, for some crumbs. You wouldn't dare to leave a crumb on the table. You would put anything in your mouth.

I don't think anything hurts as much as hunger. You become wild. You are not responsible for what you say and what you do. You become an animal in the full meaning of the word. You prey on others. You will steal. That is what hunger does to us. It dehumanizes you. You're not a human being any more.

Sara Grossman-Weil, 1937. Authors

Slowly, slowly the Germans were achieving their goal. I think they let us suffer from hunger, not because there was not enough food, but because this was their method of demoralizing us, of degrading us, of torturing us. These were their methods, and they implemented these methods scrupulously.

Therefore we had very many, many deaths daily. Very many sick people for whom there was no medication, no help, no remedy. We just stayed there, and lay there, and the end was coming.[60]

Before death came, however, the inmates of the ghetto were photographed for the German public. It was a cynical tautology in which the humiliation of the Jews was the reason for their humiliation. "The sights are so appalling and also probably so well-known to the editorial staffs that a description is superfluous," the party ideologue Alfred Rosenberg reported to the Reich press department after visiting the Warsaw ghetto. "If there are any people left who still somehow have sympathy with the Jews then they ought . . . to have a look at such a ghetto. Seeing this race en masse, which is decaying, decomposing, and rotten to the core will banish any sentimental humanitarianism."[61]

"SENTIMENTAL HUMANITARIANISM" HAD been banned from Germany long before Rosenberg's trip to the ghetto and was denied many people in addition to Jews. In late 1938 an increasing number of letters arrived at the National Socialist Party office that handled Hitler's private business, including personal appeals to him by family members of mentally handicapped people requesting the "mercy death" of their loved ones. Hitler was intrigued by the entreaty of a certain Mr. Kauer from Leipzig. Kauer's child had been born blind, appeared idiotic, and did not have a leg and part of an arm. Hitler instructed his personal physician, Dr. Karl Brandt, to examine the child and, if the father's description was correct, to kill the youngster. Brandt obeyed. Hitler was pleased, and authorized Brandt and Philipp Bouhler, the head of the department receiving the letters, to treat similar cases in the same way. They were happy to oblige and in August established the Reich Committee for the Scientific Registration of Serious Hereditarily and Congenitally Based Illnesses. That same month the Reich Ministry of the Interior decreed that midwives and physicians had to report infants born with various conditions to the Reich committee. Investigators on the committee examined the information submitted, and authorized the murder of "positive" cases in special pediatric departments established in thirty asylums.

The facility in the asylum at Egelfing-Haar, near Munich, was among the first to open. Its director, Dr. Hermann Pfannmüller, hosted a large site visit of officials of the National Socialist Party, the army, and the SS on 16 February 1940. "Dr. Pfannmüller approached one of the fifteen cots which flanked the central passage to the right and left," a member of the delegation remembered after the war.

> "We have here children aged from one to five," he pontificated. "All these creatures represent for me as a National Socialist 'living burdens' . . . a burden for our nation. . . . In this sense, the Fuhrer's action to free the national community from this overburdening is quite simply a national deed, whose greatness non-medical men will only be able to assess after a period of years if not decades. We do not carry out the action with poison, injections or other measures which can be recognised . . . for then the foreign press and certain circles in Paris or London would only have new opportunities for propaganda against us. . . . No, our method is much simpler."
>
> With these words he pulled a child out of its cot. While this fat, gross man displayed the whimpering skeletal little person like a hare which he had just caught, he coolly remarked: "Naturally, we don't stop their food straight away. That would cause too much fuss. We gradually reduce their portions. Nature then takes care of the rest. . . . This one won't last more than two or three more days."[62]

Five thousand children were killed in this way.

Satisfied with the pediatric program, Hitler instructed Bouhler's department to organize the murder of adults unfit for life.[63] After consultation with Albert Widmann, the chief of the Chemical Department of the Criminal Technical Institute, Bouhler's deputy, Viktor Brack, recommended the use of bottled carbon monoxide produced by BASF. At a meeting attended by, among others, Professor Werner Heyde, a well-known psychiatrist, a friend of Himmler's, and the leader of the operation; Professor Hermann Paul Nitsche, also a psychiatrist and the director of the Sonnenstein asylum near Dresden; a police officer, Paul Werner; and chaired by Brack, the decision was taken to kill between 65,000 and 75,000 asylum inmates by carbon monoxide poisoning.[64]

The first experimental gassing was conducted by Widmann in an unused prison in the town of Brandenburg eight weeks later. Christian Wirth, a police officer from Stuttgart, had built the gas chamber, installed the gas cylinders, and designed the fake showers. One of Widmann's collaborators recalled after the war that the gas chamber was "similar to a shower room which was approximately 3 metres by 5 metres and 3 metres high and tiled. There were benches round the room and a water pipe about 1" in diameter ran along the wall about 10 cm off the floor. There were small holes in this pipe from which the carbon monoxide gas poured out. The gas cylinders stood outside this room."[65] Between eighteen and twenty patients were brought to an anteroom, undressed, and led into the gas chamber. The door was locked, Widmann turned the valve, and the patients died within minutes. Their bodies were cremated in two mobile incinerators brought in for the occasion.

The operation, code-named T4 for the operation's headquarters at Tiergarten 4, began a few weeks later with the gassing of a first transport of inmates to the Grafeneck asylum (west of Ulm). Brandenburg came into operation in February, followed by Hartheim (near Linz), and Sonnenstein (near Dresden) in May, Bernburg (south of Magdeburg) in September, and Hadamar (north of Frankfurt) in January 1941.[66] The procedure was always the same. Institutions sent information on their patients to the Reich Committee. Three physicians assessed each file; the names of those judged "positive" were put on a list which was sent back to the asylum. The patients were transported to one of the six killing centers on buses with darkened windows. Stripped naked upon arrival, they were conducted to a room where a physician checked their files. "Someone then stamped them," a stoker in the crematorium at Hartheim recalled. "An orderly had to stamp them individually on the shoulder or the chest with a consecutive number. The number was approximately 3–4 cm in size. Those people who had gold teeth or a gold bridge were marked with a cross on their backs." They were then led into the gas chamber and killed. After an hour and a half, the fans were turned on, and the stokers went in to move the corpses to the mortuary which "was a difficult and nerve-racking task. It was not easy to disentangle the corpses, which were locked together, and drag them into the mortuary." When the incinerator was ready, the gold was removed from the corpses marked with a cross. Then the body was laid on a pan, "pushed in and left there just like with a baking oven."[67]

The victim's family received a letter a few weeks later informing them that their relative had been transferred to a new asylum and fallen ill and that "all attempts by the doctors to keep the patient alive were unfortunately unsuccessful." After the usual condolences, the letter explained that "in accordance with police instructions we were obliged to cremate the corpse immediately. This measure is designed to protect the country from the spread of infectious diseases which represent a serious threat in war time and we must strictly abide by it."[68]

Inmates from asylums in East and West Prussia and the Wartheland were not brought to a T4 death chamber. They were gassed in a special truck operated by a Sonderkommando, or Special Squad, headed by Herbert Lange. Stationed in Posen, Lange had the job of driving to an asylum, presenting a list of names to the staff, and loading the inmates into the airtight cargo area of a large Kaiser's Coffee truck. After they had left the grounds of the asylum, the driver opened the valves of the carbon monoxide cylinders stored in his cabin and connected to the cargo area, and killed his passengers.[69]

From the perspective of its management, operation T4 was an unqualified success. In 1939 Bracht and his colleagues estimated that 65,000 to 75,000 asylum inmates were candidates for death. When Hitler stopped the program on 24 August 1941, the T4 officials congratulated themselves that "70,273 persons have been disinfected."[70] They also took pride in the 885,439,800 marks they calculated they had saved the Reich.[71] Their report did not mention that, at the termination of the operation, its personnel had been offered jobs in the East. Nor did it mention that while the 70,273 victims amounted to one in five of all institutionalized patients, it included all Jewish inmates. Their papers had not been given even a cursory glance.

CHAPTER 5

A PARADISE OF BLOOD
AND SOIL

O N A COLD WINTER DAY IN JANUARY 1940 HEINRICH HIMMLER ARRIVED IN the western suburbs of Przemysl, at the easternmost edge of the German sphere of influence. Accompanied by his friend the writer Hanns Johst, Himmler walked to the bridge over the San River, a tributary of the Vistula, and since 28 September the official border between German-occupied central Poland and Soviet-annexed eastern Poland. And there he waited.

Himmler and Johst had traveled to Przemysl to witness the arrival of the last train of ethnic German peasants from eastern Poland. These Germans had found themselves on the Soviet side after the division of Poland through the Ribbentrop-Molotov pact. Himmler, upset by the prospect of losing valuable Germans to the Bolsheviks, persuaded Hitler to negotiate with Stalin to evacuate those ethnic Germans who preferred to live in National Socialist Germany. At Hitler's request, Himmler took charge of their resettlement in the German-annexed parts of Poland: West Prussia, Posen, and eastern Upper Silesia. Throughout November and December groups of evacuees had crossed the new border. By January 1940 the government-sponsored repatriation of this community of ethnic Germans was coming to a happy conclusion.

The Soviet and German officers in charge of the crossing met at the middle of the bridge for a final consultation. Then the first vehicle began to move.

Johst recorded the scene. "Two small trotters pull a cart covered with a hand-woven runner to the gate of the bridge—to us. Halfway across the bridge a woman's hand pops out and unfolds a swastika flag—and the wagon stands in front of us. A man's bearded face, framed by the dark arc of the wagon cover, leans forward, far beyond his hard hands holding the reins. He looks the Reichsführer in the eyes and says without whining yet with tears flowing from his eyes, solemn and deep from his chest, 'Now we are here!' " He spoke like a farmer used to talking against the elements, Johst noted. "He wipes his hand, which seemed to be carved from wood, over his eyes. Tears freeze and hurt like salt stones. 'Our father has called us! We have come, now we are here!!' " It was too much for Johst, as it was for his readers; his euphoric book, *Call of the Reich—Echo of the Nation*, was a best-seller. "Open your heart, reader, and bid welcome, join us who stand precisely in the middle of the bridge, on the border between here and there, bid welcome with us to our new compatriot!" As one cart after another clattered over the metal bridge, Johst heard "a paean of love for *Heimat*, and the happiness of homecoming."[1]

Johst was touched by the simple peasants whose ancestors had come to the western parts of Poland from Germany in the Middle Ages and who, generations later, had been brought for their own protection to the eastern Polish region of Volhynia after their refusal to participate in the 1830 Polish uprising against the Russians. Volhynia, with its largely White Russian population, had not joined the rebellion, and the Germans had rebuilt their lives there. More than a century later, their descendants were on the move again.

Johst turned to his friend Heinrich Himmler. After all, he was there as much to report on Himmler's project to acquire control over a piece of Germany's foreign policy as to report on the utterances of the Volhynian pawns in that program. "The Führer chose Reichsführer-SS Heinrich Himmler to initiate, lead, and complete this migration—one of many. For all those who leave their century-old home of choice, this will create a new, true, and natural home of blood." Although he saw the repatriation of ethnic German communities as one of the greatest undertakings in German history, Himmler did not seem daunted by his enormous responsibility. "One must have the faith of a Heinrich Himmler, one must be close to the heart of the Führer and have forgotten the word 'impossible' a long time ago not to become faint-hearted in the face of this task." Johst saw in his friend's "happy eyes" only "youth, trust, and confidence in victory."[2]

Himmler reached out to the Volhynian peasant and shook his hand. And

Heinrich Himmler greets an ethnic German returnee at Przemysl, January 1940. Thoss,
Heimkehr der Volksdeutschen *(1941). Sterling Memorial Library, Yale University.*

Johst could not but interpret it as the beginning of the Apocalypse that completed world history. "Time is fulfilled, and the Greater German Reich is about to be realized! The bloodstreams, the protuberances of dissipating national powers come together into a new, greater ethnic body. There is no more outside and inside. All German consciousness and Germanic existence in this world is one unified organism given life by one heart, given spirit by one soul, disciplined by one power, led by one will—educated and led by its maker Adolf Hitler!" Himmler extended the Führer's welcome, "and all the returnees bow deeply and faithfully to this greeting, which is for them a promise and the host of infinite happiness."[3]

HIMMLER'S PRESENCE ON the bridge was the direct result of rapid action on his part four months earlier, after a visit by Erhard Kroeger, the leader of the ethnic German National Socialist movement in Latvia. Kroeger had been informed by the SS that Estonia and Latvia had been given to Stalin. "The only thing that rushed through my mind was the salvation of an essential and closely linked ethnic group which, it seemed to me, was at this moment already threatened with certain destruction without even knowing it," he recalled. "There was no time for faltering or hesitation: my task was to ensure that the ethnic German communities of both countries would not fall into the hands of the Bolsheviks."[4] Kroeger reminded Himmler of the vicious war that had been fought in 1919, and the ensuing Balt-Bolshevik enmity. "Himmler considered this for a moment and then said that only the Führer could decide on the question at large. He would raise it with him that same night and request a general directive. Himmler wondered whether the Balt community was disciplined enough to undergo the resettlement without internal conflict and open opposition, which the Soviets surely would exploit. And then he raised the question of where the Balts were to be settled. Was Lithuania an option?" Kroeger was not enthusiastic, but he was more concerned with establishing the principles that would determine the site than with identifying a particular place. "First a compact settlement within a contained space, and no scattering over all the provinces of Germany. And second, it would be a good idea for the Balts to undertake the same ethnic-political task they have had until now, which means not somewhere in the center of Germany, but 'at its marches.' "[5] With this Kroeger was dismissed.

The next day Himmler received him for a second time. He had spoken to Hitler, and he told Kroeger that "the Führer agreed with the evacuation of the Balt community as a whole, but stipulated that this should be done with the approval of the Soviet government." Himmler also reported that the Balts were to be settled in those parts of Poland annexed to the Reich, including Posen and West Prussia.[6] With that Kroeger was dismissed again.

Hitler was true to his word, and when the Border and Friendship treaty which divided Poland between Germany and the Soviet Union along the Bug River was signed four days later, it included a secret protocol to allow for the resettlement of Germans, White Russians, and Ukrainians on the "wrong side" of the line. "The government of the Soviet Union will create no obstacles for those German citizens and other persons of German descent who live in their sphere of influence who wish to resettle in Germany or in the German sphere of influence," the accord declared. "The resettlement will be organized by a plenipotentiary of the German government in cooperation with the local authorities, and the property rights of the emigrants will be preserved."[7] The German government, of course, had the same obligation vis-à-vis White Russians and Ukrainians in the German part of Poland.

Himmler wanted to be the "plenipotentiary of the German government" who would control resettlement. To strengthen his hand, he consolidated all his police responsibilities. Combining the Sipo (*Sicherheitspolizei,* or Security Police)—which consisted of the Gestapo and the Kripo—and the SD into one new organization, the RSHA (*Reichssicherheitshauptamt,* or Reich Security Main Office). He appointed his faithful crony and henchman Heydrich, the SD chief, as its head.

Heydrich had proven himself up to new challenges during the past two months. In July he had obtained an agreement from the top officials of the army to attach seven mobile-police formations totaling 2,700 men to the regular troops. These Einsatzgruppen (Operational Groups), manned by members of the Sipo and the SD, were to subjugate the conquered territory in an operation code-named Tannenberg.[8] Heydrich had already sent Einsatzgruppen into Austria (March 1938), the Sudeten (October 1938), and Bohemia and Moravia (March 1939) to "comb out," as the *Völkischer Beobachter* of 10 October 1938 put it, "Marxists, traitors and other enemies of the State from the liberated territory."[9] In these areas of Central Europe the Einsatzgruppen had not committed public atrocities, but they knew no restraint in Poland. Operation Tannenberg, Heydrich asserted in July 1940, was able to "deal heavy blows to those world movements hostile to the Reich directed by the *emigré,* freemason, Jewish and politically hostile ecclesiastical camp, and also by the Second and Third International."[10]

Reinhard Heydrich, 1940. Illustrierte Zeitung, *no. 4958 (1940). Sterling Memorial Library, Yale University. Heydrich was head of the internal political police of the National Socialist movement, the* Sicherheitsdienst des Reichsführer-SS *(SD des RfSS, or Security Service of the* Reichsführer-SS). *The SD became very powerful when Hitler assigned* Reichsführer-SS *Himmler the newly created office of chief of German police in 1936. As a result, Heydrich acquired direct control of all police intelligence and, soon thereafter, state security.*

Heydrich's charge to the Einsatzgruppen was blunt and brutal. "The leadership class in Poland is to be rendered harmless," he told the commanders on 7 September. The elite was to be incarcerated in already functioning concentration camps in the Reich, "while temporary concentration camps will be established on the frontier behind the *Einsatzgruppen* for the lower classes who then can be deported to the remaining part of Poland [the Government General] immediately."[11] Two weeks later, Heydrich addressed the central issue of the so-called Jewish Problem in a follow-up memo to the commanders. For the Germans, the need for a "solution" had become acute. They had tried to reduce the German Jewish population through emigration. Of the more than 800,000 Jews who in 1933 lived within the area that in September 1939 was to comprise the Greater German Reich (the German Reich, Austria, the Sudeten, and Bohemia and Moravia), more than 450,000 had left. With the conquest of Poland, however, the National Socialists found themselves with another 2 million Jews under their control. Of these, between 600,000 and 700,000 lived in areas incorporated into the Reich. In other words, when the Polish campaign came to an end, there were approximately one million Jews in the Greater German Reich, and that number did not include those in the Government General. For the German leadership it was as if six years of work to resolve the Jewish Question through emigration had been in vain.

Heydrich realized that this—as he saw it—emergency situation demanded a new approach. "I would like to emphasize once again that the *overall measures envisaged* (i.e. the final goal) must be kept strictly secret," he wrote to the Einsatzgruppen leaders.

A distinction must be made between.

    1. the final goal (which will require a lengthy period) and

    2. the stages towards the achievement of this final goal (which can be carried out on a short-term basis).

The measures envisaged require the most thorough preparation both in the technical and in the economic sense.

It is obvious that the tasks which are desirable cannot be defined in every detail from here. The following instructions and directives serve simultaneously the purpose of encouraging the chiefs of the *Einsatzgruppen* to reflect on the practical issues. . . .

The first preliminary measure for achieving the final goal is the concentration of the Jews from the countryside in the larger cities. It must be speedily implemented.

A distinction must be made:

1. Between the territories of Danzig and West Prussia, Posen, eastern Upper Silesia and

2. The other occupied territories.

If possible, the areas referred to under 1. are to be liberated from Jews, or at least the aim must be to establish only a few cities as concentration points.

In the areas referred to under 2. as few concentration points as possible should be established so that later measures are facilitated. In this connexion you should ensure that only those cities are designated which are either railway junctions or at least lie on a railway line.[12]

The day he became chief of the new Reich Security Main Office (27 September 1939), Heydrich addressed the heads of its various departments and the commanders of the Einsatzgruppen. He told them that Himmler was to be in charge of the Germanization of the annexed territories, and that these were to form an "east wall." Farther east, a non-German-speaking gau, which would be the Polish homeland, was to be a protective zone. Repeating his instructions of 7 September, Heydrich noted that the leaders of the Einsatzgruppen in eastern Upper Silesia, Danzig, and West Prussia faced a complex problem. He realized that, especially in industrial Upper Silesia, there was a conflict between the desire to deport the Polish population and the need to maintain production levels; how, "on the one hand one can integrate the primitive Poles into the work force while at the same time expelling them." His solution was in a simple and time-honored tradition: "The aim is for the Poles to remain permanently seasonal and migrant workers; their main place of residence must be the district of Cracow."[13] While the resolution of the Polish Problem may have had to accommodate nearly contradictory German needs, the solution to the Jewish Problem had no such constraints. "The deportation of the Jews to the foreign Gau . . . has been approved by the Führer," Heydrich emphasized. "The systematic evacuation of the Jews from German territory" was to be organized "via goods-trains."[14]

While Heydrich assured the Einsatzgruppen leaders that the Führer had approved large-scale deportations, Hitler unfolded his vision of Poland for Rosenberg. He intended to divide his part of Poland in three, he explained. The eastern area between the Vistula and the Bug would be reserved "for the whole of Jewry (from the Reich as well) as well as all other unreliable elements." Hitler's plan, Rosenberg wrote in his diary, was to Germanize and colonize the western part. "This would be a major task for the whole nation: to create a German granary, a strong peasantry, to resettle good Germans from all over the world." The Poles were to be allowed some kind of homeland, for the time being at least, in the middle. "The future would show whether after a few decades the cordon of settlement would have to be pushed further forward."[15]

It is clear that Heydrich and Hitler were in complete agreement, and Himmler's appointment of Heydrich as chief of the Reich Security Main Office must have convinced Hitler that he, as Heydrich's immediate superior, was the best candidate to take responsibility for the resettlement operations. With Himmler, Hitler got Heydrich too. Of course, Himmler may not have needed the additional advantage of having Heydrich on his staff. His own vita was sufficiently compelling. He not only controlled the SS, which was identified with racial policy and settlement, but through the SD and Vomi he also had good connections with the ethnic German communities. Perhaps most important, he had privileged access to crucial bureaucrats in the German ministries as a result of his practice of giving them honorary SS ranks.[16] On 28 September, Hitler offered Himmler the job of settlement plenipotentiary in the annexed territories. His task was to coordinate the reconstruction of the German East. Himmler accepted with alacrity. The head of the Reich Chancellery, Hans-Heinrich Lammers, immediately authorized the finance minister to provide Himmler with an initial grant of ten million marks "for the resettlement from abroad of German citizens and ethnic Germans, as well as the establishment of agricultural settlements in the former Polish territories."[17]

Hitler signed the Decree for the Consolidation of the German Nation, which confirmed Himmler's appointment, on 7 October. It required the Reichsführer-SS to recall "those German citizens and ethnic Germans abroad who are eligible for a permanent return to the Reich," to "eliminate the harmful influence of such alien parts of the population as constitute a danger to the Reich and the German community," and to "create new German colonies by resettlement, and especially by the resettlement of German citizens and ethnic Germans coming back from abroad."[18]

Himmler's great ambition and his ideological vision of the German East shaped his plans for the new territories. In a speech to SS leaders in Posen on 24 October, he described his schemes in detail. Germans had been successful settlers in the area for three thousand years, he said; surely the National Socialists should be able to follow their example. Rejecting the settlement of farmers as a capitalist enterprise, Himmler embraced the more martial notion of *Wehrbauern* (soldier-farmers). "I have already made some preparations for this. One of these provisions is a program of obligatory savings I have introduced in the SS. The 2,000 to 3,000 marks an SS man saves in a few years is a down payment for settlement." But more than money was needed. The forced labor of concentration camp inmates in Germany would be put to use in brickyards and quarries "so that the bricks [and stones] for the construction of the settlements would be available."[19]

With his usual pedantry Himmler described the houses to be built. Designed to stimulate the propagation of large, healthy families, they were to be of brick and "neither luxurious nor primitive. The settlements must evince special cleanliness, and the arrangement of the houses should be both practical and clean."[20] Moving quickly from detail to general concept, Himmler confidently predicted that after the first fifty to eighty years, 20 million German settlers would live in the German East, 10 million of whom would have eight to ten children. By that time no more land would be available and Germany would have to push the border farther east. "The eternal course of the history of a people—always conquering and settling new lands."[21]

The exhibition "Planning and Reconstruction in the East," held in Berlin, early 1941. Federal Archive, Koblenz. Heinrich Himmler (center, with glasses) explains a model of a prototype farm to be built in the German East to Rudolf Hess (fingers interlaced). Immediately to the right of Himmler is Martin Bormann (head down), and next to him Himmler's chief adviser on the reconstruction of the East, Professor Doktor Konrad Meyer (forehead).

THE DECREE DEFINED Himmler's authority only vaguely. Although the job went beyond the boundaries of his old jurisdictions, the relevant ministries had not yet agreed to surrender some of their authority to him, and therefore he was not given the appropriate official title of *Reichskommissar* (which would have formally accorded him plenipotentiary power). But official or not, Himmler assumed the title and, as no one protested, in his role as architect of the German East he was referred to as *Reichsführer-SS als Reichskommissar für die Festigung deutschen Volkstums* (Reichsführer-SS as Reich Commissioner for the Consolidation of the German Nation, abbreviated as RFSS-RKfdFdV, RFSS-RKFDV or, most economically, RFSS-RKF).

The Decree for the Consolidation of the German Nation stipulated that Himmler work through existing structures. It specifically stated that the Ministry for Food and Agriculture was to oversee the settlement of rural areas. No other agency was designated, but the spectrum of institutions involved soon became apparent. The Labor Ministry and the German Labor Front were to coordinate settlement in towns and cities, the Vomi was to repatriate the ethnic Germans, the Reich health führer and the SS Race and Settlement Office were to screen the evacuees medically, the Reich Security Main Office was to weed out politically unreliable elements among the ethnic Germans and to deport Poles and Jews, and the governors of the provinces were to exercise direct executive control over the whole operation, advised by Himmler's representatives, the provincial higher SS and police leaders.[22] Göring's Office of the Four-Year Plan, the army, and the Reich Authority for Spatial Planning were to participate in general planning. In short, Hitler's decree is a classic example of the division of power to maintain ultimate absolute authority that was characteristic of the National Socialist state: "In cases where agreement between the Reichsführer-SS on the one hand and the competent highest Reich authority . . . on the other hand cannot be reached on measures which by reason of legislation and administrative organization require such agreement, my [i.e., Hitler's] decision is to be obtained."[23]

Himmler exercised direct control over the Vomi, the SS Race and Settlement Office, and Heydrich's Reich Security Main Office—insofar as anyone controlled Heydrich. But his relations with the other agencies was more problematic. Himmler's earlier friendship with Darré had cooled due to irreconcilable differences between Himmler's plans and Darré's vision of the reconstruction of the German East. Himmler sought to establish large *Wehrbauernhöfe* (soldier-farmer farms) in the border areas. He believed that farming was a privilege reserved for the racial and political elite, and he intended to establish estates which could generate a substantial income and which also would offer employment and training opportunities for Germans who had served in the SS. The gentlemen farmers were to be recruited from those cadres; those who wished could earn their own farm through seven years of service on their estates.[24] Darré opposed any such neofeudal scheme. First, estate owners tended to limit the size of their families whereas small farmers had many children because they needed them for labor. Darré, who saw the small farmer as the keystone of Germany's future, thought that the settlement

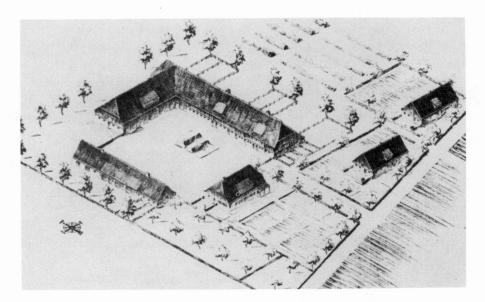

Bird's-eye view of the prize-winning design by Max Halpaap and Carl Nagl for a large German farm in the annexed territories. Monatshefte für Baukunst und Städtebau *(1942). Authors. The design was praised because it embodied East German architectural traditions. The attention paid to the accommodation of the farmhands (right) was a break with tradition. The Junkers had preferred to hire Polish seasonal laborers to work their estates and had housed them poorly. The National Socialists opposed the use of Polish labor and wanted to make the job of farmhand attractive to young Germans. The architects therefore paid special attention to their dwellings, which included a small stable, a large vegetable garden, and enough room to raise a large family. The farmhands, according to National Socialist ideology, would have the opportunity to earn their own farm. The large farm was a site not only of agricultural production but also of vocational training for a new generation of farmers and for the consolidation of the German nation.*

of North America should be taken as a paradigm. Hundreds of thousands of families from SS and SA circles should be allowed to follow the army in its conquests, to take the land and build a new society with their own hands.[25]

Another source of tension was that, as minister of food and agriculture, Darré insisted that the process of settlement not lead to a decline in food production, while Himmler contended that the long-term political significance of the settlement policies was more important than the immediate economic effects. Finally Darré felt, justifiably, that Himmler's appointment challenged his control over what had been a source of important achievement. As minister of food and agriculture, Darré had been officially responsible for rural settlement since 1933; between 1933 and 1939 his ministry had overseen the settlement of 16,000 farmers all over Germany. Darré and his staff were proud of their success, and they believed that their accomplishments had given them the right to organize settlement in the annexed territories. The decree of 7 October officially recognized their position. "In so far as reconstruction of a German agricultural society is concerned, the duties allotted to the *Reichsführer-SS* will be carried out by the Reich Minister for Food and Agriculture in accordance with the general instruction of the Reichsführer-SS."[26] The exact meaning of the last clause remained a source of conflict.

Other organizations also claimed authority in the field of settlement. The first was the Homestead Office of the German Labor Front, the single labor association that had supplanted all the former labor unions, and an arm of the Party apparatus. It was in the Homestead Office that the ideal of rural settlement, formulated in the 1920s by the Artamans, found an official place within the National Socialist Party.

The Reich Authority for Spatial Planning, the national planning office that had been established in 1935, was another contender for control over the reconstruction of the German East. This agency was responsible for the formulation of one comprehensive plan for the spatial ordering of the Reich. The core was the Reich Study Group for Spatial Research, headed by the geographer Konrad Meyer, a respected academic, but also an *Obersturmbann-führer* in the SS, and it was his ideology that shaped this program. While the agency had been charged with coordination of planning in the whole Reich, Meyer's study group concentrated on the German East. Its members were delighted with the acquisition of the incorporated territories which offered ideal conditions in the fall of 1939: easily seized (Jewish or Polish) property and no entrenched provincial bureaucracies. Unfortunately for them, how-

Konrad Meyer (third from left, fist clenched) *explaining the design of a village to the governor of Upper Silesia, Fritz Bracht* (glasses, right). *Federal Archive, Koblenz.*

ever, there were significant differences between Himmler's vision for the East and their own. Critical of Himmler's ambition to transform the region into an agrarian utopia, they sought to industrialize the area. But as the Reich Authority for Spatial Planning had no clearly defined executive power, it was forced to accommodate Himmler's vision. To ensure full compliance, Himmler invited Meyer to become chief of the planning department in his Office of the Reich Commissioner, and the latter accepted.

Meyer's perspective was colored by his tenure at the Reich Authority, and in a report he presented to Himmler at the end of 1939 he explained that to prevent *Landflucht* to the West the annexed territories had to be developed industrially as well as agriculturally. Meyer suggested that 35 percent of the population be farmers which, while lower than Himmler's ideal, was 170 percent more than the German average. But while tempering Himmler's agricultural utopia with industrial realism, Meyer endorsed his chief racist ideology: the success of reconstruction of the German East was to depend on the farmers. "Their work on the soil absolutely determines the consolidation of the German nation and the ultimate ownership of the land conquered by the sword. The rate and the extent of the Germanization of the eastern territories is determined solely by the number of appropriate families that can be deployed in the next years to create a new farming population."[27] Of the projected total population of 9 million, 3.15 million farmers were needed; of these, 70 percent, or 2.2 million, were to be German. As there were already 740,000 Germans in the area, 1.46 million Germans, or 200,000 households, were required immediately.[28] The precedent set by Frederick the Great in the eighteenth century and Bismarck's encouragement of a new migration to the East in the nineteenth loomed large for Meyer; he explicitly compared his own program to these historic events. In numbers alone Meyer had greater plans in mind: while some 28,000 families had been resettled by the Prussian Settlement Commission in Posen and 75,000 families had been relocated under Frederick, his project called for 200,000 households to be moved straight away. Building on the experience of the past and framing his aims within that context, Meyer envisioned the Germans of 1939 striding forward, moving east, towards their destiny.

The settlers were to be alive to their geopolitical task. Repudiating the pervasive perception that farming was a declining activity in an increasingly urbanized world, "the farming population will 'attack' in a truly soldierlike political sense, and it will stand in the middle of the nation and its ethnic changes."[29] Meyer proposed three kind of farms. The most important were the *Wehrbauernhöfe* (soldier-farmer farms). Resembling "the *Schulzenhöfe* (the farms of the Schulz), or the *Rittergüter* (estates) of the medieval colonization of the East,"[30] these establishments would employ agricultural workers and train them for economic independence. Meyer made it very clear that the estates were central to his plan. "The owners of these large farms have to provide leadership not only in national, defensive, and political matters. They also have the obligation to be exemplary managers and pioneers in the agricultural, technical, and economic aspects of farming. We must therefore demand the most from the owners of these farms. It goes without saying that they should be eligible for the SS, and that in their family life and the number of children produced they must have fulfilled their duty towards the nation. But they also must have proven that they are good managers."[31] Second in social status, but largest in absolute numbers (155,000), were single-family farms.[32] Finally, 72,000 miniature farms were planned to root agricultural workers

Oſtland –

Land der Sehnſucht und Erfüllung unſerer kampf-
erprobten Männer

*"The Land of the East: Land of
Nostalgia and Fulfillment for
Our Men Who Have Been Tested
in Battle." Pamphlet. Authors.
Soldiers were to be rewarded with a
plot of land in the German East.*

and craftsmen in the land. Farmhands who had worked diligently on a soldier-farmer estate and who had run their miniature farm in an exemplary fashion would be eligible to receive a one-family farm after five to eight years.[33] Himmler adopted Meyer's plan as his own and convened a meeting in Posen on 24 January 1940, at which the latter presented the program to the heads of the provincial planning agencies of the designated areas.[34]

Himmler's appointment of Meyer, and his acceptance of the latter's expertise, neutralized the competing claims of the Reich Authority for Spatial Planning for control of development in the East. The execution or actualization of Himmler's program required the cooperation of the provincial governors, who oversaw well-entrenched regional planning authorities, but the Reich commissioner's relations with the provincial governors of East Prussia, Danzig–West Prussia, Wartheland, and Silesia proved problematic. All four of the governors—Albert Forster (Danzig–West Prussia), Erich Koch (East Prussia), Arthur Greiser (Wartheland), and Josef Wagner (Silesia)—were veterans of the National Socialist Party. Their provinces were their own bailiwicks which they expected to rule with minimal intervention; they were uneasy with the increasingly powerful Himmler, and they were suspicious of the *Höherer SS—und Polizeiführer* (senior SS and police führer) whom Himmler attached to their offices. Nominally subordinate to the governors, these SS men listened only to Himmler.

As the settlement of the German East was to commence during the war, Himmler also needed the cooperation of the army. The High Command of the Armed Forces trusted the Reichsführer-SS even less than the governors did. Hitler had bought the army's unconditional loyalty in 1934 in exchange for the promise that it would be the sole bearer of arms in the nation. Himmler, however, planned already at that time to transform his Adolf Hitler Bodyguard and the Political Alarm Squads into the nucleus of a personal army. By 1935 his SS army counted nine battalions. The Wehrmacht resented these armed units and only grudgingly accepted service in the Waffen SS (so named in 1940) as official military duty. In an attempt to delimit Himmler's power, the army insisted that he work through its structure in the occupied territories, and a clause to that effect had been included in the Decree for the Consolidation of the German Nation.

Within weeks after the decree had been signed, the army's administrative role in Poland diminished. The western part of Poland was annexed to Germany, and a civilian administration in the Government General was established. But the army remained a power Himmler had to accommodate. He needed settlers for the German East, but the army prohibited recruitment of settlers within the Reich. Arguing that soldiers also should be eligible for the farms and businesses on offer in the new provinces, and insisting that no one could be discharged from military service during the war to become a settler, the army demanded the postponement of Himmler's settlement programs. Hitler was convinced, and he ordered Himmler to settle only ethnic Germans who had been dislocated, or war invalids. Officially responsible for the latter, the army approved their preferential treatment.

The army not only obstructed Himmler's ambition to build up the German East through German immigration; it also prevented the intended wholesale deportation of the Polish and Jewish populations from this area. Although the German government had designated the Government General as a dumping ground for deportees, this part of Poland bordered on the Soviet Union and had great strategic significance. When the army began to prepare for war with the Soviet Union early in 1941 it shut down immigration to the Government

General. With no site at which to unload unwanted populations, Himmler's program of ethnic cleansing in the annexed territories came to a halt.

There was one final and massive obstacle to Himmler's ambition: Reich Marshal Hermann Göring. The plenipotentiary for the implementation for the Four-Year Plan was absolutely uninterested in questions of settlement. But he had a great appetite for Polish property, especially businesses and industries. In October 1939 he established, by decree, the Main Trusteeship Office East to register and confiscate all publicly and privately owned properties in the annexed territories and the Government General. The decree did not mention the *Reichskommissar für die Festigung deutschen Volkstums*. It was an enormous setback for Himmler, who had hoped to finance part of the resettlement through the sale of nonagricultural assets. He negotiated a considerable measure of control over the requisition of agricultural property, but his plan had been thwarted.

Forced to work with different agencies and to reckon with intense rivalries, Himmler began to create his own power base. Immediately after his appointment as *Reichskommissar* he established his own operational staff, the Office of the Reich Commissioner, headed by Ulrich Greifelt. This office was not an official authority charged with executive responsibility, but Himmler meant it to wield considerable power. Its primary tasks, he wrote, were "the direction and promulgation of general orders and directives" and "the execution of certain tasks which can only be dealt with centrally."[35] And indeed, Greifelt's office grew into a massive bureaucratic apparatus. It officially became an SS department in June 1941. With a head office in Berlin and branch offices in the provinces, it never ran smoothly. Throughout his tenure as *Reichskommissar*, Himmler's passion for control was frustrated because he was forced to operate, in part, through people over whom he had only limited influence.

WHILE THE FUTURE of the annexed territories was, and was to remain, the object of intense rivalry, the evacuation of ethnic German populations from the Baltic, Volhynia, eastern Galicia and, later, Bukovina, Bessarabia, and other places, and the concomitant deportation of Poles and Jews from the annexed territories to the Government General, was effected with depressing ease. Indirectly responsible for the former and directly controlling the latter, Heydrich saw the two operations as one. For him it was an accounting operation, a debit and credit ledger, deportations against settlement. "The deportations carried out so far involved around 87,000 Poles and Jews from the Warthegau

who provided space for the Baltic Germans who were to be settled there,''
he reported in January 1940. The "evacuation" of another 120,000 Poles,
30,000 Gypsies, and all remaining Jews in the annexed territories was "for
the sake of the Wolhynian Germans."[36]

Heydrich had a clear grasp of the larger issues at stake, and a logical
approach to the particular parts of the operation. He established the Central
Immigration Office to oversee and centralize the naturalization process of the
ethnic Germans, check the racial and biological background of each family,
assess its political reliability, and assign it a parcel of land or a house. The
Central Immigration Office operated as a conveyer belt. People were led from
one room to another to be interviewed by black-clad policemen, brown-
clad Party officials, and gray-clad civil servants. The security police inspected
papers, and conducted interrogations if necessary. A comprehensive health
examination followed to assess body proportions, skin and hair color, and nose
form. (It is no accident that one of the doctors in the Posen office was Josef
Mengele, the notorious physician in Auschwitz.) Having determined the immigrant's racial value, bureaucrats of the Interior Ministry decided whether the
ethnic German immigrant could be naturalized or should be given a lesser
status. Property left behind was registered. Then it was time to find a job,
and representatives of the Labor Front, the Labor Ministry, and the Ministry
for Food and Agriculture decided on the where and how of settlement. Most
immigrants were offered settlement in the annexed territories, and eventual
property compensation, acre for acre, building for building, tool for tool.
Some were refused an independent farm or shop, but offered employment in
the Reich and government bonds as recompense for the property left behind.
And then there were those whose loyalty, racial purity, or nationality was in
doubt. They remained in the transit camps, to be transferred to concentration
camps or to be returned to their country of origin.[37]

Heydrich provided an ideology for resettlement, as well as organizing and
managing its practical aspects. As we have seen, the operation had begun on
25 September in response to the implications of the Ribbentrop-Molotov pact
for ethnic Germans. Immediately after he assumed a central role, Heydrich
sent a memorandum to Ribbentrop in which he creatively reinterpreted the
fate of the Balts. He praised them for having formed "a wall against the Asiatic
East" for seven centuries. That mission had come to completion in the Baltic
campaign of 1919. "When today it is necessary to evacuate this old German
position . . . a recognition of a centuries-long achievement for the good of

the whole nation must follow." No one less than Hitler himself should give the Balts their new task, and it should utilize their ability to deal with non-German populations and to shape and mold a space in a German way. Because the Balts were to be the avant-garde in the German East, Heydrich wrote, "we must prevent resettled members of this group from seeking shelter within the Reich on their own initiative. There is a risk that this could happen because many Balts have close family ties all over the Reich, and because there is a great lack of specialized labor in the labor market. To prevent this fragmentation, until further notice each member of this group must be put to work under an induction order and thus be limited in his freedom of action. Those men who qualify for induction into the SS must be called up immediately in a special SS regiment, and trained." With their special ability "to give a German face to areas which have not been very heavily settled and organized by Germans," the Balts should be settled in the province of Posen, Heydrich suggested, "or areas east of the old border of 1914, like that close to Warsaw."[38]

Heydrich transformed a problem that invited ad hoc crisis management into an event framed in the history of the German East. The liquidation of the Balt community was presented not as the hasty retreat that it was but as the beginning of a glorious new chapter in the history of the German Push to the East. Having fulfilled the task given to them in the thirteenth century by a Germany manifested in the Holy Roman Emperor and embodied in the Teutonic Order, the Balts were now to initiate a new project assigned to them by history, manifested in the Führer, and embodied in the SS. The German government officially adopted Heydrich's ideological position. "The Balts do not come as refugees, and absolutely not as emigrants, but to receive from the hands of the Führer new tasks and a new home," the Foreign Ministry instructed its embassies on 21 October 1939. They were not to be so defined, because this would imply that the German government had sold the Baltic countries to Stalin (which of course it had done). "Therefore its must be stressed that the Balts have been recalled by the Führer from the position they have loyally defended for centuries because he has given them *new* tasks and *therewith* gives them a new home."[39]

Even the Balts bought the official line—or in any case those Balts whom the National Socialist regime permitted to publish their sentiments and experiences.

Balts in Riga boarding a ship for Germany, November 1939. Federal Archive, Koblenz.

On Sunday 8 October my mother ran into my room with a newspaper in her hand. There it was: immediate repatriation into the Reich. First it seemed as if the earth had disappeared beneath our feet. But yet, above everything was the call of the Führer. This call was like a magnet. The Führer called us back to the Reich. He wants to give us a new and great task. Especially us, as the first of all ethnic Germans. And as one man our national group of 60,000 people stood there and said: yes, we will come. From the beginning there were no questions of yes or no. It was so self-evident that all of us said yes. . . . Great is our time and great is the man who steers the destiny of all Germans, and great is the confidence and even greater the faith in our Führer and our people. How else would one be able to explain that 60,000 to 70,000 people instantly were ready to leave all that had given meaning to their lives until then, to go blindly to an uncertain, totally unknown future? Yes, Latvians and Jews cannot understand the Germans' blind trust in their Führer. They cannot grasp how one gives up safe positions, how one abandons property, only because a man tells a part of the nation, "Come here, I need you."[40]

The evacuation of the ethnic Germans from the Baltic, eastern Poland, and northern Romania occurred under the pressure of international events and under conditions imposed by foreign governments. The only policy that applied was to get as many people out as quickly as possible with as little friction as possible with the local authorities. Within eighteen months, the numerous German communities of five sovereign states (Latvia, Estonia, the Soviet Union, Romania, and Lithuania) were evacuated and resettled in the annexed territories. The procedure was straightforward. First, the German Foreign Ministry negotiated a bilateral treaty with the foreign government to regulate property transfer and compensation. A short but intensive propaganda campaign followed, to convince the ethnic Germans that they had better answer "the call of the Führer." And then they came home. German ships were sent to pick up the Balts, while in the Soviet Union and Romania SS-trained and -controlled Resettlement Teams crossed into the ethnic German districts (Volhynia, Galicia, Narev and North Bukovina, Bessarabia, South Bukovina, and Dobrudja, respectively) to locate and register ethnic Germans, inform them about their situation and their options, and aid them in the evacuation by horse-drawn wagons, trains, or riverboats.

For Himmler this was an enormous achievement. He had brought a total of 490,640 ethnic Germans home to the Reich in a little over a year and a half. For most Germans this was an event of epic proportions. Celebrated in Gustav Uczicky's movie *Heimkehr* (Return),[41] in novels like Karl Götz's *Die grosse Heimkehr* (The Great Return), and in countless chronicles and nonfiction reports, ranging from prosaic works like Alfred Thoss's *Heimkehr der Volksdeutschen* (Return of the Ethnic Germans) to Hanns Johst's poetic *Ruf des Reiches—Echo des Volkes* (Call of the Reich—Echo of the Nation), this feat no doubt left everyone very impressed. Johst, for instance, was enraptured by a meeting he attended in the government house of Upper Silesia, located in the town of Kattowitz. Himmler and the military and civilian authorities in the region talked openly about the policies to be enacted to accommodate the returnees. "They present the hard facts, and they ask Heinrich Himmler, in his capacity as chief of resettlement, concrete questions. In his final answer he gives these gentlemen and their bureaus clear and forcible directions." Johst was enthralled. "It is wonderful to experience how here one organizes, calmly and dispassionately, the migration of whole nations. Hundreds of thousands of people stream into the Reich, and are settled in the East . . . others are deported . . . and all this occurs while the nation fights the greatest defensive

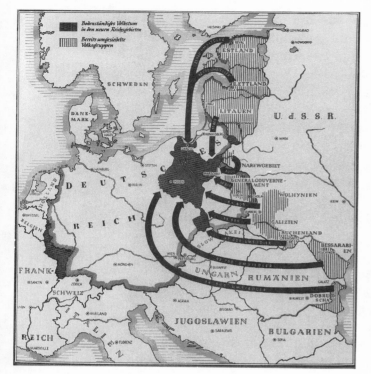

"Resettlement in the German East." Federal Archive, Koblenz. In eighteen months Himmler repatriated a total of 490,640 ethnic Germans "home to the Reich." The resettlement included Balts (October to December 1939); Volhynian, Galician, and Narev Germans (November 1939 to January 1940); ethnic Germans from the Chelm and Lublin region (summer 1940); Bessarabian Germans, North Bukovinian Germans, South Bukovinian Germans, and Dobrudja Germans (September to December 1940); and Lithuanian Germans and Balts who had chosen to remain behind in the fall of 1939 (January to March 1941).

battle for its existence. Everything happens as if it were the most obvious, the simplest issue in the world!'' And he concluded, ''At such moments I almost understand the hatred of the Western world for everything German. Nothing was ever so hateful as superiority, as natural superiority, by virtue of the belief in an idea, by virtue of the achievements, and by virtue of the results.''[42]

''ANYONE WHO WANTS to build up,'' Walter Geisler announced, ''must begin with cleansing, which means that everything that does not fit the new plan, or that opposes it, must be destroyed or removed.''[43] Geisler was professor of geography at the newly established Reich University in Posen. A National Socialist philosopher of geopolitics, he was one of the primary ideologues for resettlement and deportation. The bureaucrat Ulrich Greifelt, head of the Office of the Reich Commissioner, decided which population was going where. And it was Heydrich, of the Reich Security Main Office, who provided the muscle. Greifelt and Heydrich were primarily responsible for the cleansing operation to which Geisler referred, and they lost no time getting down to business. Within days after Himmler had established Greifelt's division and Heydrich's new security apparatus, decisions were taken to deport Polish leaders hostile to the Germans, the Polish intelligentsia, and 550,000 Jews to the Government General. Greifelt worked out plans to confiscate all property that belonged to the Polish state and to persons who had been deported or executed, to prepare for a census in December, to organize ethnic German settlement in the annexed areas, to register their claims, and to make temporary arrangements for them.[44] Himmler was eager for his subalterns to act quickly. By 1 March 1940 the annexed areas had to be cleared of Jews, he decreed (30 October 1939). Furthermore, all Poles who had lived in the Russian part before 1919 had to have left Danzig–West Prussia.[45]

Himmler's decree reflected a general acceptance of the comprehensive population policies initiated in the secret protocol of the Border and Friendship Treaty of 28 September and publicly articulated by Hitler in his speech of 6 October. It was obvious to the German government and its bureaucrats that if their ethnic countrymen were to be resettled, the Poles and Jews would have to go. Poles who had settled in the Corridor and in Posen after 1919 were especially resented and were deported ruthlessly. Significantly, the first major town to be cleansed was Gdynia, which the Germans regarded as a symbol of Polish arrogance. In the beginning of October it was designated a major port of arrival for the Balts, and the returnees were to be given the homes of the erstwhile Polish population. Two days before the first shipload of Balts left the harbor of Tallinn, the deportations began in Gdynia.

On October 17, 1939, at 8 a.m. I heard someone knocking at the door of my flat. As my maid was afraid to open, I went to the door myself. I found there two German gendarmes, who roughly told me that in a few hours I had to be ready to travel with my children and everybody in the house. When I said that I had small children, that my husband was a prisoner of war, and that I could not get ready to travel in so short a time, the gendarmes answered that not only must I be ready, but that the flat must be swept, the plates and the dishes washed and the keys left in the cupboards, so that the Germans who were to live in my house should have no trouble. In so many words, they further declared that I was entitled to take with me only one suit-case of not more than fifty kilograms weight and a small handbag with food for a few days.[46]

The Matschak family awaiting deportation, 1940. Federal Archive, Koblenz.

A three-day journey in bolted cattle cars to the Government General followed, but what happened to these Poles was of no concern to Greifelt; his responsibilities ended at the border of the Government General. The German authorities on the receiving end dumped the deportees on local town officials and philanthropies. "At Koniecpol or Radom twenty persons are put in one room, sleeping on foul straw which has not been changed for three months," a report to the Polish government-in-exile in London lamented. "As the quarters are not heated, the damp and mildew reach a yard and a half up the walls. They are given food once a day from a cauldron; it consists of potato soup without any fat. Bread for the refugees costs a zloty for a loaf weighing a kilogram (2¼ lbs). At Czestochowa the situation is still worse, for neither bread nor potatoes can be bought." The results were dire. "The poor exiles drop with weakness, and many are seriously ill; dysentery and typhus are spreading. The lack of clothing—for they were deported just as they stood—the lack of bedding and linen leads to many of them freezing to death."[47]

The towns that had been emptied of Poles lost their life. In January 1940 a Swedish newspaper commented on the situation in Gdynia, which the Ger-

Poles deported from their farms under army escort, 1940. Federal Archive, Koblenz.

mans had renamed Gotenhafen (Goth Harbor), that Totenhafen (Death's Harbor) was more appropriate. "A town which formerly had a population of 130,000 now has 17,000 inhabitants. There are only a few hundred Poles left in Gdynia, and their lot is very hard. They are hungry, because they do not share in the rationing." The new inhabitants, Balt repatriates, had chosen the nicest flats and houses of the deported Poles. "The port is completely dead. The equipment is being dismantled and shipped to Germany."[48]

The reduction in the population of Gdynia occurred in part because more Poles were moved out than Balts moved in, and in part because the Polish alternative to German Danzig had no future after Hitler's triumphal entry into the older city. But it was also due to Himmler's ambition to reduce the population density in the annexed territories. One of the planners on his staff, Josef Umlauf, set a goal of 85 to 90 people per square kilometer (in comparison with the current figure of 111.8), a reduction of 21.7 percent in the total population (9,901,878 to 7,756,088). The rural population was to be cut from 5 million (51 percent of the total population) to 2.9 million (38 percent of the envisioned population). Only thus could the many small farms be united in economically viable, one-family farms. The urban population, comprising those who lived in towns with more than 2,000 inhabitants, was to drop from 4.8 million to 4.5 million.[49] Two cities in the planning area were permitted to have more than 200,000 inhabitants: Litzmannstadt (Lodz) was to be reduced from 650,000 to 400,000 ("more or less the population of 1939–40 without the Jews"),[50] and Posen, the designated center of the new Balt settlement in the Wartheland, was to grow from a town of 285,000 mostly Polish inhabitants to a city of 350,000 German citizens.

Umlauf's numbers boded ill for both gentile and Jewish Poles. People were thrown out of their homes with only minutes of warning, and then "the Gestapo came and stole any objects of value, after which the houses were swept and given to the *Baltendeutsche*."[51] The latter showed little curiosity

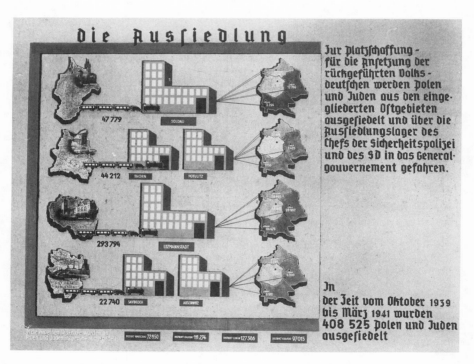

"The Deportations." Federal Archive, Koblenz. Panel from the exhibition "Planning and Reconstruction in the East," held in Berlin, early 1941. The text claims that between October 1939 and March 1941, 408,525 Poles and Jews were deported into the Government General. Of these, 22,740 came from Upper Silesia, and they were transported via Saybusch and Auschwitz.

about the provenance of their new property. Perhaps greed overwhelmed any scruples they may have had, or the rhetoric of their age-old civilizing mission convinced them that the acquisitions were right and proper. The Balt farmer Klawan, for example, noted in his diary that, on arrival in the Wartheland, he attended a meeting at which a German official urged the audience to be "pioneers in the East, bearers of culture. The province must be made German." The Balts were electrified. "Our eyes lit up. His hand points to a great map. 'Here in the north . . . are such opportunities, and in the south such a soil and such conditions. Here in the east . . . ' he hesitates and looks seriously at us, 'here I have found a terrible situation. It is indescribable misery. Here the Poles ravaged [the land].' "[52] Klawan received a farm in the eastern part of the province. It is likely that he was handed a simply worded standard document informing him that everything in the farm was his. "The Polish neighbor or the Polish farmhand will try to swindle things from you. They will claim that the former owner had borrowed tools or cattle from them. But give nothing away." The document urged the new proprietors to begin by cleaning the farm. "Do not make a face if your German neighbor got a better deal than you. There are not enough good buildings for all, as Poles

An ethnic German settler receives his ownership papers for a Polish farm in the Wartheland, 1940. Federal Archive, Koblenz.

used to live here. It is up to you to manage your farm in such a way that everyone will soon be able to see from afar that the village has become German." In this way every farmer would fulfill his duty "as a soldier in the East."[53]

From Klawan's diary it is clear he realized that only a few hours earlier the Polish owner had been deported, but he did not give it a second thought. The only thing that mattered to him was the way that Pole had left his property. "The main room is cold and dirty, and it stinks. The walls are covered with kitsch. The furniture is, with a few exceptions, good. The courtyard is filled with garbage. It is a rich farm, but everything is somehow shabby and chaotic— in short, Polish." Confronted with the dirt, the smell, and the former inhabitants' used, sticky possessions, he was about to give up hope. But then

we thought about the Führer, what he expects of us and what we owe him. We thought about our task in the East and that we had resolved not to give up. And so we gained courage. And the next day we began to clean and air out the place. My wife began the battle with the filth and the chaos, and I inspected the stables, the haylofts, the fields. Slowly, very slowly the place became a working farm again. We began to plow the fields, and to sow. Cartloads of garbage were taken from the court. Soon the filth and the stink had gone from the house, and also the kitsch and the images of saints had gone from the walls. Also gone were the decorative pieces like plaster swans, plaster hens, and shells. Now a large portrait of the Führer hangs on the wall. The swastika flutters in front of the house. We have made ourselves at home. . . . But I still had to see many terrible things. One must be hard here. Soon I was called up for service. I spent days on end in the saddle! Together with comrades we deported Poles and settled Balts. Whole villages became German again. . . . It is a great task to work and to build in the East of the Reich on behalf of Germany. We thank our Führer with our whole heart.[54]

Evidently, the Germans had taught themselves successfully to limit their compassion to those of their own nation.

KLAWAN ENDEAVORED TO eradicate the "Polish" aspects (from the stink to the saints) from, and imprint a "German" character (clean and productive) onto, the property he had been given, and he was not alone. This was the prevailing sentiment of ethnic Germans as well as the policy from Berlin. What was Polish was to be purged. The German East was to be given a Teutonic face.

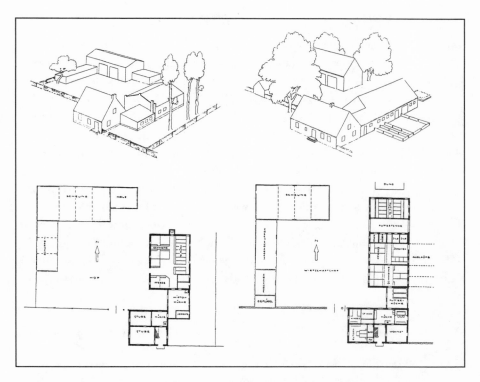

How to transform a Polish farm (left) *into a German farm* (right). *Reichskommissar für die Festigung deutschen Volkstums,* Neue Dorflandschaften *(1943). Federal Archive, Koblenz. German farmers received practical suggestions as to how to Germanize a Polish farm with minimal changes.*

At the heart of Himmler's policy to Germanize the area was the issue of agricultural workers. In a memorandum written in June 1940, he argued that the continued use of Polish agricultural labor would invite a renewal of the Polonization that had led to the losses of 1919 and 1921.[55] For the immediate future he was prepared to accept the use of Polish seasonal labor in large agricultural enterprises, or to build draining ditches, roads, villages, and towns, but he insisted that all nonseasonal agricultural laborers be recruited from other parts of Germany. Since few people (with the exception of the Artamans) had ever expressed the desire to move to the German East to be farm laborers, Himmler sought to make the job attractive by offering them their own land. Young single men who had fulfilled their military or SS service (i.e., after the war) could earn their own farm by working first as unmarried farmhands for two years and then as married agricultural laborers for three to eight years.[56]

According to Himmler's guidelines (November 1940) for the reconstruction of rural areas in the incorporated territories, the new German farms were to embody German peasant culture and be models of modern mechanized agriculture. The houses needed to be large to accommodate extended families and farmhands, and were to be well built.[57] ''The historic importance of this settlement work, and the significance of the farmers in securing our nation's future, must be expressed in the way we build. The technical execution must be solid. The use of local building materials of good quality, used in a careful, craftsmanlike manner, allows for good design.''[58]

The farms were to form villages of 300 to 400 inhabitants, and Himmler discussed their design at length: this was his vision of German settlement of the lands of the German East. The villages were to have a parade place marked by a bell tower, and surrounded by a village hall, a school and kindergarten, a Hitler Youth home, an inn, and buildings for the local farmers' cooperative. ''The landscaping of the village demands special attention, as it contributes

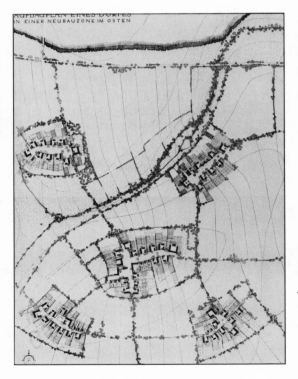

Plan of a village that follows Himmler's guidelines. Reichsheimstättenamt der deutschen Arbeitsfront, Siedlungsgestaltung aus Volk, Raum und Landschaft (1941). Art Library of the State Museums, Berlin. Designed by architects of the Reich Homestead Office of the German Labor Front, the village comprises a group of five settlements consisting of a main village in the center and four satellite villages at the periphery. Concentrating farms in groups ensured social cohesion. The arrangement was also believed to have great strategic significance.

decisively to the German face of the village. It is important to preserve our love, inherited from the German tribes, for trees, shrubs, and flowers (village oak or village linden).'' The village was part of the refashioning of the countryside into ''a healthy German cultural landscape, in which beauty and economy are brought into harmony—an environment that both respects the vital laws of nature and meets the needs of human beings.''[59]

Himmler's guidelines became the basis for an architectural competition in which twenty architects were invited to develop designs for villages in specifically designated areas of the incorporated territories.[60] Using the submitted plans and models, and the results of planning exercises conducted under his own direction, Konrad Meyer organized an exhibition entitled *Planung und Aufbau im Osten* (Planning and Reconstruction in the East) in March 1941 in the Office of the Reich Commissioner at Hardenbergstrasse in Berlin-Dahlem. It generated such great interest that it was installed later that same year in Himmler's Reich Commissioner headquarters on the Kurfürstendamm and,

View of the model of the central village. Reichsheimstättenamt der deutschen Arbeitsfront, Siedlungsgestaltung aus Volk, Raum und Landschaft *(1941). Art Library of the State Museums, Berlin.* Back, left to right: *the Hitler Youth house, the school, the village hall, and, facing the main east—west street, the inn. None of the designs for the new villages in the German East included a church.*

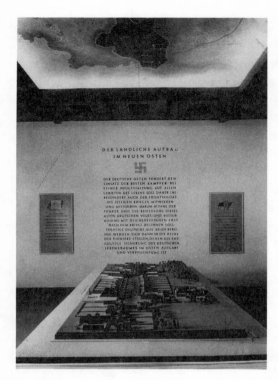

"Planning and Reconstruction in the East" exhibition. Federal Archive, Koblenz.

in October 1941, moved to Posen. The main aim of the exhibition and the sixty-nine-page accompanying publication[61] was to confirm Himmler's authority as the supreme architect of the German East.[62] This was another form of propaganda. The exhibition was mounted and the catalog printed simply and solely to ratify power in public, not to engender discussion of the issues.

HOWEVER SUCCESSFUL HIMMLER may have been in vanquishing his rivals through exhibitions in Berlin, his plans could not be implemented in the territory of his dreams. According to a decree of February 1940, only buildings needed for the war effort or which cost less than 5,000 marks could be constructed.[63] Himmler's farms did not fit either category. But he was neither discouraged nor disheartened. To the contrary: he was at home at last in the German East. According to his friend Hanns Johst, Himmler repeatedly stopped the car during their 1940 trip through occupied Poland. He climbed over the ditches, "walked into the fields plowed by grenade shells, scooped some dirt in his

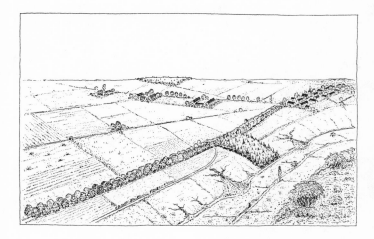

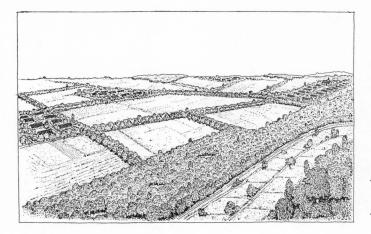

How to transform a Polish landscape (top) into a German landscape (bottom). *Reichskommissar für die Festigung deutschen Volkstums,* Neue Dorflandschaften *(1943). Federal Archive, Koblenz. German planners received practical suggestions as to how to Germanize the Polish landscape. Instead of scattered farms, the Germans should concentrate them in groups (left) or villages (right). The Germanization of the Polish landscape also meant that fields should be separated by groves, trees, hedges, and shrubs. Himmler expected that these would provide a habitat for weasels and hedgehogs, buzzards and falcons—the farmers' allies in his war against mice and vermin. He speculated that such changes in the landscape would create protection from the wind, increase dew, and stimulate the formation of clouds, force rain, and thus push a more economically favorable climate farther towards the East.*

palm, smelled it thoughtfully with inclined head, crushed the lumps of ground between his fingers, and then looked over the vast, vast space which was full, full to the horizon, with this good, fertile earth.'' Johst and Himmler discussed how the German settlers would change the appearance of the land. ''Under professional, rational, and scientific leadership, the Balt, Galician, and Volhynian returnees will do miracles,'' they predicted. The two men stood in the fields, with conquered earth in their hands. ''We smiled at each other with twinkling eyes. All of this was now German soil!''[64]

PART TWO

AMBITION AND PERDITION

CHAPTER 6

A CONCENTRATION
CAMP

HIMMLER, LIKE MANY OF HIS COMPATRIOTS IN HITLER'S GERMANY, CELE-brated the reconstruction of the German East as a return to ancestral soil. The land, the fertile, German land awaiting redemption, commanded their attention. "This earth is ancient Germanic ethnic and cultural soil. Both inheritance and victory have made it ours," Fritz Gerlach, the chief propagandist in Greifelt's office, proclaimed. The East was a land of opportunity for all those "who wish to leave the confinement of urban life and the limited space of the Reich, for all who feel within themselves the youthful power to serve the earth, and in doing so, to serve Germany."[1] This ideology was pertinent to the largely rural provinces of Danzig–West Prussia and Wartheland, but Upper Silesia, with its mine towers and smokestacks, smelting works and factories, and railway yards and canals presented a more complicated picture. As Reich commissioner, Himmler was to Germanize this region also, but he could not simply replace the cooling towers with trees, the foundries with farms, and the power lines with hedges. Upper Silesia was special. And it was precisely because of its industrial character that it was spared the brunt of the resettlement operations. Statistics of the Reich Security Main Office show that with 12 percent of the surface area of the annexed territories, and 27 percent of its population, only 4.8 percent of the deportees came from that region, and a mere 1.6 percent of the ethnic Germans had been settled there.[2]

Title page of a report on the progress of ethnic cleansing in Upper Silesia. Entwicklung, Organisation, Arbeitsleistung *(1943). Federal Archive, Koblenz.*

The population of Upper Silesia could not be moved. The labor force was largely employed (42 percent) in mining and heavy industry; of these half were Poles. They were not like their compatriots to the north who were primarily involved in farming, and therefore easy prey for expulsion. To the contrary: deporting them would not increase the number of farms to be given to ethnic Germans, but it certainly would interrupt industrial production. Furthermore, whereas in Danzig–West Prussia and the Wartheland rural and industrial settlement areas were clearly separated, in Upper Silesia the pervasive social reality of the robotmen, who traveled daily from their farms to the factories, made it impossible to cleanse even rural regions.[3] The only areas that could be evacuated according to National Socialist population policies were those

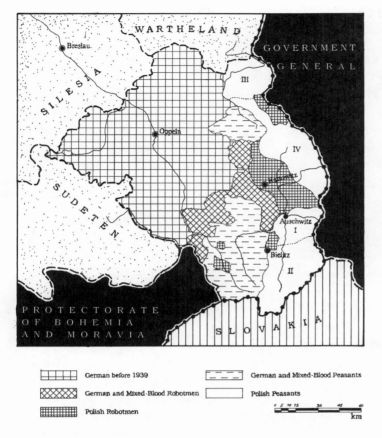

The ethnic situation in Upper Silesia as seen by the local office of the Reich Commissioner for the Consolidation of the German Nation. Drawing by Philip Doele on the basis of reconstruction by Robert Jan van Pelt. Authors. This map is a synthesis of four planning maps published in Entwicklung, Organisation, Arbeitsleistung (1943). Only Polish peasants could be moved. They inhabited the eastern edge of Upper Silesia. Soil conditions in the former duchy of Oswiecim and Zator were better (first grade [I] and second grade [II]) than those to the north (III and IV); this also encouraged German planners to concentrate the settlement of ethnic Germans in the area south of Auschwitz. The map clearly shows the geopolitical location of Auschwitz between Czech and Polish areas.

beyond commuting distance to the industries, and they were few.[4] Finally, the presence of a large group of Polonized Germans in the southern part of the province confused the situation further.[5] Himmler was ideologically committed to the recovery of "lost German blood"; this was a logical extension of the deportation policies, Greifelt explained (May 1940) to his co-workers. While "the removal of persons of alien race from the annexed eastern territories is one of the most important aims to be achieved in the German East," it is equally imperative "to regain for the German nation the German blood in these districts, even in cases where the person concerned is Polonized in language and religion." It is "an absolute national-political necessity to screen the annexed Eastern territories and, later, the Government General also for such persons of Teutonic blood, to make this lost German blood available to

our own people again.''[6] Greifelt's directive was not informed by racist idealism alone; it was expedient to conserve labor power.

Given these economic and ethnic conditions, the Germans were unwilling
to deport the Poles in Upper Silesia as they had done in the Wartheland and
Danzig–West Prussia. But they would not tolerate resistance to German rule
either, and the *Höhere SS-und Polizeiführer* of Silesia, Erich von dem Bach-
Zelewski, pressed forward to establish a concentration camp for recalcitrant
Poles.[7] If the whole population could not be carted away, at least the enemies
of the New Order could be incarcerated. His aide Arpad Wigand had identified
the former labor exchange and artillery base near Auschwitz as a possible
site, and Back-Zelewski requested permission from Berlin to start work. The
inspector of concentration camps, Richard Glücks, was skeptical, and sent a
commission led by the *Schutzhaftlagerführer* of Sachsenhausen, Walter Eisfeld,
to inspect the base in Zasole. Eisfeld was not impressed: the installations near
Auschwitz could not be transformed into a concentration camp, he reported.
(See plate 1.)

Nothing daunted, Bach-Zelewski on 25 January 1940 informed Himmler,
who was about to leave for Przemysl, that he intended to continue his search
for a concentration camp site. The situation in the prisons had become unten-
able, and the new local government officials in the recently annexed parts of
Upper Silesia flooded him with letters demanding immediate action. The police
chiefs of the Kattowitz region, which included the former duchy of Auschwitz,
also insisted on more space for prisoners. A second commission was sent to
Auschwitz, and on 21 February Glücks reported to Himmler that the former
labor exchange and Polish army base in Zasole could be used for a concentration
camp after all.

The SS headquarters in Berlin began negotiations with the army, which
had control over all former Polish military sites. Their goal was a long-term
lease. The army was willing to transfer the base to SS control, and a third
commission, led by another officer from Sachsenhausen, Rudolf Höss, traveled
to Auschwitz to inspect the site more closely. On his way to Upper Silesia,
Höss stopped in Breslau to confer with Wigand, who explained to his guest
that the camp should serve as a regional prison for opponents to German rule
and function as a holding pen from which the Polish prisoners would be
dispatched to camps in the west as slave laborers in Himmler's emerging
empire. In other words, the camp was to resume its function as a labor
exchange, except now that labor was forced. Höss was in complete accord

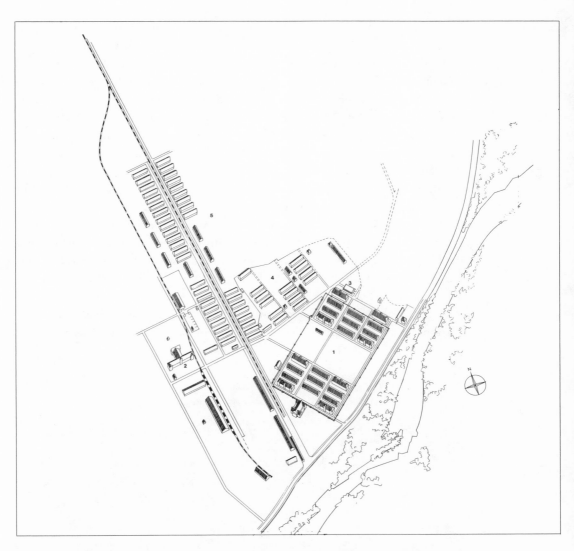

Zasole, spring 1940. Drawing by Kate Mullin. Authors. In the first months of the camp's existence, while the military barracks (1) were cleaned and surrounded by barbed wire to become the protective-custody camp proper, the Oswiecim office of the Polish Tobacco Monopoly (2) was used to accommodate the prisoners. The ammunition depot, banked by earth on the roof and three sides, became a crematorium (3). The Germans used the Polish military base stables for workshops (4). Most of the barracks lining the road to the station, previously used to house the Teschen refugees, were demolished in 1941 (5). N.B.: This is an axonometric drawing; the three-dimensional effect is derived from the exact measurements and angles of the original plan. See plate 1.

with Wigand, and together they set their sights on a large camp with a 10,000-inmate capacity.[8] Höss inspected the barracks in Zasole on 18 and 19 April and advised Glücks that the accommodations and infrastructure of the eight two-story and fourteen single-story brick barracks framing the north and south sides of the large exercise yard were workable. Glücks passed on this information to Himmler. On 27 April the Reichsführer-SS decided that a concentration camp was to be established in Auschwitz. He dispatched Höss and five SS men to prepare for construction. Shortly after his arrival in Zasole, Höss was officially appointed the camp's commandant.

As the first transports of Poles began to arrive in June, Höss focused on fencing in the prisoners' compound—the protective custody camp proper. The solution seemed easy on paper, and a plan of 22 July shows twenty of the twenty-two brick barracks surrounded with a barbed-wire fence, while two double-story barracks, the half-buried ammunition depot, the twenty-two wooden horse stable barracks, and the forty-one dwelling barracks on both sides of the road to the station (inhabited by the refugees from Teschen) were left beyond the enclosure. Delimited as that area was, Höss had difficulties cordoning it off because he was unable to obtain barbed wire. In frustration

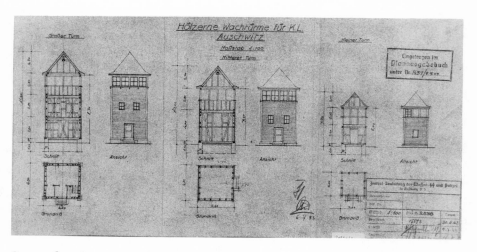

Design of watchtowers. Auschwitz-Birkenau State Museum, box BW 8–9/1, file BW 8/1. The guard towers at Auschwitz and Auschwitz-Birkenau were prefabricated and shipped in by train. The smallest model was most commonly used; the largest, only where there was a lot of traffic.

he sent thirty inmates to strip an abandoned prisoner-of-war camp for Polish soldiers. The history of the camp in Auschwitz thus began with used buildings and secondhand barbed wire. Höss managed, however, to frame the entrance to the camp with a new steel gate, forged in a hastily created workshop. Following the example of Dachau, he marked the passage into the camp with the promise *"Arbeit macht frei"*—Work will set you free.

Höss had been given the rather generous construction budget of two million marks to adapt the twenty brick barracks for the inmates (including a camp prison and an infirmary), to transform the two barracks outside the fence into offices and an infirmary for the garrison, to clean and equip existing barracks to be used as dormitories for the guards, to build a barrack for the *Blockführer* at the gate, to construct provisional guard towers, garages, and a hayloft, and to install a crematorium in the abandoned powder magazine.[9] But a budget was of no use when there was nothing to buy. In the summer of 1940 the newly established construction office in the camp, led by the thirty-nine-year-old August Schlachter (who had been an architect in the Württemberg town of Biberach and who successfully resumed his practice after the war) and his deputy Walther Urbanczyk (who had been a wholesaler in building materials), had great difficulties obtaining supplies. The office had been given a budget, but did not have the accompanying permission papers: ration allocations, bills of purchase, and transport vouchers. Höss himself did not respond to Schlachter's requests for help. Defeated, the latter announced in a report of 17 August that without building materials construction would come to an immediate halt. The complaint was filed without action.[10]

Höss and his administration began to realize the extent of the problem Schlachter faced when they asked him to supply them with sixteen rabbit-breeding cages. The architect drew up a plan, calculated the amount of building materials needed, and sent a request for lumber, nails, and fencing to them which they in turn forwarded to SS headquarters in Berlin. When nothing happened, the camp hierarchy recognized the dimensions of the difficulty: if it was impossible to get sixteen rabbit cages built, the future of their camp looked bleak.[11] Perhaps the future of Europe would have been brighter, but those damned rabbit-breeding cages appear to have stirred Höss to action. Within a fortnight the first loads of building supplies began to arrive in Auschwitz, and on 4 October Schlachter reported that he had the materials he needed. Auschwitz was back in business.[12]

It quickly became clear why Berlin suddenly had responded to Höss's

The brick barracks of the main camp during the war, 1943. Auschwitz-Birkenau State Museum, neg. 20995/36. Many of the brick buildings in the main camp were originally single-story structures. They were given a second story and a spacious attic in order to increase the compound's capacity to 10,000 inmates.

Dormitory in the main camp prisoner barracks, 1943. Auschwitz-Birkenau State Museum, neg. 20995/43.

requisition requests. The *SS-Hauptamt Verwaltung-und Wirtschaft* (SS Main Administration and Economic Office) had identified the concentration camp as a central instrument to actualize its programs in Upper Silesia. The visit of Oswald Pohl, chief of that division, in September 1940 heralded an economic future for the camp. Originally a tool of terror to subjugate a hostile population that, because of its industrial value, could not be deported and a transit camp for those arrested who were then shipped west as slave laborers, Auschwitz was put on the map of the SS financial empire by Pohl. He ordered Höss to double the capacity of the prisoner compound by adding a second story to the fourteen one-story barracks.[13] The camp was to have a stable population, which meant that Auschwitz was envisioned as a production site. The sand and gravel pits beckoned.[14]

POHL WAS WELL PREPARED, by 1940, to appreciate the proximity of a concentration camp to a production point of construction materials. Indeed, the connection between camp sites and building supplies began in 1937, when the camps had become largely superfluous in Germany as an instrument of terror. The National Socialist regime was firmly entrenched by that time and enjoyed general approval. The four concentration camps then extant within the Reich (Dachau, just outside Munich in the south; Buchenwald, close to Weimar in the center; Sachsenhausen, near Berlin in the north; and the women's camp of Lichtenburg, located between Bayreuth and Weimar) were no longer needed to subjugate dissenting Germans as they had been when Hitler first came to power. In 1937 the total number of prisoners was approximately 10,000. And while this 10,000 was 10,000 more than a decade earlier, it was far fewer than the almost 27,000 people imprisoned in the autumn of 1933. The government had not become more tolerant; the population had become more obedient. In Germany, within five years a future without concentration camps had become conceivable.[15]

Himmler was loath to abandon the camp system; he understood that it could be used to his advantage, and he thought it should be. This piece of National Socialist Germany was under his sole control by 1937, and he was ambitious. Himmler knew that Hitler was seriously committed to an enormous building program, and he realized that both manpower and construction materials were in short supply. Rearmament claimed most of the available labor, and Germany simply could not produce the materials Hitler's chief architect, Albert Speer, needed for the urban reconstruction plans the Führer had approved. In 1937, for example, Speer estimated that for Berlin alone he would need two billion bricks the following year. The German brickyards could supply him with just over 350 million; the rest had to be purchased abroad, and the government did not have the foreign currency to do so.[16]

Himmler saw his opportunity. The Reichsführer-SS decided to transform the concentration camp system, originally established to eliminate political opposition through political reeducation, into an SS-owned and inmate-oper-ated building materials industry. When the inmate population had dropped to nearly its lowest point in half a decade, Himmler opened two new concentra-tion camps: Buchenwald, five miles from Weimar and adjacent to large loam and clay deposits, to provide that city with bricks, and Sachsenhausen, in the town of Oranienburg twenty-five miles north of Berlin, to supply bricks to the capital. A few months later (early 1938) he founded the German Earth and Stone Works (DESt) to set up and run the brick works at Buchenwald and Sachsenhausen and to open new and exploit existing granite quarries. The first DESt initiative was the brickyard at Buchenwald, with a planned annual production of seven million bricks. DESt then began construction (with a subsidy of 9.5 million marks allocated by Speer) of the largest brick works in the world. Located along the Hohenzollern canal in Oranienburg, which facilitated direct transport to Berlin, this factory was designed to produce 150 million bricks annually. That same year DESt bought a closed brickyard near Hamburg and planned a 40-million-brick-a-year establishment to supply recon-struction projects in Hamburg. A new concentration camp, Neuengamme, was built adjacent to the factory.

In Hitler's Germany, granite was a primary building material for public buildings and, since it was as important in Speer's plans as brick, DESt lost no time monopolizing that market as well. Its acquisition pattern was straight-forward: first, quarries were identified for quantity and quality of stone and assessed in relation to transport and markets. Then they were leased or pur-chased. With the works securely under DESt control, the SS built concentration camps nearby. Thus, for example, among the first quarries in the DESt empire were the famous pits close to the Upper Austrian town of Mauthausen, near Linz. The Mauthausen mines had supplied most of the granite used in Vienna, Budapest, and the smaller cities of the former Austro-Hungarian empire; the stone was much valued and the town was on a major transport corridor.[17] After the Anschluss of 1938, a new market opened. Hitler had designated Linz, the town where he had spent his youth, as the fifth *Führerstadt*. Like Berlin, Munich,

Nuremberg, and Hamburg, the town where the Führer hoped to retire was to become a monumental expression of the new Thousand Year Reich. Himmler was avid for DESt to be the main supplier of the granite required.

A few days after the Anschluss, Himmler and Pohl toured the Mauthausen area. Pohl returned two months later with the inspector of concentration camps, Theodor Eicke, and the chief of the SS construction office, Herbert Karl. They selected two granite works owned by the city of Vienna: the Vienna Ditch quarry, near Mauthausen, and the Bettelberg quarry, near Gusen. The city leased the pits to DESt, and the SS promptly built two concentration camps: a main camp next to the Vienna Ditch, and a satellite camp next to Bettelberg.

Conditions in the camps did not improve when the labor of the inmates became important to the wealth of the SS. To the contrary: the conditions under which the inmates lived and worked deteriorated rapidly. When the original pedagogical purpose was abandoned and forced labor took its place, the inmates became slaves. Notwithstanding DESt's alleged intention to exploit these works efficiently from an economic point of view, they became death traps for the prisoners. Malnourished, badly equipped, lacking protective gear, and constantly harassed by the guards, the inmates had little chance of surviving the arduous labor of the brickyards or granite quarries. Eugen Kogon, arrested in Austria for anti-Nazi activities immediately after the Anschluss and sent to Buchenwald, described the harsh regime of work in the loam pits: ''Every night saw its procession of dead and injured, trundled into camp on wheelbarrows and stretchers—oftentimes there were two or three dozen. The mistreatment was indescribable—stonings, beatings, 'accidents,' deliberate hurlings into the pit, shootings, and every imaginable form of torture.''[18]

The quarries and brickyards produced the materials to actualize the designs of Speer and his colleagues, but they are not discussed in the large-format volumes tracing the development of the architects' plans for Berlin and Nuremberg. Ironically, perhaps, Speer's conceits were never built, but the suffering they engendered echoes still.

THE ESTABLISHMENT OF the concentration camp at Auschwitz did not follow precisely the model set by Buchenwald, Sachsenhausen, or Mauthausen. As we have seen, the initial purpose of the camp was to terrorize the local Polish population which, engaged in industrial occupations, was not deported by the Germans. Auschwitz was a transit camp for the arrested recalcitrant Poles, who were shipped to camps in the west as slave laborers. Oswald Pohl, however, quickly realized that the camp could take on another function. The sand and gravel pits of Auschwitz were well known, and on his visit to Auschwitz he confirmed their usefulness for the DESt enterprise. Concrete was a much needed building material and, as both the pits and the camp were already in place, Auschwitz easily could be transformed into a DESt site.

It was the potential resource of building materials which ensured the future of Auschwitz; it was due to the sand and gravel pits that Pohl ordered Höss to enlarge the camp to house a permanent, slave labor population. But building materials were the very thing the architects and engineers at Auschwitz lacked. Few construction projects in the camp were unaffected by the initial scarcity. As we saw in the introduction, architectural plans are a unique source of historical information. In this case, the blueprints prepared by Schlachter's construction office illustrate the overarching vision of those in charge of the development of the camp. They depict what the Kommandantur, or camp officials, wished to build. The supply bills, by contrast, identify precisely what was constructed and when. In the dialectic between a design in which everything is possible, and the daily reality in which nothing was feasible, the synthesis of setting priorities is clearly revealed. In other words, with limited resources, what was built first? It is no accident, and indeed is highly significant, that the two projects undertaken with the initial materials allocated by Berlin were a camp prison to instill dread and a crematorium to burn the dead. Just like Sachsenhausen, Buchenwald, or Dachau, Auschwitz also had a prison and a crematorium. With these two installations the Kommandantur ruled with brutality and got rid of the bodies of the people they killed along the way— not to hide the evidence of their cruelty, but simply to make the environment more hygienic for themselves.

A two-story building at the southern corner of the prisoner compound was transformed into the prison.[19] Later to be known as block 11, this building quickly became the most feared place in the camp. On the first and second floors were large communal cells, in which more than a hundred people were crowded together. (See plate 2.) The ground floor rooms housed the penal company prisoners. In the basement were small, dark cells along narrow corridors. Pery Broad, one of the SS men employed in the camp's own Gestapo office—the so-called political department—visited these cells often to help his boss, Maximilian Grabner, ''dust out'' the cellars; that is, select the prisoners to be shot. A minor SS official in the camp, Broad was taken prisoner by the British

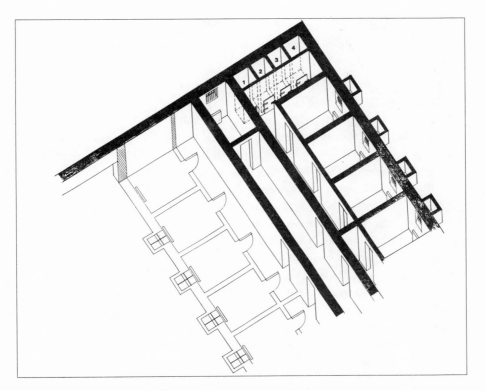

*Block 11, fall 1940. Drawing by Kate Mullin. Authors. The central corridor leads to
different groups of cells. The four tiny standing cells (1—4) are at the upper
right side. N.B.: This is an axonometric drawing; the three-dimensional effect is derived
from the exact measurements and angles of the original plan. See plate 2.*

in 1945, and in 1946 he wrote a report on conditions in Auschwitz for them.
"Breathing was almost impossible," Broad explained. Many of the cells had no
window, only a narrow vent that allowed little air. Terrible as these conditions
were, the four so-called standing cells spelled death. "Many prisoners were
doomed to spend there, naturally without a single ray of light, terrible hours or
even weeks. It was out of the question to sit down. The prisoners cowered in
the darkness. When the cold in the winter was severe, it was impossible to get
warm by moving about."[20] Up to four prisoners were consigned to the standing
cells at a time. Those who had tried to escape were left in the standing cells to
die; others who had committed minor offenses were locked in for a set number

of nights. Among the last was Wieslaw Kielar, one of the 728 men who had come to Auschwitz with the first transport of Poles on 14 June 1940.

> On my hands and my feet—otherwise I would not have been able to get in—I crawled into the black opening of the standing cell. The *Blockführer* helped me with my clumsy stumping into the tiny cell, which stank of excrement, by hitting my stretched buttocks with all his power. "Faster, faster, you dog!" he urged me impatiently. . . . In the pitch dark I felt the used breath of three fellow victims on my face. One of them had great diffulty breathing and whimpered weakly from time to time, "Water! Food! Water!" He hung against me with his whole weight seeking support and warmth. I felt his emaciated body shaking from cold and exhaustion, and he stank terribly. Compared to his stench the vapor of the worst phlegm or diarrhea seemed like the smell of sweetest perfume. The other two were in slightly better condition. They told me that they had already stood in this cell without food or water for two days. . . . They complained that I had been sent to their cell. There was only one hope left: that this other one would die before the next day. Then there would be three again, and it would be possible to change one's position, move one's feet, and stretch one's arms.[21]

Their wish was fulfilled. He died before the night was over.

Most inmates committed to block 11 died not in the standing cells but in the execution yard on its north side. The condemned undressed in a room adjacent to the courtyard. Before the tattooing of prisoners was introduced in March 1942, "the helpers wrote the prisoners' numbers on the naked bodies of the victims with indelible pencils, to make the identification of the bodies in the mortuary or in the crematorium possible."[22] The naked inmates were led into the courtyard. A strong prisoner took two victims at a time in an iron grip and pushed them against the black wall. The victims, who often had spent months in the small cells below and could hardly stand, had no strength to resist. An SS man of the political department or Duty Officer Gerhard Palitzsch shot them in the neck. Prisoners loaded the corpses onto stretchers and dumped them in a heap at the courtyard gate. When the executions were finished, the bodies were loaded on a cart and brought to the crematorium at the other side of the camp.[23]

The crematorium had been installed in the ammunition depot, and the transformation had been a remarkably smooth operation. (See plate 3.) In June 1940 Schlachter obtained an efficient and technologically advanced double-muffle (i.e., two openings, one per corpse), coke-heated furnace from Topf & Sons for 9,000 marks.[24] It had the capacity to incinerate seventy corpses in twenty-four hours, which seemed more than sufficient in the summer of 1940. Just a few months later, however, the camp authorities sent a letter to Topf requesting a second double-muffle incinerator, explaining, ''The present use of the incinerator that has been supplied by you has shown that the facility is still too small.''[25] This request was justified to SS headquarters in Berlin: ''The past use of the crematorium has shown that even at a rather good time of year the incinerator with two muffles is too small. Both the Kommandantur and the Political Department have approached the SS-New Construction Office with an urgent request for a two-muffle expansion of the facility. The SS-New Construction Office then contacted the Topf & Sons firm in Erfurt, which built the first incinerator. We discussed the expansion of the installation with Chief Engineer Prüfer of Topf at the crematorium, and it seems that the enlargement will not be too difficult. The price for a two-muffle expansion is 7,753 marks.''[26] Topf reduced the price because the second incinerator could be attached to the ventilator of the first.

A third incinerator was needed a year later. ''Third incinerator urgently needed,'' the new chief of the Auschwitz building office, Karl Bischoff, wired Topf on 11 November 1941. ''Cable when construction will occur and facility will be completed.''[27] Bischoff's telegram was in direct response to the dramatic increase of deaths in the camp. Of 9,908 Soviet prisoners of war who arrived in October, 1,255 were murdered that same month.[28] Then a special commission of the Gestapo led by Dr. Rudolf Mildner arrived from Kattowitz early in November to identify and liquidate the ''fanatical Communists'' (some 300) or ''politically suspect'' (some 700) among the remaining prisoners of war.[29] In the first five days of November the names of 1,238 Soviets were entered in the Auschwitz death register.[30]

Mildner was a regular visitor to the camp, and each visit ended with mass executions. The Gestapo Summary Court, which he chaired and which had its seat in the camp, increased the functions of the camp. In addition to being a concentration camp where inmates were killed, Auschwitz became, with the court, an execution site for ''outsiders'' who were never registered there. The purpose of the court was to interrogate, convict, and execute Polish resisters from all over eastern Upper Silesia. These Polish men and women

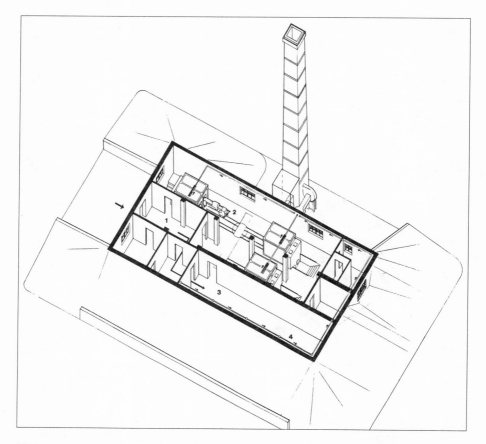

*The main camp crematorium, fall 1941. Drawing by Kate Mullin. The vestibule (1) gives
access to an incineration hall equipped with three double-muffle ovens (2) and to
a morgue which was transformed into a gas chamber in September 1941 (3). The ventilation
system (4), originally designed to extract foul odors, was used to extract the Zyklon
B fumes after gassing. The idea to use the extant machinery for lethal purposes was an
essential step in the transformation of the concentration camp into a murder site.
N.B.: This is an axonometric drawing; the three-dimensional effect is derived from the exact
measurements and angles of the original plan. See plate 3.*

were brought to Auschwitz solely to stand trial and face execution; they were
not inmates. Mildner's court convened in block 11, and initially the executions
took place in the courtyard between blocks 10 and 11. It soon became clear,
however, that it would be more efficient to bring the condemned to the crematorium and kill them in the mortuary. ''The walls were stained with blood, and

in the background there lay the corpses of those already shot," Broad wrote after the war. "A wide stream of blood was flowing towards the drain in the middle of the hall. The victims were obliged to step quite close to the corpses and formed a line. Their feet were stained with blood; they stood in puddles of it. . . . The right-hand man of the camp leader, *SS-Hauptscharführer* Palitzsch, did the shooting. He killed one person after another with a practised shot in the back of the neck."[31] The stench was so foul that in the summer of 1941 the chief of the political department, Grabner, prevailed on Schlachter to install a more sophisticated ventilation system that not only extracted the air he found sickening but also brought in a fresh supply from the outside.[32]

The corpses were burned in the incineration room next door. Filip Müller, a Slovak Jew who arrived in Auschwitz in April 1942 with one of the earliest Jewish transports, was put to work as a stoker in the crematorium. By the time Müller, a slave laborer, was detailed to the Sonderkommando (Special Squad), the morgue had evolved to its nadir: from corpse cellar to execution ground by bullet in the neck, to (as we shall discuss in chapter 9) execution ground by gas. It was Müller's job to drag the corpses from the morgue (now gas chamber) to the crematorium and to keep the fires burning steadily. One of the few of the Sonderkommando to have survived, Müller after the war described the procedure and the equipment used to move the bodies, to keep the system in operation. Rails had been laid across the crematorium, Müller explained, and "this track was about 15 metres long." (See plate 4.)

Leading off from the main track were six branch rails, each 4 metres long, going straight to the ovens. On the main track was a turn-table which enabled a truck to be moved onto the branch tracks. The cast-iron truck had a box-shaped superstructure made of sheet metal. . . . An iron hand-rail went right across its entire width at the back. A loading platform made of strong sheet metal . . . jutted out in the front. . . . Open at the front, the platform was not quite as wide as the mouth of the oven so that it fitted easily into the muffle. On the platform there was a box-shaped pusher made of sheet metal, higher than the side walls of the platform and rounded off at the top . . . [which] could be moved back and forth quite easily. Before the truck was loaded, the pusher was moved to the back of the platform. To move the truck from one track to another one had to hold onto the turn-table to prevent the truck from jumping off the rails as it left the turn-table.

To begin with, the corpses were dragged close to the ovens. Then, with the help of the turn-table, the truck was brought up to a branch rail, and the front edge of the platform supported by a wooden prop to prevent the truck from tipping during loading. A prisoner then poured a bucket of water on the platform to stop it from becoming too hot inside the red-hot oven. Meanwhile two prisoners were busy lifting a corpse onto a board lying on the floor beside the platform. Then they lifted the board, tipping it sideways so that the corpse dropped on the platform. A prisoner standing on the other side checked that the body was in correct position.

When the truck was fully loaded two corpses were lying on either side facing the oven while a third was wedged between them feet first. Now the time had come to open the oven door. Immediately one was overcome by the fierce heat which rushed out. When the wooden prop had been removed, two men took hold of the front end of the platform on either side pulling it right up to the oven. Simultaneously two men pushed the truck from behind, thus forcing the platform into the oven. The two who had been doing the carrying in front, having meanwhile nipped back a few steps, now braced themselves against the hand-rail while giving the pusher a vigorous shove with one leg. In this way they helped complete the job of getting the corpses right inside the oven. As soon as the front part of the pusher was inside the oven, the truck with its platform was pulled back. In order to prevent the load of corpses from sliding out of the oven during this operation, a prisoner standing to one side thrust an iron fork into the oven pressing it against the corpses. While the platform—which had been more than three-quarters inside the oven—was manoeuvred on its truck back onto the turn-table, the oven door was closed again.[33]

A body was burned in each of the six muffles (three double-muffle ovens) every twenty minutes.

In 1940, two bodies were incinerated in the double-muffle oven every twenty minutes; some months later, the rate had doubled with the addition of the reduced-price second two-muffle oven. In 1941, crematorium I had reached its maximum capacity of eighteen bodies per hour. It did not matter whether the victims had been shot in the courtyard of block 11 or killed in the morgue next door. The process of cremation was as Müller described it. The Germans found more and more people to liquidate—Polish partisans, Russian prisoners of war, and finally, on 15 February 1942, the first transports of Jews—but the rate-limiting step of their murder machinery was the disposal of bodies. This was the horror of Auschwitz I.

AS WE HAVE SEEN, the concentration camp at Auschwitz initially existed to subjugate the local population. After Oswald Pohl's visit in September 1940 and his greedy assessment of the sand and gravel pits, the camp took on an economic role. Terror and production were not special to Auschwitz but rather the staples of concentration camps in Germany in the 1930s. A few months later, in November, the Gestapo Summary Court gave Auschwitz another function, new to a camp in the occupied territories—it became a killing site for outsiders, for people who were not inmates. Then came a fourth dimension, unique to Auschwitz's place in the Germans' myth of the German East. Located between an industrial area to the north and the west, and a rural region to the south, the camp became an agricultural center to help ethnic Germans adjust to local farming conditions. The settlers were appropriating the farms of the Polish agricultural population to the south, designated for evacuation, and in part actually deported. Himmler envisioned Auschwitz as a support agency for incoming homesteaders. Thus, while the camp played no part in deportation actions, it had a distinct role in resettlement. The first detailed proposal to integrate Auschwitz into the ethnic-cleansing campaign dates from November 1940, but the groundwork was laid half a year earlier.

In the spring of 1940 Himmler identified the districts of Wadowitz, Saybusch, and the eastern part of Bielitz—precisely the territory of the former duchy of Auschwitz—as a geopolitically crucial region that cried out for reconstruction. "The population density of this area is extraordinarily high," the minutes of a discussion between the Reich Commissioner for the Consolidation of the German Nation and the Reich Authority for Spatial Planning reported. "The result of this population density is the emergence of a markedly impoverished peasantry. . . . The condition of the houses is so bad, and the present arrangement of the fields is so fragmented, that a completely new settlement is inevitable and necessary."[34]

The Germans found the Poles' miniature holdings an enormous problem; they calculated that, on the average, nine Polish properties were required to establish one viable farm, while in Saybusch forty-six such farms were needed.[35] But if the former duchy of Auschwitz presented immense difficulties, it also offered unusual prospects. Wholly Polish and totally agricultural, the local population could be deported without careful screening or the diminution of industrial production.[36] Furthermore, according to Gerhard Ziegler of the provincial planning office in Breslau, German settlement in the former duchy of Auschwitz would create a wedge between the Poles and the Czechs who, it was feared, were in communication through the Moravian Gap.[37] Ziegler suggested this geopolitical aspect of the situation to Himmler's chief planner, Konrad Meyer, who needed no convincing.[38] Meyer had already decided to assign the area the status of settlement zone 1 (which meant that, as an area of immediate Germanization, it would receive planning priority) and had drafted proposals to begin the resettlement of the region with ethnic Germans from Galicia.[39] At that time twenty-one camps in Upper Silesia held 8,341 ethnic German returnees from eastern Poland.[40] Following Meyer's recommendations, Himmler ordered (in June 1940) the installation of 5,000 of these settlers in Saybusch.[41] Milovka, a larger village to the south, was to be one of the four communities in the annexed territories which would serve as a model for other resettled hamlets.[42] The Galicians were to receive one-quarter of the property; the rest was to be reserved until after the war for farmers from the German Reich.[43]

Ulrich Greifelt visited the area and confirmed the policies drafted by Meyer and the other planners. He approved of their idea to destroy communications between the Czechs, the Slovaks, and the Poles through German settlement in the region between the Biala and Skava. "It is imperative to create a purely ethnic German corner at this point, positioned at the southern edge of the Upper Silesian industrial area and flanking the important passage to the south also. Later it will be possible to build a connection between this area [of ethnic German settlement] and the [German] Sudeten as well as to the ethnic German wall of settlement in the north." Greifelt suggested that resettlement "begin at first with the ethnic transformation in the western parts of the areas mentioned before."[44] He identified fifty-five of the ninety-three communities of the district of Bielitz for occupation by the ethnic Germans, including the town of Auschwitz, which, with 10,590 inhabitants, was the second-largest town to be included on the list.[45]

Himmler, Bracht, Bach-Zelewski, and Greifelt met in mid-September to discuss the latter's ideas, which were then adopted as official policy.[46] Bach-Zelewski, who as senior SS and police commander was in charge of the whole operation, chaired a meeting of the local civil servants of the Kattowitz region a month later to discuss the impending political and social changes. A map created for this conference designated the former duchy of Auschwitz as *Sied-*

Planning map showing the Upper Silesia districts identified as Zone of Settlement I and Zone of Settlement Ia in 1940. Federal Archive, Koblenz, coll. R 49, file 902. The former duchy of Auschwitz, that is, the Saybusch district, the eastern part of the Bielitz district, and the western part of the Wadowice district, was included in Zone of Settlement Ia. Compare with p. 165.

lungszone 1a (settlement zone 1a), which meant that it had been given the highest priority.[47] On 23 November Greifelt announced that the physical and social transformation of the former duchy of Auschwitz should begin immediately after the official division of Silesia on 1 February 1941 into two provinces—Lower Silesia and Upper Silesia. Auschwitz fell to the latter.[48]

Deportation of the Polish population from Saybusch had begun in September. Fritz Arlt, Greifelt's representative in Upper Silesia, the district councillor of Saybusch, and the SS and police officers who were to lead the operation had met earlier that month to discuss the details of the operation. The first item on the agenda was money. The action, Arlt calculated, would cost 370,000 marks: 10 marks for each of the 20,000 Poles evacuated to the Government General, 100,000 marks to feed the deportees during their journey, and 70,000 marks to cover the food and lodging costs of the German policemen. This sum was to be recovered "by seizure of all the valuables, money, and jewelry of the Poles who will be evacuated."[49] Customs officials were to search the Poles in local transit camps before their deportation to a central transit camp in Litzmannstadt (Lodz). The plan was for "a police detachment of 400 men, that is, two men per family, to move at 5:00 A.M. into the part of the village that will be evacuated. One official will bring a family to the transit camps that have been established in Saybusch, Rajcza, and Sucha. The second will guard the farm until the German family has arrived. The Poles are to be subjected to a racial screening in the transit camps. They will be brought

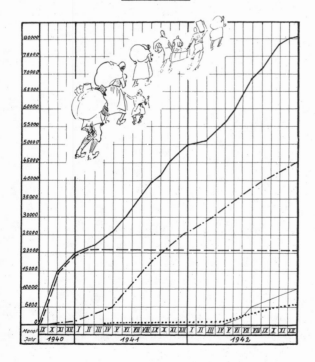

Die im Zuge der Ansiedlung in Oberschlesien ausgesiedelten und umgesetzten Fremdvölkischen.

3

Gesamtzahl der bei Umsetzungen erfaßten Fremdvölkischen
———·—·— Interne Umsetzungen
— — — — Umsetzungen in das Gen Gouvernement
············ in das Altreich vermittelt
————— Polen-Lager

Deportation from Upper Silesia.
Entwicklung, Organisation, Arbeitsleistung *(1943). Federal Archive, Koblenz.*

————— = *the total number of non-Germans deported*

—·—·— = *evacuation within Upper Silesia*

— — — — = *deportation to the Government General*

············ = *deportation to the Reich*

————— = *incarcerated in camps*

The diagram makes clear that deportations from Upper Silesia started in September 1940.

separately to Litzmannstadt. The trains leave one day after the evacuation at 1:00 or 2:00 P.M."[50] Within three days an even more detailed system was organized. The action was to begin on Sunday, 22 September, and trains holding 1,000 deportees each were to leave Saybusch on Monday at 2:48 P.M., Rajcza on Wednesday at 1:46 P.M., and Sucha on Friday at 1:15 P.M. Every Wednesday the need for trains for the following week had to be confirmed with the chief of Office IV D 4 of the Reich Security Main Office. The nerve center of the whole operation would be Greifelt's SS staff in Saybusch who would establish and maintain an alphabetically ordered card system. The guidelines also mentioned that there was no need to inform Göring's Main Trusteeship Office, East, as only agricultural properties were to be affected.[51]

The decision as to which farms were to be seized (and which families deported) was taken on the basis of a detailed survey made by roving teams that visited every property and noted the condition of the house and the stables, the number and health of the cattle, and the state of the farm equipment; local ethnic Germans served as interpreters. The day before an action the policemen got their instructions from their officers. "The units obtain a detailed list of the designated farms, the number of family members that will have to be transported. Surprise is essential to prevent sabotage through the abduction of cattle and other inventory. Therefore the village is to be surrounded between 5 and 6 A.M. and sealed off from the outside world. Two men go to each farm, instruct the inhabitants to pack their necessities, and order them to follow to a central meeting place. . . . They can take only what they can carry."[52] Polish underground sources reported that the deportees were treated roughly. While the Poles were lined up outside their house with machine guns trained on them, the policemen helped themselves to watches, money, and wedding rings. "The deportees were allowed to take with them only one suit of clothes and a little food. As they were driven out of their houses they were kicked and beaten with the butts of guns, neither old folks, women nor children being spared. In consequence several were wounded, and even killed, for example at Sól and Jelesnia. Several women as they were trying to escape were shot among the farm buildings. One woman had her infant in her arms. Then they were kicked and knocked about, packed into lorries, and transported to concentration camps at Jacza and Zywiec."[53]

A team arrived at eight in the morning to clean and disinfect the houses and stables, hoist the swastika, hang a portrait of Hitler in each house, and put up a sign next to the well saying that all drinking water should be boiled until the completion of laboratory tests. At three in the afternoon the new owners took possession. The policeman who had remained to oversee the cleaning and disinfection was instructed to lend a festive aspect to their arrival. The Poles, in the meantime, were brought to the transit camps where "there were terrible scenes of suicides and childbirths." Then they were loaded into the trains and, after a stop in Litzmannstadt, brought to occupied Poland. The journey in unheated railway cars frequently lasted three days. According to a report from the Polish underground, "on arrival at their destination they were divided into groups of ten or so, who were assigned to one farmer, this being equivalent to being condemned to a life of beggary. A few of the younger men and the stronger women were transported to Germany in special trains to do compulsory labour there."[54] The resettlement continued until 6 June 1941 when Fritz Arlt, who had overseen the operation, submitted a final report to Bracht. Arlt looked to the future with hope. Resettlement marked a new beginning. With the future reconstruction of the medieval *Waldhufendörfer*, a healthy relation between the land and the people was to be reestablished.[55] His report was released to the press and the *Ostdeutscher Beobachter* reported enthusiastically that "775 peasant families comprising 3,713 people were settled in an area of 11,385.12 hectares, as well as 131 artisan families with 412 people. They occupy ancient German *Waldhufen* villages in the former Duchy Teschen-Auschwitz."[56]

The reference to the German legacy was not accidental; for the German public of the 1930s and early 1940s the continuity with that medieval past was important. Popular publications emphasized that, despite its Polish appearance, Auschwitz and its surroundings had once been under German sovereignty. "German farmers and burghers settled these districts, and German knights and judges administered them: the ruling dukes considered their lands fiefs of the Reich, and their families were connected to the leading houses of the old German Reich," Arlt reminded the readers of his eagerly received book on the future of eastern Upper Silesia. Published by a commercial press, this work was one of a series underwritten by the office of the Reich Commissioner to inform the public of his policies and programs in the East. Arlt reviewed the medieval settlement history of the region. A "great trek of young, land-hungry farmers, of able and future-oriented merchants and action-prone noblemen" re-Germanized an area where Germans had lived before the Hun raids. In the thirteenth and fourteenth centuries "the whole left bank of the Oder was won back for German-Germanic blood," and by the end of the fourteenth century

Resettlement in the Saybusch district, 1941. Oberschlesischer Heimatkalender *(1943). Authors. Upper Silesia's Gauleiter Fritz Bracht* (in uniform) *and Minister of Finance Lutz Schwerin von Krosigk visit ethnic German returnees. Fritz Arlt* (glasses) *can be seen third from the right.*

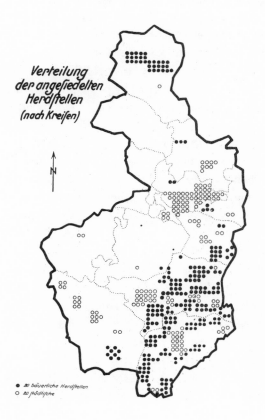

Verteilung
der angesiedelten
Herdstellen
(nach Kreisen)

N

● 20 bäuerliche Herdstellen
○ 20 städtische

German settlement in eastern Upper Silesia. Entwicklung, Organization, Arbeitsleistung *(1943). Federal Archive, Koblenz. Each black dot represents twenty transplanted farming families; each white dot represents twenty transplanted urban families.*

"the German form of settlement (*Waldhufendorf*) and German peasant law ruled in the region that stretches from Friedek to the gates of Cracow." It was the Germans who had established trade routes, laid roads, and founded "towns such as Oderberg, Freistadt, Teschen, and Jablunka; the towns of Skotschau, Bielitz, Kenty, Andrichau, and Wadowitz sprang up along the great connector between Vienna and Cracow and Lemberg and the towns of Auschwitz, Zator, and so on along the road between Gleiwitz and Cracow. These towns were founded according to German law . . . and carried German names and German culture." Even after five centuries of Polish occupation, these towns betrayed their German origin. Arlt did not confine his praise to the cities, the settlement forms alone. It was the settlers themselves who were to be lauded and their legacy honored. "The German farmer and the German burgher were robbed of the German law basis of their existence. Some left for the East, others were linguistically, socially, and culturally Polonified." Nevertheless, despite "the administrative separation from the Reich and the German cultural community [and] the immigration of a fertile Slav population, the conscious and systematic Polonification failed to destroy our knowledge of this old German settlement area in the regained areas of Upper Silesia." The German who moved into eastern Upper Silesia under the National Socialist aegis should remember "that he drives his plow in land his ancestors tilled, that he wields his ax in forests tamed by people of the same blood, that he establishes his workshop or business in towns and villages founded by German settlers."[57]

But the ethnic Germans needed more than land to prevail. As Himmler had noted in a speech of 24 October 1939, their success depended on practical support. They had to be educated about local conditions and provided with livestock. He suggested the creation of estates to provide training for the farmers and house "nurseries for the production of seed corn, garden seeds, berries, fruits" and for trees and "livestock (horses, pigs, cattle, hens)."[58] Meyer, as usual, agreed with Himmler and developed the practical implications of the latter's ideas in his first detailed plan for the region, written in the fall of 1939. Identifying good-quality livestock as crucial to resettlement, Meyer projected an immediate need for 32,500 cows, 32,500 young stock, 4,000 bulls, 100,000 pigs, 2,500 boars, 150,000 sheep, 50,000 goats, and 200,000 hens.[59] Clearly, agricultural support centers were essential, and in his book on the East Arlt explained that Upper Silesia was slated for seven such estates.[60] One of them was in Auschwitz, to be set up and run by the concentration camp Kommandantur with the forced labor of the inmates.[61]

It was Himmler's idea to use the concentration camp to establish a large

Wood engraving depicting the ideology of recovery. Heimatkalender des Beskidenkreises Saybusch *(1941). Authors. The land that was to be tilled had been sanctified by the toil and sacrifice of German farmers, burghers, and knights seven centuries earlier.*

agricultural estate. When Höss had visited him in November 1940 hoping to gain additional resources, Himmler had been entranced by Höss's maps, plans, and diagrams. (See plate 5.) The huge security zone of 5,000 acres which was already under direct control of the camp, and which would be unencumbered by civilians in a few months' time, had potential: the area could be a large manorial estate worked by a pool of inmates. Himmler "became very lively and started planning, issuing one directive after another, or made notes about all the things that needed to be done on the estates around Auschwitz," Höss recalled in his memoirs. He was pleased with the sudden agricultural enthusiasm of Himmler, his fellow Artaman. He still hoped to obtain a farm for his own family.[62] The two men began to plan the transformation of Auschwitz into an agricultural experiment station which would service the entire region.

The possibilities which existed here had never been possible in Germany itself. Certainly there were enough workers available. Every necessary agricultural experiment was to be tried out there. Huge laboratories and plant cultivation departments had to be built. Cattle breeding of all types

and breeds of animals was to become important. Major Vogel was supposed to immediately recruit the necessary experts. The marshlands were
to be drained and developed. A dam was to be constructed on the Weichsel
River. Compared to all these difficulties, the deplorable conditions in the
camp were nothing. In the near future he was going to see for himself
what Auschwitz was like. He continued with his agricultural planning even
down to the smallest details and stopped only when his adjutant called his
attention to the fact that a very important person had been waiting for a
long time to see him.[63]

Himmler decided that the experiment station would employ most of the camp's
projected population of 10,000 inmates.[64] While he had no intention of giving
up the lucrative sand and gravel pits, they had no charm for him. It was the
metamorphosis of the camp into an agricultural estate worked by slaves that
caught his fancy; it fitted his fantasy of the German East, and he was enraptured
by the vision of Auschwitz playing a central role in the reclamation of that
area.

Himmler's project encountered opposition from the beginning. The plan-

*Barn built by inmates for the Auschwitz agricultural estate, 1943. Auschwitz-Birkenau
State Museum, neg. 20995/188.*

Pigsties built by inmates for the Auschwitz agricultural estate, 1943. Auschwitz-Birkenau State Museum, neg. 20995/162.

ning office of the Kattowitz region feared that expansion of the camp would have serious consequences for the district, and the provincial planning authority in Breslau noted that the area could be better used for market gardens and industries which required a great deal of water.[65] Furthermore, Himmler's agriculture scheme clashed with a need to develop coal resources south of Auschwitz.[66] Bracht, soon the *Gauleiter* of Upper Silesia, supported Himmler's ambition, however, and told the planners that an estate at the camp would be temporary; when resettlement had come to an end and the ethnic Germans had learned to work the land successfully, the experiment station would be shut down. Ultimately the area could be used for privately owned agricultural enterprises.[67]

The concentration camp at Auschwitz sat on a swampy corner of land wedged between the Vistula and the Sola. The ground was little higher than the rivers, and the region flooded regularly. Water (rain, melting snow, flood waters) could not drain into the rivers, nor could it seep into the earth; the soil was impervious marl, 200 feet thick. If this land were to be transformed into an agricultural estate, the tremendous drainage problem would have to be solved. On 15 February 1941 Vogel asked the soil engineer Professor

The greenhouses built by inmates at Rajsko, 1943. Auschwitz-Birkenau State Museum, neg. 20995/167.

Zunker to examine the site. Zunker, Vogel, and Höss toured the area on 7 March, and three weeks later Zunker submitted a thirty-three-page report suggesting major hydrological improvements of the Vistula and the Sola to prevent flooding. He also recommended reconstructing the lake-sized fish ponds in the southern part of the area, cleaning up the existing drainage channels and digging new ones, and laying a massive network of 3.6 million drainage pipes in 3,000 acres of future farmland. Considering the number of pipes needed, Zunker noted that it would be cheaper to purchase a pipe factory than to buy them from regular suppliers.[68] By the end of the year a more detailed program of improvement had been drafted; it concentrated first on the improvement of the fish ponds by the removal of the muck on the bottom, the fertilization of adjacent fields with that same muck, and the cleaning and digging of drainage canals.[69]

Zunker's plan was adopted, and the program that was to demand the labor of tens of thousands of prisoners and claim the lives of thousands began. There was no earth-moving equipment, and every day for four years squads of inmates were sent out to excavate the heavy clay. On starvation rations and beaten by the kapos (inmates in charge of work details), they dug for twelve hours

Inmates digging a drainage ditch, Auschwitz, 1943. Auschwitz-Birkenau State Museum, neg. 20995/346.

without rest. This was women's work in Auschwitz.[70] As soon as women prisoners began to arrive, in the early spring of 1942, they were assigned to the agricultural estate squads. It was their job to actualize the projects Zunker had recommended: to construct and maintain the riverbanks, build roads, dredge the fish ponds, clear tree stumps from crop fields, and dig drainage ditches. The then fifteen-year-old Kitty Hart-Felix was on one of the early transports of women. Born in Bielsko (Bielitz), Poland, she and her mother had gone into the Reich illegally on forged papers, to work as Catholic Poles. Ultimately betrayed, they were shipped to Auschwitz (ironically within fifteen miles of their hometown), and Kitty was detailed to a road repair unit. "We were divided into work parties of about 200 and marched out to the sound of the band. . . . For miles we marched. An hour, two hours, seeing nothing but the vast stretch of the camp until we came to fields and deserted farmhouses; all the little villages and farms in the region had been evacuated." Without resting, the girls were put to work carting stones for a road.

I stared. Lifting any one of them would be beyond me, let alone carrying it any distance.

"*Schneller, du Arschloch.*" The kapo gave me a jab in the back.

I stooped and tried to lift a stone: it wouldn't budge. As the other girls tugged away and stones from the top of the mound began to crash down, I looked for the smallest. But they were all enormous. With an effort I got one up into my arms and tottered away with it. After three trips, I was finished. My back felt as if it was breaking and I had a pain in my stomach. Not the ache of a twisted muscle, but the sickening wrench of diarrhoea. My guts were going to drop out. And they did—or at any rate, a filthy mess ran down my legs. That was another of the things you had to get used to if you worked so many hours a day and were beaten so often. And beaten up I was. As soon as I faltered, an SS woman with a dog came racing up towards me.[71]

The women died or were killed, but the work went on. Magda Somogyi was deported from her small town in Hungary to Auschwitz in June 1944. It was more than two years after Kitty Hart-Felix had arrived, but she too was assigned to a road-building detail. And she too was beaten. "I was in Auschwitz, and we were working on the road. Once I dropped a great stone because it was so heavy. I couldn't carry it, and it fell down. The SS came to me and he whipped me. From this time, every day when I began to work, first he whipped me and then I could go to work. He told me, 'You understand? You will learn that you do not need to drop the stone.' He was right. I didn't drop the stone any more. I could carry it."[72]

Magda and her seventeen-year-old sister were thought to be twins and were sent to special barracks where such siblings were subjected to medical experimentation. Kitty went on to other agricultural labor details, drainage ditch digging among them. By then it was late summer and fearfully hot. "We were issued with heavy spades. I leaned on mine, got my foot on it, and tried to push it into the ground. All I achieved was a slight scratch on the iron-hard surface. It was impossible to cut through the solid crust, let alone dig any soil out. None of us had the physical strength any more for that sort of task." By the end of the day, "many of the girls had collapsed; scores were unconscious on the ground as the whistles blew for our return to camp, and the rest of us, in not much better shape, had to drag them along or improvise stretchers from building material on the edge of the men's work site." Those who could not

Hannah Kent-Sztarkman on the ship to America, 1946. Authors.

stand on their own two feet for the evening roll call "ran the risk of being declared unfit for further work and taken away. You didn't ask where. Those who were dead were piled up in heaps ready for collection by cart or, if there were a lot of them, by tip-up lorry."[73]

The agricultural work details continued to operate until the very end of the history of the concentration camp. Shortly before Auschwitz was evacuated in January 1945 and the forced march of the 60,000 remaining prisoners into Germany began, Hannah Kent-Sztarkman, who had turned fifteen in October, was sent out on a riverbank detail. "It was winter and they [the Germans] decided that they wanted to even up the banks of the Vistula River. They sent a bunch of us women to work on the banks. We were dressed completely inappropriately. We didn't have any warm clothes and the Polish winters are cold. We didn't have shoes." She and the other women stood in the icy water all day and she developed frostbite, from which she suffers still.[74]

Himmler's agricultural estate project was carried on with the naked strength of the (mostly women) slave laborers. His bucolic fantasy engendered a brutality that exceeded the conditions in the sand and gravel pit industrial work assigned to men. The women simply had no machinery of any kind to help them. It was lethal work. Many died, and nearly no one survived without permanent injury.

It was too great an assault for anyone to sustain, and it is possible that one day early in October 1942, women slave laborers at the agricultural farm in the Auschwitz subcamp of Budy tried to break out. German women kapos killed the approximately ninety French Jews with poles and axes, claiming to suppress an uprising. Not one of the prisoners survived that day.[75]

CHAPTER 7

IG FARBEN

W HILE HIMMLER AND HÖSS WERE PORING OVER MAPS OF AUSCHWITZ TO determine the contours of an agricultural estate, the thirty-nine-year-old Dr. Otto Ambros, chairman of the Committee for Rubber and Plastics at the German chemical giant IG Farben, was reviewing regional maps of Upper Silesia. Ambros's expertise was in the design of synthetic rubber plants, and he had examined factory sites and construction in Russia, France, and even America. Now he needed to find the perfect place for a new factory requiring over 525,000 cubic feet of water per hour. It had to be a flat stretch of land one square mile at a minimum, and have good railroad connections. As he studied the map, he paid particular attention to the meeting point of three rivers: the Sola, the little Vistula, and the Przemsza. From the cartographical markings, he identified a broad, unbuilt, level plain, close to the river but sixty-five feet above it and therefore safe from flooding. Geologically the site seemed ideal. Furthermore, three railroad lines converged to the west on a settlement which the map, produced a few years earlier, identified as the town of Oswiecim.[1]

Ambros became interested in Auschwitz without having heard of it before. He was an engineer in search of synthetic fuel and rubber, not an Artaman longing for land. His inheritance flowed from seventy years of German scientific preeminence in chemistry and its related industries, not seven centuries of

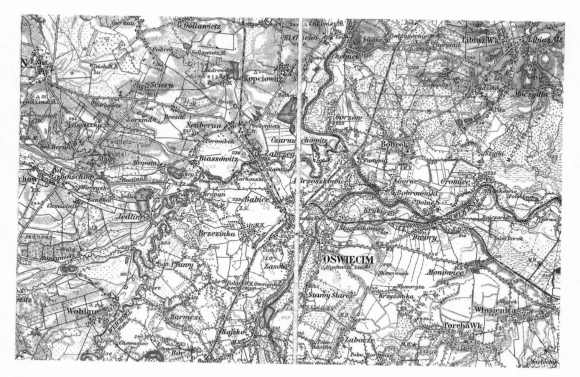

"Myslowitz and Oswiecim." Austro-Hungarian topographical map, 1905. Authors. Studying this map, Otto Ambros noted the confluence of three rivers—the Weichsel (Vistula), the Przemsza, and the Sola—at an altitude of 228 meters. Just south of this point, between Oswiecim, Dwory, and Monowice, are the numbers 251, 242, 246, and so on. They indicated a large, unbuilt plateau which, at an elevation of between 14 and 23 meters above the river, was ideally suited for industrial development.

German settlement in the East. By a very different, equally German path, Ambros, like Himmler and Höss, came to focus his attention on Auschwitz—in his case simply and solely because it was important to the future of IG Farben.[2]

IG Farben was the largest corporation in Europe and, after General Motors, United States Steel, and Standard Oil of New Jersey, the fourth largest in the world. In the 1920s and 1930s the German conglomerate was determined to produce synthetic rubber and gasoline economically by treating coal with hydrogen gas at high pressure and temperature, the "hydrogenation" of coal.

IG Farben advertisement.
Illustrierte Zeitung, *no. 4956
(1940). Sterling Memorial Library,
Yale University.*

IG Farben expected that, given the increase in motorization and the predictions of a world fuel crisis, the process would yield high profits.

The collapse of rubber and oil prices in the depression, and technical difficulties with the production of synthetic rubber and gasoline, dampened IG Farben's interest but, with the National Socialists ascent to power and their rearmament program, political considerations of reduction in imports began to weigh heavily. IG Farben turned to the development of a high-octane aviation gasoline, and it was successful. The development and production of synthetic rubber stalled, however. Although the basic procedure had been developed, involving the molecule butadiene and the element sodium (Na)—hence the name buna—the production technology did not work. New plants were needed, which required significant investment, while the demand for buna was relatively low. But Hitler insisted on the creation of a synthetic-rubber factory, and in late 1935 IG Farben began construction of a plant in the central German town of Schkopau with a planned production of 12,000 tons of buna annually. The following year, when Germany began to prepare seriously for war, Hitler ordered the massive expansion of synthetic production regardless of price. The Four-Year Plan consolidated this policy. "Germany must be wholly independent of foreign areas in those materials which can be produced in any way through German ability, through our chemical and machine industry, as well as through our mining industry,"[3] the plan proclaimed. Rubber production was specifically mentioned, which meant that the manufacture of buna became a high priority. Göring demanded that production at Schkopau double, and Hitler ordered the establishment of a second plant, which was built near Hüls, on the northern edge of the Ruhr area.

The first commercial buna was produced in January 1937, and it received the gold medal at the International Exposition in Paris. Still, manufacture remained slow. When Germany invaded Poland, there was a mere two-month supply of rubber stockpiled. IG Farben hastily planned a third plant—at Rattwitz, near Breslau—but the project came to naught. In the summer of 1940 the German government believed that its triumph over France would lead to peace with England, the recovery of the colonies Germany had lost in 1919, and the renewed availability of natural rubber. By then the two plants at

Buna production facilities in the Reich. Jünger, Kampf um Kautschuk *(1942). Authors.*

Schkopau and Hüls were able to meet the annual rubber consumption need of 115,000 tons. The plant at Rattwitz was canceled.

In the fall of 1940 the German High Command began to prepare an attack on the Soviet Union, code-named Operation Barbarossa. On 18 December Hitler ordered the military to invade in May, and mobilization commenced. The troops were augmented from 130 divisions to 180, and the need for buna increased. As Churchill had refused to sue for peace, the promise of a steady supply of natural rubber had not materialized, and the Reich Ministry of Economics wanted to boost buna production to 150,000 tons a year through the addition of two plants, one in Ludwigshaven and another in Silesia. In a letter of 8 November the ministry instructed IG Farben to "undertake the initial negotiations for financing immediately and settle the question regarding the site, so that . . . the final date on which construction will be started can be set for January at the latest."[4]

When the letter arrived at the IG Farben headquarters, it seemed most prudent to revive the project to build a plant at Rattwitz in Lower Silesia. The situation had changed since that decision had been taken, however. The large coalfields of eastern Upper Silesia, lost in 1921, had returned to German control in the fall of 1939. Together with lime (also available in the area), coal was the most important raw material for the production of carbide, which in turn was processed into buna.[5] Calculations of the coal reserves showed that exploitable deposits in that region were nearly twice as large as those in the Ruhr, but the annual production was just half. Clearly, there was great potential for development.[6] Furthermore, the composition of the coal suggested its use as a raw material for the chemical industry; it could not be made into coke but lent itself well to the production of carbide.[7]

Upper Silesia's coal supply could support eighteen large chemical plants, but it was not feasible, for physical reasons, to locate such facilities immediately adjacent to the mines. The dry industrial heart of Upper Silesia lacked the great quantity of water and the large, geologically stable sites required for synthetic rubber and gasoline factories. These plants would be better placed at the periphery of the industrial area along the Oder or the Vistula. Such a policy also made sense from a social point of view. Housing conditions in the mining region were poor, and the dearth of cultural institutions and health facilities precluded the rapid generation of a standard of living acceptable to the German managers, engineers, and skilled laborers IG Farben would move in from the west. As it transpired, provincial planners had already decided to create seventeen towns in a new development zone surrounding the industrial conurbation of Gleiwitz, Hindenburg, Beuthen, and Kattowitz.[8] IG Farben could take advantage of this program for its employees, the local authorities would have a large influx of the Germans they had hoped to attract and, as the workers would be close to the factories, they would relieve the central problem of Upper Silesia: the persistence of the robotmen. Everybody was happy.

The sole remaining question was to determine geologically satisfactory sites in the new belt which would support large hydrogenation plants. Ambros turned to the map of Upper Silesia and identified the fields between Auschwitz, Monowitz, and Dwory. Acting on his recommendation, the company sent a busload of experts to Auschwitz in the beginning of December 1940. They agreed that the area offered an excellent site about two miles downriver from the confluence of the Vistula, Przemsza, and Sola, fifteen miles from the coal mining districts near Cracow and in central Upper Silesia, and six miles from the mines in Brzeszcze, Jawiszowitz, and Dzieditz. The committee also noted that it would be easy to find housing for the workers and staff.[9] It was well aware of the National Socialist population policy, and it presumed that the Jewish inhabitants would have been deported by the time construction began. As a result, suitable quarters would be available to accommodate construction workers and, later on, factory staff. Finally, further investigations revealed that other useful raw materials such as lime and salt were readily available.[10] Auschwitz, in short, was the perfect place for IG Farben's project.

Ambros promptly wrote to the mayor of Auschwitz, requesting specific information about the town, water levels in the rivers, and so on. The district of Auschwitz—which included the villages of Birkenau, Babitz, Broschkowitz, Klutschnikowitz, Dwory, Wlosienitz, Poremba-Wielka, Stare-Stawy, Zaborze, and Monowitz, as well as the town—counted 25,507 inhabitants, the mayor replied on 9 January 1941. Of these 7,000 were Jews. There was only one large elementary school, but Herr Gutsche promised that he would consider the establishment of a high school ''as soon as sufficient numbers of Reich Germans arrive.''[11]

The IG Farben leadership was interested in Auschwitz, but other options were still under consideration, particularly the extension of the buna plant in Hüls and the construction of a new facility at Heydebreck, in Lower Silesia, primarily because the Oder supplied more than twice the amount of water at that point than the Vistula did at Auschwitz. As the IG Farben managers weighed the advantages of one site against the other, those responsible for the ethnic and social reconstruction of Upper Silesia became involved in the situation. As we have seen, the former duchy of Auschwitz had been given the highest priority for resettlement a few months earlier, and ethnic cleansing of the Saybusch district was already under way. The goal of Himmler's local representative, Arlt, was to deport just over a million Poles and Jews and replace them with 320,800 families, of whom 300,000 breadwinners would be employed in mining and industry, 1,800 in trade and crafts, 15,000 in agricultural labor, 3,000 as independent farmers, and 1,000 as employees and civil servants.[12] The settlement of farmers was going well, but Arlt had not yet developed a workable plan to substitute the Polish industrial workers with Germans, especially as wages were some 20 percent lower in Upper Silesia than in the rest of Germany. If IG Farben moved to Auschwitz, it would create a pool of high-wage jobs in the eastern part of the province, and certainly bring in highly skilled German workers from the west. Arlt was well pleased. This would also consolidate the racial political changes initiated in 1940.

For Arlt, IG Farben's investment in Auschwitz was not merely a question of numbers: such a move also fit his ideology. He found it appropriate in view of the historic destiny of the region. Himmler certainly agreed. It is not clear how information about IG Farben's intentions reached Himmler—perhaps from Ambros, who was an old school friend of Himmler, or from Walter Dürrfeld, IG Farben's chief architect, who held an honorary SS commission— but as early as 8 January 1941 the issue of the corporation's investment and its effect on the local population came up in a meeting chaired by Heydrich and attended by various representatives of the SS, the Office of the Reich Commissioner for the Consolidation of the German Nation, and the army. Their aim was to decide a target figure for deportations from the annexed territories in 1941. As Heydrich noted, 340,000 Poles and Jews had been dumped into the Government General in 1940, and he proposed to set a goal of 800,000 people for 1941. "The representative of the Government General accepted the challenge without blinking. The matter was not discussed,"[13] the protocol of the meeting recorded. Heydrich provided a detailed justification for the 800,000 figure. It included 458,000 deportees to make room for ethnic Germans, 20,000 Polish refugees who had fled to the Warthegau and were now to be moved out, and 237,000 Poles from areas claimed by the army. Finally, he mentioned that 55,000 gentile and Jewish Poles were to be deported into the Government General "for the Auschwitz project in Upper Silesia."[14]

———

CLEARLY, HIMMLER HAD decided to make Auschwitz as attractive as possible for IG Farben. If the corporation established a plant there, it would suit his ideology as well as his agenda. The influx of money would enable him to build up the town to its proper Germanic proportions, the incoming Germans would help to realize his population policies, and the camp inmates already under his control would work in the buna plant and provide him with cash revenue. IG Farben had money and access to building materials. Himmler had slave labor and dreams of what the area around Auschwitz should look like and be. It was to be a lethal wedding.

As Himmler thought about how to encourage IG Farben to establish a factory at Auschwitz, the company's managers considered the difficulties. Auschwitz itself was a major drawback. ''Apart from the large market place, the town itself makes a very wretched impression,'' they remarked. And it would be there that the German workers would live. ''The inhabitants of Auschwitz consist of 2,000 Germans, 4,000 Jews, and 7,000 Poles. The Germans are peasants. The Jews and Poles, if industry is established here, will be turned out, so that the town will then be available for the staff of the factory.''[15]

The state of the town was a real obstacle for the IG Farben management.

Postcard. West side of the Auschwitz market square, 1940. Towarzytwo Milosnikow Ziemi Oswiecomskiej.

The company was proud of the way it took care of its employees. Strong supporters of Hitler since 1932 and staunch advocates of the National Socialist blood and soil ideology, IG Farben managers sought to apply that vision to industrial laborers. Committed to reforming the living conditions of the working class in accordance with Party principles, they had established exemplary worker housing units, complete with little plots of land to be cultivated for market gardens, near their factories in Germany.[16] Auschwitz, they felt, did not lend itself to such a social project, and they began to reconsider the site at Rattwitz.

Two of IG Farben's construction experts, Erich Santo and Max Faust, traveled to Rattwitz at the end of January and met with provincial authorities from Lower Silesia, who were very keen to see the plant built there. Upper Silesia would become a separate province within a fortnight (1 February), and the bureaucrats did not want to lose the revenue of an IG Farben plant to another administrative district. The governor of Lower Silesia, Karl Hanke, and the governor-designate of the new province of Upper Silesia, Fritz Bracht, competed for the business, and the latter prevailed. When Santo arrived in Kattowitz, the capital of the new province, the chief regional planner, Froese, allayed his doubts about Auschwitz. Promising that the Jews and Poles would be deported the following spring, Froese told Santo that the soldier-farmers would settle the countryside and that plans for the development of the town of Auschwitz were already under way. Indeed, the Breslau architect Hans Stosberg had been hastily appointed earlier that month as special agent for the master plan for the town of Auschwitz. Furthermore, Froese announced, "the concentration camp already existing with approximately 7,000 inmates is to be expanded. Employment of prisoners for the building project possible after negotiations with the Reichsführer-SS."[17]

Six days later Ambros and the IG Farben director Fritz ter Meer met Carl Krauch, who as plenipotentiary general for special questions of chemical production within the Four-Year Plan oversaw Germany's chemical industry. They explained that from a technological and economic perspective Auschwitz was ideal, but that "an extensive settlement program will be unavoidable, to induce German workers to settle" there.[18] A few days later a report by one of IG Farben's chemical experts, who had conducted a four-day inspection of the town, once again confirmed what everyone already knew: everything would be ideal if only the town were nicer. "Auschwitz and villages gives an impression of extreme filth and squalor," the report complained. "The most difficult problem will be that of organizing a plant staff.'' Most of the trained workers would have to come from the west. "Construction of a large-scale settlement, including schools, cultural centers, et cetera, must therefore be started at least at the same time as the factory building in order to create living conditions for the staff which would provide even a modicum of comfort."[19] In addition to the town improvement issue, there was another problem to resolve. On the one hand, the local residents had to be deported to create space for the Germans; on the other, these people were a valuable source of construction labor. Given these difficulties, it would take much longer to establish the buna plant than originally anticipated.

Krauch, upset, approached Göring, who decided that the production of buna was to have top priority and that the plant should be completed as soon as possible even if it meant a delay in other building projects essential to the war economy.[20] Göring promptly wrote to Himmler requesting the immediate deportation of Jews from Auschwitz "for the purpose of clearing their apartments in order to accommodate the construction workers for the buna plant,"

Deportation of Jews from Auschwitz, March 1941. Auschwitz-Birkenau State Museum, neg. 20829/13.

and the use of "the largest number of skilled and unskilled construction work-ers" from the concentration camp.[21] Göring estimated that between 8,000 and 12,000 men would be needed during the construction phase. Himmler was overjoyed. The camp in Auschwitz, which only nine months earlier had been established to maintain a German hold on the local population, suddenly had become the linchpin in an immense highest-priority project.

Göring's decision, good news as it was for Himmler, posed problems. He had already committed most of the camp's planned 10,000 inmates to the agricultural estate, and he did not want to give up this project.[22] Clearly the camp had to be at least double in size. Faced with important decisions concern-ing the future of Auschwitz, but with no direct knowledge of the site, Himmler changed his planned visit to Breslau on the first weekend of March, where he was to address the Bukovinian German returnees waiting in transit camps for settlement in Upper Silesia, to include a trip to Auschwitz. In the meantime he took intermediate steps: he ordered the deportation of the local Jews and instructed Richard Glücks, the inspector of concentration camps, to get in touch with IG Farben "to aid the construction project by means of the concen-tration-camp prisoners in every possible way."[23]

On Saturday, 1 March, Himmler, accompanied by his adjutant Karl Wolff, the designated liaison with IG Farben, and Heinrich Vogel, met with IG Farben officials and provincial authorities in Gleiwitz.[24] It probably was then that Himmler played his trump card: his considerable power in eastern Upper Silesia. He would guarantee that the town of Auschwitz became a model German settlement in the East.[25] Everyone then drove to Auschwitz, where Himmler briefed Höss on the developments of the last weeks and told him to make himself indispensable to the project. As a token of good will, the camp population was increased from the November projections of 10,000 inmates to 30,000. Höss was shocked: only six months earlier his men had been unable to build rabbit cages; now he was to construct the largest concentration camp in the German Reich.[26] Himmler told him not to worry. The buna plant had been given the highest priority, and large quantities of building materials would be allocated to the town of Auschwitz. If inmate labor was indeed crucial to the construction of the plant, it would not be difficult to persuade the IG Farben managers to direct some of it to the camp.

DR. HEINRICH BÜTEFISCH, an IG Farben manager and a personal friend of Himmler, and two IG Farben engineers, Dürrfeld and Faust, met in Berlin

(20 March) with Wolff and Glücks to discuss cooperation between the company and the camp. They agreed that 700 inmates would be put to work immediately, and Glücks promised to scour the other concentration camps for skilled construction workers and technicians to send to Auschwitz. He also volunteered to create workshops in the camp to support construction.[27]

A week later Höss, Dürrfeld, Faust, and various other SS men and IG Farben officials met in the camp to work out details of this symbiotic relationship. According to the minutes, the discussion was "exceedingly objective and yet very friendly. The concentration camp showed its willingness to assist in the construction of the plant as far as it could." The participants agreed that the camp would provide 1,000 inmates immediately and that this number would be increased to 3,000 in 1942, if the anticipated expansion of the camp to 18,000 inmates—to provide the labor for the construction of both the camp and the plant for IG Farben[28]—had been realized. IG Farben, for its part, and as Himmler had predicted, would secure additional building materials for the camp. The creation of a second story on existing barracks, the report explained, at present was "held up by the lack of steel reinforcements for the floors and ceilings. We [IG Farben] undertook to see whether we could help the camp to obtain this more quickly." When the camp reached its projected maximum capacity of 30,000 the number of workers allocated to IG Farben would be augmented. The success of the deal depended on how fast iron could be acquired. It was needed to build additional quarters for the inmates and to build a bridge over the Sola to connect the camp and the plant. "A narrow-gauge railroad is to be laid over the same span so that the inmates can be transported to and from the building site by this light railway."[29]

The financial aspects of their collaboration were worked out easily. "A payment of RM 3 per day for unskilled workers and RM 4 per day for skilled workers is to be made for each inmate. This includes everything, such as transportation, food, et cetera, and we [IG Farben] will have no other expenses for the inmates, except if a small bonus (cigarettes, etc.) is given as an incentive."[30] Of course, labor was not Himmler's only salable commodity. As we have seen, the SS-owned DESt corporation operated the Auschwitz sand and gravel pits. IG Farben desired its gravel, and DESt agreed to deliver a fixed amount every day. DESt also promised to supply all the bricks for the project from SS-controlled factories.[31]

A high-level meeting to confirm the arrangements was held on Monday, 7 April, in Kattowitz with representatives of the Reich Authority for Spatial

Planning, the Reich Office for Economic Development, Upper Silesia's provincial planning office, the provincial water authority, the municipal government of Auschwitz, the IG Farben corporation, and Greifelt's Office of the Reich Commissioner for the Consolidation of the German Nation. The Reich Office for Economic Development explained that because of the continuing war with England, production of synthetic rubber had to be increased. IG Farben, the world leader in the field, had chosen Auschwitz as the site for the buna plant, to which would be added a synthetic gasoline plant.[32]

Ambros addressed some of the technical dimensions of the problem they faced, and the relationship between new scientific knowledge and IG Farben's choice of site. "Recent research indicates that coal, as a chemical basis, is becoming increasingly important in the production of buna," he informed the other participants—"the decisive reason why the *Silesian buna plant* should be built in the immediate vicinity of *Silesian coal* and not, as originally planned, near Breslau." Coal played an essential part also in the production of synthetic fuel, critical for the war effort. It made sense, scientifically and financially, to build the two plants close to each other. Ambros predicted that these two factories were just the beginning of major new industrial developments in Upper Silesia. From these "must grow new branches of organic chemistry; as for instance, plastics, resins, lacquer binding media, textile auxiliaries, et cetera. The latent potentialities of this branch of chemistry provide the stimulus for the development of a subsidiary industry in Upper Silesia, which will deal with the processing of these basic raw materials into finished articles."[33]

Ambros then turned to the problem of construction, slave labor, the German work force and its needs, and IG Farben's commitment to the German East. "By order of the Reichsführer-SS, extensive assistance from the Auschwitz concentration camp has been promised for the construction period," he assured the others. Many construction workers will be brought in from Germany. They "will be accommodated, if possible, in vacant homes in Auschwitz; for the remainder, cantonments will be erected." The IG Farben management understood that "a large-scale building program for the town of Auschwitz, foundation of schools and hospitals, will be absolutely necessary." Ambros was very clear about the scope and the significance of the undertaking. "With the Auschwitz project, I.G. Farben has designed a plan for a new enterprise of giant proportions. It is determined to do everything in its power to build up a virile enterprise, which will be able to shape its environment in the same way as the many plants in West and Central Germany do. In this manner the

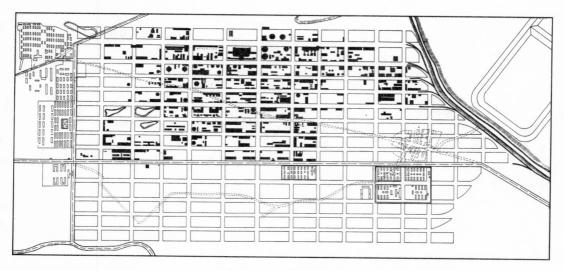

The layout of the IG Farben buna plant and its adjacent facilities, fall 1944. Based on blueprint AZ 5926–1 (3 October 1944) in Osobyi Archive, Moscow, coll. 502/5, file 13. Drawing by Harun Rashid and Robert Jan van Pelt. The plan was simple and functional. The production process went from north to south, and therefore the plant was organized in consecutive east–west zones, each corresponding to a specific phase of the process. The raw materials (water, coal, and lime) were to be taken in on the northern side, and buna was to be collected on the southern side. As can be seen from this drawing, the plant was only partly built by the time of the German withdrawal. The Poles completed the northeastern part of the plan after the war. The southern half of the grid remains farmland to this day. The huts that served as temporary offices and dwellings for the civilian construction crews are to the west of the plant. Just south of the obliterated village of Monowitz, on the southeastern edge of the factory grounds, is the satellite concentration camp Auschwitz III, or "Buna." Main roads that are public throughways today are indicated with a broken line in the axis. The two east–west connector roads to the town of Auschwitz are Jaroslawa Dabrowskiego (top left) and K. Olszewskiego (bottom left); the major east–west road that runs along the southern side of the present plant is the Fabryczna.

IG Farben corporation fulfills a high moral duty to ensure with a mobilization of all its resources that this industrial foundation becomes a firm cornerstone for a powerful and healthy Germanism in the east.''[34]

Ambros's presentation met with general approval, and various government officials confirmed their willingness to support the plant. The problem of labor and its relation to Himmler's vision of the German East in general, and his population policies in particular, remained on the table. The goal of those present

Wood engraving depicting the contribution of science and technology to the German war effort. Illustrierte Zeitung, *no. 4956 (1940). Sterling Memorial Library, Yale University.*

was to secure the Germanization of Oswiecim, of the town the Germans always had called Auschwitz. The representative of the Reichsführer-SS had good news: all Poles would be deported from Auschwitz. "It is the aim of the Reichsfuehrer to create on this spot an exemplary eastern settlement—particular attention being paid to settling here German men and women who are particularly qualified."[35] Chief Engineer Santo reminded everyone that the construction of a settlement for the IG Farben employees had the highest priority. And the recently appointed town architect, Stosberg, presented his plan for a new Auschwitz with 40,000 inhabitants. Clearly, they were well on their way to achieving their objectives. It was, the chairman concluded, "an important moment in the fulfillment of the ethnic-political tasks of the East."[36]

As soon as the symbiotic relationship between the SS and IG Farben had been secured, the Auschwitz Kommandantur and SS headquarters in Berlin went wild. They already had power; now they believed they had the resources to develop their kingdom as they wished. In Berlin the architects of *Amt II* (Office II) of the SS-Hauptamt Haushalt und Bauten (SS-Main Office Household and

The first master plan for Auschwitz, June 1941. Drawing by Kate Mullin. In the center is the main camp, with the barracks of the former labor exchange (1), a large roll call place flanked by an entrance pavillion (2), a prisoner reception building (3), the camp kitchens (4), and a storehouse for prisoners' belongings (5). Along the road to the station is the extension, with thirty-two dwelling barracks (6), a camp hospital (7), a camp prison (8), and a crematorium (9). Northeast of the camp are the barracks for single SS men (10) and a village for married SS men (11). Southwest of the camp are the offices of the commandant (12), the heating plant (13), and workshops (14). N.B.: This is an axonometric drawing; the three-dimensional effect is derived from the exact measurements and angles of the original plan. See plate 6.

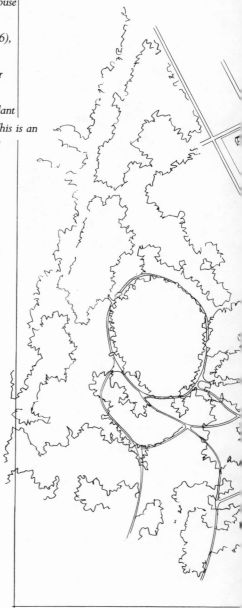

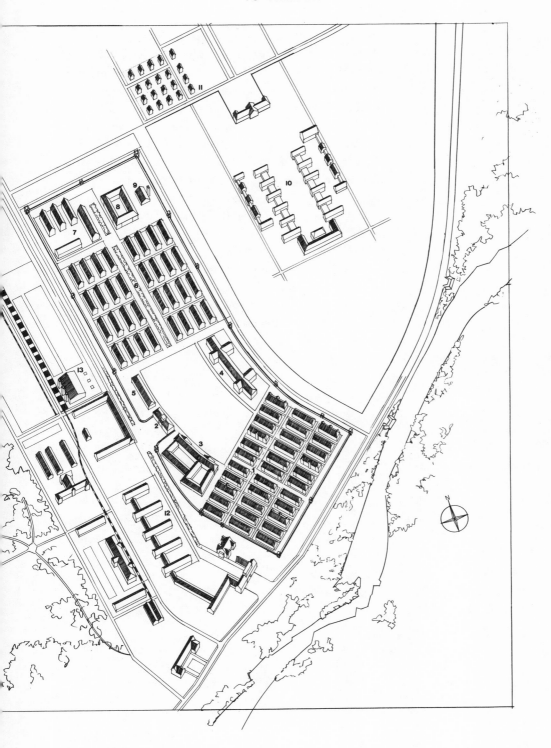

Buildings) designed a general plan for expansion, which included a camp for 30,000 inmates with a large Kommandantur, agricultural projects, a private SS railway station, an SS-owned industrial corporation, an SS settlement, and so on.[37] (See plate 6.) Höss discussed these plans in Berlin on 13 and 14 June with the new chief of Office II, Hans Kammler, a free corps veteran, old-time Nazi, and accomplished air force architect.[38] Kammler ordered the completion of the work already begun and the immediate construction of thirty new two-story barracks, a delousing facility, a laundry, garages for the Kommandantur, housing for the Kommandantur's staff and for officers, a camp for civilian employees of construction firms, a drainage and sewer system, a drinking-water installation, streets, and new offices for the so-called New Building Office, which had to design and plan all the new construction.[39] There were no designs for these structures, and no one knew how much the expansion would cost. Despite repeated requests from Berlin, the Auschwitz New Building Office did not move quickly. It took Schlachter two months to submit a partial budget, accompanied by only five plans and just one explanation of the whole project.[40] Neither the budget nor the documents have been preserved; evidently they did not impress Berlin. As Höss later recalled, Schlachter was "a nice enough fellow," but he "lacked bold ideas."[41]

Recognizing Schlachter's inability to expand the camp, Kammler sent for Karl Bischoff, one of his subalterns in the air force. Bischoff had been building airfields in northern France during the Battle of Britain, and there he had gained a reputation as a troubleshooter. According to Höss, he was a "tough, headstrong and stubborn construction expert. He saw everything from the viewpoint of a builder." He had little eye for the aesthetic side of architecture and during his tenure at Auschwitz was to rely on the design skills of his direct subordinate Walther Dejaco, a civilian architect named Georg Werkmann, and the urban designer Lothar Hartjenstein. But Bischoff had talents which, in a period of scarcity, were essential. He "exceeded himself when it came to obtaining construction material of all kinds," Höss recorded. "Whatever could be gotten in Germany or from the occupied countries, Bischoff got it. He had several buyers constantly on the move."[42]

Bischoff arrived in Auschwitz on 1 October. Within a few weeks he had compiled a budget: he would need 13.6 million marks for the first phase of the project, and another 7 million to complete building the whole camp. Significantly, the budget stated that "a license number will be given by the chemical industry through IG Farben,"[43] which meant that the camp would

Karl Bischoff. Berlin Document Center. Höss recalled after the war that Bischoff was "constantly at war with everyone. . . . He always blamed the poor work of the prisoners for the lack of progress in construction. And, of course, he used this excuse to avoid meeting the deadlines. He did everything in his power for Auschwitz. No one else could have accomplished more."

receive material allocations from the resources at the disposal of Krauch, the plenipotentiary general for special questions of chemical production. Kammler approved the budget and forwarded a copy to Krauch, who was taken aback by the proposal. He contacted Ambros who, in turn, raised the issue at a construction conference on 18 November, noting wryly that "the management of the concentration camp has made full use of the promise of support in the procurement of construction material for the expansion." He was unequivocal as to the position IG Farben should take: "The Plenipotentiary General for Special Questions of Chemical Production cannot give support to any such extent."[44] A few weeks later Dürrfeld and Faust visited the camp and told Höss that such demands "could not be considered under present circumstances"; in fact, any amount over 2 million marks was out of the question. The camp building office would have "to reduce its demands accordingly." The Kommandantur should remember there was a war on, they admonished Höss. Good will was maintained. "The officials of the concentration camp showed understanding for the present situation."[45]

In response to IG Farben's unwillingness to support a 20.6 million operation, Bischoff proposed two plans. The first, budgeted at 2.02 million marks, was called "Provisional Expansion of the Concentration Camp Auschwitz O/S [Oberschlesien, or Upper Silesia]," which was to be built with construction material supplied through IG Farben.[46] Its main purpose was to demonstrate responsibility to the corporation. The second plan, "Building Project Ausch-

The second master plan for Auschwitz, February 1942.
Drawing by Kate Mullin. In the center is the
main camp, with the barracks of the former labor
exchange (1), a large roll call place flanked
by an entrance pavillion (2), a prisoner reception
building (3), the camp kitchens (4), and a
storehouse for prisoners belongings (5). Along the road
to the station is the extension, with dwelling
barracks (6), a camp hospital (7), a camp prison (8).
Southwest of the camp are the offices of the
commandant (9), the heating plant (10), and
workshops (11). An important new element is
the large crematorium, located at the eastern edge of
the original compound (12). This is the five-
triple-muffle furnace facility designed in the fall of
1941 which, ultimately erected in Birkenau,
became known as crematorium II. N.B.: This is an
axonometric drawing; the three-dimensional
effect is derived from the exact measurements and
angles of the original plan. See plate 7.

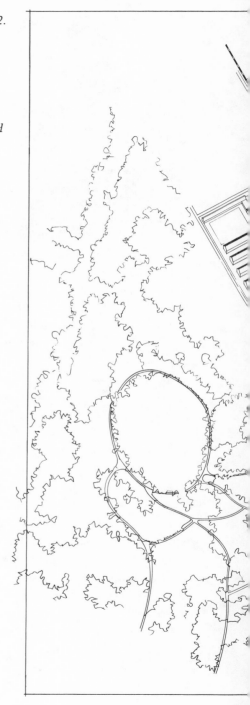

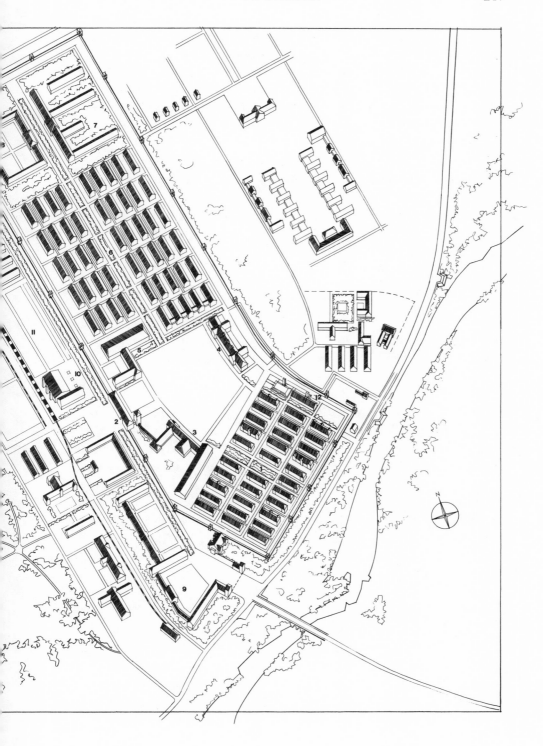

witz,'' budgeted at 20.6 million marks, was Bischoff's real agenda.[47] The agricultural estate costs were calculated separately at 3.5 million marks. Building Project Auschwitz was the joint work of the SS design offices in Auschwitz and Berlin. Completed in February 1942, Bischoff's new master plan differed from the design of the previous June.[48] (See plate 7.) The protective custody camp—the prisoners' compound—was enlarged considerably, with seventy-six instead of sixty-five two-story barracks, five interconnected workshops, and a more spacious entrance, a delousing facility, a camp hospital, and a camp prison. The crematorium was moved from its location in the June plan, on the north side of the camp's extension, to the southeast side of the camp adjacent to the existing crematorium. It too had been enlarged. Significantly, the February plan illustrated that the architects were no longer designing solely for the camp. They drafted themselves into the plan, and they clearly thought they would be there for some time. Their plan included their own compound with a private garden.

BY FEBRUARY 1942 many of the buildings in Bischoff's master plan had reached an advanced state of design development in close consultation with Berlin. In their general arrangement, these structures followed plans worked out by Kammler. His office had developed twenty-five type sheets, or pages, providing explicit design instructions for the buildings required to construct a model 5,000-person concentration camp. These designs, Kammler explained, ensured ''the orderly, functional, and quick construction'' of the necessary facilities.[49] For Kammler, the type sheets were a perfectly responsible and rational enterprise. After all, camps were being founded almost daily, and the people in the field needed information.[50] To maximize efficiency, economy, and standardization throughout the concentration camp kingdom, Kammler also had prepared more-detailed designs of the technically complex and expensive delousing facilities and crematoria. These were mentioned in his first annual report (December 1941). ''Model designs have been drawn for permanent and provisional delousing installations for the Waffen SS, the police, and concentration camps, and for provisional and permanent crematoria, incinerating sites, and execution grounds of various kinds,'' he explained.[51]

Using Kammler's type sheets, the architects in Auschwitz turned their attention first to the prisoners' reception and delousing building. Their goal was to prevent the spread of contagious diseases, which were rife in Auschwitz. The camp was overcrowded, the hygienic conditions were poor, and the inmates were ill fed, ill clothed, and ill shod. Dysentery, typhoid fever, and typhus felled the inmates and threatened the Germans. Typhus, transmitted by lice and carried by human beings and rats, was the most fatal of the three and therefore the most feared. The Germans had experience in this area from the First World War when they developed delousing units to control the disease on the eastern front, where it was endemic. The soldiers were bathed and their clothes fumigated in mobile units, thus destroying the lice. But the vermin were ubiquitous: buildings, mattresses, sofas, and chairs became infected. The Technical Committee for Pest Control of the German War Ministry founded the firm Deutsche Gesellschaft für Schädlingsbekämpfung (German Company for Pest Control), or Degesch, in 1917 to deal with the problem.[52] One of its most powerful and popular disinfestation products was the extremely toxic hydrocyanic, or prussic, acid. Sold in a crystal form and packed in sealed tins, it carried the trade name Zyklon (cyclone). As the German word for prussic acid is *Blausäure*, for the deep blue stains it produces, the poison was also known as Zyklon-Blausäure, or Zyklon B. It was commonly used to fumigate lice-infested buildings, which were sealed during the operation and could be entered safely only after having been aired for twenty hours. Even then, as a company manual warned, "mattresses, straw mattresses, pillows, upholstered furniture and similar items must be shaken or beaten for at least one hour in the open air."[53]

Zyklon B had been introduced in Auschwitz in July 1940, when it was used to fumigate the Polish barracks which, according to Höss, "teemed with lice, fleas, and other bugs."[54] Later that year Schlachter created primitive gas chambers in block 26, and some months thereafter in block 3, to fumigate the prisoners' clothing; existing rooms were sealed and powerful fans installed. The Polish inmate Andrzej Rablin operated the facility in block 3.

> We received the Zyklon-B from Kapo Mau, a German, who was the only one to have the key to the store. Bezucha, another prisoner, and I did the gassing. We put on our gas masks and went in the room naked or wearing underpants. We did that because of the lice. There were very many lice in the clothes. Sometimes, filling the gas chamber with clothes took as much as two days. The lice fell on the floor and formed a layer about 50 cm across under the clothes. When we went in to spread the gas, the lice jumped on us and the layers disappeared very fast. . . . After throwing the crystals we went out, closed the door and stuck strips of paper over the gaps. Twenty-four hours later, we put our gas masks on again, the

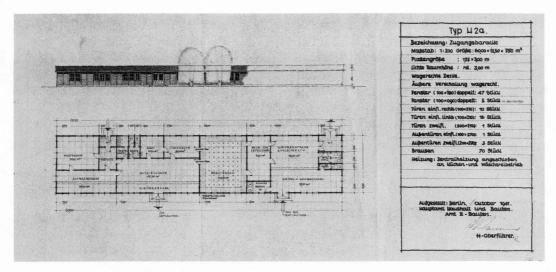

Type sheet. Design of a prisoner reception and delousing facility for a camp of 5,000 inmates. Auschwitz-Birkenau State Museum, box BW 3,3a, file BW 3/5. Barracks type Häftlinge *2a (prisoners 2a) is one of the twenty-five type sheets issued by Hans Kammler in the fall of 1941 to standardize concentration camp design. Prisoners enter at the left* (arrow), *proceed via a small vestibule into a waiting room* (Warteraum) *and a registration room* (Aufnahmeraum) *and arrive in an undressing room* (Auskleideraum). *There they hand in their clothes to attendants, who carry them via a covered gallery (see figure on facing page) to the Zyklon B delousing chambers. The naked prisoners proceed to the physician* (Arzt), *the barber* (Scheerraum), *and the shower room* (Brauseraum). *The showers separate the soiled from the clean side. After the showers the prisoners proceed to a drying room* (Raum zum Abtrocknen) *and end up in the dressing room, where they receive their own deloused clothes, or inmate uniforms* (Kleiderempfang/Ankleideraum).

extractor fans were switched on and [we went in and] we opened the windows. The ventilation continued for two hours.[55]

Effective as the procedure was, the camp authorities found it irritatingly inefficient. Too much Zyklon B was needed and it took too long to exterminate the lice. The Degesch engineers addressed this problem in an article they sent to the building office in July 1941. They recommended the installation of many small heatable gas chambers designed to be used with the standard 200-gram tin of Zyklon B. Heating the space to over thirty degrees centigrade helped the gas to evaporate from the grains quickly and completely, and shortened the exposure time needed to kill the lice to one hour. A sophisticated ventilation

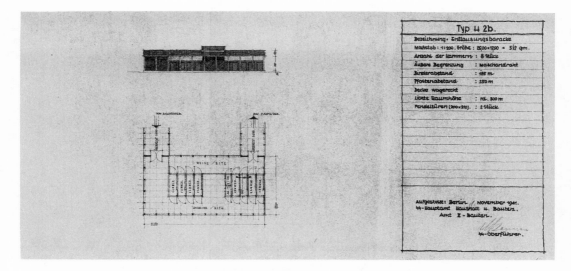

Type sheet. Design of delousing gas chambers for a camp of 5,000 inmates. Auschwitz-Birkenau State Museum, box BW 3,3a, file BW 3/5. The open pavillion with delousing gas chambers is connected via two galleries to the prisoner reception and delousing facility depicted in previous figure. The eight gas chambers are filled on the soiled side (unreine Seite) *and emptied on the clean side* (reine Seite), *to be returned to the prisoners in the dressing room depicted in previous figure* (Kleiderempfang/Ankleideraum).

system not only ensured the rapid penetration of all the garments with prussic acid but also permitted the clothes to be worn safely fifteen minutes after fumigation.[56] During this seventy-five minute procedure, the owners of the infested garments could be deloused also: the hair on their heads and bodies would be shaved, and they would wash under a shower.

The Degesch offprint arrived a few weeks after Kammler had instructed Höss to prepare for the construction of the prisoners' reception building, which was to include registration, delousing, bath, and laundry facilities.[57] Given its budget of 2.7 million marks, it is not surprising that the project was temporarily dropped after Dürrfeld and Faust's visit to the camp in December 1941 and that it did not appear in Bischoff's 2.02-million-mark budget for the "Provisional Expansion of the Concentration Camp Auschwitz."[58] It was to be built on the southwest side of the existing camp, between the new roll call place and the road to the station. The architects had drafted an E-shaped structure, with an arm for the laundry, the delousing chambers, and the baths, and the connecting wing for the "reception" facilities. (See plate 8.) This

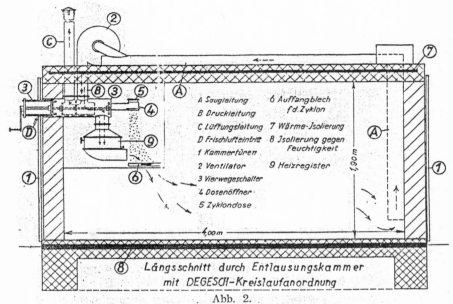

Abb. 2.

Längsschnitt durch eine Entlausungskammer mit Kreislaufeinrichtung
(Vergl. Beschreibung der Arbeitsweise im Text)

Design of a Degesch Zyklon B gas chamber. Osobyi Archive, Moscow, coll. 502/1, file 322.
The tin with Zyklon B (5) is opened by a lever (3) connected to a tin opener (4); the
Zyklon B crystals fall on a tray (6) and are heated by a hot-air blower (9) to facilitate evaporation.

permitted building in stages and, when completed, allowed for "an assembly line operation," as their explanatory notes emphasized.[59]

The prisoner reception building was one of the few designs in Bischoff's overly ambitious plan to be realized. A violent typhus epidemic erupted in Auschwitz-Birkenau in the summer of 1942, and the whole lice-infested camp—barracks, offices, and workshops—had to be fumigated with tons of Zyklon B. Convinced of the value of better prophylactic measures, Kammler finally gave Bischoff approval to proceed. Even so, progress was slow; by the time the facility was fully operational, the wartime history of the camp was coming to a close.[60]

The prisoners continued to arrive, however. They were "processed" in less perfectly designed but similarly structured reception facilities. And while those structures may have been only marginally effective in depressing the lice population, they were tremendously effective in depressing prisoner morale.

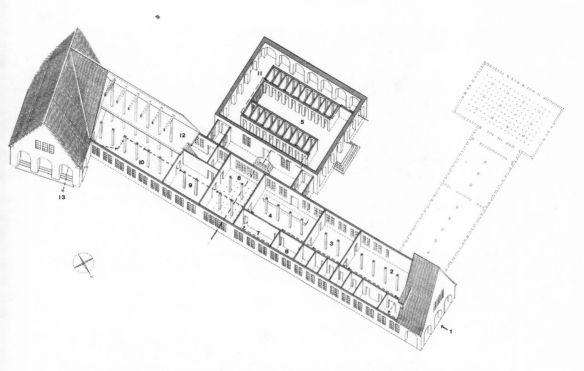

The center wing of the prisoner reception building in the main camp. Drawing by Kate Mullin.
Sandwiched between the laundry (left) and the baths (right), the center wing houses
the prisoner reception facilities and the pavillion with nineteen delousing chambers. The plan
is a monumentalized version of barrack type Häftlinge *2a issued by Hans Kammler*
in the fall of 1941. Prisoners enter at the right (1) and proceed via a small vestibule into a
waiting room (2) and a registration room (3) and arrive in an undressing room (4).
There they hand in their clothes to attendants, who carry them through a covered gallery to
the "soiled" side of the nineteen Zyklon B delousing chambers (5). The naked prisoners
proceed to the physician (6), the barber (7), and the shower room (8). After the shower, the
prisoners proceed to a drying room (9) and end up in the dressing room (10), where
they receive their own deloused clothes from the other side, the "clean" side, of the delousing
shed (11) or inmate uniforms from the storage rooms above (12). They exit at 13.

"I was cold and bewildered," Sherry Weiss-Rosenfeld recalled. "The feeling
was something indescribable; it was a feeling of total despair. I never, ever in
my life had the same feeling. . . . I saw the desperate situation we were in.
And I said to myself, 'Even if I were to sprout wings all of a sudden, I could
not fly out of here.' "[61] "We were ordered to undress, to leave everything

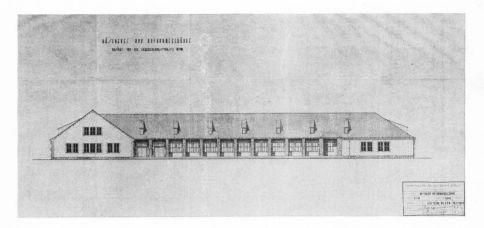

Early sketch of the entrance elevation of the main camp prisoner reception building, 1942. Architect Walther Dejaco. Auschwitz-Birkenau State Museum, box BW 160/3, file 160/10.

The showers of the "Central Sauna" in Birkenau, 1944. Auschwitz-Birkenau State Museum, neg. 20995/477. The inmates are about to enter the drying room, as indicated above the door (Trockenraum). *So doing, they enter the clean part of the building* (r[eine] Seite).

that we had and to undress,'' Hannah Kent-Sztarkman explained. They showered. ''Then our hair was shaved. We looked at each other, and we couldn't recognize anybody. We were thrown a dress, no underwear, nothing, just a dress and some shoes. And then we were tattooed.''[62] The Czech-born Alexander Ehrmann, eighteen at the time, later remembered how important that identification number was. ''We were told, 'Forget your name. From now on your number; that's all you are. Remember that. Your name is not important.' ''[63] For Mania Salinger-Tenenbaum, who was deported to Auschwitz after nearly two years in a slave labor camp in Pionki, the ritual of ''reception'' was overwhelming. She had remained resilient throughout her previous experiences, but after passing through the room-by-room enactment of a step-by-step metamorphosis from *Mensch* to *Untermensch*, she lost her optimism: ''When my head was shaved, and I had striped clothing, and my arm was tattooed, and they took my clothes and shoes away, I just did not feel like living. I turned around and went straight to the electric fence. I started running to the fence. I felt that I was going to die anyway. I was so humiliated. At that point I felt that I was not a human being any more. My sister saw me. She started to scream, and some people ran after me and shlepped me back. And all my optimism and strength just left me completely.''[64]

WHILE THE RECEPTION building for prisoners was designed, approved, and constructed, and while the prisoners continued to arrive in ever larger numbers, the architects of the building office in Auschwitz and from the SS offices in Berlin planned a monumental five-section headquarters, from which the commandant would run the camp and welcome the public. Budgeted at no less than 3.3 million marks,[65] the Kommandantur was never built, but the designs themselves are informative. They reveal the grand ambitions of the SS, their confident expectation of tremendous support from IG Farben, and their equally confident expectation of great wealth to be derived from the slave labor of their prisoners. Significantly, the administrative office complex was to face the large road which had been built from the camp, over the new bridge crossing the Sola, directly to the IG Farben buna plant in Monowitz. This was to be the entrance to Auschwitz, marked with a colossal five-arch gate. It reoriented the camp 180 degrees: prisoners arrived at the train station through the ''back door'' and were to come and go between Auschwitz and Buna through the ''front door.'' That ''door,'' the gate, was not built, but the reorientation took root.

The headquarters itself consisted (on paper) of five sections surrounding a

The third and final master plan for Auschwitz, summer
1942. Drawing by Kate Mullin.
In the center is the main camp, with the barracks of the
former labor exchange (1), a large roll call square flanked by an
entrance pavillion and a tower to house the offices of the
Lagerführer (2), a prisoner reception building
(3), the camp kitchens (4), and workshops (5). Along the
road to the station is the extension with dwelling
barracks (6), a camp hospital (7), and a camp prison (8).
Southwest of the camp are the offices of the
commandant (9), apartments for Himmler and higher SS
officers (10), accommodations for SS
noncommissioned officers (11), the heating plant (12),
and workshops (13). The large crematorium,
located in the second master plan at the eastern edge of
the original compound, has been relocated to
Birkenau. N.B.: This is an axonometric drawing; the
three-dimensional effect is derived from the exact
measurements and angles of the original plan. See
plate 11.

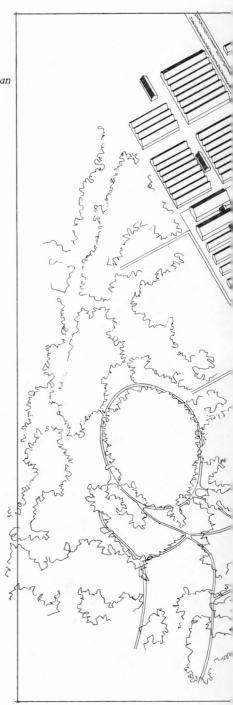

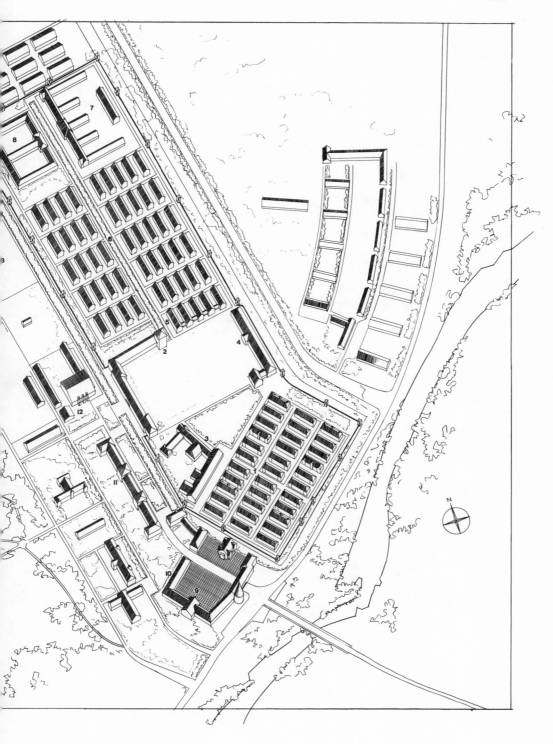

large courtyard. Sections I and II were parallel to the river and formed the formal entrance façade of the whole concentration camp. Located to the right of the five-fold gate, Section I included living quarters for seventy-five sentries, ten runners, and five roving patrols, a mortuary for SS men and their families, and a double garage for the hearse. Section II stretched to the left of the gate. The ground floor was to be occupied by a suite of twenty-five rooms for the camp administration in charge of the housing, food, and clothing of the garrison and the prisoners, and rooms for the camp engineer who, as Höss recalled, supervised the camp's water supply, its drainage and sewage, the fire brigade, and "the security installations, such as the electrified barbed-wire fence, inside and outside camp lighting of the walls and fences, the spotlights, and the sirens."[66] On the floor above were thirty-six rooms for the commandant. This suite included a spacious tower room that allowed him to oversee the traffic at the main entrance and provided a view of the chimneys and carbide towers of the buna plant in the distance.

Section III was to occupy the southern side of the courtyard. A large ceremonial hall for festive occasions was at the center of that wing. A mail and telex station, a library, rooms for the National Socialist Party local branch, a suite of eighteen rooms for the agricultural estate department, and nineteen rooms for the camp's radio communication center were also planned. It is interesting to note that while Kammler's standard type allocated 530 square feet for this function, the suite in Auschwitz was seven times as large. Sections IV and V were on the west side of the courtyard. The former had seventeen apartments for officers, each consisting of a living room, bedroom, bathroom, and hall, and

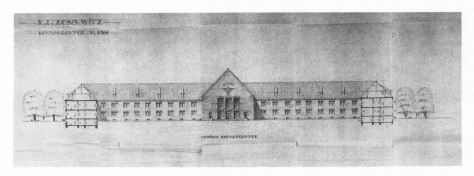

Elevation of the courtyard of the projected Kommandantur. Architect Georg Werkmann. Auschwitz-Birkenau State Museum, box BW 173/1, file BW 173/1. At the center is the official entrance to the Kommandantur with the great hall for festive occasions.

The great hall of the
Kommandantur. Auschwitz-
Birkenau State Museum, box BW
173/1, file BW 173/28.

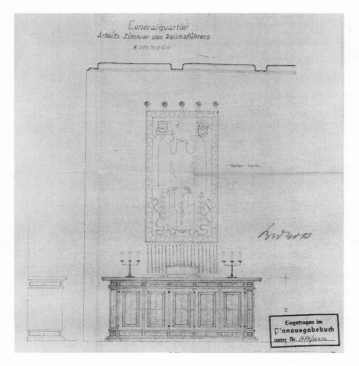

Design of a wall
hanging for
Himmler's study in
Auschwitz.
Auschwitz-
Birkenau State
Museum, box BW
40/2, file BW
40/6.

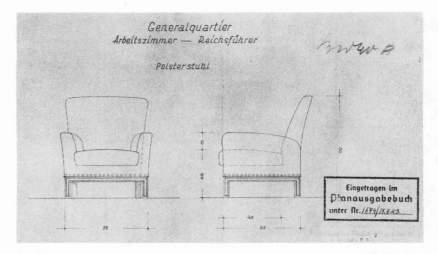

Design of a chair for Himmler's study in Auschwitz. Auschwitz-Birkenau State Museum, box BW 40/2, file BW 40/6.

a very spacious suite with specially designed furniture for Himmler.

Section V, appropriately separated from the continuous complex formed by the first four sections, was to house the two inspectorates that oversaw the management of the camp and the activities of the Central Architectural Office. The northern end of the courtyard, between section I and section IV, was to be screened off from the protective custody camp by a grove of trees and the existing theater building, which was planned to become an SS casino (and which became a Carmelite convent in the late 1980s). The road connecting the concentration camp gate to the entrance of the protective custody camp ran between sections IV and V. This road passed through another five-arch gate, located in the L-shaped section VII, where SS privates and unmarried SS noncommissioned officers were to live. At the end of this wing was a plaza with a heating plant. The monumental entrance to the prisoners compound, with a very grand tower for the *Schutzhaftlagerführer*, the offices for the inmate labor department, and the rooms of the camp Gestapo, was directly opposite the plaza. Finally, between sections V and VII, the architects projected a one-story building, section VI, to join the square within the Kommandantur to the road that led to the station and the entrance to the protective custody camp. A cheerful timber-framed gallery, section VI was designed to provide visitors to Auschwitz with a permanent exhibition of the camp's great contribution to the future of the German East.

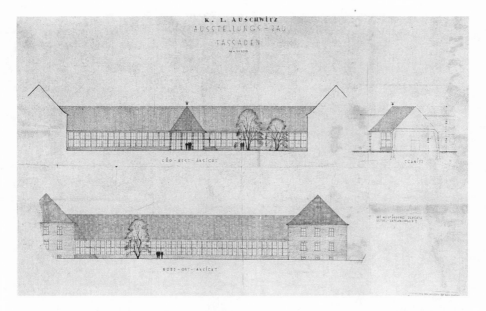

Design of the exhibition pavillion of the Kommandantur. Auschwitz-Birkenau State Museum, box BW 173/3, file BW 173/11.

HIMMLER, HÖSS, AND SS architects in Auschwitz and Berlin presumed that these grandiose designs, and many more equally monumental plans for the town, the SS settlement, and the camp, would be built with the financial and material support of IG Farben and the slave labor of the concentration camp inmates. Furthermore, as Ambros had emphasized during the conference of 7 April, "it is in accordance with the plans of the Reich Office of Economic Development, the Reich Ministry of Economics, and the High Command of the Army that, in the first stage of building operations, the buna plant should be built with the utmost speed." For the plant to be built quickly, the camp had to be enlarged, and for the plant to operate efficiently, the German workers would have to be accommodated appropriately in town. Rapid action was both required and desired, and it led to incredible violence. Rudolf Vrba, who was brought to Auschwitz in June 1942, explained that there were only two kinds of workers at the buna site: the quick and the dead.

Men ran and fell, were kicked and shot. Wild-eyed kapos drove their blood-stained path through rucks of prisoners, while S.S. men shot from

Construction in the extension of the main camp. Auschwitz-Birkenau State Museum, neg. 20995/51. The buildings in the back are prisoner barracks, the building in the front is one of the five interconnected workshops facing the projected roll call place (see p. 227, no. 5).

the hip, like television cowboys, who had strayed somehow into a grotesque, endless horror film; and adding a ghastly note of incongruity to the bedlam were groups of quiet men in impeccable civilian clothes, picking their way through corpses they did not want to see, measuring timbers with bright yellow folding rules, making neat little notes in black leather books, oblivious to the blood-bath. They never spoke to the workers, these men in the quiet grey suits. They never spoke to the kapos, the gangsters. Only occasionally they murmured a few words to a senior S.S.N.C.O., words that sparked off another explosion. The S.S. man would kick viciously at the kapo and roar, ''Get these swine moving, you lazy oaf. Don't you know that wall's to be finished by eleven o'clock?'' The kapo would scramble to his feet, pound into the prisoners, lashing them on, faster, faster, faster.[67]

Norbert Wollheim, a German Jew who was brought with his wife and three-year-old son to Auschwitz in 1943, testified after the war that following his separation from his wife and child he was taken to a subcamp at Monowitz, where he was robbed of all his possessions, deloused, registered, and tattooed with the number 107,984. The next day he was brought to the buna plant.

> There were scarcely any streets. The buildings, except for those in which the directors and senior foremen worked, were mostly unfinished. As initiation, as was the general rule, we were given only the hardest and most strenuous work, such as transportation and excavation work. I came to the dreaded "murder detail 4," whose task it was to unload cement bags or construction steel. We had to unload the cement from arriving freight cars all day long at a running pace. Prisoners who broke down were beaten by the German IG foremen as well as by the kapos until they either resumed their work or were left there dead. I saw such cases myself. . . .
>
> I also noticed repeatedly, particularly during the time when the SS accompanied our labor unit themselves, that the German IG foremen tried to surpass the SS in brutalities.[68]

Sergeant Charles J. Coard, one of the 1,200 British prisoners of war employed at the site, corroborated Wollheim's testimony with regard to the brutality of both the kapos and the IG Farben overseers. "One time I saw several civilian employees of the Farben firm beat six inmates while they were working in the factory while three or four other civilians looked on. They beat them with pieces of iron and wood for not doing their work properly. They were badly beaten and left to lay on the ground." The camp inmates were involved in every aspect of construction work. Malnourished and suffering from a plethora of illnesses and ailments, they carried on, and carried on quickly, in the full knowledge that if they did not they would incur still greater injury. "They tried to do the work even though it required more strength than they had. They could not slow down because the foreman and the kapo were always around. . . . On many, many occasions I saw civilians and kapos strike an inmate down with a piece of wood and then kick him. They would just let him lie there—sometimes all day."[69]

Injurious as were the beatings, they were not yet purposefully lethal, but it did not take long for murder to follow. The nexus of the concentration camp at Auschwitz, the building site at Monowitz, and the gas chambers at Birkenau followed from Himmler's decision to exploit the labor of the inmates, and the different parts of this fateful triangle began to emerge at the end of the first year of construction. Inmates no longer able to perform to the satisfaction of the SS were selected for death. This direct relationship between IG Farben's drive to begin the production of buna and the murder of inmates broken by the pace set by the SS and the corporate employees was clearly articulated by Paul M. Hebert, one of the judges at the postwar trial of IG Farben. ''It was Farben's drive for speed in the construction of Auschwitz which resulted indirectly in thousands of inmates being selected for extermination by the SS when they were rendered unfit for work. The proof establishes that fear of extermination was used to spur the inmates to greater efforts and that they undertook tasks beyond their physical strength as a result of such fear. It is also clear from the proof that injured or ill inmates frequently refrained from seeking medical treatment out of fear of being sent for extermination to the gas chambers at Birkenau.''[70] It is baffling, but nevertheless a matter of record, that Judge Hebert's view was a dissenting opinion. The majority of the tribunal accepted the far-fetched defense contention that the utilization

The buna works at Oswiecim after the war. Authors.

of slave labor by IG Farben had occurred within the framework of cruel and inhuman regulations imposed by the Reich government.

To the inmates it mattered little who set the work pace. What mattered was the all-consuming slave labor on the construction gangs. "The Carbide Tower, which rises in the middle of Buna and whose top is rarely visible in the fog, was built by us," the chemist, survivor, and author Primo Levi wrote in his autobiographical *If This Is a Man?* "Its bricks were called *Ziegel, briques, tegula, cegli, kamenny, mattoni, téglak*, and they were cemented by hate; hate and discord, like the Tower of Babel, and it is this that we call it:—*Babelturm, Bobelturm*; and in it we hate the insane dream of grandeur of our masters, their contempt for God and men, for us men." Ironically, the Carbide Tower was of no greater use to the Germans than the Tower of Babel had been to the Babylonians. "The Buna factory," Levi reminds us, or perhaps reassures us, "on which the Germans were busy for four years and for which countless of us suffered and died, never produced a pound of synthetic rubber."[71]

Limpid as is Primo Levi's prose, the irony he underlines is, in the end, irrelevant. And what if a million pounds had been produced?

CHAPTER 8

BIRKENAU

THE CONSTRUCTION OF THE BUNA PLANT AT MONOWITZ, THE AGGRANDIZE-
ment of the town of Auschwitz, and the expansion of the concentration camp
were intimately interrelated and interdependent projects. IG Farben, Himmler,
Göring, and the provincial authorities of Upper Silesia were in complete agreement
on these programs. The problem they faced was how to proceed within the
constraints of wartime regulations, limitations, and stoppages.

According to a special decree of December 1940, these bureaucratic obstacles could be bypassed by municipal and provincial governments in war-dam-
aged areas. Although Upper Silesia was as yet untouched by war, the provincial
authorities nevertheless turned to the German minister of the interior, Wilhelm Frick. Faced with the combined might of Göring, IG Farben, and Himmler, Frick proposed to extend the decree to eastern Upper Silesia because it
was *as if* the province had been damaged by war. Arguing that "the economy
of the area will achieve its potential" when "working people in all parts of
the province have roughly the same conditions of life and work," Frick concluded that radical intervention was needed to improve the social and cultural
conditions within eastern Upper Silesia.[1] This could be done only if Provincial
Governor Bracht were given the special powers provided by the December
1940 decree. To be sure everyone understood the urgency of the situation,

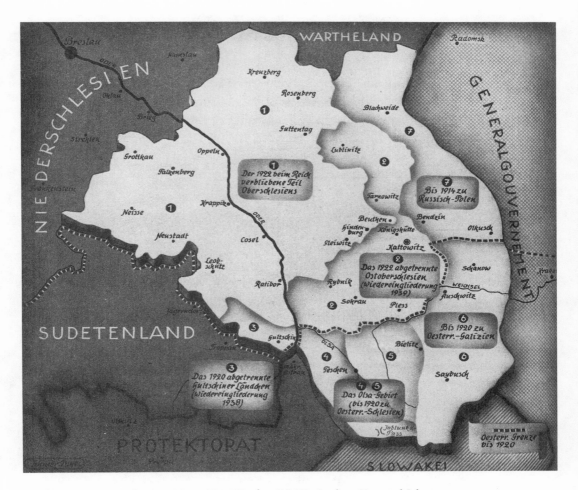

The fragmented state of Upper Silesia. Die Woche *(1941). Sterling Memorial Library, Yale University. Upper Silesia is a patchwork of regions with different histories and infrastructures.*

1 = remained German after the plebiscite

2 = Polish between 1922 and 1939

3 = German before 1920 and Czechoslovak between 1920 and 1938

4 = Austrian Silesia before 1920 and Czechoslovak between 1920 and 1938

5 = Austrian Silesia before 1920 and Polish between 1920 and 1939

6 = Austrian Galicia before 1920 and Polish between 1920 and 1939

7 = Russian Poland before 1914, German occupied during the Great War, and part of Poland between 1919 and 1939

Frick emphasized that rapid reconstruction was imperative for this "excellent, important, and valuable industrial area to reach its full war production potential."[2]

Frick's argument reflected concerns that had surfaced in the popular press subsequent to the establishment of the new province. The illustrated weekly *Die Woche*, for example, had printed a graphic representation of Upper Silesia's problematic structure in its issue of 16 April 1941. The map of the newly created province identified no fewer than seven different districts of varying degrees of political, social, and economic development. While unification of this patchwork was essential, the area that included the town of Auschwitz, "an old area of German settlement," required special attention. "Its re-Germanization is one of the most necessary cultural and administrative tasks of the new province of Upper Silesia."[3]

If the popular press found the development of Upper Silesia a newsworthy item, the professional press found it a potential problem. In a special number of *Raumforschung und Raumordnung* (Space research and space ordering), the monthly journal of Konrad Meyer's Reich Study Group for Spatial Research, the chief planner of Upper Silesia, Gerhard Ziegler, announced that the area around Auschwitz had been designated a *Neubauzone* (area for new construction); officially it was recognized as an area that needed to be rebuilt entirely. Ziegler compared their mission to that of their ancestors six hundred years ago. "Only when we consider our task from that perspective can we become conscious of our responsibility and obligation. Just as we look back at the total transformation of the Silesian landscape in the twelfth and thirteenth centuries, so our descendants will look back to our time and judge if we came to solutions worthy of our age."[4] Auschwitz, Ziegler argued, was an ideal place to begin the urban reconstruction of Upper Silesia because although it was located in a *Neubauzone*, there was much that deserved to be salvaged. "Its original face, shaped by German inhabitants and builders, still shimmers through later excrescence."[5] Indeed, in an accompanying sketch of the projected development of the region, Auschwitz was the only fixed point among twelve possible sites for new towns.

Frick obtained the approval of the numerous concerned agencies and ministries to apply the December 1940 decree to Upper Silesia. Significantly, the final decision justified this action not only on the grounds he had given but also because the construction projects were "to shape the space of the province according to the demands of the consolidation of the German nation."[6]

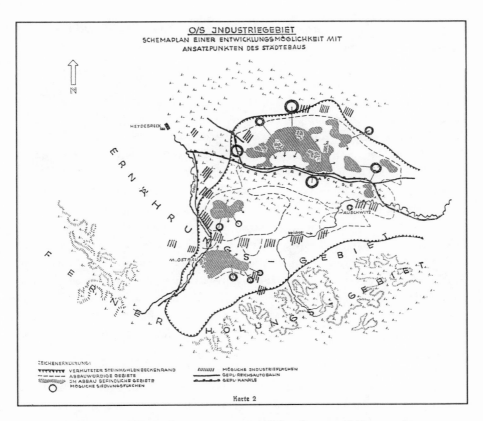

Planning sketch of the future of Upper Silesia. Raumforschung und Raumordnung
(1941). Rackham Library, University of Michigan.

▼▼▼▼▼▼▼▼	likely extent of coal deposits	/////////	possible areas of industrial development
− − − − −	area to be exploited	———————	planned super highway
//////////	area presently exploited	▬ ▬ ▬ ▬ ▬	planned canal
O	possible areas of settlement		

GIVEN THIS EXTRAORDINARY convergence of powerful interests, it is not surprising that part of the reconstruction of the town of Auschwitz occurred during
the war. Analyzed with care, the buildings that were erected and the plans
that have been preserved lay bare the ideology of National Socialism and the
mythology of the German East as they structured and shaped the Germans'
view of Auschwitz. They show us that, to the best of his ability, Himmler

kept his word when he promised IG Farben that Auschwitz would become a paradigm of settlement in the annexed territories.

Himmler had definite ideas about the qualities and properties of an ideal National Socialist town, which he had derived from such theorists as Walter Christaller, Gottfried Feder, Josef Umlauf, and Karl Neupert. It was Christaller, for example, who informed Himmler's understanding of the proper relation between a town and the surrounding countryside.[7] Like so many others in Hitler's Reich, Christaller was inspired by the medieval settlement pattern in which urban and rural life had been balanced in a healthy symbiosis. The industrial revolution had destroyed that harmony, the countryside was no longer valued by the town, and the latter lost its identity as a result. Following Artaman ideals, Christaller argued for the restoration of the original relationship between country and town, which meant that the latter was to be considered from a rural perspective. His goal was to create a social, political, and economic hierarchy that linked the smallest to the largest element, household or farm to city.[8] Adopting a hexagonal grid as the basic structure, Christaller proposed that the needs of six villages be met by the smallest town, the *Marktflecken* (market hamlet); the *Landstädtchen* (rural town) was to service six market hamlets and their dependent villages; the *Kreisstadt* (district town), six rural towns; and so on.

Konrad Meyer liked Christaller's scheme and arranged for his appointment as a planning consultant to Himmler. In cooperation with Meyer, Christaller began to test the honeycomb pattern he had developed by studying southern Germany against the empirical realities of the German East. He modified his system as a result. The smallest unit in the East was to be the *Gruppendorf* (village group). At the center of this conglomeration of seven villages, he envisioned one main village to provide various services and to host the National Socialist Party local chapter. Going up in the hierarchy, Christaller proposed an administrative district with an administrative town at its center; a district with a district town as its capital, and finally, a *Gau*, or province, with its *Gauhauptstadt* (provincial capital).

Using his model as a measuring stick, Christaller concluded that a main cause for "the cultural decline in the East" was the lack of viable villages. Towns were on the lowest rung in the hierarchy. Clearly, this needed to change. "Careful planning and the loving development of 'main villages' in the new East is essential to root the future settlers from the west and the south, and to allow them to find a new home in the expanse of the East."[9]

As Christaller was identifying the hamlets to be developed into main villages, and the small towns to be turned into district towns, others in Meyer's planning department were busy preparing guidelines for the design of the cities themselves. Their most important source was Gottfried Feder's *Die neue Stadt* (The New Town). Feder had a remarkable curriculum vitae. He was one of the original founders of the small German Workers' Party and, according to Hitler himself, it was one of his speeches that inspired the future Führer to join the party in 1919.[10] Hitler and Feder became friends, and the latter continued to mentor the former. Throughout the 1920s Feder was considered to be one of the intellectual leaders of the movement and a prominent member of the National Socialist Reichstag caucus. His influence began to wane in 1930 when he introduced a bill to expropriate unprofitable East Elbian estates to permit a massive resettlement of the German East by peasants. At that time Hitler had begun to approach Junkers for support, and he was told to distance himself from Feder. Hitler had no trouble doing so, and in 1934 he booted his onetime mentor into semiretirement as Reich settlement commissioner, and in 1936 he pushed him into the political wilderness as professor of urban design at the Technical University of Berlin. This gave Feder the opportunity to develop a comprehensive and radical National Socialist theory of urban design which, after 1939, paralleled Himmler's vision of urban reconstruction in the annexed territories.

Feder claimed that only a midsize town of around 20,000 inhabitants could provide the proper environment for a truly National Socialist community. These towns, Feder argued, avoided big-city problems such as low birthrates, mobile populations, and traffic congestion, as well as the limitations of village life with its lack of facilities, culture, and politics and its simple economy. Furthermore, midsize towns offered the advantages associated with cities, like the administrative bureaus, industry, commerce, culture, mass transportation, sense of participation in public life, and choice of careers, while maintaining the comfort of villages: the proximity to nature and the soil, economic self-sufficiency, and a healthy environment.

Feder formulated four practical questions to serve as the basis of urban design: "1. What belongs in a town? 2. How many of these buildings are necessary? 3. Where should these be located to minimize travel? 4. How large should these buildings be?"[11] He provided a detailed answer for a town of 20,000. It needed fifty-two different kinds of public buildings, and he analyzed them in detail with regard to their size, number, and location.[12] Feder also listed commercial businesses that must, should, might, and, in very special

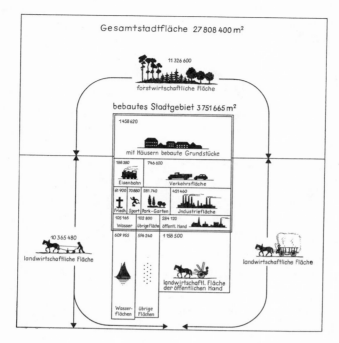

Diagram from Feder's book. Feder, Die neue Stadt (1939). Authors. A town of 20,000 requires 2,780.84 hectares, of which 1,132.66 hectares are to be forested, 1,036.55 are agricultural, and 375.2 will be built up.

cases, could be present. Finally, he calculated the investment needed to create the ideal National Socialist town of 20,000 inhabitants: the total bill was 50 million marks, or 2,500 marks per person. A true bargain.[13]

Politically, Feder's town roughly embodied the hierarchical structure of the National Socialist Party, moving from household to block, cell, local group, district, and, finally, province. "Where the community that lives along a street constitutes a block, and the street communities or blocks that form a subcenter relate to the cell, and where three to five subcenters or cells form a center or a local group with 2,000 to 3,000 people, and where again six to ten local groups or centers form a district and simultaneously a town, we see a pleasing parallel between the service, political, organizational, and traffic structures of the whole. Thus one can say that our town is 'total' in every sense of the word."[14]

For Feder the parallel had been a welcome outcome of his studies, but he had not identified it as a principle of town planning. One of his students, however, tried to work out the spatial implications of Feder's suggestions in an urban design. The result was awkward, but suggested viability if handled by a competent architect. Many ambitious designers accepted the challenge

Lfd. Nr.	Einrichtung Anzahl	Symbol	♟ = 5 Beschäftigte	Grundstücksgrößen	beb. Fläche ungefähre Baumaße Fläche aller Geschosse (einschl. Nebenräume) (Jeder der Einzelquadrate bedeckt eine Fläche von 100 m²)	Besonderes	Bemerkungen
I. Einrichtungen höherer Ordnung							
1	Justizgebäude * 1		70	5000 m²	Schwankt nach Geschoßzahl • 4550 m²	Personalzahl des Landgerichts: etwa 32	* Amtsgericht, Landgericht und Gerichtsgefängnis zusammen (darunter 2—3 Säle von rd. 200 m²)
1a	Amtsgericht		37—38	4000 m²	600 m² 1680 m²		
2	Finanzamt		58	2800 m²	700 m² • 1700 m²	Einwohnerzahl des erfaßten Bezirks: durchschnittlich 71000	* reine Nutzfläche: 1250 m²
3	Arbeitsamt 1		48	1400 m²	720 m² 1450 m²	Zahl der Arbeitnehmer: 44000 Zahl der Arbeitgeber: 9400	
4a 4b	Landratsamt Kreissparkasse		a) 60 b) 33	4100 m²	800 m² 1950 m²	b) Einwohnerzahl des Kreises: etwa 71000	
5	Partei 1		hauptamtlich * 5—6 NS-Schwestern 6—7	1900 m²	550 m² 1100 m²	Kreisleitung, Leitung der NSV., NS-Wohlfahrts-, NS-Jugendamt, Verwaltung der DAF., Hauptbüro von KdF., NS-Schwesternheim	* dazu kommen zahlreiche ehrenamtliche Angestellte
6	Gemeinschaftshaus		Bewirtschaftung an Unternehmer verpachtet	4800 m²	1600 m² 2400 m²	Anzahl der Sitz- und Stehplätze: etwa 2000	
7a	Personenbahnhof 1		225	zusammen 160000 m²	1300—1500 m²		* Empfangsgebäude
7b	Güterbahnhof 1				1100—1200 m²	Länge des Ladegleises: 2500 m** vorzusehen	* Güterschuppen ** davon ausgebaut: anfangs nur 2000 m
7c	Flugplatz * 1		unbestimmbar	100 × 13500 = 1350000 m²	unbestimmbar		
8	Reichspost 1		124	2500 m²	a) 870 m² b) 280 m² 2460 m²	Beförderte Briefe: 7000000 Beförderte Pakete: 290000 Ein- und Auszahlungen: 10900000 RM.	a) Hauptgebäude b) Nebengebäude
II. Kommunale Verwaltungen und Sicherheit							
9	Rathaus 1		81—91	3000 m²	960 m² 2600 m²		mit Polizei, Feuerwehr und Rettungswache
10	Polizei * 1		30	1000 m²	285 m² 285 m²	Einwohnermeldeamt: Nutzfläche: etwa 45 m² Personal: 3	* meist im Rathaus
III. Versorgung							
11	Wasserwerk 1		10	30—32000 m²	800 250 m²	Wasserabnahme je Kopf der Bevölkerung: 35 m³/i. J. Gesamtförderung: 700 000/i. J. Angeschlossene Haushalte: 6300 Leitungslänge: 50000 m	2 Hochbehälter mit je 400 m³ Inhalt
12	Elektrizitätswerk 1		* 35	5—6000 m²	250 m² ** 1200 m² 500 m² 1200 m²	Stromabgabe je Kopf der Bevölkerung: 103 kWh/i. J. Angeschlossene Haushalte: 6000	* davon 15 Lohnempfänger ** Verwaltungsgebäude im Obergeschoß Wohnungen
13	Gaswerk 1		* 30	8900 m²	2300 m² ** 250 m²	Gasabgabe pro Kopf der Bevölkerung: 61,5 m³ Angeschlossene Haushalte: 4130 Rohrlänge: 45000 m	* davon 20 Lohnempfänger ** Verwaltungsgebäude (bebaute Fläche)
14	Städtischer Wirtschaftshof		Bei dem städtischen Verwaltungspersonal inbegriffen	4500 m²	800 m² 1000—1100 m²		

Diagram from Feder's book indicating precise number and type of institutions, employees, and space required, etc. Feder, Die neue Stadt (1939). Authors. Feder took three pages to summarize the public institutions for his town, and three more to depict commercial life. Depicted on this page are his statistics regarding (1) the courts; (2) the municipal treasury; (3) the labor office; (4) the county office and the county savings bank; (5) the National Socialist Party; (6) a community hall; (7) the railway station; (7a) a freight station; (7b) a municipal airport (optional); (8) a post office; (9) a town hall; (10) a police station; (11) the waterworks plant; (12) the power station; (13) gas works; (14) municipal works.

with greater or lesser success.[15] It was Carl Culemann, the municipal architect of Marienburg and, later, Danzig, who developed the most comprehensive system of urban design based on the hierarchy of the National Socialist Party. He claimed that, unlike architects, the party organizers had solved the problem of organizing large masses through careful division of each larger unit into a discrete number of smaller ones, ending at the household. "The sense of a mass that is generated by arithmetic limitlessness is thus destroyed at its origin," Culemann observed.[16]

Culemann realized that the parallel would work only if immediately apparent to the eye. Arguing that this could be achieved by using a hierarchy in which each following urban unit was three to four times larger than the preceding one, Culemann justified his three-four system on the organizational principle of the German army. A similar multiplication factor structured the relationship of smaller to larger military units: soldier (one man); troop (3–4 soldiers); group (10 men); platoon (3 groups); company (3 platoons); battalion (3–4 companies); regiment (3–4 battalions). Culemann claimed that in the army hierarchy, every second step (group, company, regiment) had a special significance in establishing and maintaining the chain of command, while the intermediary steps were important to provide a sense of place for each of the units within the larger structure.[17] With some pushing and shoving, he managed to press the hierarchy of the National Socialist Party into his numerological straitjacket. From this he derived the building blocks of the city in which the house, the group (10 houses), the urban cell (100 houses), the local group (1,000 houses), and the district (10,000 houses) carried a primarily political significance, and the intermediary elements a primarily social one: neighborhood unit (3–4 houses); cell part (30–40 houses); urban district (300–400 houses); town (3,000–4,000 houses).[18] Finally, having established the ideal National Socialist structure, Culemann proposed that each level should have commercial facilities appropriate to its size.[19]

Josef Umlauf, who oversaw urban design issues in the Office of the Reich Commissioner for the Consolidation of the German Nation, adopted Culemann's principles as the point of departure for urban development in the German East. Culemann's system, Umlauf argued, permitted Germans from disparate backgrounds to forge a community instantly "amid the most violent ethnic struggle."[20] It also fit the model of the medieval urban development in the German East—when growing populations were accommodated not in suburbs but in new towns adjacent to the existing one.[21] In the twentieth-

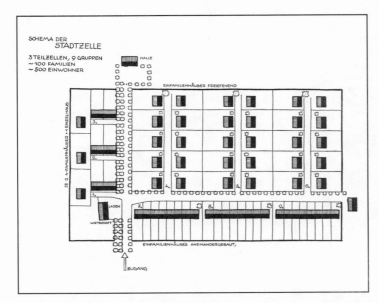

Culemann's proposal for an urban cell. Raumforschung und Raumordnung (1941). Rackham Library, University of Michigan. The cell, the basic building block of the town, consists of 33 single-family homes, 24 townhouses, 24 apartments, a few shops, a school, and a community center.

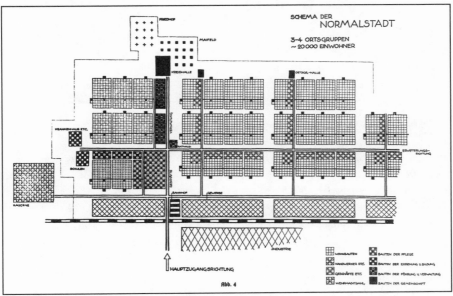

Culemann's proposal for a town of 20,000 people. Raumforschung und Raumordnung (1941). Rackham Library, University of Michigan. The town consists of three to four local groups of 1,000 houses each, subdivided in turn into three urban districts of 300–400 houses, with four urban cells of 100 houses apiece.

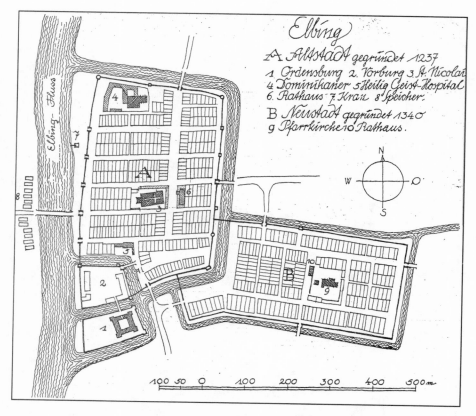

Elbing in East-Prussia. Gruber, Die Gestalt der deutschen Stadt *(1952). Seeley G. Mudd Library, Yale University. Himmler's architects were inspired by the fact that, in the medieval German East, towns accommodated a growing population by repeating the original foundation next to the existing town. The new town was independent and complete in itself, with its own market, church, and town hall. Famous double cities were Berlin, Breslau, Thorn, and Elbing. There were triple cities like Rostock and Königsberg, and Danzig was a quadruple city that consisted of the original settlement* (locatio), *the town of the Teutonic Order (1330), the new town (1343), and the suburb (1360).*

century reconstruction of the German East, the local group would be the basic building block of the new towns, and growth would proceed unit by unit.[22]

Umlauf's architects integrated Culemann's system of urban development, Christaller's hierarchy of villages and towns, and the history of medieval German urbanism in the East. They were not the only ones. Angling for a role in the reconstruction program, Karl Neupert and his architects at the Reich

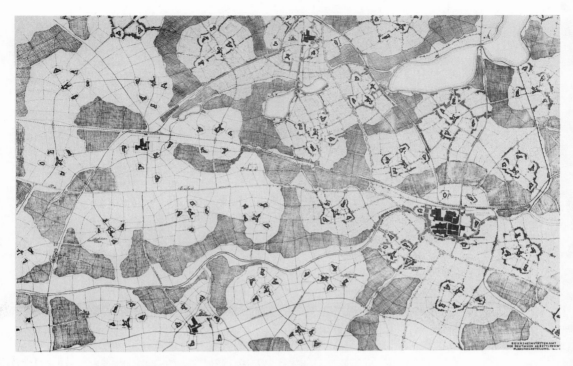

Neupert's Heimatlandschaft. *Reichsheimstättenamt der deutschen Arbeitsfront,*
Siedlungsgestaltung aus Volk, Raum und Landschaft *(1941). Art Library of the*
State Museums, Berlin. Neupert proposed a hierarchically ordered landscape in which the largest
urban unit was the town of 20,000 (right), *divided into four local groups of 5,000*
people, surrounded by concentric rings of villages and then by smaller market towns of 5,000,
each of which was itself the center of a circle of satellite villages.

Homestead Office of the German Labor Front developed parallel proposals
which they explicitly characterized as a resurrection of the *Weichbild* of the
Middle Ages. "The medieval image of settlement," Neupert claimed in 1941,
"gave the Germans a true understanding of *Heimat* that transcends all confu-
sion." The *Weichbild* was based on, and its vitality demonstrated, "the close
connection between the national and the political aspects of life."[23] He confidently predicted that he and his colleagues would be able to reconstruct "a new
and simultaneously age-old German *Heimatlandschaft* in the East."[24] Indeed, the
architects went so far as to claim strategic significance for their designs. "The
history of the German people has shown that an area of settlement was only
fully appropriated when this space was shaped according to the will and in the

consciousness of the whole nation,'' the Reich Homestead Office planning guide asserted.[25] This was the mysterious reason why, against all odds, East Prussia had remained German both in 1466 and in 1919.

Himmler's ten-page general directive ''Guidelines for the Planning and Design of Towns in the Annexed Territories,'' drafted by Umlauf, borrowed heavily from him and from Christaller, Culemann, and Neupert. The aim of building activity in the German East, the guidelines declared, was ''the consolidation and augmentation of a racially superior German ethnic group.'' To that end ''a healthy relation between country and town'' was required to ensure that the political, economic, and cultural life in the annexed territories would reach the level of ''Germanic-German cultural landscapes.''[26] Towns were part of a settlement hierarchy that logically connected the smallest to the largest unit. The town of 20,000 with its ''organic connection between town and country'' was to be the backbone of the German East.[27] Himmler's guidelines acknowledged, however, that large corporations would need to be serviced by more populous centers; towns of 50,000 people would provide the appropriate compromise between economic and technological realities and social and political ambitions.[28]

THE NEWLY APPOINTED architect for the aggrandizement of Auschwitz, Hans Stosberg, shared this admiration for medieval predecessors who had been ''urban designers of a most daring stature with a comprehensive, visionary perspective that looked centuries ahead.''[29] Rebuilding the town was a challenging proposition: the allocated space was squeezed in between the concentration camp's agricultural areas to the west, the buna plant to the east, and the floodplains of the Sola and the Vistula to the south and the north. Yet Stosberg made the best of it. (See plate 9.) In an explanation of his first design he described the location—''amid a fertile, loessial landscape'' and ''at the center of the Moravian, the Upper Silesian, and the Polish industrial areas''— as excellent, and he applauded the good sense of his thirteenth-century predecessors in building the German town on a defensible outcropping of land.[30]

Stosberg aimed to build a new town for 35,500 inhabitants, who would be employed in government, trade, crafts, light industries, and services, in the buna plant and other industries, and by the railways, the SS, and other economic endeavors.[31] They would live in the medieval center, in a new district between the old town and the IG Farben plant, and in a new district to be located in Zasole. An extra 11,500 people would find homes in the satellite

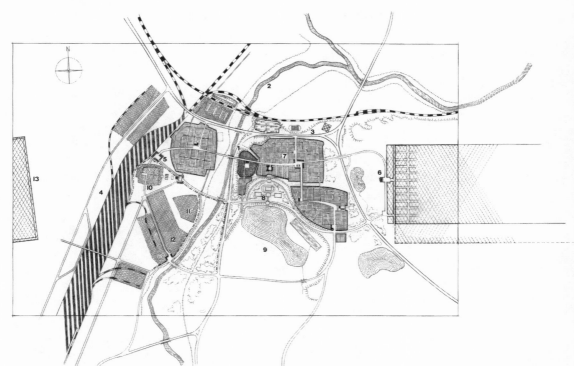

Second master plan for the expansion of Auschwitz by the town architect Hans Stosberg, spring
1941. Based on drawings in the Osobyi Archive, Moscow, coll. 502/2, file 93. Drawing
by Kate Mullin. The old town of Auschwitz (1) is located at the junction of the Sola (2), the
main road Gleiwitz—Zator (3), and the railway yard (4). A major avenue connects the
old town to the station (5) and the industrial area to be developed by IG Farben (6). The new
town (7) is developed on the high grounds between the old town and the synthetic
rubber plant. The low grounds south of the town are designated for recreational activities such
as sport (8) and sailing (9). South of the station are the SS village (10), the SS barracks
(11), and the concentration camp (12). The area defined by the dotted line is the camp's zone
of interests. Birkenau (13), to the west, is not marked on Stosberg's original drawing.

villages of Stare-Stawy and Zaborze. Stosberg projected a population density
of 115 inhabitants per hectare, which would call for two-story buildings in
general, while major streets would be lined with three-story structures. Green
belts were to separate the eastern district from the buna plant, the settlement
area adjacent to the station from the SS base, and the SS base from the concentra-

tion camp proper. An avenue running from the station, over the existing Sola bridge, through the old town, via the eastern district and the green belt to the main gate of the plant was to be the town's spine.[32]

Drafted in February 1941, Stosberg's initial plan guided design development for the next two years. (See plate 10.) Only a portion of it was built but, as we have seen, the designs themselves offer a unique view of the ideology of the men wedded to the project of their ancestors, and the politics of urban development in the National Socialist German East. The plans and their accompanying documents reveal, for example, that in compliance with IG Farben's demand for a special 6,000-inhabitant company settlement, Stosberg developed a paradigm of urban design in the new German East. It was precisely the size of a local chapter of the Party, which constituted a basic urban development building block. Stosberg followed Feder's and Culemann's recommendations and specified that this urban unit be serviced by one midwife, two restaurants, three doctors, four butchers, bakers, and barbers, five shoemakers, seven grocers, and so on.[33] Following both IG Farben guidelines and Himmler's vision of industrial workers' right to participate in the mysteries of "blood and soil," Stosberg provided a garden for every house and, in the green areas surrounding the settlement, an allotment garden for every apartment.[34] "The organic formation of the space cannot stop at the edges of the settlement, but must also embrace the whole town landscape beyond," he wrote, using language informed by Himmler's general directive. The new Auschwitz was to transform "a piece of desolate earth" into "a true cultural landscape."[35]

Stosberg had more difficulty achieving ideological purity in the other parts of Auschwitz. While the 3,206-inhabitant old town may have been a "testimony to the spirit of medieval German settlers" and an "important monument of old German urban history,"[36] it was too small to support a local Party chapter of 6,000 people. The 13,600-inhabitant New Town East was too large, but there was not enough space to divide it into two clearly articulated urban groups. Nevertheless, Stosberg attempted to match his plan to Feder's and Culemann's prescriptions. He designed a stadium, parade grounds, and six other sports facilities and—on paper—located twenty playgrounds, six daycare centers, and six primary schools on the edge of the neighborhoods, as well as two junior high schools, two high schools, and three vocational schools. Anticipating that the new Auschwitz would attract tourists, Stosberg projected one hotel at the station, another overlooking the Sola, and a third close to the buna plant.[37]

Stosberg was constrained in the development of his design by the main

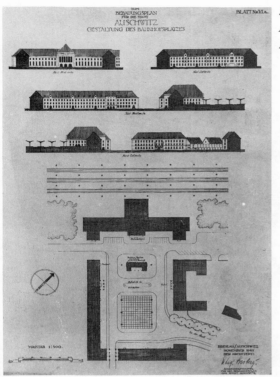

Stosberg's design for the railway station in Auschwitz, 1942. Auschwitz-Birkenau State Museum, neg. 21321/6.

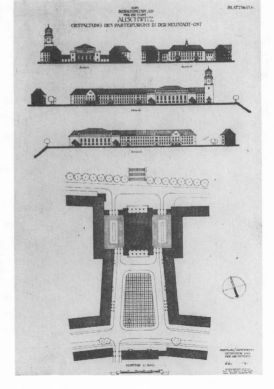

Stosberg's design for the County Party Headquarters at Auschwitz, 1942. Auschwitz-Birkenau State Museum, neg. 20586. The square is located on a wide avenue connecting the railway station to the IG Farben site. Between the square and the large sports fields to the south is the great gathering hall, which follows the neoclassical aesthetics of National Socialist monumental architecture as conceived by Adolf Hitler, developed by Ludwig Troost, and perfected by Albert Speer.

A part of Stosberg's Auschwitz that was built. Photo by Robert-Jan van Pelt. Authors.
While Stosberg designed the urban plan, the Ludwigshafen architect Klemens
Anders, who had done work for IG Farben before, designed the houses.

concentration camp in Zasole and the claims of the SS in their master plan of
June 1941 to a terrain for an SS settlement. Stosberg wanted that area for his
New Town West, but Kammler refused to give in and instructed his subaltern,
the urban designer Lothar Hartjenstein, to develop a new master plan for an
SS settlement between the railroad and the Sola.[38] (See plate 11.) It ran aground
with Stosberg, who still wanted to use the site for the southern half of a densely
built-up, self-sufficient community of Reich Railway employees. Complaining
that Hartjenstein's proposal reduced his plan to a "torso," Stosberg also
emphasized that the cozy one-family homesteads set in large gardens of the SS
garden city contradicted the strongly urban character of his own design. There
were two solutions to the problem: either the SS settlement had to conform
to the urban density of Stosberg's plan, or the SS had to move the garden city
to another site within its zone of interests. Stosberg was supported by the
provincial planner Ziegler and by the provincial bureaucracy. But the camp
also had strong supporters, not the least of whom was Himmler. The two
parties argued for almost a year, pushing the border between the city and the
camp backwards and forwards. Ultimately the SS yielded to the city because

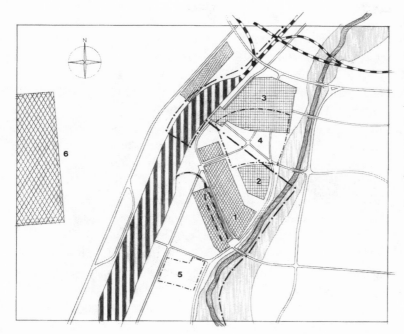

Diagram showing the conflicting territorial claims of the SS and the municipality of Auschwitz. Drawing by Kate Mullin. Authors. 1 = concentration camp; 2 = SS barracks; 3 = neighborhood planned by Stosberg; 4 = SS settlement planned by Hartjenstein; 5 = final location of the SS settlement; 6 = Birkenau.

Oswald Pohl, the business administrator of the SS empire, felt that as more and more transports of Jews rolled through the Auschwitz station, he could not afford to offend the province and the town and ask them at the same time to close their eyes to what was happening in the camp.[39] Hartjenstein was ordered to draft a new design, with the SS settlement located elsewhere.[40]

Hartjenstein completed the new plan on 12 November 1942 and Pohl approved it on 5 December. At that time the camps in Auschwitz and Birkenau counted 30,000 inmates, of whom 8,200 were women. What was happening to them, live human beings, while Pohl considered what to do with Hartjenstein's paper designs? In the twenty-three days between 12 November and 5 December, 2,000 prisoners were gassed, 461 sick inmates were killed with phenol injections, 25 were executed, 2 were shot "in flight," 1 was hanged, and 1 was tortured to death. Another 837 people died as a result of "natural causes"—starvation, exhaustion, or a combination of both. This totaled 3,327 murdered human beings. The true situation was even more ghastly; these official statistics applied only to officially registered inmates. During the same twenty-three days, 13,000 people were sent immediately upon arrival to the gas chambers of bunkers 1 and 2 in Birkenau.[41]

———

THE CREATION OF THE camp at Birkenau, which by the end of 1942 had become a major center for the annihilation of Europe's Jews, was directly connected to Himmler's program to transform Auschwitz into a paradigm of German settlement in the East. To convince IG Farben that Auschwitz was just what the company desired, Himmler had to do more than make promises. On his first visit to the camp in March 1941, he therefore proposed not only to increase the camp population to 30,000 but also to establish a huge satellite camp of 100,000 prisoners in the agricultural estate area. Himmler "discussed this," Höss recalled, "and pointed out the approximate area that he wanted me to use." If Höss was surprised, the provincial authorities were chagrined. Upper Silesia was poor in water, and they had identified the wetlands around Birkenau as a major source.[42] Furthermore, they realized immediately that 100,000 prisoners would create a massive sewage problem. "Himmler just smiled and disposed of their objections saying, 'Gentlemen, this project will be completed; my reasons for this are more important than your objections!' "[43]

Himmler's visit to Auschwitz and Birkenau and his instructions to build what became a graveyard for more than one million Jews was an event carefully staged to impress the directors of IG Farben. He had no intention of beginning construction right away—that order came more than six months later—but to declare his commitment to the future of Auschwitz. By ordering the establishment of a 100,000-inmate camp Himmler had taken care of labor availability, which (as we have seen) was key to development of the region. Furthermore, the precedent of using inmates for municipal projects had been established in December 1940 when the camp and the town agreed that chain gangs of prisoners would improve the dikes along the Vistula and the Sola, and the trajectory of the two rivers; a few months later crews were put to work at demolition sites in the town.[44] Himmler's gesture in Birkenau was to impress on the rest of the entourage that the camp would be able to service the town reconstruction project. All those present—IG Farben officials; Provincial Governor Fritz Bracht and other civic authorities; the SS liaison with IG Farben, Karl Wolff; and the SS head of agricultural affairs, Heinrich Vogel; as well as the camp officials—heard him, as did SS leaders a year later. The deployment of a massive army of slaves was a simple necessity in the cause of laying a stable foundation for a German future in the East, Himmler told his men. "If we do not create the bricks here, if we do not fill our camps with slaves—in this room I state these things precisely and clearly—with work slaves who will build our cities, our villages, and our farms, irrespective of losses, then, after a long war, we will not have the money to create settlements that will allow a truly Germanic people to live with dignity and to take root within one generation."[45]

Who was to fill the camp? In previous discussions with IG Farben, the complete eviction of all the Jewish and Polish residents of Auschwitz had been promised so that the town would "be available for the factory staff." Deportees were to be incarcerated in a camp "in the immediate neighborhood of Auschwitz" and used as unskilled construction workers.[46] The political situation had changed, however, and Himmler's pronouncements about Jewish and Polish forced labor were a smoke screen. Himmler knew by 1 March 1941—but the others did not—that Hitler had decided to attack the Soviet Union in the spring. It was clear to Himmler that Soviet prisoners of war would provide him with the labor force he needed for the reconstruction of the German East. Of the Jewish and Polish inhabitants of Auschwitz, only 50 percent or so would be able to do actual work; the rest—children, old people—were useless mouths to feed. The Soviet prisoners, by contrast, were relatively young men. If the Soviet draft board had decided they could handle a rifle, Himmler presumed they could handle a spade.

HAVING IMPRESSED IG FARBEN in the fields of Birkenau, Himmler returned to Berlin and for the next six months did not think much about the reconstruction of Auschwitz. As the invasion of the Soviet Union, code-named Operation Barbarossa, approached, he had other things on his mind; the town could wait. On Sunday, 22 June 1941, the German army surprised its neighbor with an early morning offensive. The justification was neither political nor practical, but purely ideological. While the war with Poland was to right the wrongs wrought at Versailles, the attack on Russia passed no such test. The Soviet Union had not gained a square inch of German soil after the Great War. The energy for the assault was the geopolitical urge to conquer *Lebensraum* in the East,[47] and the unconditional imperative to rise up against the Judeo-Bolshevik conspiracy to rule the world. The first of these was firmly rooted in mainstream German *Kultur* by 1941; the second was the core of Hitler's ambition. The largest mobilization in world history, the destructive fury of the assault and the initially unprecedented military successes forged the two concepts into a new crusade.

Within weeks of the onslaught, and in the wake of stunning victory after

*The Shadow. The Stürmer, 1937. In the early 1920s Hitler came to believe that the Russian
revolution had been a Jewish revolution, and that Bolshevism was Judeo-Bolshevism—that is, the Jews'
tool to control the Russian masses. In* Mein Kampf *he wrote that "Marx was only the* one
*among millions who, with the sure eye of the prophet, recognized in the morass of a
slowly decomposing world the most essential poisons, extracted them, and, like a wizard, prepared
them into a concentrated solution for the swifter annihilation of the independent existence
of free nations on this earth. And all of this in the service of his race." The result was an ideology
in complete opposition to Hitler's conviction that those of higher* Kultur *(read Germans)
had the right and the duty to rule those of lower culture (read Slavs and Jews).*

victory, Franz Lüdtke, the National Socialist historian of the German East,
wrote a propaganda book distributed to soldiers in which he recast the war
into a European-Asian conflict. "As these lines are written we witness the
final confrontation in the European East," he told the men. "All the destructive
forces of the space stretching east of our nation's soil into Asia have gathered

in the crucible of Bolshevism, from which a wind of destruction blows. Under the command of the Führer, Germany has become the savior not only of German culture but of all of Western culture." Lüdtke believed that the war made it clear that "German National Socialism and Jewish Bolshevism could not coexist. One had to yield. . . . In the new millennium, the East will stand in the sign of the swastika."[48]

Lüdtke's belief that 1941 marked a truly historic moment in not solely German but European history was shared by all committed National Socialists, including the thirty-one-year-old award-winning poet Gerhard Schumann. A National Socialist student leader in the early 1930s, and a high official in the SA, Schumann represented the view of the typical SS man which, tempered neither by experience nor compassion, reduced the war with the Soviet Union into an apocalyptic struggle between cosmic forces. "The issue at stake is not if we preserve the life itself of the West, . . . the issue at stake is to defend with flaming arms the soul and the value of Man against the satanic instinct for destruction of a soulless demonic power that wants to drown the world in its blood, to dissolve the meaning of history up till now and that seeks to erect on the ruins of the sacred, human world a world domination of the *Untermensch.*"[49] Through language such as this the relative became absolute, and bad became evil. The myth of the Judeo-Bolshevik conspiracy, formulated a generation earlier by the party philosopher Alfred Rosenberg, now reached its full potential.

Propaganda, however, was not primarily in the hands of poets, no matter how famous or how well recognized as the voice of National Socialism. It was Minister of Propaganda Josef Goebbels's task to orchestrate the publicity campaign of the war, and he was well prepared. In a conference of 27 June 1941, Goebbels instructed his staff to describe the struggle as a conflict between the whole of Europe (most of which was occupied by that time) and Asia. The Occident was "on the march against the common enemy. With unique singleness of purpose [Europe] is rising, as it were, against the suppressor of all human culture and civilization. The hour of the birth of the new Europe has arrived without pressure or compulsion from Germany."[50] The German East now became the European East. Goebbels directed the media to report the war in those terms. If Russia had been an outpost of Asia before, its fate now became an example of that of any European country that fell for Bolshevism, "the greatest Jewish swindle of all times." Called "The Veil Drops," Goebbels's propaganda campaign was designed to reveal Soviet society as a "gigantic system of cheats and exploiters, in which the workers are compelled by the most bloody terrorization to live an indescribably pitiful existence in inhuman conditions." There was no doubt who was responsible for the pitiful hovels, lice-ridden homes, neglected roads, and filthy villages: "By means of their diabolical system of bolshevism, the Jews have cast the people of the Soviet Union into this unspeakable condition of deepest misery." The German press was instructed to compare "the inhuman conditions in the Soviet Union" and "the social progress, the high cultural standard and the healthy *Lebensfreude* of the working man in National Socialist Germany" and, using a carefully designed photo layout, to contrast "the bestialized Bolshevik types with the free and open gaze of the German worker, filthy Soviet hutments with Germans' workers' settlements, muddy tracks with the German Reich highways."[51]

From this it was only a small step to a rhetoric pitting the European/German *Mensch* against the Asiatic/Soviet *Untermensch*, which had come to mean a Russian in the clutches of Judeo-Bolshevism. The simple polarization of human being and subhuman was graphically depicted in *Der Untermensch*, an SS publication released simultaneously in fifteen European languages to arouse enthusiasm across the Continent for the German crusade in the East. An organ for Himmler's view of history, the book was structured on a mirror-image principle: the wonderful situation of children under German protection (for example) was shown on the right while the contrasting deprivation of children in the Soviet Union was depicted on the left. Under a picture of Soviet prisoners of war, the caption explained, "Now they are here again, the Huns, caricatures of human faces, nightmares that have become reality, a blow of the fist into the face of all that is good."[52]

Influenced by such propaganda and responding to increased Red Army resistance, the German military leadership decided that rules of war as established by custom and formulated in international law did not apply to the war in the East. The notorious "Guidelines for the Treatment of Political Commissars," better known as the "Commissar Order" (6 June 1941), abolished the usual protection of prisoners of war. Captured Soviet political commissars were to be denied prisoner-of-war status and shot immediately after identification. The army concluded an agreement with the SS three weeks later that allowed the latter to enter the prisoner-of-war camps and select and execute commissars, Communist functionaries of all ranks, agitators and fanatical Communists, and "all Jews."[53] The army's position was clear and unequivocal: "the special situation of the Eastern campaign . . . demands special

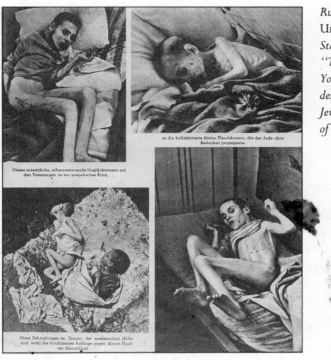

Russian Children. Reichsführer-SS, Der Untermensch (1942). Hoover Institution, Stanford University. The large caption reads, "This is the picture of the Soviet 'State Youth!' These are the results of the systematic destruction of the family wrought by Jews!—Even centuries will not dry up this sea of children's tears."

Children in Germany's Europe. Reichsführer-SS, Der Untermensch (1942). Hoover Institution, Stanford University. The large caption reads, "We, however, know how to appreciate the mothers of the nation.—We honor them as the eternally fertile sources of enduring life.—We recognize motherhood as the highest happiness in this world and are infinitely reassured to realize that the female youth of the Aryan-European family of nations have again become conscious of their mission." Four pictures of cheerful mothers with their children depict "the same happiness of mothers everywhere—in Switzerland, in the Netherlands, in Croatia, and in Denmark."

Hun/Mongol horsemen. Reichsführer-SS, Der Untermensch *(1942). Hoover Institution, Stanford University. An organ for Himmler's view of history,* Der Untermensch *emphasized the centuries' old conflict between the European* Mensch *and the predecessor of the Soviet* Untermensch, *the Hun and Mongol horseman, whom the National Socialists both conflated and confused. "The challenge of the* Untermensch *began with the bloody rides of [the Hun] Attila and [the Mongol] Genghis Khan," explains the text. "On ugly little horses, almost grown together with the skin of their animals, dashed the Hun hordes against Europe. Their split eyes glowed with lust to kill, and behind them they left only wilderness, murder, fire, and destruction."*

„Nun sind sie wieder da, die Hunnen. Zerrbilder menschlicher Gesichter, Wirklichkeit gewordene Angstträume, Faustschlag in das Gesicht alles Guten ..."

Soviet prisoners of war. Reichsführer-SS, Der Untermensch *(1942). Hoover Institution, Stanford University. The caption continued on the opposite page, "Now they are here again, the Huns, caricatures of human faces, nightmares that have become reality, a punch in the face of all that is good."*

measures." Until then, "the regulations and orders concerning prisoners-of-war have been based solely on military considerations, while now a political objective must be attained, which is to protect the German nation from Bolshevik inciters."[54]

In the months that followed, high-ranking officers toed the Party line. In early October the commander of the German Sixth Army reminded his soldiers that their task was "the complete destruction" of the Soviet army and "the eradication of the Asiatic influence on the European cultural sphere." The troops had tasks "which go beyond the conventional unilateral soldierly tradition. In the East the soldier is not only a fighter according to the rules of warfare, but also a carrier of an inexorable racial conception and the avenger of all the bestialities which have been committed against the Germans and related races."[55] Some weeks later Colonel General Hoth explained to his men, "Here in the East spiritually unbridgeable concepts are fighting each other: German sense of honour and race, and a soldierly tradition of many centuries, against an Asiatic mode of thinking and primitive instincts, whipped up by a small number of mostly Jewish intellectuals." Their "mission," he said, was "to save European culture from the advancing Asiatic barbarism. . . . This battle can end only with the destruction of one or the other; a compromise is out of the question."[56]

Three major international conventions—the First Hague Convention (1899), the Second Hague Convention (1907), and the Geneva Convention (1929)—had established minimal standards of prisoner maintenance. As the Soviet Union had not signed the last convention, which had merely clarified certain points, the German High Command chose to assume that none of the conventions applied. As a result, by early summer 1941 conditions had grown catastrophic in the camps holding Soviet prisoners of war. "Camps" is a euphemism: a camp consisted of fields surrounded by a barbed-wire fence. The inmates had to build the shelters themselves, but no materials were provided. Höss recalled after the war that one such camp—Lamsdorf in Silesia, which reportedly held some 200,000 prisoners—"was simply a square area of land where most of the Russians huddled together in huts made from the earth which they had built themselves. Food distribution to the camp was irregular and totally inadequate. The prisoners cooked for themselves in fire pits in the ground."[57] A camp near Chelm in Poland held 150,000 prisoners. According to a local eyewitness:

> The marl soil on which the camp stands turns after rain into thick mud,
> in which the prisoners must sleep, without even a handful of straw. Food

is worse than poor. The prisoners are actually dying of hunger and eat grass, straw and odd bits from the refuse heap. An epidemic of dysentery is spreading alarmingly among them. They are black with dirt, and eaten up by lice. No medical attendance is available. Their treatment is barbarous. The German guards torture them, beating them with the butt-ends of their rifles or with whips, and stabbing them with bayonets. Persecution goes on in broad day-light, before the eyes of the people living in the neighborhood of the camp. Naked prisoners are fastened to the fence surrounding the camp in such a way that they have to stand on their toes. Their hands are tied behind their backs and fastened to the fence. A string is passed round their necks under their chins and fastened to the fence. A man cannot stand long in such a position: he gradually sinks down, his arms turn round, and the string tightens round his neck and slowly strangles him. Such scenes may be observed every day.[58]

Maddened by despair, many prisoners lost all restraint. It merely confirmed the prejudices of the guards; as one wrote to his friend, "What would become of our cities and of our women if this horde ever succeeded in invading Germany? Fortunately, our *Führer* has foreseen everything and will prevent this evil."[59]

For Himmler, the Soviet prisoners of war were a gift from heaven. To deliver on promises made to IG Farben, he needed them for forced labor. Things were not going well in Auschwitz. Ambros and Dürrfeld were increasingly pessimistic. "The plant is under construction on what was once Galician soil with, by German standards, the lowest civilizatory and cultural level," they wrote to Krauch. "There is no water, no decent sewage system, no inn, no schools, no German cinema in the 'town' Auschwitz! . . . All of this makes it very difficult to hire and settle German employees."[60] Immediate action was required. "In this construction year we must begin to build 1,000 houses to domicile at least the qualified workers who will settle here from western and central Germany. Ten German shops, an inn, and a hospital will have to be established to service the Germans."[61] Himmler knew they were discontented and he understood that if he wanted to preserve his project he had to act quickly. He approached the army and offered to take 100,000 Soviets off their hands. The generals happily obliged.[62]

WHEN THE FIRST 10,000 Soviet prisoners arrived in Birkenau in early October, no camp had been built for them. But the newly appointed Bischoff acted promptly and instructed the thirty-three-year-old Bauhaus graduate Fritz Ertl to draw up a plan.[63] Ertl proposed a two-part camp for a projected 97,000 inmates. (See plate 12.) The smaller part, Bauabschnitt I (Building Sector I, abbreviated as BA I), designed to hold just under 17,000 prisoners, was a quarantine camp; BA II and BA III constituted the regular camp. The two sectors were separated by a "neutral zone." This plan was modified at a mid-October meeting, and the second version became the basis for the fourteen-page accompanying document explaining the design.[64] The single most important change was an expansion of the camp's capacity from 97,000 to 125,000 inmates. One drawing, illustrating a section of the standard hut to be built, makes it absolutely clear that this increase was achieved simply by cramming more inmates into the same space. The original drawing, signed by Bischoff on 8 October, listed a capacity of 550 men. A week later Bischoff crossed out "550" and replaced it with "744."[65] (See plate 13.) Nothing else had changed. Perhaps Bischoff's decision was inspired by the arrival of the first prisoners of war. Like so many other Germans, he perceived the starved, ill, and emaciated men as subhumans entitled to even less living space than he originally had allotted them. But while he may have despised them, he also feared them. Visions of anarchy led to another modification. The main camp (BA II and BA III) was now subdivided into twelve smaller, self-sufficient

Fritz Ertl, 1938. Berlin Document Center.

"camps." This arrangement, which recalls Culemann's urban building block design principles, was to persist through all subsequent modifications. Finally, a rail spur to connect the camp directly to the railway junction a mile to the east was included. In the future, prisoners were to arrive by train.

Working in a hurry, Bischoff had been drafting plans without informing Berlin, and without a sense of how much money would be available. Reminded by SS headquarters that his designs would be funded only if he followed the usual procedures, he created a package hastily.[66] The total budget was to be 8.9 million marks, and BA I was already under construction and would be finished in fourteen days, Bischoff wrote in an accompanying letter. It was not the last time that

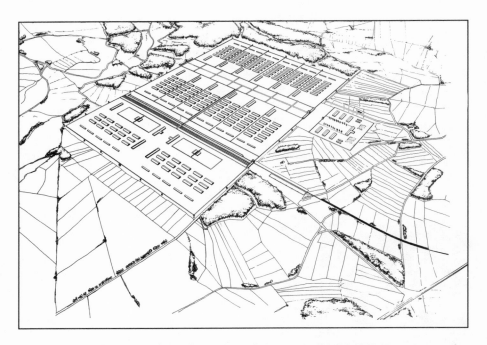

Bird's-eye view of the second design for Auschwitz-Birkenau, October 1941. Reconstruction and drawing by Robert Jan van Pelt, Peter Gallagher, and Paul Backewich. Authors. South of the railway terminus is the quarantine camp with two delousing stations, two kitchens, thirty barracks each accommodating 744 men, five toilet barracks, and five washrooms. To the north of the terminus are twelve camps, each with twelve barracks, one kitchen, one toilet barracks, and one washroom. The quarantine section was completed as planned; the main camp was expanded in size and changed further as a result of Hans Kammler's decision to replace the brick barracks with prefabricated wooden horse stables.

Bischoff was far too optimistic about both money and speed of construction. The Soviet prisoners were, as Höss observed, "perfectly willing to work but were unable to accomplish anything because of their weakened condition. . . . The entire body organism was finished and could no longer function."[67] Berlin saw the matter differently. The SS head office reduced the total cost from 8.9 million marks to 7.7 million, as the standard rate for labor costs did not apply; the prisoners were to build the camp themselves, free of charge.

The designs illustrate the ideology reflected in Bischoff's stroke of the pen through the number 550 and insertion of 744. The German identification of the Soviet soldier as an *Untermensch* was translated into architectural terms. Prisoners were to be housed in 174 barracks, each barrack subdivided into sixty-two bays, and each bay having three "roosts." A roost was originally supposed to hold three prisoners, but Bischoff's numerology increased the capacity to four. To sleep, sit, and keep his belongings, each prisoner was now provided with "private" space that amounted to the surface dimensions of a

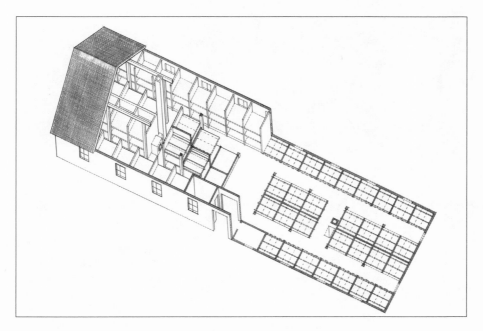

A brick barrack at Auschwitz-Birkenau. Drawing by Kate Mullin. Authors. N.B.: This is an axonometric drawing; the three-dimensional effect is derived from the exact measurements and angles of the original plan. See plate 13.

*Postcard. Interior of a
Birkenau barrack after
liberation by the Red Army,
spring 1945. Authors.*

large coffin or the volume of a shallow grave. The cost per barrack was to be
12,400 marks, or 16.67 marks per inmate.

Inmates were denied the minimum space needed to exist. Tadeusz Borowski, who was interned in Auschwitz in 1943 as prisoner number 119,198,
described the conditions in the camp as more horrendous than medieval fanta-
sies about hell:

> If the barrack walls were suddenly to fall away, many thousands of people,
> packed together, squeezed tightly in their bunks, would remain suspended
> in mid-air. Such a sight would be more gruesome than the medieval

paintings of the last Judgement. For one of the ugliest sights to a man is that of another man sleeping on his tiny portion of the bunk, of the space which he must occupy, because he has a body—a body that has been exploited to the utmost: with a number tattooed on it to save on dog tags, with just enough sleep at night to work during the day, and just enough time to eat. And just enough food so it will not die wastefully. As for actual living there is only one place for it—a piece of bunk. The rest belongs to the camp, the fatherland.[68]

This design showed a blatant disregard for international law protecting prisoners of war, who were to be treated like German soldiers.[69] Not only were they not treated like German soldiers; they were not even on a par with German concentration camp inmates. A comparison of the Ertl-Bischoff plan and the official SS standards for concentration camp barracks, issued that same month by Kammler, reveals that the concentration camp inmates had almost six times the space allocated to the Soviet *Untermensch*.[70] The standard concentration camp barrack provided eighteen times as much light. In Ertl's design for Birkenau the toilets and washrooms were housed in sixteen wash barracks

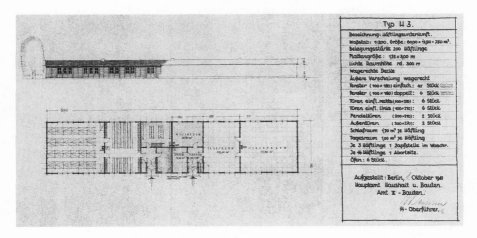

Type sheet for a barrack. Auschwitz-Birkenau State Museum, box BW(B) 3,3a, file BW 3/5. Barrack type Häftlinge 3 *(prisoners 3) is one of the twenty-five type sheets issued by Hans Kammler in the fall of 1941 to standardize concentration camp design. One barrack was to house a total of 200 inmates in two sections. Each section contained a day room, a dormitory, a washroom, and a toilet room.*

and eighteen latrines, or one wash barrack per 7,800 inmates and one latrine hut per 7,000 inmates, while the figures for concentration camp inmates were twenty times and twelve times more generous, respectively.

The design of the wash barracks and the privies was, in fact, lethal. Terrence Des Pres has argued that the Germans' "excremental assault" on the inmates was the result of a deliberate policy to destroy the last vestiges of the prisoners' sense of self-worth. It was not enough to kill the prisoners. They were to be killed when they were totally broken. Only when the inmates were crushed would the SS "reach the orgasmic peak of their potential domination. . . . Spiritual destruction became an end in itself, quite apart from the requirements of mass murder."[71] Des Pres is incorrect that the defilement was the result of the SS's desire to exercise total power. Architects and bureaucrats are to blame: the design was inadequate, and not enough material and financial resources were allocated for the camp's construction. Whether the architects designed to degrade the prisoners or not, the result was the same: with the latrines submerged in excrement, with very little water to be had at very few points, and with mud everywhere, what remained was an inmate population without the means to preserve any outward sign of human dignity. As Des Pres asked, "How much self-esteem can one maintain, how readily can one respond to the needs of another, if both stink, if both are caked with mud and feces?"[72]

Were the architects simply incompetent? The "privy" meant to serve 7,000 inmates was a shed with one concrete open sewer serviced by far too little water, no seats, no "shame walls" for privacy, and one long beam as a back support. The result was a catastrophe. Gisella Perl, an inmate of BA I after it had become the women's camp of Birkenau, succinctly described the situation the prisoners faced. "There was one latrine for thirty to thirty-two thousand women and we were permitted to use it only at certain hours of the day. We stood in line to get in to this tiny building, knee-deep in human excrement. As we all suffered from dysentery, we could rarely wait until our turn came, and soiled our ragged clothes, which never came off our bodies, thus adding to the horror of our existence by the terrible smell which surrounded us like a cloud." The construction itself was an affront. "The latrine consisted of a deep ditch with planks thrown across it at certain intervals. We squatted on these planks like birds perched on a telegraph wire, so close together that we could not help soiling one another."[73] Ertl and Bischoff's structure was an assault and a biological disaster.

THE ATTENTION THE Auschwitz architects failed to give the latrine design was focused on the crematorium. Shortly after Bischoff had begun work on Birkenau in October 1941, he realized that the existing crematorium of the concentration camp (later to be known as crematorium I), designed for an inmate population of 10,000, would not suffice to service the prisoner-of-war camp. He summoned the Topf engineer Kurt Prüfer, who had supplied the incinerators of the crematorium in the main camp.[74] Arriving in Auschwitz on Tuesday, 21 October, for a two-day design session, Prüfer suggested combining three muffles (openings for corpses) in a single furnace. As Birkenau promised to be a temporary camp, it would be a waste of money to build an expensive structure such as a crematorium on a site that was going to revert to farming a few years later.[75] Therefore the crematorium would be built in the main camp across from the administration building and next to the existing crematorium.

Prüfer could advise Bischoff on the technological side of the project. For the architectural aspects, Bischoff relied on Kammler's type sheets. As we have seen, Kammler had announced the model designs he had developed "for provisional and permanent crematoria, incinerating sites, and execution grounds of various kinds" in his annual report.[76] The model Bischoff used conformed to civilian law regarding crematoria and included a coal supply room on one side of the large incineration hall and an autopsy room on the other. (See plates 14 and 15.) Below the autopsy room, underground, were three morgues leading off a vestibule. A two-door elevator, opening onto both the autopsy room and the incineration hall, ran to the vestibule below, thus facilitating the transfer of corpses between floors.[77]

Werkmann developed preliminary designs which Kammler approved in late November and sent to Auschwitz on the basis of Prüfer's calculations and Kammler's type. Bischoff's office, which now had more responsibilities and the new name of Zentralbauleitung der Waffen SS und Polizei, Auschwitz O/S (Central Building Authority of the Waffen SS and the Police, Auschwitz in Upper Silesia), worked with Werkmann's design to produce eight blueprints for a new crematorium.[78] (See plate 16.)

As the architects were developing these plans, Prüfer was busy calculating the implications of his suggestion to unite three muffles in one incinerator. It proved to be a difficult problem. Prüfer had no experience with triple-muffle furnaces, and he had increased the size of each muffle. Furthermore, new air flow systems were needed. Greater power was required for the forced-air

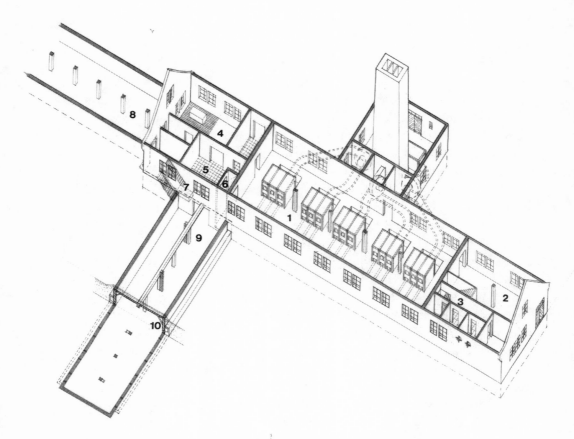

The crematorium, originally designed for the main camp but ultimately erected in
Auschwitz-Birkenau as crematorium II. Drawing by Kate Mullin. The
incineration hall with the five triple-muffle furnaces occupies the center of the building
(1). To the right are the fuel storeroom (2) and the rooms for the inmates working
the installation (3); to the left are the two dissection rooms (4 and 5) and the two-door
elevator (6) opening onto both the incineration hall and the first dissection
room. The elevator descends into a vestibule that is connected to the outside by two
staircases and a chute for corpses (7). The two large morgues (8 and 9) extend
far beyond the footprint of the building. One of the morgues is equipped with a double
ventilation system (10) to draw in fresh air and extract foul odors. This piping
made it possible to transform the morgue into a gas chamber with little effort. N.B.:
This is an axonometric drawing; the three-dimensional effect is derived from the
exact measurements and angles of the original plan. See plate 16.

system to fan the flames of the incinerator; the furnace room, the autopsy rooms, and the largest of the three corpse cellars required a ventilation system that extracted the hot, foul air; and the second-largest mortuary was to have a fresh-air supply also.[79]

There is no indication that either Bischoff or Prüfer envisioned any homicidal use for these rooms and machinery but, from its inception, the presence of the powerful ventilation system charged the design with a genocidal potential which would require small modifications to actualize.[80]

FROM THE MOMENT of their arrival, the Soviet prisoners of war had died more rapidly than the SS expected. As Höss recalled, "the situation really became terrible during the muddy period in the winter of 1941–42. They could bear the cold, but not the dampness and wearing clothes which were always wet. This together with the primitive, half-finished, hastily thrown-together barracks at the start of Camp Birkenau caused the death rate to steadily climb."[81] Snow began to fall at the end of November. Höss sent a report to Berlin suggesting that a catastrophic situation had developed. Kammler phoned Bischoff in response (3 December) demanding a full report within twenty-four hours. Bischoff's reply introduced the bad news with some statistics to impress his boss in Berlin with how much work had been done: in a little over one month 140,000 cubic feet of earth had been moved, 1,600 concrete foundations poured, and 86,000 cubic feet of brickwork erected, using 1.1 million bricks. Furthermore,

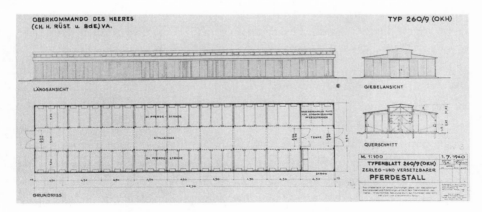

Design of the standard army horse stable barrack. Auschwitz-Birkenau State Museum, box BW (B) 3,3a, file BW 3/1. The horse stable barrack came as a kit and could be easily erected and dismantled.

600 concrete posts had been erected for the fence and 100,000 feet of barbed wire put into place. The bad news was that only two of the huts in BA I had been completed, twelve were partially completed, work could begin on the girders in seven, and the walls of nine were under construction.[82]

A major reason for this slow progress, Bischoff explained, was that the Russians had not been supplied with building materials. According to his own original brief of October, ''the barracks will be built from brick, as there is no wood available, and the material will be derived in part from the demolition of the hamlet of Birkenau,''[83] but the SS overseers had not given the Soviets the tools with which to cannibalize the houses in Birkenau. The houses were to be pulled down with their bare hands and the barracks built likewise. This had contributed to the high mortality rate; in the month of October, 1,255 Soviets had died. None of this was welcome news to SS headquarters in Berlin, where the prisoners were considered an asset. Kammler assigned Birkenau 253 prefabricated wooden huts that had been designed as horse stables for the army, each of which would house 400 prisoners.[84] They could be assembled in less than a day by a crew of thirty unskilled men led by one carpenter, and with no loss of life.

Bischoff directed his staff to design a new master plan for Birkenau, substituting the prefabricated huts for brick barracks in BA II and BA III, which was duly completed.[85] As the former held fewer inmates than the latter, the number of dwelling barracks per camp section increased from twelve to twenty-eight. The latrines and washrooms, however, remained where they were at the end, which meant that prisoners in the farthest barrack had to walk a great distance to get to the toilet or to wash. Poor planning? Inadequate design? Incompetence? Criminal negligence? Whatever the reason, the result was calamitous.

Kammler's allocation did not arrive until early summer of 1942, and in the meantime the Soviets continued to die: by the end of January almost 8,000 of the 10,000 men had perished and another month would suffice to kill nearly all the remaining 2,000. The architects recognized the catastrophic conditions in the camp. At the western edge of BA II and BA III, a new zone was designated which was to include two auxiliary crematoria and ten corpse cellars. This increased the corpse storage capacity six times, which, if Auschwitz-Birkenau were filled to its joint projected prisoner population of 155,000, would bring the camp in line with the ratio found in other concentration camps. If the number of inmates decreased, however, the daily corpse storage and incineration capacities would increase.

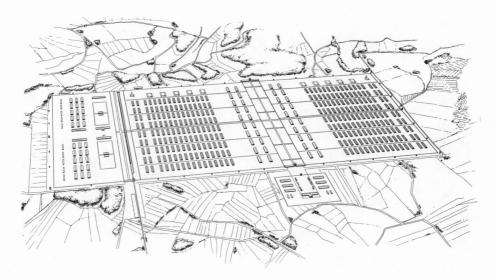

Bird's-eye view of the third design for Auschwitz-Birkenau, January 1942. Reconstruction and drawing by Robert Jan van Pelt, Peter Gallagher, and Paul Backewich. Authors.
South of the railway terminus is the quarantine camp with two delousing stations, two kitchens, thirty barracks each accommodating 744 men, five toilet barracks, and five washrooms.
To the north of the terminus are ten camps, eight of which have twenty-eight wooden horse stable barracks, two kitchen barracks, two storage barracks, two wooden toilet barracks, and two wooden washroom barracks; the other two camps are half the usual size. To the west of the living section of the camp are two strips each with two hospital barracks, five morgues, and a backup crematorium. Both of these crematoria were canceled by Kammler on 27 February 1942.

NO MORE SOVIET prisoners of war arrived. As it became increasingly clear that Operation Barbarossa had failed as a blitzkrieg, Germany had to mobilize all its resources to continue the war. With more men called up for service and more demands on German industry—especially the armaments industry— even the Soviet prisoners of war became a resource too precious to be wasted. ''The lack of workers is becoming an increasingly dangerous hindrance for the future of the German war and armament industry,'' Field Marshal Keitel informed various military agencies and ministries on 31 October. ''The Fuehrer has now ordered that the labor of the Russian prisoners of war should also be utilized to a great extent by large-scale assignment for the requirements of the war industry.''[86] A week later Reich Marshal Hermann Göring gained control over all prisoners of war and promptly announced that the Russians would be

View of horse stable barracks in Building Section II, 1943, Auschwitz-Birkenau State Museum, neg. BW 20995/431.

Postcard. Interior of one of the horse stable barracks in Building Section II after liberation by the Red Army, spring 1945. Authors. A masonry heating duct connecting the two small ovens at either side occupied the center of the barrack. In theory this contraption should have ensured the even distribution of heat throughout the space. The system did not work.

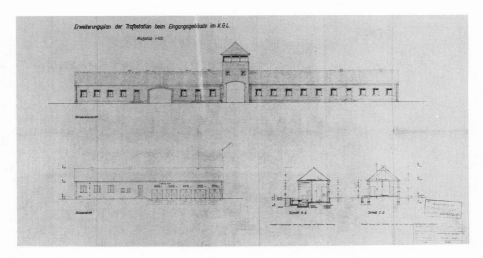

Elevation of the gate to Birkenau, 1943. Auschwitz-Birkenau State Museum, box BW
(B) 9/1, file BW 9/1. Originally the gate was asymmetrical, with the tower
and the railway entrance at the building's northern edge. At the end of 1943 the
building was expanded to the north to create space for a transformer station.

primarily employed in mining, railroad maintenance, the armaments industry, and agriculture. Building was given a low priority.

Göring charged the Labor Allocation Division of the Office of the Plenipotentiary of the Four-Year Plan with the creation and execution of a policy to exploit the labor potential of the Soviets. On 8 January the division issued a decree. All prisoners of war were assigned to the armaments industry and to a selected number of other realms, such as agriculture, forestry, and mining. None could be employed for construction work.[87]

The decree of 8 January brought an end to Himmler's plan to amass a large Soviet labor force to build the town of Auschwitz. He had to look elsewhere, and his eye fell on the Jews.

CHAPTER 9

SUMMER 1941

OSWIECIM HAD BEEN "AVOIDED BY LIFE FOR THOUSANDS OF YEARS, AS DEATH kept watch there," the Polish judge Jan Sehn claimed in his 1945 official report on the German atrocities in Auschwitz. Civilization had bypassed "the small, provincial Polish town of Oswiecim . . . far from the main railway centres and the more important lines of communication." The Germans, Sehn explained, had used both "the climate and geographical character of Oswiecim with premeditation in their criminal design."[1]

Sehn's belief that the town of Oswiecim was somehow doomed to host a German death camp, and that the SS consciously acted to realize that destiny, has become commonplace in the popular and even the scholarly literature on Auschwitz. With varying degrees of sophistication, the argument is that the wartime horrors of Auschwitz had to happen in that godforsaken, desolate, remote place in the wilds of Poland. One of the few who resisted the temptation to link the establishment of an extermination camp to some inevitable precondition was the ex-inmate Tadeusz Borowski. "Where Auschwitz stands today, three years ago there were villages and farms," he wrote the same year Sehn submitted his report. "There were rich meadows, shaded country lanes, apple orchards. There were people, no better nor worse than any other people. And then we arrived. We drove the people out, demolished their houses, levelled the earth, kneaded it into mud. We built barracks, fences, crematoria. We brought scurvy, phlegmon and lice.''[2]

Unlike Sehn, Borowski remembered that before the first Poles were beaten to death in Zasole, before the first Soviet prisoners of war were gassed in crematorium I, and before the first transport of Jews was subjected to selection in Birkenau, the ultimate transformation of Auschwitz into an extermination camp was not a foregone conclusion. More successfully than Sehn, Borowski negotiated the paradox that underlies every historical narrative: that while in everyday life each moment unfolds with no certainty of outcome, "history" is based on a known conclusion that charges an otherwise tedious chronicle with portent and pregnancy.[3] "Auschwitz used to be an ordinary town," we wrote at the beginning of our narrative, and the end was there, invisible but present. If Auschwitz had not become an extraordinary town, no one would care that it used to be an ordinary town. The end gives value, meaning, and significance to the past ordinariness of the town. Every bit of information that is included cannot but become an annunciation of the end to come. Whether we want it or not, the misery of Auschwitz dominates our understanding of its history before that evil occurred.

But evil need not have occurred. People, individual people and groups of people, nearly all German and nearly all male, enacted that evil, perpetrated that misery. The history of Auschwitz, in short, could have been a different story. As the novelist Robert Musil remarked in *The Man without Qualities*, history has neither author nor script. The course of history has only one inherent quality he explained, and that is its tendency to go off course.[4]

WHEN DID THE HISTORY of Auschwitz "go off course"? According to Rudolf Höss, Himmler discussed the transformation of Auschwitz into an extermination site as early as June 1941. Is he correct? Did he have a conversation with Himmler in June 1941? If so, did they talk about the construction of killing installations at Auschwitz? And if they did, did Himmler mean, in June 1941, that this murder machinery was to be used to kill Jews?

Höss's statements about Himmler's decision to designate Auschwitz as a death camp are our sole source of direct information about this issue. After pursuing him for almost a year, the British captured Höss on 11 March 1946 in northern Germany. They brought him to Nuremberg, where he spoke at great length for three consecutive days to an American interrogator, Whitney R. Harris.[5] In the affidavit that Harris then drafted and Höss read, corrected, and signed, Höss

Rudolf Höss after his capture. Auschwitz-Birkenau State Museum.

claimed, "I was ordered to establish extermination facilities at Auschwitz in June 1941." At least 2.5 million people "were executed and exterminated [in Auschwitz] by gassing and burning, and at least another half million succumbed to starvation and disease making a total dead of about 3,000,000."[6]

Gustave M. Gilbert, the prison psychologist at the Nuremberg trial, examined Höss. "He readily confirmed that approximately 2.5 million Jews had been exterminated under his direction," Gilbert wrote in his diary. In response to Gilbert's question as to how Höss had reacted to the order to become a mass murderer, he amplified his earlier statements. "In the summer of 1941, Himmler called for me and explained, 'The Führer has ordered the Endlösung [Final Solution] of the Jewish question—and we have to carry out this task. For reasons of transport and isolation, I have picked Auschwitz for this. You now have the hard job of carrying this out.' As a reason for this he said that it would have to be done at this time, because if it was not done now, then the Jew would later exterminate the German people, or words to that effect. For this reason one had to ignore all human considerations and consider only the task—or words to that effect." And Höss explained to Gilbert, "I had nothing to say; I could only say *Jawohl!*"[7]

On the witness stand Höss repeated his account of the origin of Auschwitz as the central site of the Holocaust. "In the summer of 1941 I was summoned to Berlin to Reichsführer SS Himmler to receive personal orders. He told me something to the effect—I do not remember the exact words—that the Führer had given the order for a final solution of the Jewish question. We, the SS, must carry out that order. If it is not carried out now then the Jews will later on destroy the German people." According to Höss, Himmler had chosen Auschwitz because it was easily accessible by rail and because the extensive concentration camp grounds ensured isolation. This was a secret matter; the "conference concerned the two of us only and I was to observe the strictest secrecy."[8]

Höss's Nuremberg confessions seemed to close the case concerning the origins of Auschwitz as a death camp. But internal inconsistencies in his statements, as well as additional indirect but pertinent evidence, suggest that Höss reinterpreted events that indeed had occurred in light of the ultimate outcome. Probably, he had a conversation with Himmler in June 1941. Probably, they spoke about the construction of extermination facilities at Auschwitz. But probably, *in June 1941*, those installations were not intended for the mass murder of Europe's Jews.

Let us look at Höss's statements more closely. In his affidavit saying he "was ordered to establish extermination facilities at Auschwitz in June 1941," he also explained that "at that time, there were already in the General Government three other extermination camps: Belzek, Treblinka, and Wolzek [Sobibor]."[9] These camps, however, came into operation only in 1942. In a detailed account of the role of Auschwitz in the genocide of the Jews that Höss wrote later that year, he again related Auschwitz to the other killing sites and again made the same mistake about the dates. "Himmler greeted me with the following: 'The Führer has ordered the Final Solution of the Jewish Question. We the SS have to carry out this order. The existing extermination sites in the East are not in a position to carry out these intended operations on a large scale. I have, therefore, chosen Auschwitz for this purpose.' "[10] In June 1941 there were no "existing extermination sites in the East."

As Höss insisted on various occasions that the conversation took place in 1941, although acknowledging that he may have been confused about the exact words, it would seem plausible that there was a meeting in June 1941 and that he was ordered "to establish extermination facilities." But how large were these meant to be, and for whom? As we saw in chapter 7, Höss visited

SS headquarters in Berlin in mid-June to discuss the new master plan of the camp, created in the euphoria of the IG Farben support. Himmler too was in town, to celebrate the fifth anniversary of his appointment as chief of the German police. Given his personal interest in the future of Auschwitz, it seems likely that the completion of the first master plan was an occasion for him to chat with Höss. It is not likely, however, that they conferred about a decision to liquidate European Jewry; most historians of the Holocaust agree that such a policy crystallized later that summer. But just because they did not discuss a planned genocide of the Jews does not mean that they did not discuss building some kind of extermination facility at Auschwitz. Again as we have seen, the building department of the SS was developing standard designs for "provisional and permanent crematoria, incinerating sites, and execution grounds of various kinds" in 1941, and it is quite possible that Himmler's instruction related to a specific design issue that came up in the examination of the new master plan, or to a general policy to equip concentration camps with killing installations that could handle larger groups of victims.

Scrutiny of the master plan under review reveals a curious design decision. The architects had chosen a far corner of the compound, behind the camp prison with its execution yard in the center, and relatively close to the hospital, for the site of a new crematorium. If everyone who died in the camp had been an inmate, this arrangement would have made sense. But Auschwitz also served the Kattowitz Gestapo as an execution ground and, according to the plan, the condemned would have had to traverse the whole camp. Someone disapproved of this arrangement: in the next master plan the new crematorium is right next to the old one, conveniently close to the back gate of the camp. That "someone" may have been Himmler.

The extant killing facilities themselves may have prompted discussion of more sophisticated capabilities. At Himmler's request, the T4 program had been extended to the concentration camps, and at the end of May a medical team had arrived in Auschwitz to select sick inmates. According to the new 14f13 (14f referred to the Inspectorate of Concentration Camps, and 13 to "the special treatment of sick and frail prisoners") program guidelines, mentally ill, chronically sick, and invalid inmates who were Jewish were automatically selected for "special treatment," while the other cases were referred to the headquarters at Tiergartenstrasse 4 for a final decision. Ultimately, 575 prisoners were approved for death. It was impossible to liquidate the prisoners within the camp without causing great commotion, so the 575 men were loaded onto a train and transported hundreds of miles to the T4 gas chamber at Sonnenstein.[11] Höss's visit to Berlin occurred after the selection had taken place but before the transport had been organized, and the camp's inability to handle the institutionalized mass murder of the 14f13 program must have been a topic of discussion, especially as he and Himmler knew that these selections were to be a regular element of camp life.

Finally, in June 1941 the Germans had another reason to equip a concentration camp with a more sophisticated facility for mass extermination. Operation Barbarossa was to begin on 22 June, and the war was to become a global conflict. The memory of the "stab in the back" of the First World War loomed large and was taken seriously. Hitler was absolutely convinced, as he wrote in *Mein Kampf*, that "if at the beginning of the War and during the War twelve or fifteen thousand of these Hebrew corrupters of the people had been held under poison gas, as happened to hundreds of thousands of our very best German workers in the field, the sacrifice of millions at the front would not have been in vain. On the contrary: twelve thousand scoundrels eliminated in time might have saved the lives of a million real Germans, valuable for the future."[12]

After the German army had begun its attack on the Soviet Union, Hitler confided to his inner clique that everything would be done to prevent a repetition of 1918. The soldiers at the eastern front did not have to worry. The stab in the back which had defeated the armies in 1918 would not recur. "I've ordered Himmler," Hitler assured his audience, "in the event of there some day being reason to fear troubles back at home, to liquidate everything he finds in the concentration camps. Thus at a stroke the revolution would be deprived of its leaders."[13] Hitler expanded on this idea on at least one other occasion: not only all the camp inmates but also rioters, opposition leaders, and Soviet prisoners of war should be killed if a "stab in the back" was attempted. "As for the justification of these summary executions, I've only to think of the German idealists who are risking their lives in front of the enemy."[14]

When Himmler met with Höss in Berlin, Heydrich was already preparing the mass murder of potential instigators of a revolution among the Soviet prisoners of war. Himmler had detailed Heydrich to negotiate with the High Command of the Armed Forces to permit his Security Police to canvass the prisoner-of-war camps to select and liquidate "Bolshevik driving forces." They reached an agreement later that month. These "special measures," the High Command claimed, were justified by the "special situation" in the East.

Drawing by A. Tippmann of an actual scene of revolutionary soldiers in Munich, November 1918. Illustrierte Zeitung, no. 3935 (1918). Sterling Memorial Library, Yale University.

''While so far the regulations and orders concerning prisoners-of-war have been based solely on military considerations, now a political objective must be attained, which is to protect the German nation from Bolshevik inciters and forthwith take the occupied territory strictly in hand.''[15]

Himmler's instruction to Höss was, we believe, a result of Hitler's instruction to Himmler. Hitler had made it clear that, if revolution was attempted during this war as it had been at the close of the last war, the participants and camp inmates were to be killed in extermination installations in the concentration camps. Himmler, anticipating Hitler's wishes, was not going to wait for trouble. The Soviet prisoners of war were the first group to be targeted, and Heydrich was already busy with that problem. The question was, Where were they going to be killed? Auschwitz was a good choice. The agricultural estate gave Himmler control over a fifteen-square-mile area in which he could do anything he pleased in secrecy, while none of the other major camps available to him at that time offered him this space. Then too, Auschwitz was located in a community in flux. Because of the ethnic-cleansing program in the region, it was easier to do unsavory things in Auschwitz than, for example, in Dachau, which was close to Munich, or in Sachsenhausen, near Berlin. Furthermore, in June 1941 Auschwitz was one of the few camps designated for rapid expansion and seemingly favored with financial, institutional, and corporate support. Himmler expected millions of marks and abundant building materials to become available for use in Auschwitz, and he may have thought it possible to include some kind of extermination installation in the IG Farben–sponsored program.

The feared stab-in-the-back opposition never materialized, but the idea of using concentration camps as execution grounds for undesirables whose very existence threatened the state bore fruit. A few hundred Soviet prisoners of war arrived in Auschwitz on 18 July. They were locked into block 11. As no extermination facility had been built yet, liquidation followed the established pattern. "They were shot in the gravel pits . . . or in the courtyard of Block 11," Höss recalled.[16] Following the arrival of the first Soviet transport and the departure of inmates to be killed under the aegis of the 14f13 program, the camp physicians began to experiment with more clinical methods of murder. Prisoners were injected with phenol, gasoline perhydrol, ether, and other substances, and after a number of trials phenol injections in the heart were found to be the most efficient.[17]

LET US RETURN to Höss's consistent connection of the establishment of extermination facilities in Auschwitz with the Final Solution of the Jewish Question in his postwar statements. Does this mean that Himmler already had decided in June 1941 that Auschwitz was to be what it became a year later? Or to ask the question differently, how did the Final Solution serve Himmler's needs, fit his ambitions, or help his career?

Throughout the twenty-one months since the war had begun, Himmler had well understood that deportation, settlement, and authority over territory went together. Authority to oversee settlement meant control of the area to be settled, and authority to oversee deportation implied control of the area to which the deported would be sent. In 1939 Himmler had acquired implicit territorial authority in the Lublin district, which was to be used as a Jewish reservation ruled by the Reich Security Main Office. He had lost it in 1940, when Governor General Hans Frank had asserted his own ambition. Himmler had once again faced the prospect of territorial authority through the Reich Security Main Office's plan in 1940 for the creation of a Jewish "homeland" in Madagascar, and again the promise of power did not materialize. In short, although neither of the two earlier attempts to find a territorial solution for the Jewish Problem had worked out, both involved the prospect of territorial powers.

In the spring of 1941 the issue of control over land was central to Himmler. His deployment of the Einsatzgruppen in 1939 to subdue German-conquered Poland through the arrest and execution of political opponents of the Germans had substantiated his claim to be Reich Commissioner for the Consolidation of the German Nation. When Hitler decided to invade Russia, Himmler antici-pated that the same pattern could be repeated on a larger scale in the new campaign. As in 1939, he would deploy Einsatzgruppen to terrorize the occu-pied lands and, also as in 1939, his reward would be responsibility for German settlement there. If in Poland his dream was the renewal of German medieval villages and towns, in Russia he hoped to take up the aborted history of the Goths, who had run a Germanic empire in the fourth century.

Hitler and Himmler agreed in February that the latter would deploy Einsatzgruppen behind the front line, and the generals agreed to the plan. Expecting victory over Russia in two months at most, and having been told that Himmler's units would operate only during the hostilities, they were prepared to accept this intrusion into their domain to preserve the army's standing with Hitler.[18] "In the area of operations, the *Reichsführer-SS* is, on behalf of the *Führer*, entrusted with special tasks for the preparation of the political administration, tasks which result from the struggle which has to be carried out between two opposing political systems," Field Marshal Keitel instructed his staff on 13 March. "Within the realm of these tasks, the *Reichsfü-hrer-SS* shall act independently and under his own responsibility."[19]

Himmler, Heydrich, the bureaucrats of the Reich Main Security Office, and the army agreed that four battalion-size Einsatzgruppen would be allowed to operate both close to the front line and in the rear, and that they would "carry out special security police tasks *outside the ambit* of the military forces." These were to include "executive measures vis-à-vis the civilian population."[20] Significantly, the agreement did not mention Jews. In a first directive, dated 2 July, Heydrich emphasized that extremist elements such as saboteurs, snipers and agitators, senior and middle-rank Communist Party officials, and "Jews in the service of the Party or the State" should be executed. Furthermore, "no steps will be taken to interfere with any purges that may be initiated by anti-Communist or anti-Jewish elements in the newly occupied territories. On the contrary, these are to be secretly encouraged."[21] According to the

Swiss scholar Philippe Burrin, these instructions were similar to the orders given in September 1939, when the Einsatzgruppen were involved mainly in liquidating the Polish ruling classes. Heydrich's directive to foment pogroms suggests, moreover, that there was as yet no general plan for extermination. "There is a world of difference in the thinking behind the covert and rational organization of the genocide and the open use of the most savage violence," Burrin has observed. "Pogroms could only trigger the impulse to flee; [in the late summer], when the extermination was under way, Heydrich's men, on the contrary, would resort to subterfuge to reassure the Jewish population, to keep it in place or entice it to return, to ensure as complete a massacre as possible."[22]

As he was preparing his men to subjugate the Russian lands ruthlessly, Himmler waited in vain for the appointment he felt was his just reward. Hitler did not extend Himmler's authority as Reich Commissioner for the Consolidation of the German Nation to include Russia, probably because he did not want to offend Göring, who as plenipotentiary for the Four-Year Plan claimed control of the wealth in that area. In 1939 Himmler had taken the land and Göring the industries, but this was not an option in 1941. In the National Socialist New Order, the East was to become the breadbasket of Europe and the industrial plants were to be dismantled. The division of spoils that had worked in 1939 could not be repeated in 1941.

Perhaps to preserve the balance of power between Himmler and Göring, Hitler turned to Alfred Rosenberg, the Balt who had been his mentor in Russian affairs twenty years earlier and who had become politically irrelevant by 1941. Rosenberg and Hitler met on 2 April to discuss the future civil administration of the occupied territories in the east, and Hitler promised his old mentor an appointment as "political advisor in a decisive capacity."[23] Rosenberg immediately drafted a program that included the destruction of Judeo-Bolshevism, the re-Germanization of ancient Livonia, and the transformation of the rest of Russia into "a dumping ground for undesirable elements of the population."[24] He also submitted a list of men to run the occupied territories, and suggested that the chief executive officer of the area should be called "Protector General of the German Reich for the Occupied Territories."[25] Himmler was not mentioned.

Hitler was convinced, and on 20 April he asked Rosenberg to establish a department to deal with Eastern Questions. Rosenberg consolidated his claim through another plan, dated 29 April, in which he called for "a general treatment" of the Jewish Problem.[26] A memorandum of 7 May was more specific.

Alfred Rosenberg. Authors.

"After the customary removal of Jews from all public offices, the Jewish question will have to undergo a decisive solution through the institution of ghettos or labour battalions. Forced labour is to be introduced."[27]

Rosenberg was prepared to yield little to Himmler. As Reichsführer-SS and chief of the German police, Himmler could appoint a permanent representative to Rosenberg's office—with no executive power. As Reich Commissioner for the Consolidation of the German Nation, he could appoint a liaison—who would operate under the direct control of Rosenberg's office.[28] Himmler was livid. He saw all too clearly that Rosenberg was laying claim to settlement operations in the eastern territories, and he refused to surrender his own stake. The two rivals turned to Hitler.[29]

Himmler's ally Martin Bormann tried to intervene with Hitler on his friend's behalf. When he was unsuccessful, Himmler realized that more drastic measures were needed. Subsequent events suggest that Himmler understood that, if he were to prevail over Rosenberg, he would have to be seen as the more brutal and efficient. If the situation were properly framed, Himmler could show up Rosenberg as a moral coward in regard to the Jewish Question. Rosenberg's proposal to establish ghettos and create labor battalions had been tried in Poland but, for the Germans, to too little effect. If Himmler were to propose a plan that would take care of all of Europe's Jews in a truly "Final Solution," he would transcend the parochialism of Rosenberg. This did not necessarily entail the murder of the eleven million Jews in Europe. At this point, Himmler probably envisioned an SS-administered reservation in Russia, like the failed Nisko and Madagascar projects. Perhaps part of his plan was that those who could not be transported so many thousands of miles would be killed. Auschwitz was a perfectly situated way station on the railway lines from the west of Europe to the east, to Russia, the territory he aimed to control and the site of the planned reservation. The Germans already had experience with deportation by train. Perhaps the facility at Auschwitz was to be used to get rid of the corpses of those who had died en route, and to unload those too weak to survive the rest of the journey. Diminishing the numbers to be transported would be an efficient use of rolling stock. Höss's repeated assertions in his postwar statements that Himmler had asked for an extermination facility to be used to kill Jews and that he, Höss, was "to observe the strictest secrecy" about this, even with his own superiors, may well have been accurate.

Succeeding developments in Auschwitz suggest this interpretation. Adolf Eichmann, the Jewish emigration specialist whose center of operations had been Vienna and Prague, was now chief of the Subsection on Jewish Affairs of the Reich Security Main Office in Berlin. It was his job to map the location of Jews throughout Europe and to devise schemes to move them out of German and German-occupied territories; it was in this capacity that he came to be responsible for railway transport. When preparations began at the end of August for the mass deportation of German Jews to Russia, Himmler sent Eichmann to visit Höss in Auschwitz. A few weeks later, an extermination facility was ready for operation. The German Jews, however, were not shipped in as anticipated, because the territories that Himmler had expected to use as a Jewish reservation remained under Soviet control.

The crematorium stood idle for the next five months. The first direct intersection between the history of Auschwitz and the course of the Holocaust, to which Höss referred in his Nuremberg statement, had been a nonevent. But in 1946, knowing full well that Auschwitz became a central site of Judeocide, Höss hardly would have considered those few months of great importance. For those, however, who seek to understand what occurred in the context of possibilities that did not materialize, it is important to recognize that there was no direct causal connection between the conversation Himmler and Höss had in June

1941, Eichmann's visit that August, and the beginning of the mass annihilation of Jews in Auschwitz in the spring of 1942. As we shall see, those murders of Jews evolved from another set of specific antecedent circumstances.

Himmler's directive to Höss to construct an extermination installation in Auschwitz set in place one piece of his campaign to extend his authority to the eastern territories. It was not his only move. A week before the invasion, he upgraded Ulrich Greifelt's Office of the Reich Commissioner into a full-fledged SS department. As the Staff Department of the Reich Commissioner for the Consolidation of the German Nation, Greifelt's bureau was equal to Heydrich's Reich Security Main Office and acquired far-reaching power within the SS and security empire. The settlement of the Russian lands would require unparalleled effort, and Greifelt now had the human resources at his command. If called upon, he was prepared.

At that same time, Himmler asked Konrad Meyer to draft a "general plan" for the East as an alternative to Rosenberg's program. Meyer finished his proposal, now lost, on 15 July.[30] From a long and critical commentary by Rosenberg's aide Dr. Erhard Wetzel, it would seem that Meyer calculated that the area to be settled was inhabited by 45 million non-Germans: Estonians, Latvians, Lithuanians, Poles, White Russians, West Ukrainians, and Jews. Of these, 31 million were to be deported over a period of thirty years, and 10 million Germans were to take their place.[31]

Meyer submitted a second and more complete version of his proposal in June 1942 which, presumably like the earlier draft, validated and substantiated Himmler's claim to authority in Russia. The first sentence of the project summary confirmed Himmler's power as Reich Commissioner for the Consolidation of the German Nation in the annexed territories (Danzig–West Prussia, Wartheland, and Upper Silesia); the second presented the logical deduction that this power applied to specifically defined areas of settlement in Russia. These so-called marches of settlement would "be under the exclusive control of the Reichsführer-SS as Reich Commissioner for the Consolidation of the German Nation."[32] "Exclusive" meant exactly that: in the areas to be settled by Germans in Russia, there was to be no interference by local governors, army commanders, Göring's agents, or Rosenberg.

THE INVASION OF the Soviet Union began on 22 June 1941, and Himmler's Einsatzgruppen followed the advancing army. The Security Police initially kept a low profile with regard to the anti-Jewish measures, standing aside while the local populations engaged in "spontaneous" pogroms. Its involvement was limited to shooting Jewish men suspected of, for instance, looting, and as Burrin has pointed out, "during the first weeks, the victims were executed according to the provisions of martial law."[33] Later on, military procedures were abandoned for the most efficient form of mass butchery. Submachine guns were now the favorite means of liquidation and, from the beginning of August onwards, women and children were killed also.

Both in the abandonment of traditional firing-squad procedures and in the inclusion of those who could not even be suspected of being guilty of anything but existence, the Einsatzgruppen moved towards the genocide of all Russian Jews. Two factors appear to have played a part. First, in the beginning of July when German victory followed victory, Hitler began to make increasingly brutal pronouncements, calling himself, for example, the Robert Koch of politics. Omnipotent, he could and would eradicate the bacillus and defend the healthy body of the German Nation. Second, Himmler, Hitler's most loyal vassal, had learned to anticipate his Führer's wishes, and the new language may have suggested to him that Hitler was ready for ruthless action against that most virulent strain of bacilli, the Judeo-Bolsheviks—that is, Russian Jews. And as of 16 July, Himmler had to take drastic action to please Hitler and to press his case.

On that fateful day in July, Hitler, Rosenberg, Reich Minister Lammers, Field Marshal Keitel, Reich Marshal Göring, and Nazi Party Chancellor Martin Bormann convened to discuss, in Hitler's words, "the task of cutting up the giant cake according to our needs."[34] In a long and passionate monologue, Hitler envisioned the creation of "a Garden of Eden in the newly occupied eastern territories." He called for the annexation and Germanization of Livonia, the ethnic German areas in the Volga, the Crimea, and oil-rich areas around the Transcaucasian city of Baku. The men argued about who was to be responsible for the civil administration of Russia. According to the minutes, someone mentioned Himmler's role in the territories to be Germanized, but no one spoke up for him: in the end the participants agreed that "Himmler was to have no greater jurisdiction than he had in Germany proper."[35] In Germany "proper" Himmler's jurisdiction was limited to the police, and in Russia he was to be in charge of security—nothing less and certainly nothing more. Hitler confirmed this circumscribed role the next day when he appointed Rosenberg Reich minister for the occupied eastern territories. He was to coordinate his policies with the military commanders, with Göring as plenipotentiary of the Four-Year Plan, and with Himmler as chief of the German police. Hitler's decree did not mention Himmler's responsibility as Reich Commissioner, but it did not state explicitly that Rosenberg was to be responsible for settlement either. The question of who was to Germanize Russia remained unresolved.

The meeting of 16 July and Rosenberg's subsequent appointment meant tactical defeat for Himmler. He did not protest. As Albert Speer recalled after the war, Himmler never appealed Hitler's decisions. "Instead he would patiently lie in wait, and then suddenly spring into action when he saw his chance."[36] In July 1941 Himmler did not just wait patiently. To show Hitler that he was still ready for the appointment, he prepared to implement Meyer's first general plan for the East in territories which were not under his jurisdiction but where his men provided the police force. The Lublin district was strategically positioned halfway between the annexed territories Himmler already controlled and the ultimate Russian area of settlement which he coveted. Furthermore, his trusted friend Odilo Globocnik was the higher SS and police leader in Lublin. The day Rosenberg received his ministry, Himmler ordered Globocnik to organize areas of German settlement around existing and projected SS police posts in the Government General and in occupied Russia. Himmler visited Globocnik in Lublin three days later. His activities in Lublin were staged to impress Berlin, but he also had some practical business to transact. His goal was to make Lublin the major supply base for SS colonization activity in Russia. To that end, he detailed Globocnik to enlarge the existing SS enterprises, which depended on Jewish forced labor, and to ensure an uninterrupted supply of manpower, directed him to establish a 50,000-inmate concentration camp in the Lublin suburb of Majdanek.[37]

As Himmler toured the central segment of his projected new zone of settlement, Heydrich took care of the rear and began to activate his end of the claim. In accordance with the pattern they had established, Himmler focused on colonization, while Heydrich took care of deportation. Now this entailed a visit to Göring. In 1941 Göring was officially responsible for "Jewish affairs," but in 1939 he had given Heydrich the task of preparing the emigration or expulsion of all German Jews. With the conquest of Russia, the space was available for a new Jewish reservation. Heydrich rightly assumed that a simple extension of the powers given to him in 1939 could strengthen Himmler's case for territorial powers in the East, and at the end of July he drafted a letter in which Göring was to authorize him to take charge of a Final Solution of the Jewish Question in Europe.

Complementing the task that was assigned to you on 24 January 1939 to find an as advantageous as possible solution of the Jewish problem through emigration and evacuation, I hereby charge you with making all necessary preparations in regard to organizational and financial matters for bringing about a complete solution [*Gesamtlösung*] of the Jewish question in the German sphere of influence in Europe. Wherever other governmental agencies are involved, these are to cooperate with you. I charge you furthermore to send me, before long, an overall plan concerning the organizational, factual and material measures necessary for the accomplishment of the desired [final] solution [*Endlösung*] of the Jewish question.[38]

Just as previous plans to solve the Jewish Question had included a territorial dimension, and therefore territorial authority, Himmler wanted this "overall plan" to carry similar powers. Heydrich visited Göring on 31 July, and the latter signed the letter.

HIMMLER'S FIRST USE of the murder of Jews as a chip for his bid for power was in Russia. Immediately after Göring signed Heydrich's letter, which confirmed Himmler's ultimate executive authority for the solution of the Jewish Question, the Einsatzgruppen began to massacre Jewish men, women, and children indiscriminately. The army, the only power that could have restrained the killing, stepped aside.[39] The generals' plans had been dashed. By the beginning of August they had to admit they had underestimated the resilience and efficiency of the Soviets, the vastness of the theater of operations, and the difficulties caused by poor roads. When they had planned Operation Barbarossa, the urge for *Lebensraum* had blinded them to the difficulties ahead.[40] As the advance of German mechanized units was hampered by mechanical breakdowns and supply problems, the Soviets quickly raised new divisions.[41] They were running weeks behind schedule, and they knew that if the Red Army was not defeated in two months, the campaign would fail and Germany would find itself in a permanent two-front war.[42] In a situation of escalating frustration and rage, the army gave a free hand to the Einsatzgruppen to mass murder Jews.

Within a month Himmler took steps to begin the deportation of German and Czech Jews to Russia. As we know, at the end of August Eichmann visited Auschwitz, which we believe was to serve as a transit point between Germany, Bohemia, and the projected reservation in the East. Eichmann discussed the design of an extermination facility with Höss, and they decided on the use of gas. They also agreed that the carbon monoxide chambers used in the T4 program would not do: the piping was too complex and the bottled gas too expensive.[43]

The Auschwitz personnel knew a great deal about hydrocyanide. In the summer of 1941 construction of delousing installations had been given the highest priority, and the lethal potential of Zyklon B was common knowledge. Höss instructed Lagerführer Karl Fritsch, who was responsible for the liquidation of the Soviets and was also in charge of the fumigation of the camp and the disinfection process in the extant gas chambers in blocks 3 and 26, to carry out a pilot experiment. Fritsch obliged with a transport of Soviet prisoners of war, whom he took to block 11 and locked into a basement cell. Fritsch threw Zyklon B crystals into the room and all the men died.

Encouraged by his success, Fritsch conducted the first mass execution with Zyklon B on 3 September. Wojciech Barcz, an inmate who worked as a nurse, recalled that a few months after the beginning of the war against the Soviet Union he was ordered to bring very ill inmates into the underground cells of block 11.

> They were locked into these cells. Around ten in the evening we heard that the SS drove a large group of people to that place. We heard screaming in Russian, orders of the SS, and the sound of beating. In the middle of the night three days later, we nurses were ordered to go to block 11. We had to clear the corpses from the basement cells. We saw that a large group of Russian prisoners simply had been gassed in those cells together with the sick inmates who we had brought there. The image we saw when we opened the cell doors was that of an overpacked suitcase. The corpses fell towards us. I estimate that some sixty corpses were pushed together in a small cell. It was so packed that they could not fall over when they died, but remained standing. . . . One could still see many signs of a terrible death struggle.[44]

The Germans were not satisfied. Some prisoners survived the ordeal, the procedure took too long, the corpses had to be transported to the crematorium on the other side of the camp, and it took two days to air out the building. The basement of block 11 was not the ideal gas chamber, but those first exercises had demonstrated that it was easy to convert any space into a Zyklon B gas chamber. Unlike the carbon monoxide gas chamber, with its system of pipes and perforated vents and its cumbersome gas cylinders, the hydrocyanide gas chamber required only a small porthole, preferably in the roof, through which to drop the Zyklon B crystals.

Fritsch remembered that the morgue of the crematorium in the *Stammlager* had a flat roof; it would be a simple matter to make one or more openings in it. He also knew that, a month or so earlier, the morgue had been equipped with a new and powerful ventilation system. As we have seen, the Political Department had begun to use the morgue as an execution site for those convicted by the Gestapo Summary Court. From the beginning, the executioners had complained about the nauseating smell, because it also served as a mortuary for the bodies of inmates who had died. Maximilian Grabner, the chief of the Political Department, had prevailed on Schlachter to install a more sophisticated ventilation system that not only extracted the foul air but also brought in fresh air from the outside.[45] Fritsch realized that such a ventilation system could deal with poisonous gas.

Fritsch's men punched three square portholes through the morgue roof and covered them with tightly fitting wooden lids.[46] The murder of 900 Soviets inaugurated the new gas chamber on 16 September.[47] "The entire transport fit exactly in the room," Höss recalled. "The doors were closed and the gas poured in through the openings in the roof. How long the process lasted, I don't know, but for quite some time sounds could be heard. As the gas was thrown in some of them yelled 'Gas!' and a tremendous screaming and shoving started toward both doors, but the doors were able to withstand all the force."[48] A few hours later the fans were turned on and the doors opened. "I really didn't waste any thoughts about the killing of the Russian POWs," Höss confessed in 1946. "It was ordered; I had to carry it out. But I must admit openly that the gassings had a calming effect on me, since in the near future the mass annihilation of the Jews was to begin."[49]

The expected transports to Auschwitz did not materialize, because the Russians were not defeated. Elsewhere, however, the destruction of Jews was triggered by the massive influx of German and Czech Jews being shipped to the east. Himmler informed Gauleiter Greiser of Wartheland on 18 September that he intended to send 60,000 German and Czech Jews to the Lodz ghetto. As there were not sufficient barracks in Auschwitz to hold so many people, the camp was not a viable transit point and the Jews were to remain in Lodz until the spring of 1942, when they would be sent on to Russia. The first transport of German Jews arrived in Lodz four weeks later, and in the next eighteen days a total of 20,000 were packed into the already overcrowded ghetto.

Greiser panicked and instructed Wilhelm Koppe, the local higher SS and police leader, to do something. Koppe did not fail him. He had, as he later claimed in print, a truly historic perspective on the situation. He believed that the Second Reich (1871–1918) had lost the ethnic war in the eastern marches because it had allowed liberal principles to prevail where the laws of war should have applied. "We National Socialists," Koppe wrote, "have learned from the mistakes of the past and the bitter experiences of the time of German powerlessness." Only the ruthless elimination of all non-German "intruders" would restore to Wartheland its historic mission: "to be a base for ethnic German penetration further to the east."[50]

Koppe not only remembered Bismarck's failure; he also recalled Herbert Lange's achievement. Lange had effected the T4 program in East Prussia, Danzig–West Prussia, and Wartheland with gas vans. Koppe dispatched Lange's Sonderkommando from Posen to the village of Chelmno, known to the Germans as Kulmhof, which he identified as the ideal "place of settlement" for the Lodz Jews. Koppe and Lange decided that between 100 and 150 Jews at a time were to be taken by truck to a country house in Kulmhof surrounded by a high fence. "The loaded lorries entered the camp grounds and stopped before the house, where the new-comers were addressed by a representative of the *Sonderkommando*, who told them that they were going to work in the East, and promised them fair treatment, and good food," Judge Wladyslaw Bednarz explained in his 1945 report.

He also told them that first they must take a bath and deliver their clothes to be disinfected. From the court-yard they were sent inside the house, to a heated room on the first floor, where they undressed. They then came downstairs to a corridor, on the walls of which were inscriptions: "to the doctor" or "to the bath"; the latter with an arrow pointing to the front door. When they had gone out they were told that they were going in a closed car to the bath-house.

Before the door of the country house stood a large lorry with a door in the rear, so placed that it could be entered directly with the help of a ladder.

The time assigned for loading it was very short, gendarmes standing in the corridor and driving the wretched victims into the car as quickly as possible with shouts and blows.

When the whole of one batch had been forced into the car, the door was banged and the engine started, poisoning with its exhaust those who were locked inside. The process was usually complete in 4 or 5 minutes, and then the lorry was driven to Rzuchów wood about 4 km (2½ miles) away, where the corpses were unloaded and burnt.[51]

By the time the gas vans had left the country house, a second truckload of Jews would arrive, unaware of what had happened to the earlier group. Unlike in the later camps in Belzec, Sobibor, Treblinka, and Auschwitz, where most people could guess that something was terribly wrong when they disembarked from the trains, those brought to Kulmhof would realize that the Germans did not mean what they said only when they saw the gas van—and then it was too late. For the Germans, Kulmhof was a great success: some 150,000 Jews were killed between 8 December 1941 and 9 April 1943. Only two survived: Simon Srebnik and Mordechaï Podchlebnik.

IN THE AUTUMN of 1941 it was clear to Himmler that Hitler was delighted with his policy to deport the German Jews to Russia. His public prophecy that, in the case of a war, the Jews would disappear from Europe was to be realized, Hitler told Himmler and Heydrich on 25 October. He had no qualms about it. "That race of criminals has on its conscience the two million dead of the First World War, and now already hundreds of thousands more. Let nobody tell me that all the same we can't park them in the marshy parts of Russia! Who's worrying about our troops?"[52] It also was obvious that the accompanying killing of Russian, Polish, and by then German Jews did not bother the Führer in the least. Even before the extermination camp at Kulmhof had come into operation, Hitler delighted his court with a saying of his old teacher Dietrich Eckart. "In all his life he had known just one good Jew," Hitler mused, "Otto Weininger, who killed himself on the day when he realized that the Jew lives upon the decay of peoples."[53]

By the end of November many individuals and agencies had taken the initiative to kill Jews: Koppe had set up his own extermination installation in Kulmhof, and Erhard Wetzel and his colleagues in Rosenberg's Ministry for the Occupied Eastern Territories were negotiating with unemployed T4 specialists to bring their expertise to Riga and Minsk. It was time to establish once and for all that Himmler was in charge.

To that end, Heydrich invited top bureaucrats of the Reich Chancellery, the Ministries of Justice, Interior, Foreign Affairs, and the Eastern Territories, and from the Four-Year Plan, the Government General, the Chancellery of the National Socialist Party, and various SS agencies, such as the Race and Settlement Main Office and Greifelt's Staff Department of the Reich Commissioner of the Consolidation of the German Nation, to a meeting to be held on 9 December in the Berlin Interpol Office, at 56 Am grossen Wannsee. The object, he said, was to secure "a uniform view among the relevant central agencies of the further tasks concerned with the remaining work on this final solution." The meeting was especially urgent because "from 10 October onwards the Jews have been evacuated from Reich territory, including the Protectorate, to the East in a continuous series of transports."[54] Heydrich included a photocopy of Göring's authorization letter of 31 July with each invitation.

For five years Himmler had been unwilling to forgo the labor potential of concentration camp inmates, and if the scheduled meeting at Wannsee confirmed his authority over the Final Solution to the Jewish Question, there was no reason not to use the labor potential of the Jews as an integral part of that solution. At Himmler's request the chief of SS construction, Hans Kammler, developed a provisional peace building program for the Waffen SS and the German police which required Jewish labor. Kammler believed that the only way the SS would get its share of the limited resources that were to be available for construction was to propose a bold plan that presupposed the allocation of money and materials to the SS, just as the armed services had such quotas.

Hans Kammler. Berlin Document Center. Höss remembered him as a tireless worker with "many good ideas; he was firmly planted in reality. . . . He hoped to achieve the impossible by force and finally had to admit that the war was stronger than he was. He lived a very simple, humble personal life and had a good family."

Kammler submitted a budget for a little over 13 billion marks, of which around 10 percent was to be spent in the annexed areas, and he ordered the design development of various projects to support the proposal.[55]

Himmler found Kammler's proposal insufficiently comprehensive, and suggested another 10 to 12 billion marks. Within two months he had come to the conclusion that this sum was laughable too. The SS building projects in the annexed territories alone would require 80 billion marks, which was sixty times the figure Kammler originally had budgeted. Himmler presumed that SS companies like DESt would supply him with stone, brick, chalk, and cement; he counted on a special arrangement with the Hermann-Göring-Werke for steel, and lumber was to be extracted from the Russian forests, but none of these materials could be produced without labor. Building construction, moreover, demanded skilled labor, which was going to be in very short supply. Himmler instructed Pohl to introduce vocational training for concentration camp inmates. "If we do not do this, then we will not get proper barracks, schools, offices, or houses for our SS men in Germany, and I, as Reich Commissioner for the Consolidation of the German Nation, will not be able to create the enormous settlements with which we will make the East German."[56]

Kammler proposed the creation of roving SS building brigades for the provisional peace program. Each brigade would consist of two regiments, and every regiment was to be divided into three battalions. The first battalion would prepare the building site, level the terrain, lay streets, and dig basements, drainage canals, and wells; the second would do the rough construction work; and the third would be responsible for painting, electrical installation, heating, and plumbing. Kammler calculated that, with all the resources of the concentration camps at his disposal, he could not muster even one brigade of 4,000 men. To cover the 1942 SS building program, he would need 175,000 workers—"inmates, prisoners of war, Jews, etc."[57]

A paradoxical situation had developed in the SS empire. For Heydrich, chief of the Reich Main Security Office, the Jews were a nuisance to be deported, while for Kammler, chief of SS construction, Jews who could work were a valuable resource—and their value was rapidly rising as it became increasingly unlikely that Himmler would receive the other 90,000 Soviet prisoners of war the army had contracted to give him. Heydrich and Kammler articulated the conflict that, at the end of 1941, troubled Himmler. There was no place for Jews in the German utopia he had dedicated himself to creating, but he could not build it without them. These apparently mutually exclusive demands were resolved at the Wannsee conference rescheduled for 20 January 1942.

Heydrich chaired the meeting, opening with a reference to Göring's letter of July. He then proceeded to assert his central objective. "Primary responsibility for the handling of the final solution of the Jewish question . . . is to lie centrally, regardless of geographic boundaries, with the Reichsführer SS and Chief of the German Police," he claimed flatly.[58] No one protested. He had prevailed, and he wrapped up the conference in ninety minutes. Too few Jews had emigrated between 1933 and 1939, and 11 million remained in Europe. "Under appropriate direction, in the course of the final solution, the Jews are now to be suitably assigned as labor in the East," he announced. "In big labor gangs, with the sexes separated, Jews capable of work will be brought to these areas, employed in roadbuilding, in which task a large part will undoubtedly disappear through natural diminution. The remnant that may eventually remain, being undoubtedly the part most capable of resistance, will have to be appropriately dealt with, since it represents a natural selection and in the event of release is to be regarded as the germ cell of a new Jewish renewal. (Witness the experience of history.)"[59] In view of the provisional peace program and discussions about the deployment of Jews in building brigades, apparently Heydrich meant what he said when he talked about labor gangs.

Himmler met Hitler three days after the Wannsee conference. There is no record of their conversation, but later that day Hitler hinted at the content of their talk. "If I withdraw 50,000 Germans from Volhynia, that's a hard decision to take, because of the suffering it entails," he complained. "The same is true of the evacuation of Southern Tyrol. If I think of shifting the Jew, our bourgeoisie becomes quite unhappy: 'What will happen to them?' Tell me whether this same bourgeoisie bothered about what happened to our own compatriots who were obliged to emigrate?" By 1942 this was pure fantasy, of course. If such a bourgeoisie ever had existed, it certainly had not raised its voice on behalf of the Jews for at least a decade. But such facts were of no concern to Hitler. "The Jew must clear out of Europe. Otherwise no understanding will be possible between Europeans. It's the Jew who prevents everything. When I think about it, I realise that I'm extraordinarily humane," he told his admirers. "I restrict myself to telling them they must go away. If they break their pipes on the journey, I can't do anything about it. But if they refuse to go voluntarily, I see no other solution but extermination." Jews were a danger and a threat. They were at the forefront of those who were ready to stab Germany in the back. "Why should I look at a Jew through other eyes than if he were a Russian prisoner-of-war? In the p.o.w. camps, many are dying. It's not my fault. I didn't want either the war or the p.o.w. camps. Why did the Jew provoke this war?"[60]

Three days after listening to his Führer, Himmler sent a telegram to Richard Glücks, the inspector of concentration camps. "As no Russian prisoners of war can be expected in the near future, I am sending to the camps a large number of Jews who have emigrated from Germany. Will you therefore make preparations to receive within the next four weeks 100,000 Jews and up to 50,000 Jewesses in the concentration camps."[61]

Having received full authority over the Final Solution, and with that over all of Europe's Jewry, Himmler was now free to dispatch Jews to take the place of the Soviet prisoners of war. Although he did not specify which camps would be affected, in only two were Soviets an essential part of the planned inmate population: Auschwitz and Majdanek. But while the idea to replace prisoners of war with Jews worked in principle, Himmler's initial plan to dispatch German Jews immediately for that purpose was not practicable. As it transpired, the immediate deportation of 150,000 Jews from the Reich and the protectorate of Bohemia and Moravia was difficult from an organizational point of view.[62] There were also delays due to the official procedures for the transfer of German Jewish property to the Reich. Himmler's telegram was premature. German Jews could not take the place of the Soviets. If a quick fix were to be found for Himmler's problem in Auschwitz, he would have to find another group of Jews who could be quickly assembled and moved and who did not warrant the attention of German bureaucrats.

THE JEWS OF Hitler's client state of Slovakia, ruled by the Fascist cleric Monsignor Dr. Josef Tiso and the National Socialist professor Vojtech Tuka, fit the bill. As the Holocaust historian Yehuda Bauer has explained, in 1940 the German government had compelled Tuka to agree to send 120,000 Slovak workers to the labor-strapped Reich. The Slovaks regretted this arrangement and dragged their feet. Finally, in the late summer of 1941 the Germans demanded the immediate transfer of 20,000 workers. Asked if they would take 20,000 Slovak Jews, the Germans declined. They were just beginning to deport all remaining Jews from the Reich.[63]

Tiso and Tuka continued to hold out. In the hope that the Germans would be prepared to take Jews instead of Christians, they concentrated thousands of young Slovak Jews into three labor camps. In January 1942 they again offered the German Labor Ministry 20,000 strong, young Jews for work in Germany. Within days a response came in the form of Dieter Wisliceny. Officially an attaché at the German embassy in Bratislava, Wisliceny was in fact Eichmann's local agent. He had learned from Eichmann that Himmler needed Jews to replace the Soviet prisoners of war in Auschwitz, and he was instructed to accept the Slovak offer of 20,000 able-bodied Jews on Germany's behalf: 10,000 would be sent to Auschwitz and 10,000 to Majdanek. The deal was made official on 16 February. "As part of the measures for the Final Solution of the European Jewish Question, the German Government is pre-pared to take over 20,000 young, strong Slovak Jews immediately and to transport them to the East, where there is need for labour," a senior official of the Foreign Office, Martin Luther, cabled the German legation in Brati-slava.[64] Tiso and Tuka were delighted.

"The order came four weeks prior to the end of March," Helen Tichauer-Spitzer, one of the targeted 20,000 Jews, recalled. "End of February. They printed large placards which were pasted on kiosks. No written invitation. They announced that Jewish girls, unmarried, I think it was fifteen or sixteen through forty-five or fifty, were ordered to assemble on a certain date. It was the twenty-first of March, I remember, on a Monday."[65]

Helen understood that nothing good would come of this, but "the order said that if you don't report, your parents will be taken instead. So it was a little bit of a tricky business. Nobody wanted to sacrifice their parents. If I would have undertaken to escape to the neighboring countries, the parents would be taken instead."

Helen, however, seemed to have another option. She was a sign writer, and her "employer, who was German, decided to ask for an exemption because there was a shortage of manpower in the profession." The employer was successful; the exemption "was signed; it was ready." But "it was that bloody Monday which was the turning point in my life. I had to leave for the collection point early in the morning, before office time, so I could not go to my employer and collect the permission. I still had to leave because if I wouldn't have reported at the gathering point, they would have picked up my parents. It was a very tricky business. It was bad luck. One day difference and I could have stayed."[66]

Helen reported to "the gathering point, an empty ammunition factory near the railway station," where she was kept until Saturday morning. When another 999 people had been assembled, the Slovak Hlinka guards loaded them onto a train, squeezing them in to boxcars. "The journey took one day, one night, and late in the afternoon of the next day we arrived. We arrived on a Sunday." The train stopped "in an open field before the [Auschwitz] railway station. We had to leave everything behind. They marched us to the main gate. I went through the *Arbeit macht frei* gate."[67]

The Slovak women were destined for Birkenau, but there had been a delay in the Germans' building schedule. Birkenau officially had been in operation since the beginning of March, when the remaining Soviet prisoners of war, a group of German criminals, and 1,200 sick male inmates from the lazaret had been moved to BA I, the area designated for the women. The transfer of the women to Birkenau had to wait; in the meantime they were packed into ten specially walled-off barracks in the base camp at Auschwitz.

"They were not prepared for us," Helen Spitzer recalled. "They didn't know what to do with us. Everything went in such a hurry. They were so quick on the trigger. When we arrived, they just pushed us in to a barrack, and the next day they shaved us and put us into some old Russian uniforms."[68]

By the end of April ten Slovak transports had arrived and 9,655 Slovak Jews had been registered. None of the transports included old people or young children, and there were no selections on the train ramps.

WHILE NEGOTIATIONS WERE carried on between the German Foreign Office and the Slovak government, Auschwitz already had become the destination for one particular group of Jews residing on Reich territory: those considered unfit for work in the so-called Schmelt program. A high-ranking SS officer and senior civil servant in the provincial administration, Albrecht Schmelt had established a special organization in 1941 to monopolize the forced labor of Jews left in Upper Silesia after the deportations to the Government General had been halted.[69] Schmelt employed some 50,000 Jews, and he felt that his program was burdened by too many mouths to feed. He knew about the Gestapo Summary Court executions in Auschwitz, and in mid-February he shipped some 400 older Jews to the camp.

The morgue of the crematorium in the main camp had been transformed in September 1941 into an effective gas chamber which could hold 900 people, so there was plenty of room to kill the elderly Jews with ease. Shortly before their arrival, the SS closed off the roads and emptied the offices that had a view of the crematorium. "A sad procession walked along the streets of the camp,'' Pery Broad remembered after the war. ''All of them had large, yellow Jewish stars on their miserable clothes. Their worn faces showed that they had suffered many a hardship.''[70]

It was not an ideal situation from the camp management perspective, Broad noted. Using the crematorium as a killing station for a transport of old people interrupted the life of the camp. Broad's superior, Maximilian Grabner, who had overseen the whole operation, had even had to run a truck engine to drown out the death cries of the victims. Whereas the Germans had felt no need to camouflage the execution of Polish hostages or resisters ''duly'' sentenced by a court of justice, the murder of elderly Jews was another matter. It was not a useful deterrent against resistance activities.

The Slovaks, in the meantime, realized that when the 20,000 young Jews they had got the Germans to take left home, many families would have no breadwinner and would become a burden on the Slovak economy. Eichmann initially refused even to discuss the matter but, after the successful ''special treatment'' of the elderly Upper Silesian Jews, concluded that the same solution could be applied to Slovak Jews unable to work.

The Germans had a few practical problems to work out. As the Slovak Jews were to be brought to Birkenau and not to Auschwitz, and as killing them in crematorium I would interrupt the life of the main camp, they considered building an extermination installation close to the new satellite camp. Hans Kammler arrived in Auschwitz on Thursday, 27 February, to meet with Höss and Bischoff. There are no minutes of this conference, but its content can be ascertained from a letter Bischoff wrote to Topf a week later. Kammler had decided to cancel their order for the backup incinerators included in the Birkenau plan of 6 January, Bischoff explained. The large crematorium with five triple-muffle incinerators that had been designated for the main camp was to go to Birkenau instead.[71] Obviously Kammler wanted construction to proceed quickly. Those furnaces had been ordered almost four months previously and he expected they would be available soon.[72] Furthermore, the designs for the crematorium that was to house these incinerators had been both completed and approved. On paper, at least, everything was ready for the crematorium they had agreed upon the previous October. A blueprint of the prisoner-of-war camp shows that Kammler decided to locate the new crematorium in the northwestern corner of Birkenau, adjacent to an abandoned cottage that had belonged to a Polish peasant named Wiechuja.[73] The interior of this cottage, known as ''the little red house,'' was converted into two gas chambers within a few weeks, and on 20 March it was put into operation

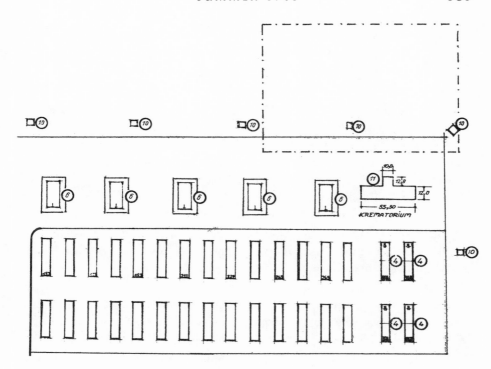

Part of a modified version of the third design for Auschwitz-Birkenau, early March, 1942.
Osobyi Archive, Moscow, coll. 502/2, file 95. In this version of the design of 6
January 1942 (see p. 273), both backup incinerators have been erased, and crematorium II
has taken the place of the incinerator in the northwest corner of the camp. Bunker
1, which was torn down in 1943, must have stood somewhere in the area defined by the
broken line (added by authors). The structures marked with a 4 are wash and toilet
barracks, 6 are morgues, 10 are guard towers, and 11 is crematorium II.

as "bunker 1."[74] The first group of victims was another transport of Schmelt Jews "unfit for work."[75]

There is no doubt that Kammler's visit led to the Germans' reversal of their decision about the mass deportation of Slovak Jewry. Once Kammler had organized the construction of the crematorium in Birkenau, the Reich Security Main Office permitted the German Foreign Office to negotiate seriously. On 3 March Tuka announced in the Slovak State Council that, pending certain financial arrangements, the Germans had agreed to take the remaining 70,000 Jews.[76] The Germans were doing them a favor and were to be compensated at the rate of 500 marks for every Jew deported. For this sum, however, the Slovak government was guaranteed that "the Jews accepted as part of the de-Judaization of Slovakia will remain permanently in the Eastern territories and will not be offered any possibility of re-immigrating into Slovakia."[77] The state was free to seize Jewish property left behind.

It took Eichmann another month to arrange the deportation of families. Several transports went to Lublin, where a selection took place just outside the station. Able-bodied men were marched to Majdanek; the "unfit for work" were forced back onto the train, which continued its journey to killing installations which Christian Wirth, the architect of the T4 gas chambers, had built at Belzec on Odilo Globocnik's instructions.

Throughout May and June, no Slovak Jews were killed in bunker 1 in Birkenau; all the victims were Upper Silesian Jews. With the destruction of these Jews, mass murder became a fixture of life in Auschwitz, but it was not yet the camp's primary purpose. The history of bunker 1 was rooted in the well-established function of the camp as an execution ground for people convicted by the Gestapo court in Kattowitz. The deportation of Schmelt Jews to Auschwitz was independent of the massive deportations overseen by Eichmann. It was, and remained, a local affair.

Bunker 1 also was used to kill sick inmates, and here too its murder function developed from earlier practices: the 14f13 program. Once bunker 1 was operational, it was unnecessary to transport victims hundreds of miles to gas them; a short truck ride to Birkenau sufficed. Regularly replenished with new arrivals from the main camp, the "isolation station" created on 13 March became a much used holding pen. Selections of inmates in the isolation station were introduced on 4 May, and an unknown number of sick prisoners were loaded onto trucks, brought to bunker 1, and killed. From that date on, periodic selections in the isolation station harvested up to 90 percent of its inmates for death in the gas chambers.[78]

Bunker 1 was not very efficient, and sometime in June Höss began to plan the transformation of a second cottage, the "little white house," into what was now known as a "bathing facility for special actions."[79] According to Jean-Claude Pressac, Bischoff attempted to improve the efficiency of this gas chamber by applying the advice given in the Degesch pamphlet on how to design Zyklon B delousing chambers, but he could not obtain the necessary equipment. Following the architectural arrangement of the Degesch delousing chambers, Bischoff divided the cottage into four long, narrow, parallel rooms with doors on each side. This allowed for ample cross ventilation after the Zyklon B had done its work.[80]

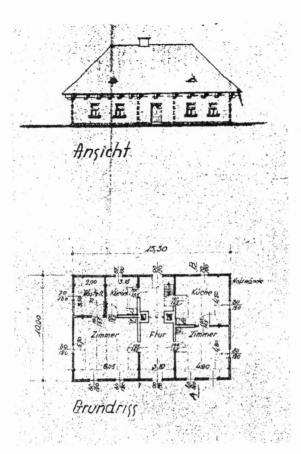

House 647, Budy, ca. 1942.
Osobyi Archive, Moscow, coll.
502/2, file 116. The cottages
transformed into bunkers 1
and 2 probably resembled this
house in Budy, drawn by
prisoner 23046 of the
Auschwitz Zentralbauleitung
in 1943.

Bunker 2 was operational by the end of June 1942. A Jewish Sonderkommando, or Special Squad, was formed on 4 July to service the killing installations.[81] That same day a first transport of 1,000 Jews was submitted to a selection on arrival. The Germans lined them up and chose 264 able-bodied men and 108 able-bodied women. The remaining 638 people were brought to the new gas chambers. André Lettich, a French Jewish doctor forced to work at bunker 2, described it as a "peaceful looking house."

More than five hundred metres further on were two barracks: the men stood on one side, the women on the other. They were addressed in a very polite and friendly way: "You have been on a journey. You are dirty. You will take a bath. Get undressed quickly." Towels and soap were handed out, and then suddenly the brutes woke up and showed their true faces: this horde of people, these men and women were driven outside with hard blows and forced both summer and winter to go the few hundred metres to the "Shower Room." Above the entry door was the word "Shower." One could even see shower heads on the ceiling which were cemented in but never had water flowing through them.

These poor innocents were crammed together, pressed against each other. Then panic broke out, for at last they realised the fate in store for them. But blows with rifle butts and revolver shots soon restored order and finally they all entered the death chamber. The doors were shut and, ten minutes later, the temperature was high enough to facilitate the condensation of hydrogen cyanide, for the condemned were gassed with hydrogen cyanide. This was the so-called "Zyklon B," gravel pellets saturated with twenty per cent of hydrogen cyanide which was used by the German barbarians.

Then, *SS Unterscharführer* Moll threw the gas in through the little vent. One could hear fearful screams, but a few moments later there was complete silence. Twenty to twenty-five minutes later, the doors and windows were opened to ventilate the rooms.[82]

The corpses of these 638 Slovak Jews, who had been promised an agricultural life in the Lublin area by their president, Monsignor Tiso, were buried in the adjacent meadow.

CHAPTER 10

THE
HOLOCAUST

L ESS THAN A FORTNIGHT AFTER THE FIRST TRANSPORT OF JEWS WAS SUB-
jected to selection in Auschwitz, Himmler breezed into the office of his
confidant and personal masseur, Felix Kersten. "This is the happiest day of
my life," he exclaimed. "Everything I have been considering and planning on
a small scale can now be realized. I shall set to at once on a large scale—and
with all the vigour I can muster. You know me: once I start anything I see it
through to the end, no matter how great the difficulties may be."[1] Himmler
was euphoric because, after precisely one year of waiting and working, Hitler
had all but told him that he would be authorized to begin settlement of Russia.

Himmler was prepared. Konrad Meyer had completed his second and final
Generalplan Ost, or General Plan East, with detailed proposals for settlement
in the East—the annexed territories, the Government General, and Russia—
and the financial and demographic implications of these projects.[2] The aim of
the Generalplan Ost was, first, to identify and describe the measures to be
taken and the resources needed to complete the Germanization of the annexed
territories begun in the fall of 1939. Meyer submitted a budget of 500 million
marks as seed money for a massive program to reforest woodland, drain and
protect agricultural property, improve the energy and transportation infrastructure, establish farms, villages, and so on in accordance with earlier guide-

lines, develop industrial jobs, and ameliorate urban areas.[3] His estimated total of 45.7 billion marks to fund this work was to come from private capital, the state, a special fund to be administered by the Reich Commissioner for the Consolidation of the German Nation, the municipalities, industry, and the German railways.[4]

Meyer emphasized that the whole enterprise depended on forced labor; ''labor gangs of prisoners of war and comparable foreign workers,'' which in May 1942 meant Jews, were absolutely essential to its success.[5] Assuming that plenty of slaves would be available for a few years after the war, but that the pool would dry up quickly thereafter, he concentrated much of what had to be done into the first decade. Beginning with an initial slave labor force of

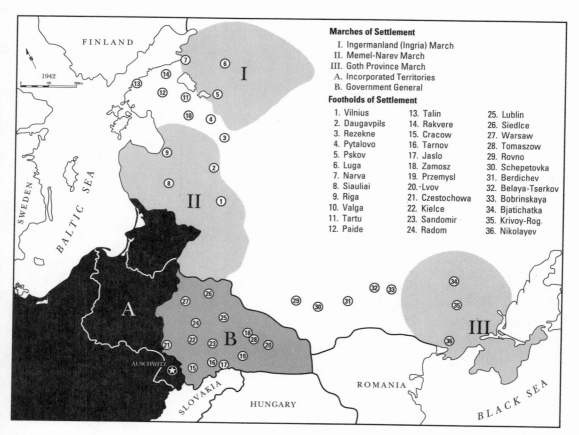

Meyer's General Plan East, map by Robert Jan van Pelt and Don Bonner.

450,000 workers, Meyer based his plan on the use of 300,000 in the third five-year period, 150,000 in the fourth, and 90,000 in the fifth. As Himmler was committed to Germanize the countryside before the towns, and as, practically speaking, forced labor was most easily used in rural conditions, Meyer focused on forests, agricultural land, roads, farms, and villages during the initial ten-year interval.[6]

In his discussion of the Germanization of the annexed territories, Meyer explicitly acknowledged the centrality of forced labor for the reconstruction of the German East. Himmler's projects of rural and urban reconstruction in Auschwitz during the preceding twenty months were now adopted as models for general policy. The Reichsführer-SS approved wholeheartedly. His goal, he announced in a speech about the plan to SS leaders on 9 June, was to "provide a stable foundation at last for the fifteen-hundred-year-old German history, a history that has seen radiant heights and infinite weaknesses and lows. With this foundation, individuals who come fifty, eighty, one hundred, or two hundred years after us can crumble or lose their heads without endangering the future of the German Empire. But, gentlemen, we still have to achieve that foundation." Most of the work, he explained, was to be done by slaves assembled in large cantonments. They were to build "our cities, our villages, and our farms, irrespective of losses. This is necessary because, after a long war, we will not be able to raise the money to create the infrastructure which would allow a truly Germanic people to live and root there within one generation."[7]

Himmler was pleased with Meyer's plan for the annexed territories. He was positively excited, however, by the second part of his proposal, which dealt with the consolidation of the German nation farther east in three "marches of settlement" and thirty-six smaller "footholds of settlement." This project anticipated the eastward migration of 3,345,800 settlers of Germanic descent, and was estimated to cost 20.9 billion marks.[8] Although financially less than half as ambitious as the program for the annexed territories, the project of the three marches and thirty-six towns and cities represented for Himmler the realization of his earliest aspirations and dreams. In the annexed territories his power as Reich Commissioner for the Consolidation of the German Nation was curtailed by many competing ministries and offices, while the General Plan East asserted that, for the anticipated twenty-five years of development, the Reichsführer-SS as Reich Commissioner for the Consolidation of the German Nation was to have sole legal, executive, and judicial authority in the marches and footholds.[9] In other words, Himmler would rule there like the

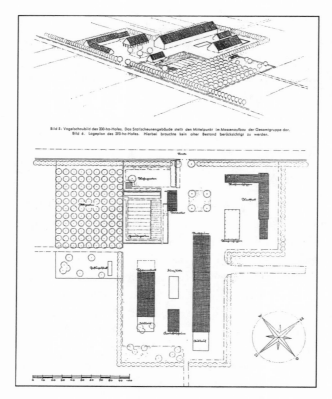

Bild 5. Vogelschaubild des 200-ha-Hofes. Das Stallscheunengebäude stellt den Mittelpunkt im Massenaufbau der Gesamtgruppe dar.
Bild 6. Lageplan des 200-ha-Hofes. Hierbei brauchte kein alter Bestand berücksichtigt zu werden.

Design of a large farm for the East. Reichskommissar für die Festigung deutschen Volkstums, Neue Dorflandschaften (1943). Federal Archive, Koblenz.

Ascanian Albrecht the Bear in Brandenburg, or the Grand Master of the Teutonic Order in Prussia. With this power, this degree of control, he could complete the Germanization of the marches in five years and that of the towns and cities in a decade and a half. With this prospect ahead, Himmler had no difficulty turning his back on the daily realities of the Germanization of the annexed territories: the incessant battles over turf, the governor of Danzig–West Prussia, who believed that most Poles in his province were really of German blood and could be Germanized after all, or the governor of Upper Silesia, who preferred uninterrupted industrial production to ethnic cleansing. If Hitler could be persuaded to adopt Meyer's plan, Himmler could walk away from all the problems and players and begin again without interference from anybody or anything.

The diaries of Felix Kersten suggest that on or around 16 July 1942 Himmler got Hitler's approval to proceed.[10] Kersten was a Balt who had fought in 1918 in General von der Goltz's German expeditionary force in Finland and with a Balt-Finnish volunteer force in Livonia. He had become a masseur famed

Marches and Footholds of Settlement	Year 1-5			Year 6-10			Year 11-15			Year 16-20			Year 21-25		
	Settlers per 1,000		Costs in Millions of Marks	Settlers per 1,000		Costs in Millions of Marks	Settlers per 1,000		Costs in Millions of Marks	Settlers per 1,000		Costs in Millions of Marks	Settlers per 1,000		Costs in Millions of Marks
	town	country		town	country		town	country		town	country		town	country	
Ingermanland	80.0	150.7	1,442.2	80.0	--	500.0	40.0	--	250.0	--	--	--	--	--	--
Memel-Narev Territory	76.0	522.3	3,739.6	76.0	--	475.0	38.0	--	237.4	--	--	--	--	--	--
Goth Province	130.0	600.1	4,563.4	130.0	--	813.0	65.0	--	406.2	--	--	--	--	--	--
Total of Marches	286.0	1,273.2	9,745.3	286.0	--	1,787.5	143.0	--	893.7	--	--	--	--	--	--
Vilnius	21.0	--	131.2	10.5	3.9	91.4	10.5	1.9	77.7	10.5	1.9	77.7	--	1.9	12.2
Daugavpils	4.5	--	28.1	2.2	3.9	38.5	2.2	1.9	26.3	2.2	1.9	26.3	--	1.9	12.2
Rezekne	--	--	--	1.3	3.9	32.6	1.3	1.9	20.4	1.3	1.9	2.4	--	1.9	12.2
Pytalovo	--	--	--	0.1	3.9	25.2	0.1	1.9	13.1	0.1	1.9	13.1	--	1.9	12.2
Pskov	6.0	--	37.4	3.0	3.9	43.2	3.0	1.9	31.0	3.0	1.9	31.0	--	1.9	12.2
Luga	2.6	--	16.4	1.3	3.9	32.6	1.3	1.9	20.4	1.3	1.9	30.4	--	1.9	12.2
Narva	2.3	--	14.7	1.1	3.9	31.5	1.1	1.9	19.4	1.1	1.9	19.5	--	1.9	12.2
Siauliai	2.5	--	15.6	1.2	3.9	31.9	1.2	1.9	19.9	1.2	1.9	19.9	--	1.9	12.2
Riga	38.5	--	140.6	19.2	3.9	144.5	19.2	1.9	132.4	19.2	1.9	132.4	--	1.9	12.2
Valga	--	--	--	1.1	3.9	31.1	1.1	1.9	18.9	1.1	1.9	18.9	--	1.9	12.2
Tartu	6.0	--	36.8	3.0	3.9	42.6	3.0	1.9	30.5	3.0	1.9	30.5	--	1.9	12.2
Paide	--	--	--	0.3	3.9	26.3	0.3	1.9	14.2	0.3	1.9	14.2	--	1.9	12.2
Talin	14.0	--	87.5	7.0	3.9	66.8	7.0	1.9	55.8	7.0	1.9	55.8	--	1.9	12.2
Rakvere	--	--	--	1.0	3.9	30.4	1.0	1.9	18.3	1.0	1.9	18.3	--	1.9	12.2
Cracow	24.2	--	151.2	12.1	4.6	104.2	12.1	2.3	90.0	12.1	2.3	90.0	--	2.3	14.3
Tarnow	4.5	--	28.2	2.2	4.6	42.6	2.2	2.3	28.4	2.2	2.3	28.4	--	2.3	14.3
Jaslo	--	--	--	1.0	4.6	34.8	1.0	2.3	20.6	1.0	2.3	20.6	--	2.3	14.3
Zamosc	2.5	--	15.6	1.2	4.6	36.4	1.2	2.3	22.2	1.2	2.3	22.2	--	2.3	14.3
Przemysl	5.1	--	31.9	2.5	4.6	44.6	2.5	2.3	30.2	2.5	2.3	30.2	--	2.3	14.3
Lvov	31.7	--	198.2	15.8	4.6	127.7	15.8	2.3	113.4	15.8	2.3	113.4	--	2.3	14.3
Czestochowa	13.3	--	83.1	6.6	4.6	70.2	6.6	2.3	55.8	6.6	2.3	55.8	--	2.3	14.3
Kielce	5.8	--	36.4	2.9	4.6	45.7	2.9	2.3	32.5	2.9	2.3	32.5	--	2.3	14.3
Sandomir	--	--	--	0.8	4.6	34.0	0.8	2.3	19.7	0.8	2.3	19.7	--	2.3	14.3
Radom	7.7	--	48.7	3.8	4.6	53.0	3.8	2.3	38.6	3.8	2.3	38.6	--	2.3	14.3
Lublin	11.6	--	70.6	5.8	4.6	64.3	5.8	2.3	50.5	5.8	2.3	50.5	--	2.3	14.3
Siedlce	4.0	--	25.0	2.0	4.6	41.2	2.0	2.3	26.2	2.0	2.3	26.2	--	2.0	14.3
Warsaw	123.2	--	770.0	61.6	4.6	413.5	61.6	2.3	400.0	61.6	2.3	400.0	--	2.3	14.3
Tomaszow	3.8	--	23.8	1.9	4.6	40.5	1.9	2.3	26.2	1.9	2.3	26.2	--	2.3	14.3
Rovno	3.5	--	15.6	1.2	5.5	42.1	1.2	2.7	25.0	1.2	2.7	25.0	--	2.7	17.2
Schepetowka	--	--	--	1.6	5.5	44.5	1.6	2.7	27.4	1.6	2.7	27.4	--	2.7	17.2
Berdichev	6.6	--	41.2	3.3	5.5	55.0	3.3	2.7	37.9	3.3	2.7	37.9	--	2.7	17.2
Belaya-Tserkov	4.6	--	28.8	2.3	5.5	48.7	2.3	2.7	31.6	2.3	2.7	31.6	--	2.7	17.2
Bobrinskaya	--	--	--	1.7	5.5	45.0	1.7	2.7	27.8	1.7	2.7	27.8	--	2.7	17.2
Bjatichatka	--	--	--	0.8	5.5	39.4	0.8	2.7	22.2	0.8	2.7	22.2	--	2.7	17.2
Krivoy-Rog	10.1	--	63.1	5.0	5.5	65.9	5.0	2.7	48.7	5.0	2.7	48.7	--	2.7	17.2
Nikolayev	10.1	--	62.5	5.0	5.5	65.5	5.0	2.7	48.4	5.0	2.7	48.4	--	2.7	17.2
Total of Footholds	368.6	--	2,302.2	191.1	162.5	2,227.7	194.1	81.3	1,721.2	194.1	81.3	1,721.2	--	81.3	508.1
Marches and Footholds	654.7	1,273.2	12,047.5	480.2	162.5	4,015.2	337.2	81.3	2,614.9	194.2	81.3	1,721.2	--	81.3	508.1

Table 2. Table summarizing the need for finances and settlers in the five marches of settlement and the thirty-six footholds of settlement. For the convenience of the reader, this table uses the present Polish, Estonian, Latvian, Lithuanian, and Ukrainian names of the footholds of settlement. The table is based on a German original in Federal Archive, Koblenz, coll. R 49, file 157c.

for his ability to alleviate nervous pains; Himmler became his patient in 1939, and by 1940 Kersten was in constant attendance. While he massaged, Himmler talked, and Kersten made notes afterwards. There is no doubt that Kersten's memoirs are self-serving and exaggerated, promoting his preventive influence on Himmler. But after careful analysis, the prominent Holocaust scholar Yehuda Bauer has concluded that his accounts are essentially accurate: ''The task is to peel off Kersten's colorful additions to get to the core.''[11]

In the beginning of July, Himmler joined Hitler at his headquarters in

Nun konnte im ganzen Lande darangegangen werden, nicht nur die Kriegsschäden zu beseitigen, sondern allmählich auch jene Zustände abzubauen, die das Land dem europäischen Kulturkreis entrückt hielten. Der Vernachlässigung und Verwahrlosung wurde überall energisch an den Leib gerückt. Arbeitskräfte waren infolge der herrschenden Arbeitslosigkeit allenthalben vorhanden. Aus Schmutz und Schlamm entstanden so allmählich überall nette saubere Städtchen, die dem Lande ein völlig neues Gesicht gaben. Ein Beispiel für viele : der Marktplatz von Jaslo in seinem früheren Zustande (im Bilde oben) und nach der Umgestaltung durch die deutsche Verwaltung (unten).

The town of Jaslo under Polish and German management. Das Generalgouvernement (1944). Authors. In October 1944 Governor-General Dr. Hans Frank reflected in the foreword of a special jubilee issue of Das Generalgouvernement—an expensive government-sponsored magazine—that five years of German reconstruction work in Poland would honor the German name. He claimed that he had transformed a rotten inheritance into a blossoming country worthy of "the heroes whose blood drenched this land, the farmers who plowed it in German fashion, and the burghers who, centuries ago, created a proud work of culture." A photo essay offered many instructive "before and after" pictures. One pair depicted the Ring of Jaslo, an ordinary town east of Auschwitz. Like Auschwitz, Jaslo was a medieval German foundation in the foothills of the Beskid Mountains. Like Auschwitz, Jaslo had become Polonifed and was to be re-Germanized once more. Unlike Auschwitz, Jaslo became one of Meyer's "footholds of settlement." In the first picture the large town square is surrounded by trees and occupied by people going about their ordinary business. In the second picture most of the trees are gone, and only one person crosses the newly paved expanse. "Thus everywhere attractive and clean towns arose out of dirt and mud, which gave the country a completely new face," the caption explained.

Zhitomir, and he told Kersten that the Führer was absolutely sure the Soviet Union would be defeated by Christmas. Everyone had begun once again to divide the Russian pie. Finally, on 16 July, Himmler got Hitler's undivided attention. "The Führer not only listened to me, he even refrained from constant interruptions, as is his usual habit," Himmler told Kersten. "No, today he went so far as to approve of my proposals, asking questions and drawing my attention to important details which I had not considered and which need additional study on my part." It was the happiest day of his life, Himmler repeated. He had been able to realize settlement only on a small scale before. Now, he said, 'I shall set to at once on a large scale—and with all the vigour I can muster.'"[12]

With these words, Himmler began an enraptured account of Meyer's Generalplan Ost and, showing Kersten the maps and architectural plans he had just presented to Hitler, expounded on the soldier-farmer villages in the German East, which were now to be established in Russia. "It's the greatest piece of colonization which the world will ever have seen," Himmler exclaimed. "When he has accomplished that, the name of Adolf Hitler will be the greatest in Germanic history—and he has commissioned me to carry out the task."[13] Victorious and jubilant, he embarked on a week-long trip to the German East to make a new beginning at Lublin, and tie up some loose ends at Auschwitz.

THERE WERE TWO items on Himmler's agenda for his three-day visit to Lublin.[14] The first was the progress of the Final Solution in that district. In 1941 he had instructed Globocnik to construct extermination camps in the area, and by the time of his visit three had been completed. Belzec had been in operation since the middle of March and Sobibor since May, and on 16 July Himmler had given the order to begin killing operations in Treblinka a week later. Accompanied by Globocnik, he visited Sobibor and signed the death warrant for Polish Jewry that same day. "I herewith order that the resettlement of the entire Jewish population of the General Government be carried out and completed by December 31, 1942," Himmler commanded. In accordance with his plans for the Germanization of the East, the "resettlement" of Jews meant the murder of all but half a million fit for slave labor. The idea of a reservation in Russia had never been anything more than a vague abstraction, while Meyer's proposal was concrete, detailed, and ideologically sound. Selection of the able-bodied could take place in the ghettos, and they would be sent to five collection camps in Warsaw, Cracow, Czestochowa, Radom, and Lublin. Everyone else would be killed. "These measures are required with a view to the necessary ethnic division of races and peoples for the New Order in Europe, and also in the interests of the security and cleanliness of the German Reich and its sphere of interest.''[15] The liquidation of Polish Jewry was code-named Operation Reinhard, in memory of Reinhard Heydrich, who had been shot in May by agents of the Czech government-in-exile.

The Jews in the ghettos of the Government General were affected immediately. "I'm broken, shattered," Chaim Kaplan wrote in his diary on 22 July. "My thoughts are jumbled. I don't know where to start or stop. I have seen Jewish Warsaw through forty years of events, but never before has she worn such a face. A whole community of 400,000 people condemned to exile.''[16] Kaplan learned the details of the order the following day. "Jews who work in the German shop-factories and the officers of the *Judenrat* and all its agencies" are not going to be deported, he reported. Furthermore—and Kaplan quoted the precise words—" 'All Jews qualified for labor are exempt from deportation and may remain in the ghetto; those Jews who were not heretofore included in the labor force may henceforth be included. They will be taken to barracks where they will work.' " Kaplan, like the other ghetto residents, recognized that deportation meant depradation. "Silver, gold, and jewels may be taken without restriction. This is understood: All of that will be stolen. . . . This tactic is already known to us." It also signaled death. "The deportees are, to begin with, taken for killing. They are not qualified for work.''[17] No one understood this more clearly than the chairman of the Judenrat (Jewish Council), Adam Czerniakow, who committed suicide rather than sign the expulsion order. The decree applied to children as well, he explained in a note to the Jewish Council, and he could not be a signatory to the murder of children.[18] Czerniakow "did not have a good life, but he had a beautiful death" was Kaplan's assessment. "There are those who earn immortality in a single hour. The President, Adam Czerniakow, earned his immortality in a single instant.''[19]

Czerniakow's immortality did not help the Jews of Warsaw. "Since 22 July every day a train, with five thousand Jews per train, travels from Warsaw via Malkinia to Treblinka, as well as a train twice a week with five thousand Jews from Przemysl to Belzec," an employee of the Directorate General for Eastern Railways wrote to Himmler's aide Karl Wolff on 28 July.[20] Wolff, in response, thanked the official "also on behalf of the Reichsführer-SS." The efficiency of the railways enabled them "to carry out this movement of population at an accelerated pace.''[21]

Globocnik, too, wrote to Wolff to express his eagerness for German reset-tlement. "The Reichsführer-SS was just here and gave us so many new tasks that from now on all our hidden ambitions will be directed towards carrying them out." The Jews, of course, would be deported quickly to clear the way for the Germanization project. "I am so thankful to him for this that he can rest assured that the thing he is interested in will be executed in the shortest time."[22] Globocnik looked forward to the first installment of the General Plan East: the creation of a "foothold of settlement" around Zamosc. Located in the fertile southeastern part of the Lublin district, Zamosc occupied a strategic position close both to Lublin, a major base of SS operations, and to the Ukraine. Zamosc was to be transformed into a foothold within a year.[23]

Globocnik "promised Himmler that within one year he was going to bring in fifty thousand new settlers as a pattern and example for the future, when huge settlements were supposed to be created further in the East," Höss recalled. "All the necessary things such as the cattle and the machinery were supposed to be supplied by Globocnik as soon as possible. However, the territory he had selected was still inhabited by Polish farmers. So he just evacuated them."[24] More than 110,000 Poles were deported. Most went to special camps created in the district; those with labor potential were sent to Germany. Some 12,000 suspected troublemakers were incarcerated in Majda-nek; 2,000 of them were shipped on to Auschwitz.[25]

On his way from Hitler to Globocnik, Himmler made a detour to Auschwitz. Much had changed since March 1941 when Auschwitz had offered him a unique opportunity to realize his dreams. By July 1942 that magic had vanished. Bigger and better things were about to come his way. In a funda-mental sense, the war with Russia had made him drunk with *Lebensraum*. Compared to the Germanization of the three marches and thirty-six footholds of settlement, the Auschwitz project appeared paltry indeed. The aggrandize-ment and amelioration of the town was progressing slowly; even if it were completed, he would have to share the credit with IG Farben and the gover-nor of Upper Silesia.

No longer the object of his ambitions and fantasy, Auschwitz nevertheless was still useful to Himmler for making money for his empire, and for advancing his own political purposes as necessary. It had become clear earlier that year that little domestic construction would be permitted until the end of the war, and Himmler had detailed Pohl to integrate the ever-expanding concentration camp system into the booming armament industry. Discussions with the newly appointed minister for armaments and war production, Albert Speer, led to an agreement to employ 25,000 inmates in Auschwitz and four other camps to produce carbines. Himmler ordered the expansion of Birkenau to 200,000 inmates and instructed Eichmann to fill the camp with Jews capable of work.[26]

Auschwitz had ceased to be Himmler's end; from 16 July 1942 on it would serve only as a means. And in July 1942 Himmler was in some need of means. With the Wannsee conference his authority over the Final Solution had been confirmed, but Heydrich, the architect of the deportations, was dead, and Himmler had taken direct personal control of the Reich Security Main Office. It was now up to Himmler to demonstrate his competence and abilities to his

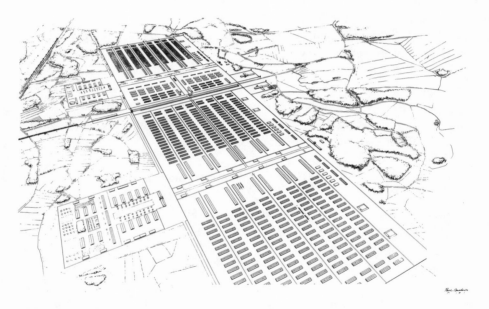

Bird's-eye view of Auschwitz-Birkenau as expanded to hold 200,000, summer 1942. Based on a plan of 15 August 1942, Auschwitz-Birkenau State Museum, box BW (B) 2/1, file BW 2/10. Reconstruction and drawing by Robert Jan van Pelt, Peter Gallagher, and Paul Backewich. Authors. The view is from the northeast. The railway station is in the neutral zone separating Building Section I with 20,000 inmates (to the south), and Building Section II with 60,000 inmates (to the north); closest to the viewer is the 60,000-inmate Building Section III, and farthest is the newly projected Building Section IV, also designed for 60,000 inmates. The two crematoria are located at the western end of the neutral zone. On the eastern side of Building Sections II and III are the SS quarters.

Führer. He could do what Heydrich had done, only better. So determined, he flew to Kattowitz, where he was welcomed by Fritz Bracht and Hans Kammler, with whom he drove on to Auschwitz. According to Rudolf Vrba, who had been deported from Slovakia two months earlier and who had reached Auschwitz via Majdanek, Himmler's visit was anticipated with great tension. Ill, unpresentable inmates had been dispatched to the new gas chambers, and those fit for show were given new uniforms. Hours before the Reichsführer's arrival, the prisoners were lined up outside the barracks while the orchestra stood ready at the gate. "And then it happened," Vrba recalled. "The catastrophe that every actor dreads. The moment of horror that only great occasions merit."

> In the tenth row outside our Block, the Block Senior found Yankel Meisel without his full quota of tunic buttons.
>
> It took some seconds for the enormity of the crime to sink in. Then he felled him with a blow. An uneasy shuffling whispered through the ranks. I could see the S.S. men exchange taut glances and then I saw the Block Senior, with two of his helpers, hauling Yankel inside the barrack block.
>
> Out of sight, they acted like men who have been shamed and betrayed will act. They beat and kicked the life out of him. They pummelled him swiftly, frantically, trying to blot him out, to sponge him from the scene and from their minds; and Yankel, who had forgotten to sew his buttons on, had not even the good grace to die quickly and quietly.
>
> He screamed. It was a strong, querulous scream, ragged in the hot, still air. Then it turned suddenly to the thin, plaintive wail of abandoned bagpipes, but it did not fade so fast. It went on and on and on, flooding the vacuum of silence, snatching at tightly-reined minds and twisting them with panic, rising even above the ugly thump of erratic blows. At that moment, I think, we all hated Yankel Meisel, the little old Jew who was spoiling everything, who was causing trouble for all of us with his long, lone, futile protest.[27]

As Yankel Meisel died, the orchestra began to play the Triumph March from Verdi's *Aida*. Himmler's car pulled in and stopped in front of the orchestra. "Himmler got out, smiling, obviously surprised and pleased by the music. He paused, listened for a moment, then strolled, chatting with Hoess, towards our Block." Vrba remembered his relief when he saw that the man whom he had imagined as an "all-powerful ogre," an "angry, ugly, bogey man who would grind our bone," moved "with the grace and easy charm of someone

from the upper-middle echelons of English royalty, relaxing in an atmosphere
that was as benevolent as that of any English garden party.'' He passed Vrba
once and, at the end of the line of prisoners, turned around, ''eyeing the
prisoners with polite interest.''

> Again he passed close to me, close enough for me to touch him, and for
> a moment our eyes met. They were cold, impersonal eyes that seemed
> to see little; and yet I found myself thinking: ''If he finds out what is going
> on, maybe he'll improve things. Maybe the food will get better. Maybe
> there won't be so many beatings. Maybe . . . maybe we'll see some justice
> around for a change.''
>   Already, you see, I had forgotten Yankel Meisel. And so had everybody
> else because Heinrich Himmler was smiling.[28]

After the inspection, ''Kammler, using maps, blueprints, and models
explained the planned or already progressing construction,'' Höss recalled.
''Himmler listened with great interest, asked about some of the technical
details, and agreed with the overall planning.''[29] Himmler probably was briefed
on the slow progress of the construction of the large crematorium. The camp
had reached an agreement with the Huta contractor firm to build the fabric
of the building for 133,756.65 marks just a few days earlier, and work was to
begin on 10 August.[30] Huta was not the only civilian firm to participate in
the erection of crematoria at Birkenau. Ultimately eleven other companies
contributed their expertise: Topf built the furnaces and the ventilation systems,
Koehler erected the smokestacks, Vedag waterproofed the gas chambers, the
Kontinentale Wasserwerks-Gesellschaft, Falck, and Triton handled the drainage of the gas chambers, Segnitz manufactured roof parts, Industrie-Bau-A.G.
installed the roof, Riedel built the shell of crematoria IV and V, Kluge helped
Topf build the furnaces for crematoria IV and V, and AEG did the electrical
installation.

Himmler and his entourage left the camp architects' offices for a tour of
the grounds. They visited ''the farms and soil enrichment projects, the dam-
building site, the laboratories and plant cultivation in Raisko, the cattle-raising
farms and the orchards.'' Then they arrived in Birkenau. ''He saw the emaciated victims of epidemics. . . . Himmler also saw the overcrowded barracks,
the primitive and totally inadequate toilet and wash facilities. He was told
about the high rate of illness and the death rate by the doctors and their causes.

He had everything explained to him in the greatest detail. He saw everything in stark reality. Yet he said absolutely nothing.''[31]

The company proceeded to the railway spur adjacent to the main line, where he watched the selection of a transport from the Netherlands. ''Himmler very carefully observed the entire process of annihilation. He began with the unloading at the ramps and completed the inspection as Bunker II was being cleared of the bodies. At that time there were no open-pit burnings. He did not complain about anything.''[32] The Reichsführer-SS went on to visit IG Farben, which he found impressive, and the site of a planned wastewater treatment plant. Much of the drinking water for Upper Silesia's industrial belt came from the Auschwitz area, and the local and provincial authorities were concerned about the untreated sewage from the camp that drained directly into the rivers. ''When I gave my permission some time ago to establish a concentration camp, I made it clear that a camp of this enormous size, situated in such an extraordinarily well-located place for industry (close to coal, at a

Heinrich Himmler and the IG Farben engineer Max Faust discuss the plans for the Buna plant, 17 July 1942. Auschwitz-Birkenau State Museum, neg. 385.

major road and railway junction, and at the confluence of three rivers), would be expected to accept many conditions in the interest of other parties or for the common good,'' the provincial planner Gerhard Ziegler had written to Himmler a few months earlier.[33] The Reichsführer-SS could do what he wanted in Auschwitz-Birkenau, but he could not pollute the drinking water of an important part of Upper Silesia. Spring and summer came and went, and the camp continued to expand. More and more sewage flowed untreated into the Vistula, and relations between the town, the province, and the camp worsened steadily. During the inspection of the proposed site for the sewage plant, Bracht reminded Himmler that a solution had to be found. As he needed a lot of good will from the province in the months to come, Himmler promised ''that Kammler would work on the matter with all his energy.''[34]

The next morning, Himmler discussed the progress of ethnic German resettlement in Upper Silesia with Bracht, and returned to the camp for another round of inspections. According to Höss, it was then that he confirmed the new role of Auschwitz as a destination for Europe's Jews. ''Eichmann's program will continue,'' Himmler announced, ''and will be accelerated every month from now on. See to it that you move ahead with the completion of Birkenau. The Gypsies are to be exterminated. With the same relentlessness you will exterminate those Jews who are unable to work.''[35] As the construction of the town was on hold until after the war, Jews fit for labor would be dispatched to other camps to work in armaments industries. In other words, Auschwitz-Birkenau would be a selection site, a killing field for those who could not work, and a holding pen for those who could. Himmler left, relieved. His ambitions were now elsewhere, and Auschwitz had been reduced from his favorite project to the garbage heap of his empire.

THE CAMP AUTHORITIES set out to implement Himmler's orders to reduce the pollution problem. Sewage treatment plants were built in quick succession.[36] Furthermore, the 107,000 corpses that had been buried in Birkenau and, decomposing, were polluting the ground water were dug up and burned on specially constructed ''roasts.'' According to Vrba, the kapos jokingly called this the real agricultural work of Auschwitz. ''It was a disgusting, dangerous job'' for the 1,400 prisoners assigned to this task. ''When the graves were opened, the stench was sickening. The prisoners had to work, mainly with bare hands, knee deep in decomposing flesh, heaving disintegrating bodies to the surface, while heavy drunken S.S. men with whips and machine guns

PLATES

Blueprints of Genocide

THE EVOLUTION OF THE AUSCHWITZ CONCENTRATION CAMP IS CAPTURED IN THE hundreds of architectural plans the Germans forgot to destroy and the Poles and the Soviets preserved in archives in Oswiecim and Moscow. A unique historical source, these materials are part of the archive of the Zentralbauleitung der Waffen SS und Polizei, Auschwitz O/S (Central Building Authority of the Waffen SS and the Police, Auschwitz in Upper Silesia). For while the Germans burned the archives of the camp Kommandantur prior to their evacuation from Auschwitz in January 1945, and Allied bombs inadvertently helped them accomplish the same task at SS headquarters in Berlin, the archive of the construction office, some three hundred yards away from the Kommandantur, was overlooked and remained intact. There is no similarly complete archive from any other concentration camp, and none of the administratively less complex Operation Reinhard death camps under the control of Odilo Globocnik (Belzec, Sobibor, Treblinka) generated such documents.

Building at Auschwitz both in the concentration camp and in the town was subject to normal civilian procedures as well as to the wartime superstructure of special permissions. Multiple copies of many documents survive with the comments and signatures of the individual bureaucrats or businessmen to whom they were sent. The Building Office generated a wide paper trail: plans, budgets, letters, telegrams, contractors' bids, financial negotiations, work site labor reports, requests for material allocations, and the minutes of meetings held in the Building Office among the architects themselves, with camp officials, and with high-ranking dignitaries from Berlin.

These papers tell us a great deal. They elucidate the thinking in the Auschwitz Kommandantur and, to some extent, at SS headquarters. Every decision Himmler took with regard to Auschwitz, or Höss took about the camp over which he reigned, had implications for the physical site. If prisoners were to be shipped in, barracks were needed; if the deportees' goods were to be claimed for the Reich, storehouses were required. If masses of people were to be murdered, incinerators to burn their bodies were essential. The documents of the Building Office archive retrace the course in reverse, from the structure back to the decision, the thinking, the idea. These materials illuminate the possibilities the Germans considered and the options they chose, their ambition as well as its outcome. And they reveal the widespread and far-flung complicity of Germans in many walks of life. As we have said before, Auschwitz was neither a preordained tragedy nor a natural disaster. The SS leaders themselves did not anticipate in 1940 what they wrought in 1944. Yet, step by step, blueprint by blueprint, the architects, at the behest of their bosses, came to plan and execute the horror we call Auschwitz and, as we have seen, they had a lot of help from bureaucrats, technocrats, and businessmen.

The following twenty-one plates are key documents. Produced on poor-quality paper and now over fifty years old, these blueprints have been reproduced here on glossy paper to facilitate interpretation. Plates 16 and 18 have been redrawn for publication.

The survey depicted in plate 1 was produced well before the SS was interested in Auschwitz as a concentration camp site. Drawn by army surveyors to record the particulars of this newly conquered territory, it was reproduced and widely disbursed. One copy was sent to the SS office in Breslau, where it was used by upper-echelon officials to determine a favorable location for a concentration camp in Upper Silesia. Settling on the region around Auschwitz, Erich von dem Bach-Zelewski wrote to Berlin to claim the area for the SS. Richard Glücks, the inspector of concentration camps, agreed, and the SS gained control. It was only a partial victory, however, as the SS officials were not allocated sufficient funding or building materials to develop the erstwhile migrant workers' settlement turned Polish army camp for their purposes. They made do—all too well— with what was at hand and had little difficulty modifying the basement of an existing structure to create torture chambers (plate 2). The ammunition depot (plate 3), built by the Polish army in the 1920s, was similarly transformed into a crematorium. At this point in the camp's history, a crematorium was needed to dispose of the bodies of those who died from the "ordinary" brutality of the concentration camp regimen, not because Auschwitz was—or would become—a mass murder site.

As the Kommandantur obtained greater resources, civilian expertise was needed to install heat, electrical, and sewage systems, to build chimneys, to provide building shells. The best known of the outside contractors was Topf & Sons from Erfurt, whose engineers' blueprints are preserved in archives in Oswiecim and elsewhere, as well as in the German Patent Office. Proud of its production of first-class incinerators used by hospitals to burn contaminated clothing and bed linen, by mortuaries to incinerate corpses, and by trash collection authorities to dispose of garbage, Topf regularly sent promotional literature to Auschwitz, a likely market with its contaminated clothes, corpses, and trash to burn. The first of Topf's incineration systems, which included a double-muffle furnace (plate 4), burned only corpses. The second Auschwitz system was designed to serve the other functions as well.

Companies and businesses were only one genre of the outside agencies with whom the Auschwitz Kommandantur negotiated. Auschwitz rail lines fell under the authority of the Oppeln regional office of the German railways and camp officials applied to Oppeln for a spur into Birkenau (plate 5). Their first request came in the winter of 1941 and, after much discussion with the camp about the best possible alignment, the regional office approved two years later.

Not only did the Auschwitz Kommandantur need outside help for technical services, and permission to extend the national transportation system into the camp; it was also subject to SS Design Office supervision at headquarters in Berlin. There was no urban designer in the camp Building Office. All plans (plates 6, 7, 11) that extended beyond camp confines to the town and surrounding region were drawn in Berlin, sent to Auschwitz for comment, and returned to Berlin to be finished. The first master plan for Auschwitz (plate 6) was produced as a presentation plan to be discussed by Himmler, Kammler, and Pohl. It reflects the SS officials' first flush of excitement after Farben decided to establish a buna plant in the area. Substantial sums of money and allotments of building materials hovered on the horizon, and the drawings in plates 6, 7, 8, and 11 illustrate the rapid evolution of the authorities' ambition for the camp. Hans Stosberg, the German town architect, was also bedazzled by the IG Farben move. Plates 9 and 10 depict his increasingly grand schemes for the town Himmler envisioned as a model German settlement in the East.

Presentation plans were rarely produced; most blueprints (and therefore most of the plans in the archive) were working drawings. Stained, folded, carried to the work site and back, they are in poor condition today. But they are significant. Their scribbled marginalia and penciled changes reveal the architects at work: their thoughts and their decisions. For example, in his plan for Auschwitz-Birkenau (plate 12), Fritz Ertl organized the main part of the camp on the basis of discrete units consisting of twelve dwelling barracks, one kitchen, one wash barrack, and one latrine. During the meeting at which this design was discussed, Karl Bischoff informed Ertl that Himmler had ordered an increase in the camp capacity from 97,000 to 125,000 Russian prisoners of war. Anticipating a need to control this mass of inmates efficiently, Bischoff took Ertl's plan and sketched, in pencil, lines indicating barbed-wire fences between the units. Thus he divided Birkenau into subcamps which, a year later, became the men's camp, the women's camp, the Gypsy camp, and the Theresienstadt family camp. Similarly, to accommodate the additional 28,000 Russian inmates, Bischoff changed the barrack capacity from 550 to 774 by a stroke of the pencil (plate 13).

At this point, as can be seen in Ertl's plan (plate 12), the latrines were still at a reasonable walking distance from the barracks. Subsequently, however, the architects stretched out the subcamps until inmates in the farthest barracks slept half a mile away from the nearest toilet. Having elongated the camp and increased the number of inmates by some 50 percent, the architects failed to change the latrine site or design, thereby creating a biological disaster and engendering even greater suffering. The latrines themselves were, in any case, totally inadequate.

The architects' germ warfare against the inmates is almost trivial in comparison with their professional cooperation in genocide. Drawings in the Building Office archive illuminate the step-by-step transformation of the crematoria from an incineration system for the efficient disposal of corpses to a lethal installation for the murder of live human beings—and then for the burning of their corpses. The plans for the so-called new crematorium (plates 14, 15, 16, 17), designed for Auschwitz I but erected in Birkenau, clearly illustrate this evolution. Originally (plates 14 and 15) the architectural style and the solidity of the material fit the vernacular of the main camp. As conceived in the autumn of 1941, this was to be a crematorium to accommodate the mortality of the concentration camp at Auschwitz and the prisoner-of-war camp in Birkenau. Like all other buildings in Auschwitz I, the crematorium had to conform to civilian building codes, which required an autopsy room. The SS had learned in the 1930s to circumvent the intrusion of civilian coroners by building its own in-camp crematoria and by having an in-camp medical service to sign off on the cause of death. It did not, however, have its own building inspectors, and therefore camp crematoria conformed to national civilian standards. In Auschwitz, these well-outfitted autopsy rooms fell into the hands of Mengele and his colleagues. They had not requested such facilities, but it took them little time to appreciate their usefulness. The autopsy rooms, built in conformance with state code, became laboratories for the Auschwitz physicians' infamous medical experiments.

The designs in plates 14 and 15 are conceptual sketches. The worked-out blueprint (plate 16) is more complex and informative. It was used to request building materials and permissions, and was given to the Huta contracting firm, which was happy to have the business. The plan was changed yet again in December 1942. With a relatively simple drawing (plate 17), Walther Dejaco transformed the basement design. He drew in an outside staircase descending from the yard next to the railway spur into a basement entrance to the crematorium. There he changed one of the two underground morgues into an undressing room and the other into a gas chamber. He canceled the planned corpse chute, which in the earlier plans (plates 14, 15, 16) had afforded the main access to the basement morgues. Live human beings descend staircases. Dead bodies are dropped through a chute. The victims would walk to their death.

Crematorium IV (plate 18), by contrast with crematorium II, was designed after Himmler's second visit to Auschwitz in July 1942. Birkenau had become a site for mass murder. All pretense of civility and civilian rules had been shed. The heimat style of Auschwitz I was replaced by the functional vernacular of Birkenau. The architects no longer bothered to draw in autopsy rooms. The space was used for gas chambers.

Even after Birkenau was completely committed to killing Jews, the last bit of economic use was squeezed out of those found fit for work. The blueprint to complete Building Section III (plate 19), drawn in the summer of 1943, depicts a plan to service satellite camps established throughout Upper Silesia solely to provide slave labor to German civilian-owned businesses. ''Labor'' was liberally interpreted. In Auschwitz, the prohibition against sexual intercourse between Germans and Jews applied to the SS but not to German kapos, camp inmate functionaries, or particularly productive ''Aryan'' prisoners. The ''Special Barrack'' depicted in plate 20 was evidently meant to house young Jewish women specially selected to be camp prostitutes.

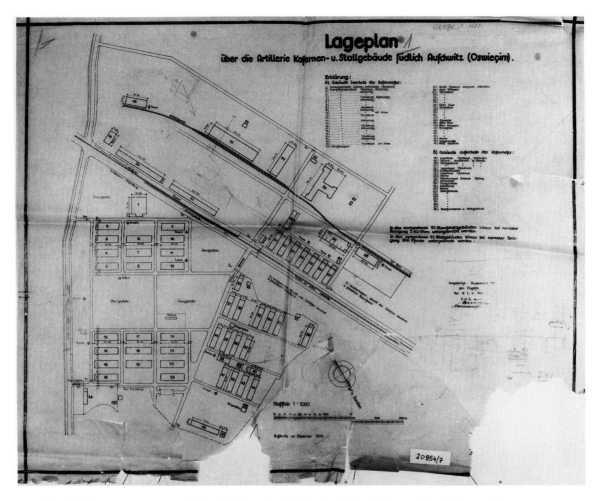

Plate 1. German army survey of Zasole, December 1939. Auschwitz-Birkenau State Museum, box BW2/1, file 2/1. In the first months of the camp's existence, building 56 accommodated the prisoners while buildings 2–23 were cleaned and surrounded by barbed wire to become the protective-custody camp proper. The Arbeit macht frei gate was erected next to building 20. Below building 23 is the half-buried ammunition depot that became the crematorium. Buildings 25–44 were used by the Poles as stables. They were to become workshops under the Germans.

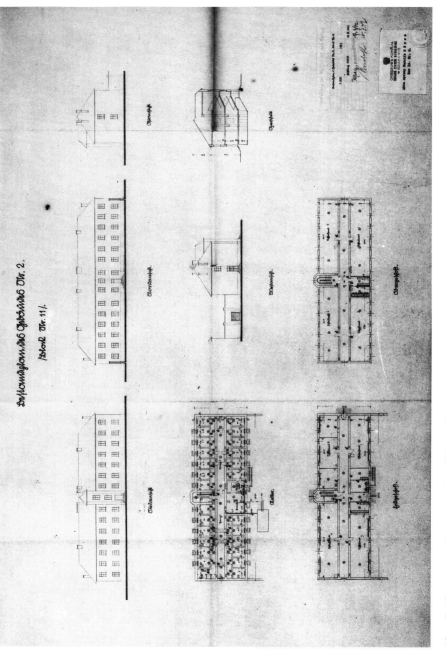

Plate 2. *Elevation and basement plan of block 11. Auschwitz-Birkenau State Museum, box BW 20/ 1, file BW 20/9. The plan shows four groups of cells. The four tiny standing cells are at the upper left side. The outside stairs which lead from the basement furnace room end in the adjacent courtyard, which was used for executions.*

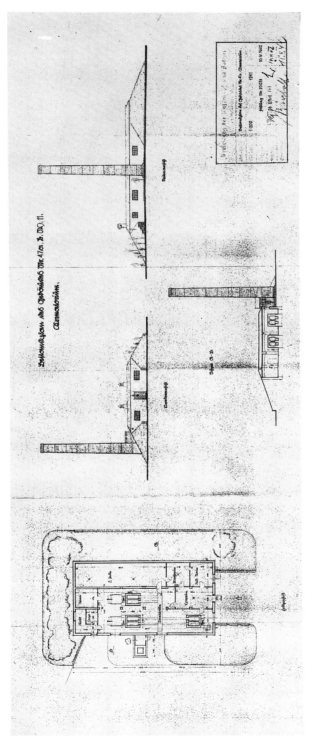

Plate 3. Plan and elevations of the crematorium of the main camp, 1942. Osobyi Archive, Moscow, coll. 502/1, file 312. The drawing, showing the location of a new chimney, was made after all three double-muffle ovens had been installed. The large space to the right of the incineration hall is the morgue, which was transformed into a gas chamber in September 1941.

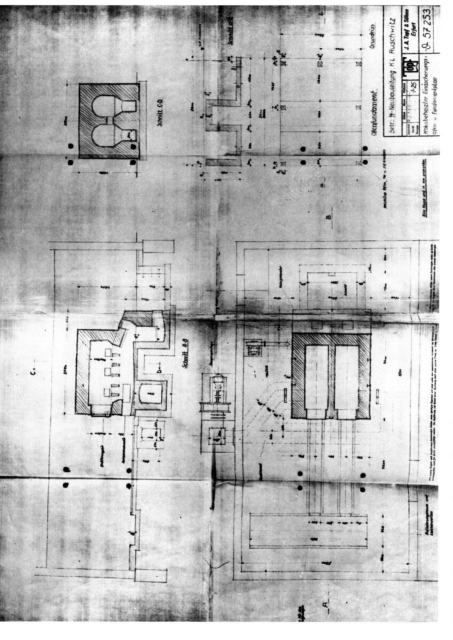

Plate 4. Blueprint by Topf & Sons for the first incinerator built in Auschwitz, 1940. Federal Archive, Koblenz, coll. NS4 Mauthausen, file 54. The section of the furnace shows a muffle (top left) separated by a grille from a receptacle for the ashes (bottom left). Corpses are introduced from the left. To the right is the coke burner (bottom left), accessible from a special stoker's pit. The plan shows the two muffles, the underground chimney flue with a damper to regulate the draft, and the outside chimney with a fan for draft reinforcement. A smaller fan located against the inner wall of the incineration room brings compressed air into the muffle.

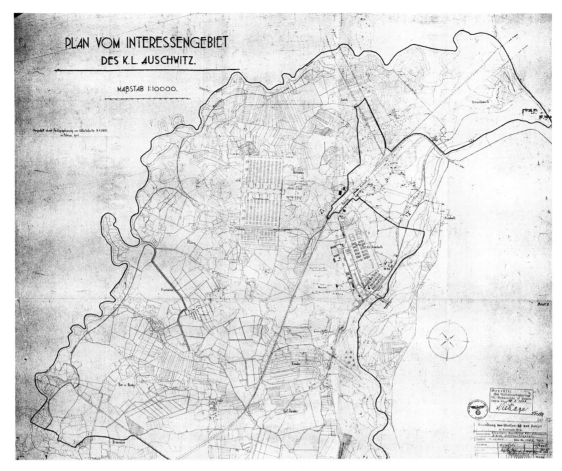

Plate 5. Map of the "zone of interest" of the Auschwitz concentration camp, 1943.
Auschwitz-Birkenau State Museum, box. BW 27, file BW 27/2. The Vistula
(left) provided the western boundary of the zone of interests; the Sola (right), the
eastern boundary. A civilian peninsula projected from the Sola into the zone to
connect the town to the railway station. The main camp (K.L. Auschwitz) can be
seen just south of the station. The plan includes the extant buildings, the only
partly realized camp extension, and buildings that remained on the drawing board.
West of the railroad station is the village of Birkenau and the Auschwitz-Birkenau camp. This
blueprint was used to obtain permission from the German Reich Railway to extend a
railway spur into the camp, and therefore the V-like rail trajectory connecting the main line
to Auschwitz-Birkenau has been emphasized.

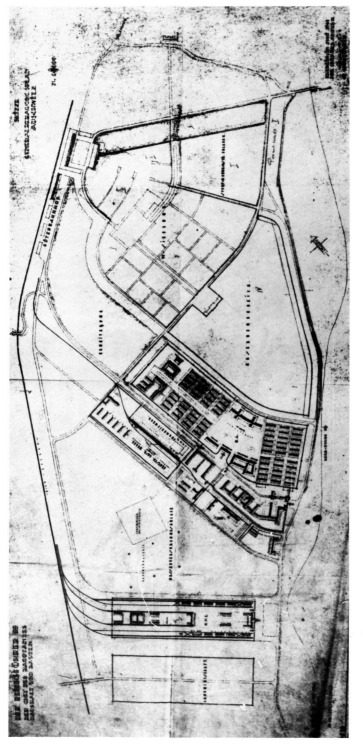

Plate 6. *The first master plan for Auschwitz, June 1941. Auschwitz–Birkenau State Museum, box BW 2/1, file BW 2/11. In the center is the main camp, with the barracks of the former labor exchange (bottom), a large roll call square flanked by an entrance pavilion, a prisoner reception building, the camp kitchens, and a storehouse for prisoners' belongings. Along the road to the station is the extension with thirty-two dwelling barracks, a camp hospital, a camp prison, and a crematorium. Northeast of the camp are the barracks for single SS men, a village for married SS men, and the station. Southwest of the camp are the offices of the commandant, workshops, and compounds with storehouses (marked T.W.L) and agricultural equipment.*

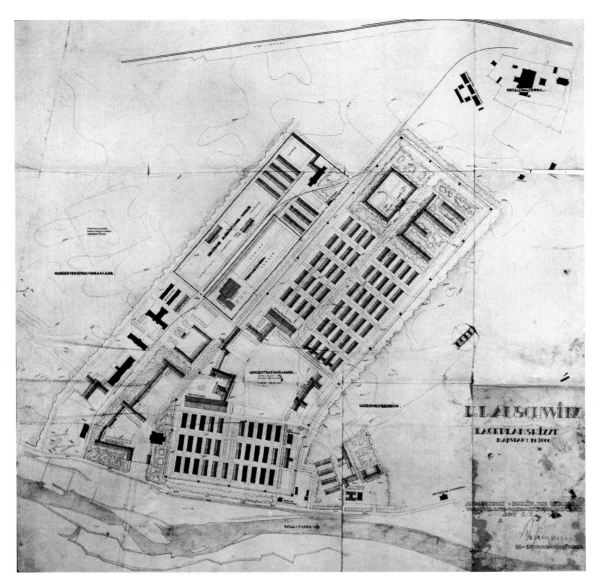

Plate 7. The second master plan for Auschwitz, February 1942. Auschwitz-Birkenau State Museum, box BW 2/2, file BW 2/17. Various elements of the first master plan have been developed. An important new element is the large crematorium, located at the eastern edge of the original compound (bottom center). This is the five triple-muffle furnace facility designed in the fall of 1941; ultimately erected in Birkenau, it became known as crematorium II.

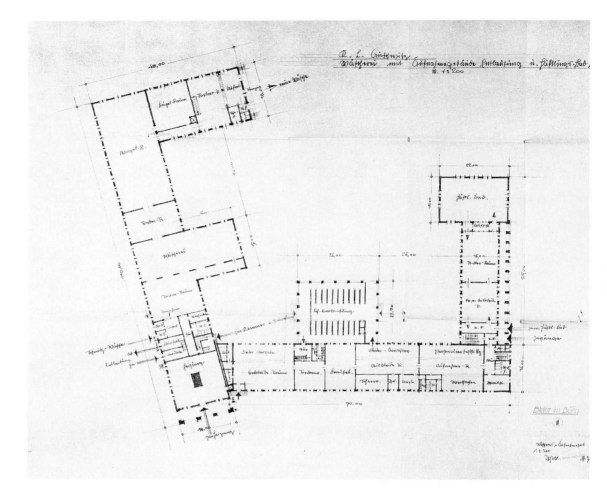

Plate 8. Early design sketch of the prisoner reception building in the main camp, 1942. Architect Walther Dejaco. Auschwitz-Birkenau State Museum, box BW 160/3, file BW 160/11. To the left is the laundry, to the right are the baths, and the center wing houses the prisoner reception facilities and the pavillion with nineteen Zyklon B gas chambers.

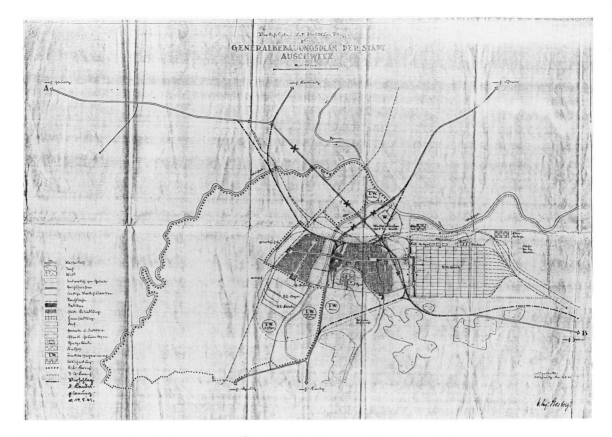

Plate 9. First master plan for the expansion of Auschwitz by the town architect Hans Stosberg, spring 1941. Oswiecim Municipal Archive. The Vistula runs from southwest (left) to east (right). The tributary river Przemsza comes from the north (top) and the Sola from the south (bottom). The old town of Auschwitz is located along the Sola. A major avenue connects the old town to the station (west) and the industrial area to be developed by IG Farben (east). South of the station are the SS barracks and the concentration camp (K.Z. Lager). The area defined by the dotted line is the camp's zone of interests. The circles with the digraph TW indicate areas with drinking-water wells. The chessboard-like rectangles are wastewater treatment plants. The plan shows one modification in the location of the main road Gleiwitz–Zator. The straight section between the turnoff to Kattowitz and the town has been canceled in favor of a new route closer to the station.

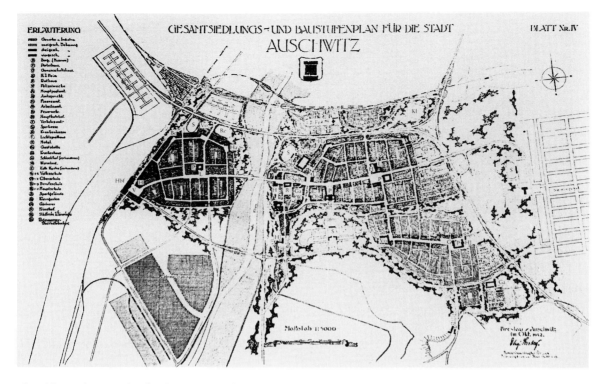

Plate 10. Final master plan for the expansion of Auschwitz by the town architect Hans Stosberg, autumn
1942. Niels Gutschow, Absteinach. The final plan reveals important modifications over the first
design. The eastern district of Auschwitz has been split into two separate units, each with its own center.
A main square, the site of Party headquarters, has been inserted east of the old town. The
connection between the camp's zone of interests and the western district of Auschwitz has changed. In
the 1941 proposal, Stosberg assumed the two areas would be adjacent. Hartjenstein's proposal
inserted an SS settlement between the SS barracks and the main road connecting the station to the rest
of Auschwitz (see fig. 145). Stosberg's final master plan includes the camp and the SS barracks.
The site that Hartjenstein claimed for the settlement is now occupied by a green belt, a second road
between the station and the IG Farben site, and the southern part of the western district.

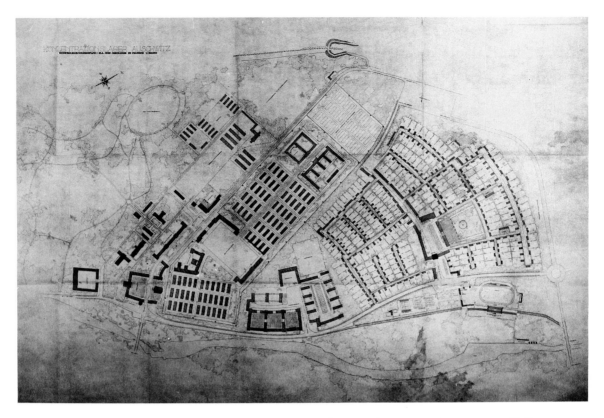

Plate 11. The SS architect Lothar Hartjenstein's master plan for the SS district at Auschwitz, summer 1942. Auschwitz-Birkenau State Museum, box BW 2/3, file BW 2/26. The left side of the drawing depicts the concentration camp. Its center is the enormous roll call square, designed to hold 30,000 inmates. Along the sides are the various administration buildings, with offices for the camp Gestapo and the Lagerführer (north and west), the prisoner reception building with the delousing installation and the laundry (southwest), and the kitchens (east). To the south are the brick barracks of the original camp, built in 1916 as a labor exchange for Polish seasonal workers en route to Germany. To the north of the roll call square are five connected workshops, forty-five newly built barracks, the camp hospital, and the camp prison. On the west side of the camp are the buildings of the Kommandantur and various industries, and to the east the SS base and the village for married SS men and their families. The center of the village includes a hotel and shops. Along the river are the SS sports facilities. The large building at the bend of the road that goes west from the village center is a primary school. It is a stone's throw from the electrified fence of the camp.

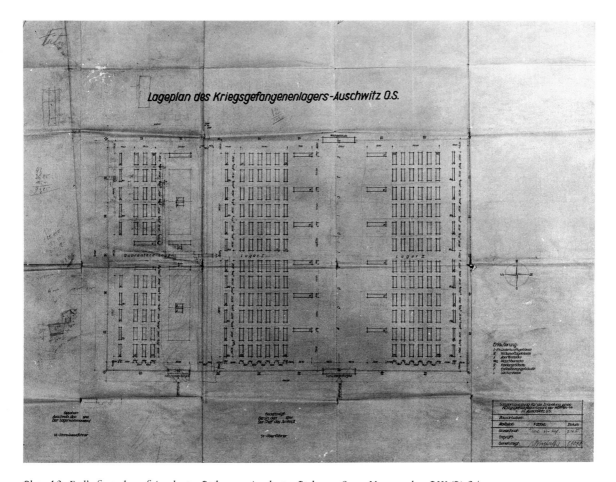

Lageplan des Kriegsgefangenenlagers-Auschwitz O.S.

Plate 12. *Ertl's first plan of Auschwitz-Birkenau. Auschwitz-Birkenau State Museum, box BW (B) 2/ 1, file BW 2/1. Ertl divided the camp into two parts. To the left is the quarantine camp for 17,000 men. Built as drawn, it became the women's camp in late 1942. To the right, centered on an enormous* Appelplatz *(roll call place), is the camp proper, designed to hold 80,000 men. In this first design the camp already was organized on the basis of discrete units, which included twelve dwelling barracks, a kitchen barrack, a wash barrack, and a latrine barrack. The plan is drawn in ink. During the meeting at which this design was discussed, Bischoff sketched, in pencil, lines indicating barbed-wire fences between the units. These became a fixed part of subsequent designs.*

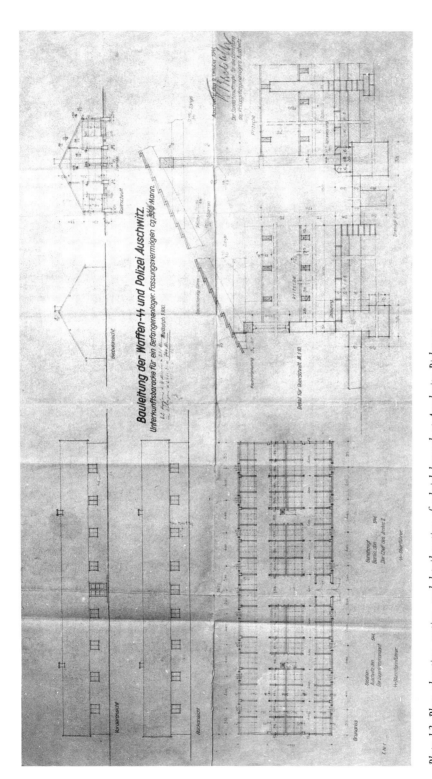

Plate 13. Plan, elevation, section, and detail section of a brick barrack at Auschwitz-Birkenau. Auschwitz-Birkenau State Museum, box BW (B) 3a, file BW 3a/1. The number indicating capacity (Fassungsvermögen) is inked in as roughly 550. Bischoff changed this, with pencil, to 744.

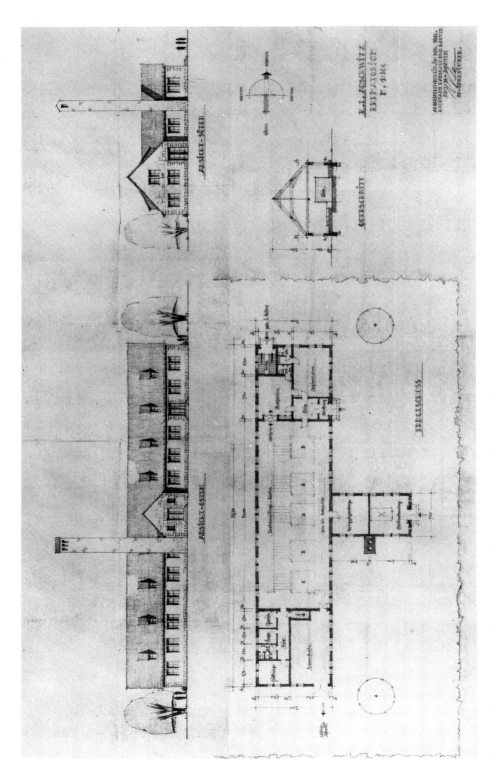

Plate 14. Ground plan and front elevation of Georg Werkmann's first design for a new crematorium in Auschwitz, autumn 1941. Osobyi Archive, Moscow, coll. 502/2, file 146. The incineration hall with the five triple-muffle furnaces occupies the center of the building. To the left are the fuel storeroom and the rooms for the inmates working the installation; to the right are the two dissection rooms and the two-door elevator (marked by an x), opening onto both the incineration hall and the first dissection room, that descends to the morgues below.

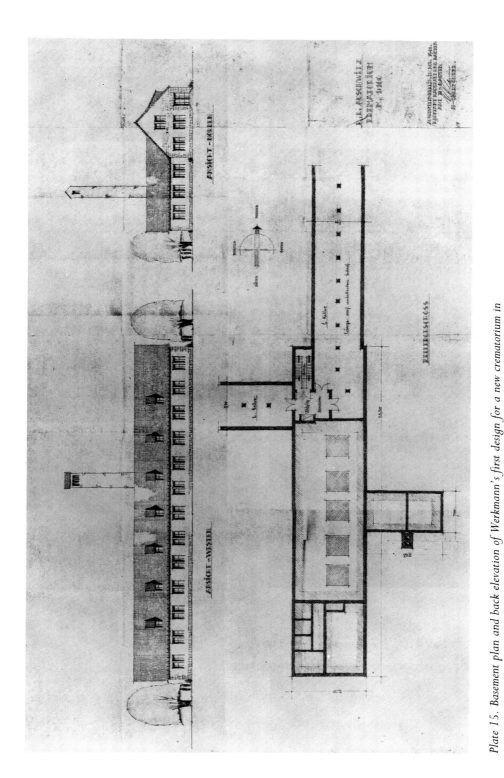

Plate 15. Basement plan and back elevation of Werkmann's first design for a new crematorium in Auschwitz, autumn 1941. Osobyi Archive, Moscow, coll. 502/2, file 146. There is no basement below the incineration hall and the fuel storeroom. The elevator (marked by an x) descends into a vestibule connected to the outside by two staircases and a chute for corpses. The two large morgues extend far beyond the footprint of the building.

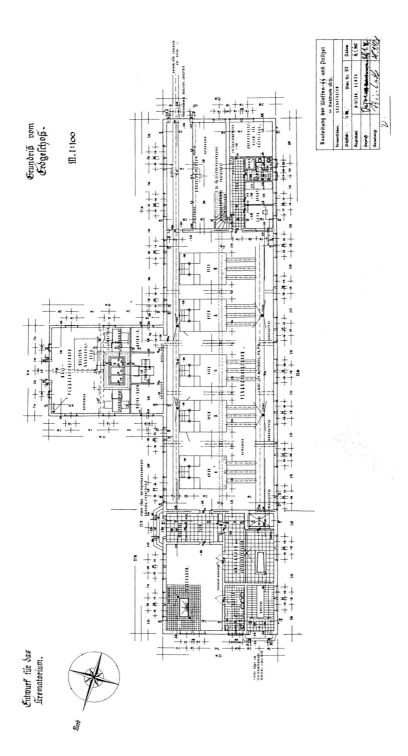

Grundriß vom
Erdgeschoß.

M. 1:100

Entwurf für das
Krematorium.

Nord

Bauleitung der Waffen-ᛋᛋ und Polizei
in Auschwitz O/S.

Plate 16. The ground plan of Walther Dejaco's modification of Werkmann's design, January 1942.
Original blueprint, Auschwitz-Birkenau State Museum, box BW (B) 30/1, file BW 30/2;
redrawn for publication by Mikolaj Kadlubowski. Authors.

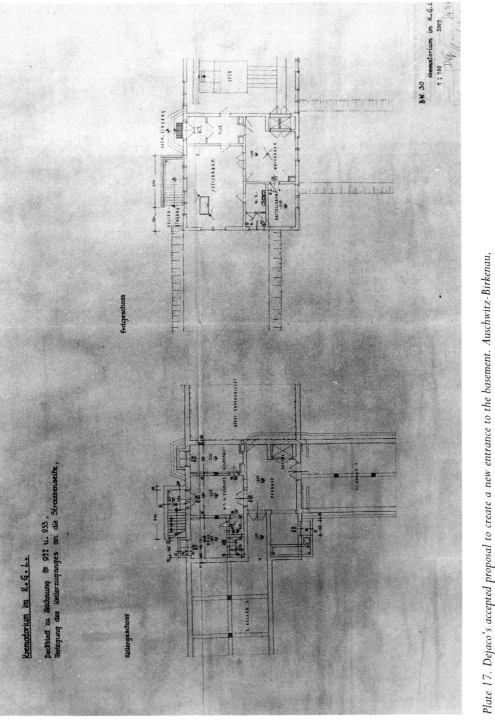

Plate 17. Dejaco's accepted proposal to create a new entrance to the basement. Auschwitz-Birkenau, December 1942. Auschwitz-Birkenau State Museum, box BW (B) 30/2, file BW 30/12. The slide, which would obstruct movement between the morgue to the left (the undressing room) and the morgue to the right (the gas chamber), has been removed.

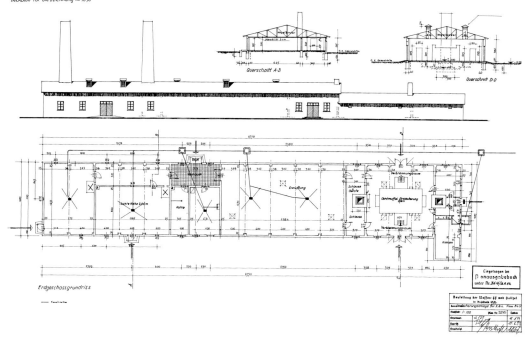

Plate 18. Final design for crematorium IV, by Walther Dejaco, January 1943. Original blueprint, Auschwitz-Birkenau State Museum, box BW (B) 30b; redrawn for publication by Mikolaj Kadlubowski. Authors. In the plan, the north is the top of the page but, contrary to convention, the elevation shows the north and not the south facade. Therefore the incineration room, which in the plan is located to the right, is to the left in the elevation, and the gas chambers, which in the plan are located to the left, are to the right in the elevation. The functional arrangement is simple and straightforward. The entrance on the north side gives access to a corridor (left, on the drawing) that opens to two gas chambers equipped with stoves to preheat the room during winter. Between the vestibule and the incineration room is a large morgue, which in the winter was also used as an undressing room. The center of the incineration room is occupied by a double-four-muffle furnace connected to two chimneys. The section through the lower part of the building shows one of the two gas chambers, the chimney of the stove of the other gas chamber, and the corridor. The section through the higher part of the building shows the furnace room.

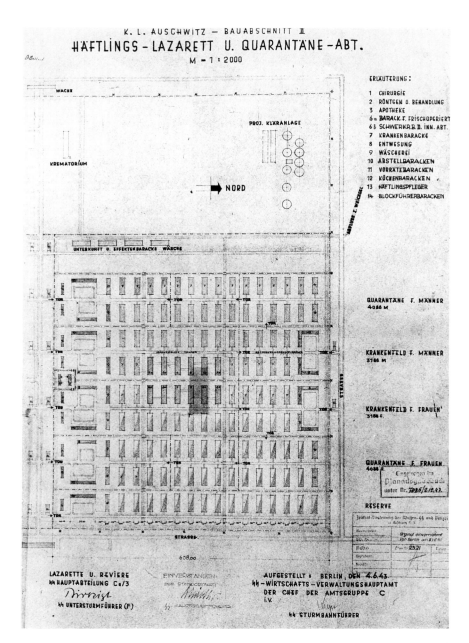

K. L. AUSCHWITZ — BAUABSCHNITT III

HÄFTLINGS-LAZARETT U. QUARANTÄNE-ABT.

M — 1 : 2000

ERLÄUTERUNG :

1 CHIRURGIE
2 RÖNTGEN U. BEHANDLUNG
3 APOTHEKE
6a BARACK. F. FRISCHOPERIERT
6b SCHWERKR. D. INN. ABT.
7 KRANKENBARACKE
8 ENTWESUNG
9 WÄSCHEREI
10 ABSTELLBARACKEN
11 VORRATEBARACKEN
12 KÜCHENBARACKEN
13 HÄFTLINGSPFLEGER
14 BLOCKFÜHRERBARACKEN

WACHE

PROJ. KLÄRANLAGE

KREMATORIUM

NORD

UNTERKUNFT U. EFFEKTENBARACKE WÄSCHE

QUARANTÄNE F. MÄNNER
4088 M

KRANKENFELD F. MÄNNER
3188 M

KRANKENFELD F. FRAUEN
3188 F.

QUARANTÄNE F. FRAUEN
4088 F.

RESERVE

STRASSE.

608,00

LAZARETTE U. REVIERE
SS HAUPTABTEILUNG C a/3

SS UNTERSTURMFÜHRER (F)

EINVERSTANDEN:

AUFGESTELLT : BERLIN, DEN 4.6.43.
SS-WIRTSCHAFTS-VERWALTUNGSHAUPTAMT
DER CHEF DER AMTSGRUPPE C
i. V.

SS STURMBANNFÜHRER

Plate 19. Plan to complete Building Section III as a large hospital and quarantine area for prisoners put to work in satellite camps, summer 1943. Auschwitz-Birkenau State Museum, box BW (B) 3ef, file BW 3e/22. In the center are two groups of six barracks housing a surgery, an X-ray department, a recovery room, etc.

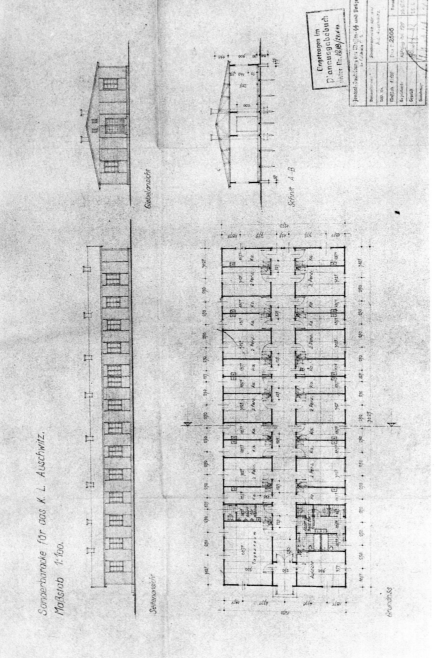

Plate 20. "Special Barrack," summer 1943. Auschwitz-Birkenau State Museum, box BW 84–93, file BW 93/1. Evidently a barrack to house the camp prostitutes. One of the incentives to increase the labor of "Aryan" prisoners was the privilege to have intercourse with a Jewish female inmate. The Auschwitz architects developed a special design for a whorehouse. Left to right: the entrance, a "dayroom" for the women and a room for the madam, washrooms for the women and visiting men, and eight "units," each consisting of two small rooms (with sinks) for business transactions and a slightly larger, two-person living room in between. Presumably it was not built; no bills for materials have been found.

bullied them and harried them.'' Each of the guards assigned to this detail was issued a bottle of liquor per day. ''They drove their slaves without mercy because they wanted to get the whole dirty business over fast; and, as they gulped down their liquor, their anaesthetic, the slender threads of their restraint snapped and they shot or beat to death those they thought were flagging.''[37] Of the initial 1,400 men, 1,100 were murdered on the job; the remaining 300 were liquidated when the work was completed.

With the appeasement of the provincial authorities, Höss and his staff were free to enlarge the camp further. Bischoff drew up a new master plan for the transformation of Auschwitz-Birkenau into a 200,000-inmate labor pool for the armaments industry. The expansion was realized by adding an extra building sector of 60,000 prisoners to the south side of BA I. To keep up with camp mortality, a second crematorium was to be built opposite the first, on the west side of the camp at the end of the neutral zone between BA I and BA II.

These two crematoria, numbered II and III (crematorium I was in the main camp), had no extra incineration capacity to handle the corpses of those gassed in the bunkers which, physically, were located outside Birkenau and which, administratively, belonged to the main camp.[38] Bischoff sketched two smaller incineration installations, each of which was to be equipped with the two stripped-down three-muffle furnaces which had been planned in January but canceled in February. Crematorium IV was to be erected next to the ''little white house,'' and crematorium V next to the ''little red house.'' Each was to have an anticipated incineration capacity of 576 corpses per day.

Topf suggested equipping the two crematoria with a new-model double-four-muffle (or eight-muffle) incinerator that had been developed for use in Russia and was readily available. Bischoff approved, and had blueprints drawn up on 14 August.[39] Prüfer visited Auschwitz a few days later and left with orders for five triple-muffle furnaces for crematorium III and two double-four-muffle ovens for crematoria IV and V.[40]

Crematoria IV and V were the first buildings designed, from inception, to operate as killing machines, with gas chambers, a morgue, and a furnace hall arranged in a functional sequence.[41] (See plate 18.) Bunkers 1 and 2, crematorium I, and, as we shall see, crematoria II and III were all transformed into extermination centers. It is likely that during his July visit Himmler had advised Höss to seek inspiration from Treblinka, which had been conceived from the outset as an extermination center.

In his Nuremberg testimony, Höss certainly compared his work to Globoc-

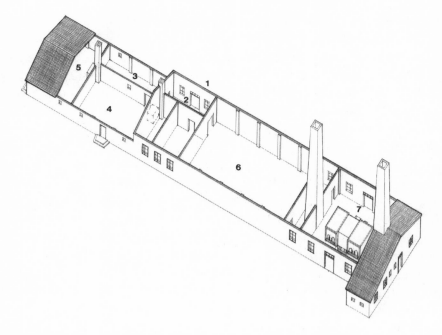

Crematorium IV. Drawing by Kate Mullin. The functional arrangement is simple and straightforward. The entrance on the north side (1) leads to a vestibule (2) and a corridor (3) to two gas chambers (4 and 5) equipped with stoves to preheat the room during the winter. Between the vestibule and the incineration room is a large morgue (6), which was also used as an undressing room in the winter. The center of the incineration room is occupied by a double-four-muffle furnace (7), connected to two chimneys. N.B.: This is an axonometric drawing; the three-dimensional effect is derived from the exact measurements and angles of the original plan. See plate 18.

nik's. Treblinka was "not very efficient," his gas chambers were larger than Globocnik's, and while victims arriving in Treblinka knew that they were going to be killed, "at Auschwitz," Höss proclaimed with pride, "we endeavored to fool the victims into thinking that they were going through a delousing process." And he added, "Very frequently women would hide their children under the clothes but, of course, when we found them we would send the children in to be exterminated."[42]

The final transformation of Auschwitz into a killing site for Jews was confirmed on 26 September 1942, when Höss received explicit instructions from Berlin about the property of gassed victims. So long as Auschwitz had been a "normal" concentration camp, it had operated under the fiction that, in principle, all prisoners could be released, and therefore their belongings were labeled and stored, on the assumption that they would be returned. Now the majority of arrivals were never to claim their property. Oswald Pohl instructed Höss to deposit German money into an SS bank account; foreign currency, valuables, and precious metals were to be shipped to SS headquarters in Berlin; rags and unusable clothes should be sent to the Reich Ministry of Economy for use as raw materials in industrial production, and all usable garments, shoes, blankets, bed linens, quilts, and household utensils were directed to the Ethnic German Liasion Office (Vomi) for distribution among ethnic German settlers. The yield was enormous. In an interim report Pohl submitted to Himmler on 6 February 1943, he noted that 824 boxcars of goods had left Auschwitz: 569 to the Reich Ministry of Economy, 211 to Vomi, and 44 to other concentration camps, various other Nazi organizations, and the IG Farben works at the other end of town.[43] "It was only later that I discovered how cleverly [these goods] were used," Vrba explained, "not only to bolster the Reich's economy,

The wooden barracks of "Canada." Auschwitz-Birkenau State Museum, neg. 20995/482.

but to manipulate the foreign exchange through Swiss banks so that the Allied economy would suffer. Only later did I learn the importance of this psychological warfare on the home front. Baby needed shoes in Berlin, for instance. Hitler found shoes in Auschwitz; and Momma wrote to Poppa on the Russian front, lauding this Saviour with the little black moustache."[44]

As the architects, engineers, and contractors built two larger crematoria to service a camp of 200,000 prisoners and two smaller crematoria for the gas chambers, the SS bureaucrats in Berlin who hoped to make the camps the linchpin of the armaments industry faced disaster. By the end of September, Speer had convinced Hitler that Himmler was incompetent in this regard. The SS bureaucracy was inept; nothing had been done in pilot projects to produce arms at Buchenwald or Neuengamme, Speer's aide Karl Saur reported to Hitler. It was easier, Saur argued, to transform established industries into armaments works. "I added a few sentences about the inadequacy of the SS business leaders," Speer recalled in the late 1960s. "Before the war they had promised Hitler that they would quickly supply bricks and granite for his buildings. But only the tiniest portion of this promise had been kept."[45]

With the cancellation of the armaments deal, there was no need to concentrate 200,000 prisoners in Birkenau, and a new master plan was drawn up which envisioned a camp of 140,000 inmates. But the second large crematorium, which had been included to service the "normal" mortality of the earlier projected inmate population, was not canceled. The sudden extra incineration capacity could be used within the context of the Final Solution. As construction progressed, Bischoff and his chief designer, Walther Dejaco, endeavored to do precisely this, with minimal change in the design. The solution was obvious: one of the two larger underground morgues that already had been completed was equipped with a powerful ventilation system.[46] In September 1941 just such a system had proved crucial in the transformation of the morgue of crematorium I into a gas chamber. This procedure could be repeated in crematoria II and III. Dejaco changed the basement plan. (See plate 17.) He drew in an outside staircase descending from the yard next to the railway spur into a basement entrance to the crematorium. This is where a vestibule, a new undressing room, and the new gas chamber were located. He canceled the planned corpse chute, which in the earlier plans had been the main access to the basement morgues. Live human beings descend staircases. Dead bodies are dropped through a chute. The victims would walk to their death.[47]

———

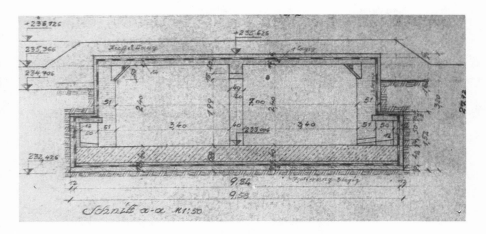

*Section of the morgue of crematorium II. Auschwitz-Birkenau State Museum, box BW
(B)30/2, file BW 30/19a. The conversion of this morgue into a gas chamber
was facilitated by the double ventilation system located where the wall touches the
ceiling and in the wall itself.*

Walther Dejaco. Berlin Document Center.

IN AUSCHWITZ, BISCHOFF and Dejaco altered the crematoria under construction. In Berlin, the German leadership decided that the Final Solution would continue to completion. In 1941, the Germans had killed some 1.1 million Jews; none was killed in Auschwitz. In 1942, approximately 2.7 million Jews were annihilated, of whom some 200,000 were gassed in bunkers 1 and 2.[48] "Beginning with the territories of the Reich and then going on to other European countries implicated in the final solution, the Jews are commonly transported to the East to large camps, in part still to be built, where they are set to work or brought still farther east," a National Socialist Party confidential report circulated to Party leaders explained. Its recipients understood that the words "farther east" meant gas chambers.[49]

The euphemism, which invoked the mythology of the German East as a domain of redemption for the German nation, stuck fast. Even Himmler adopted it. In January 1943 he ordered the chief statistician of the SS, Richard Korherr, to compile a report on the progress of the Final Solution.[50] Korherr's initial draft included the usual and unusual euphemisms current at the time. In a section on "the evacuation of the Jews," Korherr stated that 1,449,692 Polish Jews from Poland had been subjected to "special treatment"—1,274,166 in the extermination camps in the General Government (Belzec, Sobibor, and Treblinka) and 145,301 in the extermination facility in Wartheland (Kulmhof). Himmler objected to the phrase "special treatment." "The Reichsführer-SS has received your statistical report on the 'Final Solution of the European Jewish Problem,'" his secretary, Rudolf Brandt, wrote to Korherr.

> He does not wish the words "special treatment of Jews" to be used at all. On page 9, point 4 the text must read as follows: "Transportation of Jews out of the Eastern Provinces to the Russian East: [1,449,692]. Number of those passed through the camp in the General Government: [1,274,166]; through the camp in Warthegau: [145,301]." A different formulation must not appear. I am sending back the copy of the report already signed by the Reichsführer-SS with the request to make the indicated changes on page 9 and return it.[51]

Korherr made the required change, and "Russian East" became the official euphemism for a death camp and "passing through" for the process of extermination. Himmler was so pleased that he instructed Korherr to compile a summary for Hitler. Korherr complied and on 19 April sent the requested summary to Brandt. In his conclusion, underlined to catch Hitler's attention, Korherr cheerfully observed, "Altogether, European Jewry must have been reduced by almost ½ since 1933, that is to say, during the first decade of the development of power of National Socialism. Again half, that is a quarter of the total Jewish population of 1937, has fled to other continents."[52]

Korherr also recorded that 4,917 male Jews and 932 female Jews had been admitted to Auschwitz; one male Jew had been released, 3,716 male Jews and 720 female Jews had died; thus 1,200 male Jews and 212 female Jews remained. The careful statistician noted that he had not counted those who had been brought to Auschwitz "as part of the evacuation action," that is, all those who had been brought "farther east" to Birkenau.[53]

THE AUSCHWITZ PROJECT, inaugurated with so much fanfare in early 1941, officially came to an end in January 1943. As the German army faced defeat farther east at Stalingrad, Hitler ordered the cessation of all preparations for peacetime settlement. The Auschwitz town architect, Hans Stosberg, closed up shop. Before he joined the army, he filed his designs and papers so that if he did not return, a successor would be able to take up the project. It was his wish, he wrote in his final report, that "the work of our time—begun in difficult years of struggle for the existence of our nation—may continue and come to completion, and that this undertaking may stand proudly next to the creations of our ancestors, who sanctified this soil with their blood and sweat centuries ago, and who prepared the road we followed." In acknowledgment of the sacrifice of the soldiers at Stalingrad, he dedicated his effort to them.[54]

Himmler's marches and footholds of settlement in Russia were also put on hold. His dream to oversee the settlement of millions of Germans evaporated. Of all his ambitions only one could be realized now: to enact a truly Final Solution to the Jewish Question. Previously the "solution" had been a means to an end. Deportation, like settlement, had been part of his ethnic-cleansing campaign, his project to create a racially pure, unified German nation, his utopia of German blood working German soil. But now, getting rid of the Jews, cleansing Europe of them, was an end in itself. No longer part of a larger program, it was a project on its own. In January 1943 Himmler had no illusions that Germany would win the war, but at least he could dispose of the Jews. That was one good deed he could accomplish. Auschwitz once again became the object of his concern, but his focus shifted from IG Farben, the town, and the agricultural estate to the crematoria. Although concentration camp inmates continued to work at the construction of the buna plant, and although labor details went on improving the soil and repairing the dikes, their labor had ceased to be of interest to Himmler. The only prisoners who mattered were those assigned to the "Special Squads." It was their job to maintain order among the victims selected to be murdered, to empty the gas chambers after the killing, to extract gold teeth and cut the women's hair, to burn the corpses, and to sort and prepare the deportees' belongings for transport to the Reich. Each of the squads lasted for only a short time: after a few months they, too, were killed, and each new commando began its tenure with the cremation of the corpses of its predecessors—each, except the last, which rebelled in October 1944 and was massacred in the uprising.

As construction in the Reich came to a halt, Kammler, Bischoff, Dejaco, and Prüfer did everything in their power to complete the crematoria. Throughout the month of January regular transports arrived from the Bialystok district, the Netherlands, Berlin, and Theresienstadt; the bunkers were hardly able to keep up, and in February Eichmann was forced to divert trains destined for Auschwitz to Sobibor and Treblinka.

Eichmann then designated the proud, 2,000-year-old Sephardic community

Completing the roof of the underground undressing room of crematorium II, winter 1942–43. Auschwitz-Birkenau State Museum, neg. 20995/ 498.

of 55,000 Jews in Salonika for immediate liquidation. Salonika and the rest of northern Greece was occupied by German forces, but southern Greece was in Italian hands, and by the end of 1942 the Saloniki Jews had discovered that the Italians were not interested in applying the anti-Semitic policies of their Nordic allies. Increasingly large numbers of Saloniki Jews sought refuge in the south, and the Italians refused to extradite them to the Germans. Eichmann realized he had to act quickly. He knew that the killing station in Auschwitz was working at top capacity, but he also saw that the Operation Reinhard camps, which were equipped neither with crematoria nor with a holding pen for those deportees who could not be killed immediately upon arrival, could not handle the long-distance 3,000-person transports he envisioned.

Eichmann telephoned Kammler to ask him when the crematoria would be ready. Informed only by Bischoff, who was loath to admit that construction had fallen two months behind schedule, Kammler reported the current official prognosis: crematorium II would be operational on 31 January, crematorium IV on 28 February, and crematorium III on 31 March.[55]

Unexpected problems in the electricity supply to the buildings caused

Completing the roof of crematorium II, winter 1942–43. Auschwitz-Birkenau State Museum, neg. 20995/506. In front (right foreground) *we see the partially exposed end of the underground gas chamber.*

additional delays. When Bischoff and Dejaco had modified the basement plan of crematoria II and III to include a gas chamber, they had increased the anticipated electricity consumption of the building. The ventilation system was now simultaneously to extract the Zyklon B from the gas chamber and fan the flames of the incinerators. They had contacted AEG, the contractor for the electrical systems, but because of rationing AEG had been unable to get the heavy-duty wiring and circuit breakers the system required. As a result, crematorium II was to be supplied with a temporary electrical system; nothing at all was available for use in crematorium III. Furthermore, the AEG representative in Kattowitz, Engineer Tomitschek, warned the Auschwitz building office, the capacity of the temporary system would not allow for simultaneous "special treatment" and incineration.[56]

The five triple-muffle furnaces in crematorium II were test-run on 4 March with the incineration of fifty corpses of men killed in bunker 2. At forty-five minutes, the incineration took longer than planned: Prüfer thought the furnaces

Four of the five triple-muffle furnaces of crematorium II, winter 1942–43. Auschwitz-Birkenau State Museum, neg. 20995/495.

were not dry enough. They were to be heated for a week without being used.[57] In the meantime, his colleagues completed the gas chamber ventilation system.[58] On Saturday, 13 March, the machinery was ready for a trial run, and 1,492 women, children, and old people, selected from a transport of 2,000 Jews from the Cracow ghetto, were killed in the new gas chamber and burned in the new incinerators.[59] The murder itself took five minutes, but burning the bodies took two days—the managers operated the incinerators at 50 percent capacity to forestall technical failures.

Erroneously believing all the crematoria to be fully operational, Eichmann dispatched the first transport of 3,000 Saloniki Jews in mid-March. Traversing southeastern Europe via Skopje, Belgrade, Zagreb, Graz, Vienna, and Teschen, the train arrived in Auschwitz on the twentieth of that month. Crematoria III, IV, and V were still being built, and crematorium II was in the trial stage; it had not yet been handed over by the architects and engineers to the camp authorities. The physicians who conducted the selection that day admitted 417 men and 192 women to the camp; the other 2,191 deportees were designated for immediate liquidation. They would "pass through" crematorium II, the camp officials decided.[60] It quickly became clear that the building could not handle such numbers at once. Killing was easy, but as the Germans began to work the ovens at full capacity (officially 1,440 bodies per day—that is, 96 per muffle, or an average of 4 bodies per muffle per hour), they ignored the advice of the AEG engineer Tomitschek, and the electrical system caught fire. Both the forced-draft system that fanned the incinerator flames and the ventilation system to extract the Zyklon B from the gas chamber were damaged. The Germans carried on. They would not close down the installation for repair. Trains with 2,000 to 3,000 deportees were leaving Salonika according to schedule, and could not be stopped. In anticipation of these transports, the architects signed off on crematorium IV on 22 March, without having tested the incinerators.[61] They also tried to repair crematorium II and, partly successful, transferred the crippled system to the camp on 31 March.

After two weeks of intensive use in the Salonika action the double four-muffle furnace of crematorium IV cracked and, after various attempts at repair, the incinerator was decommissioned in May. Prüfer realized that the overly centralized structure of the furnace was to blame for the breakdown, and he modified the incinerator of crematorium V, which was still under construction. It was officially completed on 4 April.[62] Crematorium II initially functioned reasonably well, but after a month the internal lining of the smokestack and

Crematorium IV, summer 1943. Auschwitz-Birkenau State Museum, neg. 20995/509. The gas chambers are located in the lower wing (left) of the building.

the connecting flues to the incinerator began to collapse. It was taken out of commission on 22 May for a month of repair work. One would have hoped that, with all these technical failures, the system would have proved less fatal, but such was not the case. Despite the breakdowns, in just two months the camp personnel liquidated over 30,000 members of the Salonika community, and some 7,000 Yugoslavian, German, and Polish Jews.

Crematorium III was transferred to the camp authorities on 24 June, after Salonika had become Jew free.[63] The camp now had an official daily incineration capacity of 4,756 corpses and, according to Vrba and Höss's aide Franz Hössler, Himmler came to see what he had wrought.[64] All four crematoria in Birkenau had been completed, but the precise date is unknown. Höss himself never mentioned this visit. Himmler arrived at Auschwitz at eight o'clock and was expected to attend a gassing after breakfast at nine, Vrba has reported. The gas chambers had been well packed with Polish Jews in advance, but somehow breakfast lasted until eleven. Finally Himmler and Höss turned to business. They drove to the crematorium, ''got out and chatted for a while to the senior

Crematorium III, summer 1943. Auschwitz-Birkenau State Museum, neg. 20995/507.

officers present. Himmler listened intently, as they explained the procedure to him in detail. He ambled over to the sealed door, glanced casually through the small, thick observation window at the squirming bodies inside, then returned to fire some more questions at his underlings.'' Finally, he gave permission to commence operation. As the children, women, and men were dying inside, Himmler peeped once again through the window, asked some more questions, smoked a cigarette, laughed, joked, and observed the subsequent procedures with great interest. "Himmler waited until the smoke began to thicken over the chimneys and then he glanced at his watch. It was one o'clock. Lunch time, in fact.''[65]

THE TRANSPORTS HAD become larger, and the number of people selected for work as well as for death increased concomitantly. Birkenau had only two, relatively primitive delousing installations. These buildings could not handle so many newcomers at once, and in the late spring Bischoff proposed the construction of a new, large "central sauna," which could handle two thousand people if necessary.[66] The building, designed to operate with a minimum of personnel and a maximum of efficiency, was completed in December.

The architects of Auschwitz, 1943. Auschwitz-Birkenau State Museum, neg. 422. A "family photo" of all the German architects and engineers employed in the Zentralbauleitung. Bischoff *(lighter coat)* stands in the center, with Dejaco *(right).* Ertl is in the second row *(third from left).*

The sauna was to service not only the incoming transports but also an immense new subdivision, Building Section III, which was to support the penultimate of the many functions Himmler had added on to the camp in the five years of its existence. After the massive military losses in the summer of 1943, the German army began to draft every last German male, and the armaments industry impressed every available "free" person into its factories. Now slaves were needed for other industrial work as well as in the coal mines. Pohl negotiated with numerous businesses, and ultimately agreed to create and maintain a system of twenty-seven satellite camps located on industrial sites. The first of these was the Buna camp at Monowitz, established in November 1942; the Jawischowitz camp to operate the nearby mines at Brzeszcze and a small camp to support the Bata shoe factory at Chelmek followed in quick succession. Five more camps opened in 1943 and another nineteen in 1944. By that time, IG Farben utilized 11,000 prisoners at the Buna plant housed in the camp at Monowitz, also known as Auschwitz III, 7,000 inmates

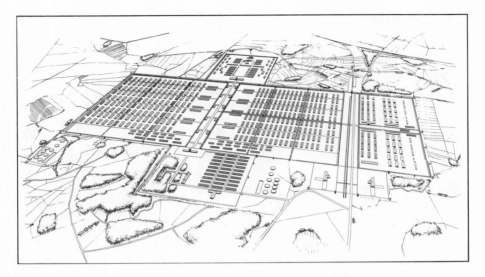

Bird's-eye view of Auschwitz-Birkenau, as planned in February 1943. Original Auschwitz-Birkenau
State Museum, box BW(B) 2/1, file BW 2/14. Reconstruction and drawing by Robert Jan
van Pelt, Peter Gallagher, and Paul Backewich. Authors. The view is from the west. Closest to the
viewer are, left to right, *a sewage treatment plant for Building Section III, crematorium V*
surrounded by trees, crematorium IV, the thirty barracks of "Canada" and the Central Sauna, a
second sewage treatment plant, crematorium III, and crematorium II.

worked at other chemical plants, 7,000 in the steel and metal industries, and
8,000 in the mines. In total, 33,000 prisoners were in satellite camps and
4,000 were barracked in Auschwitz but worked in the fuse factory next to the
camp. SS enterprises consumed another 4,500 prisoners. The camp made a
hefty profit. The Kommandantur was paid 3 to 6 marks a day, while prisoner
maintenance amounted to 1.34 marks. At the end of 1943 Auschwitz was
taking in an average of 2 million marks per month.[67]

Birkenau was to become a service station for the outlying posts, which
were too small to maintain hospitals. Divided into four subsections, BA III
was to accommodate 14,552 inmates in relatively spacious barracks: 4,088
men and 4,088 women in two quarantine camps, and 3,188 sick men and
3,188 sick women in two hospital camps. Each of the two hospital camps was
to be equipped with a six-barrack treatment center that included a surgery,
an X-ray department, and recovery rooms. (See plate 19.)

Of the proposed barracks, one-third were erected, none was completed,
and in none was the designated function carried out. As soon as the roofs were

The Central Sauna under construction. Auschwitz-Birkenau State Museum, neg. 20995/467.

closed, the buildings were crammed with deportees for whom there was no room elsewhere. There were no floors, no beds, not even roosts. The prisoners had no clothes except blankets. Someone thought they looked like Mexican Indians, and BA III became known as Mexico.

THE FOUR NEW crematoria came into operation after the Holocaust itself had peaked. The Judeocide had begun in 1941, and the Germans killed some 1.1 million Jews that year. In 1942 they murdered another 2.7 million Jews, of whom approximately 200,000 died in Auschwitz. The year the crematoria of Auschwitz came into operation, the number of victims dropped to 500,000, half of whom were killed in Auschwitz.[68] All the Jews whom the Germans could catch easily had been trapped. By the end of 1943 the Germans closed down the death camps built specifically to exterminate Jews: Kulmhof (150,000 Jews), Sobibor (200,000 Jews), Belzec (550,000 Jews), and Treblinka (750,000 Jews). In these camps there was no selection process; nearly everyone who was shipped in was killed within hours of arrival. In terms of mortality, at the end of 1943 Auschwitz ranked behind Treblinka and Belzec. But it was the only camp that remained to mop up the remnants of the Jewish communities of Poland, Italy, France, the Netherlands, and the rest of occupied Europe.

As the killing wound down, Himmler talked about the task that since January had become his unique contribution to the future Europe. "One basic principle must be absolute for the SS man: we must be honest, decent, loyal, and comradely to members of our own blood and to nobody else," Himmler declared at a meeting of SS leaders in Posen on 4 October 1943. It was now time to mention "a really grave matter" which hitherto had been surrounded by a "tactful" silence. "I am referring to the evacuation of the Jews, the annihilation of the Jewish people," he explained. "Most of you must know what it means to see a hundred corpses lie side by side, or five hundred, or a thousand. To have stuck this out and—excepting cases of human weakness—to have kept our integrity, that is what has made us hard. In our history, this is an unwritten and never-to-be-written page of glory." The liquidation of the Jews had eliminated the possibility of another stab in the back. If "we still had the Jews in every city as secret saboteurs, agitators, and demagogues . . . we probably would have reached the 1916–17 stage by now." It was difficult work, but they had managed. "We have carried out this heaviest of our tasks in a spirit of love for our people. And our inward being, our soul, our character has not suffered injury from it.[69]

WITH AN AVERAGE of 6,000 arrivals in Auschwitz during January through April 1944, the rate of murder was significantly reduced in comparison with monthly figures in 1943. The Hungarian Jews were the sole remaining major Jewish community in Europe, and the Germans occupied Hungary in March. The labor shortage had become so acute that in early April Hitler instructed Himmler to obtain 100,000 Jewish slave workers from Hungary immediately.[70] Auschwitz was now to acquire its last function which, remarkably, was identical to that which, three decades earlier, had led to the construction of the main camp. It once again was to become a gigantic labor exchange. Hungary's Jews were to be shipped in and slave workers were to be selected and shipped out again to the network of concentration camps in the Reich that served German industry. Those selected for work in Germany were to be kept in quarantine until transport to the west was available.

Jews found unfit for work were to be killed in the crematoria, and in the spring of 1944 the Germans expected that many, if not most, of the arrivals would be of no use to German industry. The crematoria were overhauled.

"Cracks in the brickwork of the ovens were filled with a special fireclay paste," Filip Müller, one of the very few survivors of the early Slovak transports and a Sonderkommando worker recalled. "New grates were fitted in the generators, while the six chimneys underwent a thorough inspection and repair, as did the electric fans. The walls of the four changing rooms and the eight gas chambers were given a fresh coat of paint."[71] Crematoria II and III also got new elevators connecting the gas chamber with the incineration room, and the gas chambers of crematorium V were equipped with a new ventilation system to speed up the extermination process.

Not only were the existing killing and incinerating installations fully repaired; bunker 2, now renumbered bunker 5, was brought back from retirement too. Behind crematorium V the newly appointed manager of the crematoria, Otto Moll, put crews of inmates to work digging two huge cremation pits. "Accompanied by his henchmen, extermination expert Moll paced up and down the large site, giving instructions for the siting of pits, a fuel depot, the spot where the ashes were to be crushed, and all the rest of the devices which he had thought up for the extermination and obliteration of human beings."[72] Müller explained that Moll's most ingenious invention was a channel "to catch the fat exuding from the corpses as they were burning in the pit."[73] Finally, Moll created a store of conifer branches, waste wood, rags, barrels of alcohol, lubricating oil, and chlorinated lime to keep the fires going.[74]

To facilitate the system, the train lines were extended into the camp. "Day and night many hundreds of prisoners were busy laying railway tracks right up to crematoria 2 and 3. On the road between the building sites B1 and B2 the construction of a loading and unloading ramp complete with a three-track railway system was in progress in order to provide a direct link between the death factories, Auschwitz railway station and the outside world."[75]

The first transport of Hungarian Jews, 1,800 people, arrived in Auschwitz on 29 April and pulled over the new spur through the gate into Birkenau. A few weeks later Himmler boasted that "at the moment we are indeed bringing 100,000, and later another 100,000 male Jews from Hungary to concentration camps to build underground factories."[76] By the end of June, in just two months, half of Hungary's Jewry—381,661 souls—had arrived in Auschwitz. With another 18,000 Jews brought in from other countries during the same period, Auschwitz received a record average of 200,000 deportees per month. One of them was the eighteen-year-old Alexander Ehrmann, who until the spring of 1944 had lived in the town of Kiralyhelmec. His transport pulled into Birkenau at night.

*Arrival of a transport of Hungarian Jews from the Carpathian Mountains, summer
1944. Hellman, Meier, and Klarsfeld,* The Auschwitz Album *(1981).
Sterling Memorial Library, Yale University.*

*The Ehrmann children, ca. 1931. Authors. In the garden in back of their home in
Királyhelmec. Left to right: Ernest, Alexander, Eva, Atyu, Sarah, Magda.*

We arrived around one o'clock in the morning in an area with lights, flood-lights, and stench. We saw flames, tall chimneys. We still did not want to accept that it was Auschwitz. We preferred to think we didn't know than to acknowledge, yes, we are there. The train stopped. Outside we heard all kinds of noises, stench, language, commands we didn't understand. It was in German but we didn't know what it meant. Dogs barked. The doors flung open, and we saw strange uniformed men in striped clothes. They started to yell at us in the Yiddish of Polish Jews: *"Schnell! Raus!"* We started to ask them, "Where are we?" They answered, *"Raus, raus, raus!"* Sentries and their dogs were there, and they yelled at us also. *"Macht schnell!"*

We got out and they told us to get in formations of five, and to leave all the luggage there. We asked one of the guys, "Tell me, tell me, where are we going?" *"Dort, geht,"* and he pointed towards the flames. We had to move on. So we formed up, true to family tradition, two parents, the oldest sister, and the next sister and the child on my sister's hand. My mother asked her, "Let me carry him," two and a half years old. She said, "No, I'll take care of my own son." So the three sisters and my two parents were walking and the two boys in the next row with three other people. We came up to Mengele, we were standing there. He was pointing left, right. My sister was the first one, with a child, and he pointed to the right. Then my mother, who had a rupture, she had a big belly, she looked like she was pregnant, she wasn't. So I guess that made her go to that side. My father and the two sisters were pointed to his left. He asked my father, "Old man, what do you do?" He said, "Farm work." And then came the next row and the two of us were told also to go after our father and two sisters; and he stopped and he called my father back. "Put out your hand!" So my father showed him his hand and Mengele smacked him across the face and pushed him to the other side. And he continued, *"Schnell!"* And the sentries were there, and the dogs and we have to move, and that's the last we saw of our parents and sister and nephew.

It started to get daylight, and we moved on to an area where there was barbed wire on both sides. We walked down an alley, a sentry so often spaced out. We kept on moving, we were prodded to move faster. We were told, "You will be coming to an area where you will be given a bath and change clothes and you'll be told what to do." We were walking, and beyond the barbed wire fences there were piles of rubble and branches, pine tree branches and rubble burning, slowly burning. We're walking by, and the sentries kept on screaming, *"Lauf! Lauf!"* and

Arrival of a transport of Hungarian Jews, summer 1944. Hellman, Meier, and Klarsfeld,
The Auschwitz Album *(1981). Sterling Memorial Library, Yale University.*
In the distance are the chimneys of crematoria II (left) *and III* (right).

Selection of the Hungarian Jews, summer 1944. Hellman, Meier, and Klarsfeld, The Auschwitz Album *(1981). Sterling Memorial Library, Yale University. Hungarian Jewish women* (left)
and men (right) *lined up in rows of five. The selection took place halfway down the platform,*
so that there were four lines in all. The mother with the infant has been pointed to the left (for us,
right); *she will cross the railway line, turn right, and walk to crematorium II or III.*

I heard a baby crying. The baby was crying somewhere in the distance and I couldn't stop and look. We moved, and it smelled, a horrible stench. I knew that things in the fire were moving, there were babies in the fire.[77]

At no other time in its history was Auschwitz less efficient as a labor exchange. Of the total 438,000 incoming Jews, between 10 and 30 percent were found fit to make their contribution to the German war effort. Most of them were dispatched to Bergen-Belsen, Buchenwald, Dachau, Gross-Rosen, Mauthausen, Neuengamme, Ravensbrück, Sachsenhausen, and 378 other camps in Himmler's empire. Alex Ehrmann and his sixteen-year-old brother were sent to Warsaw, where they were put to work in the ruins of the erstwhile ghetto ''tearing down the walls'' and ''salvaging the bricks.''[78]

At no other time was Auschwitz more efficient as a killing center. In May and June the number of people murdered exceeded the official incineration capacity of 132,000 corpses per month. Moll's pits were useful, too. The frenetic gassing

''Cremation of corpses on pyres.'' Postcard, 1952. Authors.

and burning continued through July. In two months one-third of the total number of people murdered at Auschwitz were killed, and between one-half and two-thirds of all the 600,000 Jews the Germans killed in 1944. In the thirty-two months that Auschwitz operated as a designated extermination center, from March 1942 to November 1944, between 1 million and 1.1 million people were killed, or an average of 32,000 to 34,000 a month. During the Hungarian action the Germans, with dispatch and efficiency, increased that average five- to sixfold.

In August 1944, as the Hungarian action came to an end and the crematoria stood idle, Sara Grossman-Weil, her husband Menek, her mother- and father-in-law Feigele and Wolf, her brother-in-law Adek, his wife Esther, their adolescent daughter Regina, and their little girl Mirka were herded into a train of cattle cars in Lodz, the last of the hundreds of ghettos the Germans had established to cleanse the German East of Jews.

The ghetto of Lodz, which had been organized in early 1940 as a holding

The Grossman family, Lodz, ca. 1924. Authors. Twenty years after this photo was taken, the woman standing (left) went with her grandchild Mirka to the gas chambers; thus her daughter-in-law, Esther, survived.

pen for the Nisko project, had survived at the expense of most of its inhabitants as a vast workshop. The German-appointed Eldest of the Jews, Chaim Rumkowski, had developed a policy to make the ghetto indispensible to the German war effort. If work would not set Jews free, it should at least guarantee survival. The Germans agreed, with a caveat: if the ghetto were an enormous workshop, only those who were capable to work could stay. Selections were instituted, and Sara put rouge on her gaunt cheeks to look healthy. "You would try to look straight, not to look sick. You would not bend, because this would suggest that you're not capable of doing the work you're doing. You would walk straight, or as well as you could, to show them that you are fit to remain."[79]

But there were those who could not be saved by all the rouge and posture in the world. In early September 1942 the Germans decreed that those who could not work—children under ten and old people over sixty-five—would have to leave. Forcing Rumkowski, his Jewish Council, and the Jewish ghetto police to share moral responsibility, the Germans demanded they execute the order. Their families would be exempt. When the decree was made known, it seemed that the nadir of perdition had been reached. "The sky above the ghetto . . . is unclouded," Josef Zelkowicz recorded. "Like yesterday and the day before, the early autumn sun shines. It shines and smiles at our Jewish grief and agony, as though someone were merely stepping on vermin, as though someone had written a death-sentence for bedbugs, a Day of Judgment for rats which must be exterminated and wiped off the face of the earth."[80] Like Josef Zelkowicz and everyone else, Sara witnessed dragnet operations to catch infants, toddlers, and elementary school children. "The children were taken away; thrown, literally thrown, onto the wagon. And when the mother objected, either she was taken with them or shot. Or they tore the child away from her and let her go. And all the children, small children, little ones, five-, six-, four-, seven-year-old ones were thrown, literally thrown, into this wagon. The cries were reaching the sky, but there was no help; there was no one to turn to, to plead your case, to beg."[81] Mirka Grossman was one of the few children to survive the selection.

With the action against the children and the elderly, the two-year death knell of the last Jewish community on Reich territory had begun. It ended on Wednesday, 2 August 1944, when the German mayor of Lodz informed Rumkowski that the ghetto would be resettled, workshop by workshop. "Factory workers will travel with their families," Rumkowski's final proclamation read. Sara Grossman-Weil left with her husband's family. They were herded to the train station and ordered onto the cattle cars. "You couldn't throw a pin in, one was sitting on top of the other, with the bundles. We were in this cattle car, this wagon, and we were riding, riding, riding. There was no end to it. And the little one asked, in Polish, 'Daddy, isn't it better that today it's a bad day, but tomorrow it will be better?' She was five years old. And her father said, 'Today doesn't matter, tomorrow will be much better.'"[82]

Tomorrow proved him wrong. The train with the survivors of the Lodz ghetto passed by Kattowitz and Myslowitz and crossed the Vistula at Neu-Berun. They arrived at the station of Auschwitz. The train turned into a spur and stopped. When the sun began to set, the train backed onto another spur, through a gate, and entered the enormous compound of Birkenau. It came to a halt. The bolted doors were opened. Sara Grossman, her relatives, and the rest of the people on the train were hauled out and told to form two columns, one of men, and one of women and children.

I was standing there not knowing what's going on, overwhelmed with the amount of people around us, not believing that they threw us all out from these wagons in the manner they did. How they pushed and shoved and

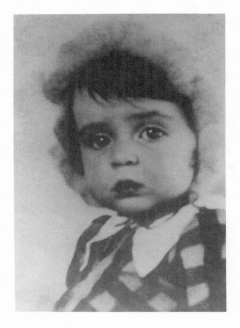

Mirka Grossman, ca. 1941. Authors.

screamed. And these SS men with the dogs in front of us. I lost sight of what was going on. It's crazy. And I was standing with my mother-in-law and my sister-in-law with her little girl, when someone approached us, and said, ''Give this child to the grandmother.'' And my sister-in-law gave the child to my mother-in-law. They went to the left, and we went to the right.[83]

Sara and the other women considered fit for work entered the camp. ''As we were marching, I saw columns of women marching on the other side in the opposite direction who were half naked, shaven heads, stretching out their arms. 'Food, food. Give me your bread!' Screaming, shouting. I was over-whelmed. I thought that I found myself in an asylum, in a madhouse, in a place with only crazy people.'' This was the place she had heard about, always in whispers and always with dread. ''They always called it Auschwitz, but we didn't know what it meant.''[84]

They arrived at the delousing station, were registered, shaved and show-ered, and handed some rags and wooden shoes.

From there they gathered us again in columns, in rags like the people whom I had seen an hour ago in the columns marching in the opposite direction. We had the same look, except we weren't shouting. We looked like crazy people, just like the rest of them. We were led to a lavatory, where we had to take care of our needs, and from there we went to a barrack, which was the house where we would be staying. In this barrack we were given a bunk. The size of the bunk was approximately the size of not quite a twin bed, I would say considerably smaller. And on this bunk bed, five people had to find their sleeping quarters. And this was our new home.[85]

Sara remained in Birkenau for ten days, and then she was brought on another transport to a munitions factory at Unterlüss, eighteen miles northeast of Celle. Most of the inmates were Hungarian women. Sara recalled that sulfur was everywhere, ''in the air, and in the bread that you were given as a ration at work, and in your mouth, eyes, hands, fingers; everything turned yellow. I was sick with the smell.''[86]

Production at Unterlüss came to an end in March 1945. The satellite camp was closed, and the inmates were sent to Bergen-Belsen, were Sara was put in a barrack with hundreds of other women. ''On the outside were hundreds of women dying of thirst, thirst, and thirst again.''

Young Hungarian Jewish women entering the women's camp (Building Section I) after delousing in the Central Sauna, summer 1944. Hellman, Meier, and Klarsfeld, The Auschwitz Album *(1981). Sterling Memorial Library, Yale University.*

It was a sight that is beyond any description or understanding or imagination. You cannot, because when you see the pictures of the dead bodies, you just see pictures. You don't see the bodies, the eyes that talk to you and beg you for water. You don't see the mouths quietly trying to say something and not being able to utter a word. You see and you feel as I did, the agony of these people for whom death would be a blessing. They are just dying and can't die.[87]

All around the camp were mounds of bodies, and Sara was ordered to move corpses to a large pit.

These mounds that you see on some of the pictures that are being shown about the Holocaust, they were real people. They were living, breathing, eating, feeling, thinking people, thousands upon thousands of them. Mothers and daughters and children. These pictures are real. And I saw it, I smelled it, I touched them. They were very, very real. This was Bergen-Belsen in March and the beginning of April in 1945.[88]

Sara survived, and was liberated on her birthday, the fifteenth of April.

THERE WERE NO mounds of corpses in Auschwitz. The crematoria took care of that. ''I was standing with my mother-in-law and my sister-in-law with her little girl, when someone approached us, and said, 'Give this child to the grandmother.' And my sister-in-law gave the child to my mother-in-law. They went to the left, and we went to the right. And I said, 'Why?' My mother-in-law took the little one and went to the left.''[89] None of the new arrivals knew what ''left'' meant, and no one who went to the left survived to give testimony. It is from the accounts and reports of the slave or willing workers, and from documents and

Hungarian Jewish woman, perhaps elderly, and four children trudge to crematoria II and III, summer 1944. We do not know their relationship, nor do we know the age of the woman. Hellman, Meier, and Klarsfeld, The Auschwitz Album *(1981). Sterling Memorial Library, Yale University.*

drawings, that we can follow the route that Feigele and Mirka took. They went
to the left, crossed a train track, and came to a road parallel to the rails, running
from the gate building at their left to two relatively large buildings at their right.
An SS man directed them to the right, towards the two buildings. Another SS
man 500 yards down the road told them to turn left, into a compound surrounding
one of the two identical brick buildings with their square, squat chimneys. They
were not led to the large entrance below the chimney, but walked past the
building and then, beyond, along a 70-yard-long terrace. At the end of the paved
asphalt they were told to take a sharp turn to the left, and descend a staircase
ending at a door leading into a basement.

Today, in 1995, that underground space and a room connected to it at
right angles are shallow pits overgrown with grass. In 1944 this place, originally
designed as a mortuary, served as the penultimate stage in a process of destruction that had begun with the identification of Feigele and Mirka as Jews, and
had continued with their incarceration in the Lodz ghetto, their deportation

*Hungarian Jewish women and children entering the compound of crematorium II, summer
1944. Hellman, Meier, and Klarsfeld,* The Auschwitz Album *(1981).
Sterling Memorial Library, Yale University.*

to Auschwitz, and their selection at the station. Robbed of their home and financial assets in 1939, of most of their other property during the four long years in the ghetto, and of their suitcases at the Auschwitz station, they now were to surrender the last things they owned: the clothes they wore. The basement they entered served as the undressing room.

Very few of the hundreds of thousands of people who entered that basement survived. One of them was Filip Müller. ''At the entrance to the basement was a signboard, and written on it in several languages the direction: *To the baths and disinfecting rooms*. The ceiling of the changing room was supported by concrete pillars to which many more notices were fixed, once again with the aim of making the unsuspecting people believe that the imminent process of disinfection was of vital importance for their health. Slogans like *Cleanliness brings freedom* or *One louse may kill you* were intended to hoodwink, as were numbered clothes hooks fixed at a height of 1.50 meters.''[90]

Feigele, Mirka, and the other Jews who had survived the Germans' abuse until that point were told to undress, and then herded into a small vestibule. Someone pointed to the right, to the doors of an oblong white-washed room resembling the one they had just left. But, as Filip Müller knew, there were some important visible, and even more important invisible, differences between the two rooms. ''Down the length of the room concrete pillars supported the ceiling. However, not all the pillars served this purpose: for there were others, too. The Zyclon B gas crystals were inserted through openings into hollow pillars made of sheet metal. They were perforated at regular intervals and inside them a spiral ran from top to bottom in order to ensure as even a distribution of the granular crystals as possible. Mounted on the ceiling was a large number of dummy showers made of metal. These were intended to delude the suspicious on entering the gas chamber into believing that they were in a shower-room.''[91] Feigele, Mirka, and the others were crammed in, the doors closed, and the lights turned off.

While Feigele and Mirka were driven into the underground room, a van marked with a Red Cross sign parked along its side, which projected 1.5 feet above ground. Two ''disinfecting operators'' climbed onto the roof of the basement, carrying sealed tins manufactured by the Degesch company. They chatted leisurely, smoking a cigarette. Then, on signal, each of them walked to a one-foot-high concrete shaft, donned a gas mask, took off the lid, opened the tin, and poured the pea-sized contents into the shaft. They closed the lids, took off their masks, and drove off.

Müller witnessed everything from a short distance. "After a while I heard the sound of piercing screams, banging against the door and also moaning and wailing. People began to cough. Their coughing grew worse from minute to minute, a sign that the gas had started to act. Then the clamour began to subside and to change to a many-voiced dull rattle, drowned now and then by coughing."[92] Ten minutes later all was quiet.

An SS man ordered Müller and the rest of the death squad workers to take the elevator down into the basement. There they waited for the ventilating system to extract the gas from the room and, after some twenty minutes, unbolted the doors to the gas chambers. Contrary to Höss's assertion that he had adopted Zyklon B as a killing agent because it offered an easy death, the victims showed the marks of a terrible struggle.

This is where and how Germans killed Feigele, Mirka, and countless other human beings. Within hours of their arrival in Auschwitz nothing of the Jews remained but smoke, ashes, and our memory of them. Their bodies were brought to the ground floor with the same elevator that Müller had used to go down to the basement, and there they were cremated in one of the five incinerators with three muffles each in the center of the crematorium.

Today we know where Feigele and Mirka died: in a town the Germans always called Auschwitz. We know they built the town in 1270, and a Polish king bought it in 1457. We know the town declined under Polish rule. We know it had a modest existence along a major railway line in the nineteenth century. We know the region became the object of German rage in the 1920s. We know the National Socialists annexed the town to the Reich in 1939. We know they intended to repeat the initiatives of the Middle Ages.

Today we know that Feigele and Mirka died in a camp that was originally created as a labor exchange, that then served as a Polish army base, and that the Germans adapted into a concentration camp to terrorize a local population too useful to deport. We know that the camp acquired one function after another: it became a production site for sand and gravel, an execution site for the Gestapo in Kattowitz, the center of a large agricultural estate to support ethnic German transplantees, a labor pool for constructing a synthetic rubber plant and a new town. We know that, throughout these transformations, Auschwitz remained the centerpiece of Himmler's ambitions in the recovery of German history in this onetime area of German settlement. We know that it became a center of extermination when he lost interest in the town and the region, and that it also served as the heart of a network of satellite camps to service various industries in the region, and that it finally became a labor exchange again, only this time the laborers were Jewish slaves.

Today we know who designed the building: Georg Werkmann, Karl Bischoff, and Walther Dejaco. We know who constructed the furnaces: the Topf & Sons company in Erfurt. We know the power of the forced-air system (over 4 million cubic feet per hour) to fan the flames. We know the official cremation capacity (thirty-two corpses) per muffle per day. We know that it was Bischoff who took the decision to change the larger morgue into an undressing room, and the smaller one into a gas chamber. We know that Dejaco drafted the plan that transformed a mortuary into a death chamber. We know the specifications of the ventilation system that made the room operable as a site for mass extermination: seven horsepower is required to extract the Zyklon B from the gas chamber in twenty minutes. We know that the building was brought into operation on 13 March 1943, when 1,492 women, children, and old people were gassed. We know about the difficulties the Germans had getting everything just the way they wanted. We know who paid the bills and how much was paid.

We know all of that. But we understand very little about many issues central to this machinery of death. Research into the history of the region, the intended future of the town, the development of the camp, and the changing design of the crematoria has been useful, but it is not the whole story about the Holocaust at Auschwitz. It is the questions of the victims and the survivors which loom large.

When Sara Grossmann faced selection upon arrival at Auschwitz in August 1944,

> I lost sight of what was going on. It's crazy. And I was standing with my mother-in-law and my sister-in-law with her little girl, when someone approached us, and said, "Give this child to the grandmother." And my sister-in-law gave the child to my mother-in-law. They went to the left, and we went to the right. *And I said, "Why?"* My mother-in-law took the little one and went to the left. Regina, Esther, and I went to the right. To the left were all the people who were led to the gas chambers, cremato- rium, however you call it.

"Gas chambers, crematorium, however you call it." Half a century later, Sara Grossman was not precise. What mattered was that the men were sepa- rated from the women, and that the grandmother Feigele and the little girl

Mirka went to the left, and the adolescent Regina, and the two sisters-in-law Esther and Sara to the right. And she is correct. That process of selection is the core and moral nadir of the horror of the Holocaust—the selection, and not the gas chambers and crematoria. The Germans and their allies had arrogated to themselves the power to decide who would live and who would die. ''As though,'' Hannah Arendt accused Eichmann, ''you and your superiors had any right to determine who should and who should not inhabit the world.''[93]

Mirka, Sara, and hundreds of thousands of other deportees lined up for selection by a physician. Had he worked alone, he could have done little harm. But he did not. His work was but a small part of a system envisioned by ideologues, organized by bureaucrats, financed by industrialists, serviced by technocrats, operated by ordinary men, and supported by millions of Germans whose daily lives were improved by the goods shipped home to the Reich for their use.

And Sara's question remains: ''And I said, 'Why?' ''

EPILOGUE

OWNING AND DISOWNING AUSCHWITZ

L UXURIOUS GERMAN CARS FILL THE PARKING LOT OF THE AUSCHWITZ-
Birkenau museum. Most European and nearly all American tourists come by
tour bus from Cracow, and Polish visitors use public transport, but Oswiecim is
within an easy day's drive from the German border and the Germans arrive
in their Audis, Benzes, and Bimmers. They make up the single largest group
of foreign visitors.

"When I went to school [the Holocaust] was a taboo subject," Hanna
Delius, one such German tourist, told a *New York Times* journalist in January
1995. Like many of her compatriots, she decided to visit Auschwitz herself.
"I was in such anger and rage when I walked here yesterday. The thing was
planned. It was really drawn up: this should be here, that there, this here. I
can't say I feel guilty, but I do feel responsible in some way."[1]

Half a century after the Red Army liberated the camp, many individual
Germans such as Hanna Delius feel the need to go to Auschwitz. It is, they
say, a moral obligation to face their own history; to recognize, confront,
and ultimately accept historic responsibility for the atrocities committed by
German citizens against others in foreign lands. They hold themselves in some
way accountable for the people—not the place. The actions of their fathers
and grandfathers bind them to Auschwitz, not ownership of a German town

The German East, 1996.
Map by Robert Jan van
Pelt and Don Bonner.

in the German East. Geographically, Auschwitz is like Babi Yar in Ukraine, Lidice in the Czech Republic, or Oradour in France: it is a foreign city in a foreign country. They do not think of Auschwitz as a town founded by Germans and honored with a 700-year German history. Just fifty years after the war, such thoughts do not even cross the tourists' minds.

Once so eager to claim Auschwitz as theirs, the Germans have disowned it completely. This is in part due to the cold war. In the divided Germany of 1948 to 1989, the history of the former German East and the way this history was read by the men who built Auschwitz was condemned as politically incorrect. General Secretary Ulbricht buried the problem in a rhetoric of fraternity between his German Democratic Republic and the Polish People's Republic, while Chancellor Adenauer successfully presented the Federal Republic as a new, democratic Germany that looked westward.

It was not always so easy for West Germany to maintain this stance. With refugees and expellees from the German East accounting for 16.5 percent of the population, the politicians were tempted to pander to the League of Expellees' call for unrelenting opposition to the Potsdam agreement which had brought all the German lands east of the Oder-Neisse under Polish and Soviet administration.[2] But the majority of West Germans did not believe that East Prussia, Pomerania, or Silesia were worth a quarrel with Paris, London, or Washington. And the territories certainly were not worth a war with the Soviet Union. In any case, as the well-respected author and, later, publisher Wolf Jobst Siedler noted in 1964, postwar Germans did not want to think about the eastern territories at all. The memory of the German East not only evoked the image of the westward flight (1944–45) and the postwar deportation of German inhabitants (1945–47); it also conjured up the specter of Jews in cattle cars relentlessly rolling in the opposite direction during the preceding years. Unpleasant as it might be, Siedler urged Germans to resist this comfortable amnesia. It was, he said, important to remember the lost cities as well as the forgotten camps.[3]

Despite Siedler's admonition, first-rate German historians who have made important contributions to a balanced understanding of the history of the region between the Elbe and the Bug simply ignored the concentration camp at Auschwitz and its role in the history of the German East. For instance, the late Walter Kuhn, who grew up close to Auschwitz and who wrote a number of excellent histories of the medieval development of Upper Silesia in general and Auschwitz in particular, referred to the camp only twice in all his works. In 1941 he took students on an excursion to Upper Silesia, he recalled in his memoirs. ''I wanted to show them some Polish dwelling types and settlement forms close to Auschwitz. Suddenly we stood in front of a large iron gate with the inscription *'Arbeit macht frei.'* Without knowing it, we had reached the concentration camp and, deeply shocked, we turned around.''[4] He did not mention the camp again in that memoir. Kuhn limited a discussion of that other Auschwitz to a brief lament in an excellent and scholarly essay on the medieval settlement of the duchy of Auschwitz, published for the first time in 1975. ''In the Second World War the name 'Auschwitz' gained a new and horrible meaning which largely overshadows the older historical interpretation of that land, insofar as one ever existed.''[5]

With the fall of the Berlin Wall in 1989 and the unification of the two German states in 1990, the German East has become topical once again. Immediately after the border opened, the American historian Gordon Craig predicted in *Der Spiegel* magazine that with reunification "sooner or later someone would remember the lost territories in the East."[6]

Craig was correct. The German East quickly became a rallying point for German neo-Nazis.[7] It also acquired a prime place in German bookshops. One of the major publication ventures undertaken after unification is the ten-volume series *German History in the East of Europe*, published by Wolf Jobst Siedler. Siedler has gone out of his way to emphasize that the books do not serve a political aim and that the German history in the east of Europe is irrevocably in the past. Germans have no place or function there any more. "With this history the survivors and the descendants of the catastrophe [the loss of the German East—not the Holocaust] say farewell to a great and tragic millennium of German history."[8] The title itself reflects the publisher's attempt to produce a politically correct commemoration of what an older generation still glorifies as a *German* East. "*German History in the East of Europe* clarifies two things: that *German* history occurred in that historic space, but that east-central Europe cannot be wholeheartedly subsumed in German history. Clearly, this world— its origins and its subsequent history—cannot be read merely as 'German,' but neither can it be understood in its historic individuality without the Germans."[9]

The time had come for a measured, nuanced interpretation of east-central Europe. "The pain of the loss of the homeland has lost its sting, and the outrage over the often so horrible last epoch of German *Ostpolitik* lessens, as can be seen in symposia of German, Polish, and Russian historians. Both sides [Slavs and Germans] try to understand each other, and thereby themselves, in a more balanced way. Since the turning point [*die Wende* in 1989], the Baltic peoples, the Poles, Czechs, Slovaks, and Hungarians very much wish to be part of Europe. Thus both sides, Slavs and Germans, are increasingly conscious of the common heritage that connected them over centuries."[10] The Jews, the people most singularly affected by Germany's mid-twentieth-century *Ostpolitik*, are ignored totally. They have been written out of this history.[11] An accompanying map indicates such important sites of German historical activity as Danzig, Reval (Talinn), and Kiev but excludes Auschwitz. Rudolf Augstein, the publisher of *Der Spiegel*, summarized this attitude critically and ironically in the sentence "*Ja, wenn da nicht das leidige Auschwitz wäre!*" ("Yes, if only that tiresome Auschwitz simply were not there!")[12] But it was, and it is, and it makes short shrift of the sanctimonious sentimentality of a common heritage.

Map showing significant sites of German history in the East of Europe. Siedler, Prospectus. Authors.

The author of the volume on Silesia in Siedler's series, Norbert Conrads, has gone further than to erase the Jews from the history of the German East. He effaces the *Germans*. ''Not without apprehension we must raise the question in a book about Silesian history: Was Auschwitz, located in the enlarged [province of] Upper Silesia at the time of murder, part of Silesian history, its last and its most sinister? We may, in all good conscience, reply in the negative.''[13] To do otherwise, Conrads argued, would be to accept the position that, in view of its medieval history, the German annexation of Auschwitz in 1939 was legitimate.

WHILE THE GERMANS have disowned Auschwitz, Poles and Jews contend for spiritual ownership of the camp. Auschwitz is the most significant memorial site of the Shoah, and it is also the most significant memorial site of Polish suffering under German rule. Every aspect of the camp is an object of contention and conflicting interpretation, even its shape and location.

There are many component parts to what we call Auschwitz, and while a number are still to be seen, some are no longer discernible. Auschwitz I, the *Stammlager*, remains at the edge of the town of Oswiecim; Auschwitz II, or Birkenau, borders the village of Brzezinka, a few miles to the west. It is these sites which are visited. Auschwitz III, Buna, has disappeared, although the synthetic rubber factory functions still, and no one visits it now. Only stones mark the satellite camps at Rajsko, Chelmek, Brzeszcze-Jawiszowice, Trzebinia, and other places; occasionally a building survives, like the greenhouses and laboratory in Rajsko, but there is no indication that they were part of the Auschwitz complex.

Auschwitz I alone appears to be intact. The presentation of the buildings conveys a sense not of abstract history but of tangible actuality. Former inmates take sightseers through the site, instilling them with lived memory—or so we are to believe. For Auschwitz I, though apparently unchanged, is quite different from the camp the Soviets liberated in 1945. At present, it is essentially as it was after the initial 1940–42 program to transform the labor exchange into a German concentration camp. As we have seen, however, Auschwitz I was changed further with the completion of the first stages of a plan to quadruple the size of the camp; another project created a separate industrial area triple the original camp. The edifices erected in these building programs remain intact today. The pleasant, yellow stucco structures visible to the visitor who arrives at the parking lot of the memorial camp belonged to the Auschwitz of the Shoah, although there is no indication to that effect. Partly hidden by a grove of trees and a concrete wall, these erstwhile work halls and barracks are now used as military quarters for the Polish army and as low-income housing. They are off-limits to the tourists. Yet they were part of the camp when it was liberated. A misconstruction of history begins right in the parking

Former concentration camp barracks now used by the Polish army, Oswiecim, 1990.
Photo by Robert Jan van Pelt. Authors.

lot: visitors think they have arrived at the periphery of Auschwitz I; in fact, they are already in the middle of the camp as it existed in 1945.

Practical and theoretical considerations prompted the severance of the stucco barracks from the memorial camp. There was a crippling lack of housing in Poland in 1945, and these structures were spacious, well-built, intact, and available for immediate occupancy. Then too, it was easier to transform the camp into a museum with a specific, controlled, ideological message when the site was confined to a more limited area. Furthermore, the excellence of Walther Dejaco's design and the solidity of the barracks built during the war would have suggested that the architectural history of Auschwitz was more complex and multilayered than our immediate postwar era assumptions led us to believe. The image of the shoddy horse stable barracks in Birkenau had quickly become a canonical representation of the Germans' contempt for concentration camp inmates, and the new barracks of the main camp did not fit that image.

There may have been another reason why part of the camp was excised, and it has to do with the role of the *Arbeit macht frei* gate. For the post-Auschwitz generation, that gate symbolizes the threshold that separates the human community from the Planet Auschwitz. It is a fixed point in our collective memory, and therefore the canonical beginning of the tour through the camp. In fact,

Gate to Auschwitz I, Oswiecim, 1990. Photo by Robert Jan van Pelt. Authors.

however, the arch did not have a central position in the history of Auschwitz. It played no role in the Judeocide. Indeed, very few of the Jews deported to Auschwitz ever saw that gate. Arriving at the so-called *Judenrampe* just outside the Auschwitz station, the Jews were marched or taken by truck to Birkenau; later a spur rail line was laid and the transports went there directly. Furthermore, although the arch was the main gate to the living area of Auschwitz I in 1940 and 1941, in the expansion program the following year it became an internal structure separating the original camp from the extended domain. From 1942 to 1945, the main entrance to the living area of the camp was exactly at the point where one now enters the parking lot—a passage currently marked by a kiosk for the parking attendant. If more building materials had been allocated to the camp in 1942, visitors now would pass through a monumental, two-story gate complex worthy of the importance of the camp within the Germans' plans for the New Order.

Yet our memory clings to the inscription above the gate as the modern version of Dante's *Lasciate ogni speranza* (Abandon all hope) at the entrance of Inferno. Nothing is labeled or inscribed before that point, and therefore visitors to Auschwitz I remain ignorant of what may be the most interesting exhibit: the reception center adjacent to the parking lot. Today it is a multipurpose building to meet tourists' needs, with a restaurant, cafeteria, post office, currency exchange, cinema, bookshop, guest rooms, and Slawomir Staszak's Galician Antiquariat. Most visitors assume that the structure was built after 1945, even though the quality of both the workmanship and the materials far exceeds anything built in postwar Oswiecim. In fact, it was conceived in 1941 and constructed between 1942 and 1944. It served as the prisoners' reception center and included a delousing installation with nineteen gas chambers for clothing, a bathhouse for the prisoners, a laundry, and so on. Visitors who now enter the building to the left of the restaurant do so at precisely the point where, as we discussed in chapter 7, civilians were inducted into the camp. The little vestibule is still largely the same, but current visitors are herded through a new corridor along the northeast side of the building which was created after the war. During the war the prisoners passed through a series of large rooms, each designated for a specific function. Entering this labyrinth as a captured civilian, the registered, tattooed, robbed, disinfected, shaved, and striped-pajama-clad prisoner left through the porch facing the gate with the inscription *Arbeit macht frei*. The oral testimonies and memoirs of survivors attest to the shattering impact of this ritual of humiliating baptism into the kingdom of death. The building where it occurred ought to have been marked by an inscription, but it was not, and now stands incognito.

Visitor reception center, Oswiecim, 1990. Photo by Robert Jan van Pelt. Authors.

The architecture designed to enact the metamorphosis from *Mensch* to *Untermensch* was intact when the Soviets liberated the camp in 1945. All traces of it were removed subsequently. The guidebook for sale in the bookstore does not mention the building at all. Perhaps the men and women who created the museum could not reconcile its implications with their ideology of a resistance: an ideology that denied total victimization. Perhaps it was simply a question of resources and the need for tourist services. Whether for doctrinal or practical reasons, the destruction of the original arrangement within the present visitor reception center is a postwar obfuscation and a loss.

There have been additions to the camp the Russians found in 1945 as well as deletions, and the suppression of the prisoner reception site is matched by the reconstruction of crematorium I just outside the northeast perimeter of the present museum camp. With its chimney and its gas chamber, the crematorium functions as the solemn conclusion for tours through the camp. Visitors are not told that the crematorium they see is largely a postwar reconstruction.

When Auschwitz was transformed into a museum after the war, the decision was taken to concentrate the history of the whole complex into one of its component parts. The infamous crematoria where the mass murders had taken place lay in ruins in Birkenau, two miles away. The committee felt

Crematorium I, Oswiecim, 1990. Photo by Robert Jan van Pelt. Authors.

that a crematorium was required at the end of the memorial journey, and crematorium I was reconstructed to speak for the history of the incinerators at Birkenau. This program of usurpation was rather detailed. A chimney, the ultimate symbol of Birkenau, was re-created; four hatched openings in the roof, as if for pouring Zyklon B into the gas chamber below, were installed, and two of the three furnaces were rebuilt using original parts. There are no signs to explain these restitutions, they were not marked at the time, and the guides remain silent about it when they take visitors through this building that is presumed by the tourist to be the place where *it happened.*

THE AUSCHWITZ-BIRKENAU State Museum presents only the main camp at Auschwitz to visitors. One can enter Birkenau, but on one's own. The standard guided tour does not include a visit to the principal site of the Judeocide, although it was there that the countless transports arrived and the four chimneys smoked. Auschwitz I alone was designated to be the permanent exhibit. There were, as always, practical reasons. Birkenau had been largely dismantled when most of the portable stables used as barracks were taken away after the war to shelter construction crews in Warsaw. But there were also deeper, more compelling motivations for the decision. First, the fate of the Jews did not have an important place on the national agenda of postwar Poland. And second, Auschwitz I had been established as the Germans' instrument to subjugate the *Poles* into serfdom—an enslavement the Poles rightly interpreted as the initial steps toward a "solution" to a Polish problem. Auschwitz I was a tremendously significant site in Polish history, and the 1947 law that established the museum explicitly stated that the site was to commemorate "the martyrdom of the Polish nation and other nations in Oswiecim." Given this directive, it made sense that the museum would concentrate the state's meager resources on the part of Auschwitz where Polish resisters and hostages had suffered and died.

The result of this combination of expediency and historical experience is an exhibition that relies on a few paltry exhibits in blocks 4 and 5 of Auschwitz I to relate the mass murder of Jews perpetrated in Birkenau. In block 4, two rooms are dedicated to a description of the process of extermination to which Jews—and not Poles—were subjected in the death camp. In one of these rooms the history of Birkenau is presented through the large model of crematorium II referred to in chapter 1. This graphic, almost pornographic, depiction of people entering, undressing, and dying is not, and was not meant to be, informative. Its intention is, literally, to "re-present," to make the fate of the Jews symbolically present in Auschwitz I. That goal is also achieved through the transposition of hair, eyeglasses, crutches, suitcases, and so on from Birkenau to block 5 in Auschwitz I. These endow the commemorative camp with the history of the nearby murder machinery.

The main camp first and foremost preserved Polish—not Jewish—history, and the decision to relegate Birkenau to a position of secondary importance reflects a specific ideology of remembrance described by the Canadian sociologist Iwona Irwin-Zarecka: "Auschwitz . . . is *not*, for Poles, a symbol of Jewish suffering. Rather, it is a general symbol of 'man's inhumanity to man' and a symbol of the Polish tragedy at the hands of the Nazis. It is a powerful reminder of the evil of *racism*, and not a singular reminder of the deadliness of anti-Semitism. In the most literal sense of memories evoked on site, it is an 'Auschwitz without Jews.' "[14]

This ideology elucidates the extraordinary significance of block 11 (which we described in chapter 6) to the Poles. They rightly claim "The Block of Death" as their site of martyrdom, and recently it has been so recognized by the Roman Catholic Church. Father Maximilian Kolbe, the central protagonist in the story of block 11, volunteered to die in the place of another man, a father with children. Kolbe's moral choice fits the traditional notion of martyrdom, and his example is one of the few moments of grace in this abyss of misery. But it is also almost

Father Kolbe's cell, block 11, Oswiecim, 1990. Photo by Robert Jan van Pelt. Authors.

irrelevant. Father Kolbe's death was exceptional because, ultimately, he died a free man while nearly all the other millions of victims never had a choice at all. In a fundamental way his memorial in block 11 fits the conventional, chivalric ideology of a hero who fights and dies on behalf of someone else. Pervasive and dominant, this concept of heroism is reflected in the official symbol of the memorial camp, a shield with two drawn swords, and the official banner which flies over block 11 in Auschwitz I and the monument in Birkenau, the red triangle of the gentile political prisoners superimposed on the uniform motif of vertical blue and white stripes. There is no room in this ideology for women like Mrs. Zucker, who, during the selection in Birkenau on 22 August 1944, held fast to the hand of a little girl she knew. As her then fifteen-year-old daughter, Esther, recalled, "This was the last time I saw my mother. She went with that neighbor's child. So when we talk about heroes, mind you, this was a hero: a woman who would not let a four-year-old child go by herself."[15]

A VISIT TO AUSCHWITZ I takes time, and visitors from abroad who spend the preceding night in the relative comfort of the Holiday Inn in the somewhat distant city of Cracow have little time left after their late arrival in Auschwitz, their lunch, and their guided tour to undertake more than a cursory trip to the enormous site

Landscape Building Section I, Oswiecim-Brzezinka, 1990. Photo by Robert Jan van Pelt. Authors.

at Birkenau. Late in the afternoon the buses drop them off in front of the gate, and most groups limit their visit to a pilgrimage along the ramp to the monument at its end. For many Jewish visitors there is a sense of relief; the lack of information at Birkenau at least spares them the pain of the official interpretation provided at the main camp. The bleakness of Birkenau fits the Jewish memory of the genocide as Shoah: total devastation and ruin. The site has not been appropriated, or falsified, by transposed objects, as in Auschwitz I. The bronze medallion nailed to the monument and depicting drawn swords, the red-triangle banner hanging from a flagpole, and the large cross in front of the Kommandantur of Birkenau (which was transformed into a parish church for the inhabitants of Brzezinka) are certainly inappropriate in the place where more than a million Jews died. But they are physically so insignificant in relation to the overwhelming desolation of the site that most people fail to notice them.

Nevertheless, time and again, Birkenau too is annexed, albeit insidiously. As the vast expanse of the camp can easily accommodate large crowds, the monument has become the focus of public ceremonies. Inexact allusions, snatches of misinformation, and inappropriate metaphors uttered at such gath-

Landscape Building Section II, Oswiecim-Brzezinka, 1990. Photo by Robert Jan van Pelt. Authors.

erings generate histories that corrode the history of the Judeocide. The most stunning of these revisions occurred on the occasion of the pope's visit on 7 June 1979. At that time the church represented one of the two pillars of Polish resistance against communism (the other was Solidarity), and it seemed opportune to the church leadership for the pope to visit Auschwitz, a martyrium of the Polish nation. Many in those heady days hoped that the church would provide spiritual leadership for a reconciliation of Polish and Jewish history. It did not. Standing amid the ruins of the crematoria where three generations of Jews burned and in front of a memorial that remembered the "Six Million," the pope interpreted the Polish inscription to mean that "six million Poles lost their lives during the Second World War: a fifth of the nation."[16]

The pope made a true historical statement, yet the place where he chose to do so, between the ruins of crematorium II and crematorium III, gave it a

Monument, Oswiecim-Brzezinka, 1990. Photo by Robert Jan van Pelt. Authors.

new and infelicitous significance. Speaking as a Pole to a Polish audience, the pope gave a further twist to the scandal of "Auschwitz without Jews." As Iwona Irwin-Zarecka has observed, "the persistent commemoration of six million Polish victims of genocide:—a figure which includes the three million Polish Jews—testifies to the ease of appropriating the Jewish dead as one's own." But, she continued,

> the figure of "six million Poles" does more than that. It also grants the dead Jew the status of a Pole, in a post-mortem acceptance of the Jews' membership in the Polish family. And this renders a reading of the past which makes that past unrecognizable. The Jew not only appears to be mourned on a par with others—which he was not—he also appears to have always belonged, which he did not. The destruction of the Jewish community, when reclaimed as the loss of Polish lives, acquires a sense of trauma which it did not have, at least for the majority. And the sharing in suffering, together with assigning all the blame to the Nazis, helps eliminate questions about the Poles' action and inaction towards the Jews.[17]

The issue of usurpation is neither simple nor straightforward. When the pope took the decision to go to Birkenau, the process of appropriation began, no matter what he would say. The choice to go to that site was the first step. But there is a hierarchy of arrogation, and a concomitant hierarchy of responsibility. Falsifying the boundaries of a site, or the purpose of certain structures (as in Auschwitz I), constitutes one level of appropriation; the pope's visit to Birkenau is another; and the words he spoke yet a third. The onus for each varies. We are less responsible for a site we inherit than for words deliberately uttered there.

In direct response to the pope's call for a beacon of (Catholic) piety amid the evil of Auschwitz-Birkenau, a few Carmelite nuns sought and obtained permission to found a convent in a building just outside the camp's perimeter but close to block 11. The structure they chose had been a theater before the war. During the occupation it functioned as a storehouse; plans to transform it into an SS casino and a centerpiece in the new Kommandantur were never carried out. The nuns moved in unobtrusively and conducted their business quietly. Other buildings around the camp are used for various purposes, and the establishment of the convent was not particularly remarkable until Belgian Catholics exploited the situation. In an appeal to raise money for the sisters,

Carmelite convent seen from the prisoner compound of Auschwitz I, Oswiecim, 1990. Photo by Robert Jan van Pelt. Authors.

the Catholic charity Aide à l'Eglise en Détresse presented the convent as a "spiritual fortress and a guarantee of the conversion of strayed brothers from our countries as well as proof of our desire to erase the outrages so often done to the Vicar of Christ."[18] Triumphalist in its premise, militant in tone, and offensive to Jews, this statement of purpose triggered a five-year battle of quarrelsome assertions, self-righteous statements, sanctimonious professions, frivolous pronouncements, irreverent protests, and even physical tussles that must prove, as far as the history of the memorial site at Auschwitz is concerned, of only passing significance: in 1993 the nuns vacated the building at the fence and moved to a new center of prayer, built at the respectful distance of 550 yards from the perimeter of the camp.

This painful episode has left an unresolved issue: the legacy of Edith Stein and its role in the memorial camp. A convert to Roman Catholicism, Stein had entered a Carmelite convent under the name of Sister Benedicta of the Cross. For the Germans, however, Sister Benedicta was still a Jew. She was arrested and transported to Birkenau, where she was killed a few hundred yards northwest from the present monument. She was one of the thousands of victims in the first mass murders of Jews in Birkenau in the summer of 1942, when eight hundred people at a time were exterminated in bunker 2, a peasant cottage with crude gas chambers.

Stein's death was a tragic footnote in the history of Birkenau until John Paul II announced his intention to initiate the beatification process for "the Carmelite Sister Benedicta of the Cross . . . who was a descendant of a Jewish family living in Wroclow."[19] Stein had died because she had been born a Jew, yet on his 1979 visit the pope claimed her for the church. According to him, she had died the death of a Christian martyr *and* a daughter of the Jewish people. As a prominent Catholic theologian, Joseph Cardinal Ratzinger, has explained, "It is important to note that Edith Stein, agnostic, atheistic, once she became a Catholic was saying: 'Now I feel myself back to true Judaism.' Because not only did she regain the faith in God, but finding the faith in Christ, she entered in the full heritage of Abraham. . . . Entering the union with Christ, she entered in the heart of Judaism. Following the thought of St. Paul we can say that becoming a Christian, I became

Marker recording Edith Stein's martyrdom at bunker 2, Oswiecim-Brzezinka, 1993. Photo by Robert Jan van Pelt. Authors.

a true Jew.''[20] In short, Auschwitz was a new Golgotha, and the Jews had died there, as John Paul II declared in a speech of 1 May 1987, with Christ's cross placed over their shoulders.[21]

This Christian, triumphalist appropriation of Jewish suffering is clearly manifested around the remains of bunker 2. Pious visitors placed a cross in the ruins of the gas chambers where Jews, including Stein, were killed. Upset by this, Jews erected a Star of David affixed to a post. A battle of symbols and a proliferation of crosses and stars ensued. One star was even nailed to the top of a ten-meter-high utility pole. This star-and-cross war ended when a group of Warsaw schoolchildren erected a large cross with a Star of David nailed to it. To the children it seemed a fitting compromise. Unfortunately, however, the union of the two symbols reflects very precisely one of the church's triumphalist doctrines: the significance of the death of the Six Million (Jews) as witnesses to the truth of His Cross.

THE COMMEMORATION ceremonies for the fiftieth anniversary of the liberation of Auschwitz reflected the continued legacy of disparate claims on Auschwitz. The collapse of communism had done nothing to resolve the tensions between Poles and Jews over spiritual ownership of the site. Led by President Lech Walesa, the Polish government initially refused to acknowledge the Holocaust of the Jews at the official observances scheduled for 26 and 27 January 1995. Outraged by this high-handed marginalization of their co-religionists' suffering, Jewish groups organized a separate ceremony in Birkenau.[22]

Some fifteen hundred Jews assembled for the ceremony in Birkenau on 26 January. They were joined by Roman Herzog, the president of Germany and the only dignitary to absent himself from the official function in Cracow. "Although we know that God is merciful, please God do not have mercy for those people who created this place," the survivor, author, and Nobel laureate Elie Wiesel pleaded. "Remember the nocturnal procession of children, of more children, and more children, so frightened, so beautiful. If we could simply look at one, our heart would break. But it did not break the hearts of the murderers." At the Jagiellonian University, thirty miles away in Cracow, Walesa lamented the Germans' attempts to destroy Poland's "intellectual and spiritual strength." He did not mention the Jews.[23]

Tensions between Jews and Poles increased as the day progressed. That evening Elie Wiesel met privately with Lech Walesa. They had much to discuss. In 1988, when the then Solidarnosc leader had not been permitted to leave the country, Wiesel had organized an entire planeful of Nobel laureates to go to Poland to meet the labor activist. Together, Wiesel and Walesa had traveled to Oswiecim, and there Wiesel had asked Walesa to extend his solidarity to the Jews who had died at that site. It was, Wiesel had suggested to Walesa, the new Nobel laureate's duty to be the custodian of the memory of the Jewish victims at Oswiecim. Walesa had accepted that responsibility, and on Thursday, 26 January 1995, Wiesel reminded Walesa of his promise.[24]

Walesa arrived at Auschwitz I the next day and, flanked by the Jewish European politician Simone Weil and by Elie Wiesel, he entered the camp through the *Arbeit macht frei* gate and walked to block 11. There he delivered his address. ''The distance we have walked from the sign that says 'labor liberates' to this death house is a symbolic journey. A journey down the road that stands for the suffering of many nations, especially the Jewish nation.'' The ceremony at the *Stammlager* was followed by observances at Birkenau. Prayers for five groups of victims were said, beginning with Kaddish, the Jewish prayer for the dead, recited by the rabbi of Warsaw. President Walesa spoke once more, and this time he particularly noted the suffering of the Jews and the fate of the Gypsies.[25]

THE POLISH GOVERNMENT should have been better able to avoid such bitter controversy. Recognizing the complexity of the ongoing legacy of Auschwitz, then Prime Minister Tadeusz Mazowiecki established a commission in the autumn of 1989 to transform the memorial camp into a site acceptable to all concerned. As an international conference on ''The Future of Auschwitz: Should the Relicts Be Preserved?'' held in the summer of 1993 revealed, the commission faced a nearly impossible task. The exhibits in Auschwitz I are deteriorating rapidly, and the physical remains of Auschwitz-Birkenau are falling apart. The museum conservators therefore posed very practical questions on the conference agenda: What should be done with the hair, the suitcases, the brushes? Should the disintegrating barbed wire in Birkenau be replaced?

The participants quickly found themselves caught in the web of the many, contradictory functions and meanings of Auschwitz. It is a destination of mass tourism (in 1989 alone 700,000 people from eighty-nine countries visited the camp), a Polish museum to preserve the physical remains of the Germans' crimes and to educate future generations, and it is a place of pilgrimage, a cemetery for mourners. Inseparable and entangled, these three functions clash at every spot.

The Auschwitz-Birkenau State Museum staff listened to the foreign guests and presented their own plan to construct a memorial consisting of slabs of glass inscribed with the names of the people who died in the camp complex. These slabs—hundreds of them—are to be installed in the Central Sauna. If executed, the memorial would obliterate a unique architectural record of the National Socialist system for dehumanization: the interior of the Central Sauna building. This was German industry at its most effective; the designer of the building took pride in the fact that it worked "like a conveyer belt."[26]

We proposed moving the presentation of the *Shoah* from blocks 4 and 5 of Auschwitz I to Birkenau, where the Jews were murdered. Auschwitz I, we believe, should focus on the significance of the camp in the history of Polish-German relations. We argued that the present resurgence of the kind of ethnic troubles that contributed to Germany's annexation of Danzig, Pomeralia, Posen, and eastern Upper Silesia in 1939 provides a powerful impetus to refocus the exhibition in the *Stammlager*, which should explain Himmler's policies as Reich Commissioner for the Consolidation of the German Nation in the annexed territories. We also argued that the present visitor reception center should be stripped of its tourist services and, restored to its original internal arrangement, preserved as a major relic of the German regime. Most important, Auschwitz I needs to be recognized as a central site for Poles in particular and Christians in general; the didactic labels and informational plaques cannot collapse the history of Auschwitz I and II.

The genocide of the Jews and the mass murder of Gypsies and Soviet prisoners of war took place at Birkenau, where a memorial museum has not yet been developed. At the moment, visitors enter the camp through the well-known gate and hurry along the tracks to the monument at the end of the axis, which discourages exploration of the rest of the site. It would be helpful to give visitors a sense of the sheer scale of the place and of the megalomaniac ambition of the Germans. Our proposal includes a permanent exhibition to present the history of the *Shoah* on the site of 'Canada' because of its specific role, its location between the three gas chamber sites, and its moral significance.

Exiting the exhibition, the visitor can proceed along the wastewater treatment plant to the ruins of crematorium III, the monument, and the ruins of crematorium II. Only then will the visitor follow the railway tracks, but in counter-movement to the arriving cattle cars in the 1940s. This is consistent with the dominant ideology of our project which emphasizes that we cannot experience the fate of the victims; at best, we can be witnesses to their suffering.

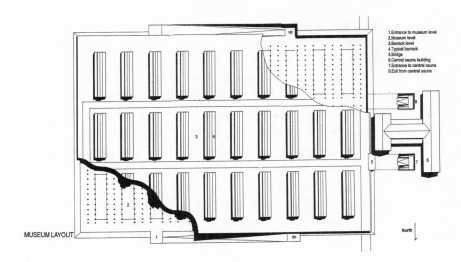

Plan of underground museum design, Auschwitz-Birkenau, 1993. By Paul Backewich and Robert
Jan van Pelt. The exterior of the museum presents a reconstruction of the horse stable barracks of "Canada,"
which will function as large skylights for the exhibition space below ground. The exhibition space
sandwiches the visitor between the two planes of floor and ceiling, which are normally
taken for granted but here invested with significance. The barracks/skylights will be separated
from the space below by a iron grid "ceiling" on which are deposited, visible to those
below, the eyeglasses, crutches, suitcases, and other personal possessions found in "Canada" after
the German retreat. Similarly, important objects and information will be located in the
floor beneath the visitors' feet. The center of the exhibition will be one of the most important
architectural relics at Birkenau, the Central Sauna.

An excellent solution to this problem was formulated decades ago. In the late
1950s, a group of Polish architects and sculptors led by Oskar and Zofia Hansen
submitted a radical proposal to the international competition for a monument in
Auschwitz-Birkenau that gave form to the chasm between the 1.1 million dead
and the living, an abyss the latter cannot traverse. Their design refused to allow
the ruins of the camp to become objects for others to arrogate. It made no
suggestion that there was some way in which the living could trace the steps of
the victims, understand their experiences, or share their memory.[27]

The architects proposed to close the infamous gate of Birkenau through
which the trains transporting the victims had rolled to the platform and the

selections. No one was ever to pass through that gate again. But they knew that it would be unacceptable, indeed reprehensible, simply to close the camp as if it were a place of lethal contamination. If no one entered it, the site and the event would slip into oblivion, and this the architects did not want at all. It was their goal to *confront* the living with oblivion, to bring them face to face with the essential truth of the site: the fact that, ultimately, no memory could connect them to Birkenau's past. Their plan forced the visitor to the desolate realization that one merely passes along the event one hoped to grasp.

The designers proposed to remove a few meters of the barbed-wire fence north of the main gate to the camp, thus creating the illusion that the visitors had to sneak through an accidental opening. But they were not to walk on its soil. A special path of granite, 60 meters wide and 1,000 meters long, was to slash diagonally across the grid of the camp, towards the ruins of the crematoria. Slightly elevated, it was to float over the camp, along the remains of the barracks. The path would not touch them and would provide no devotional stations. The only interruptions of the granite strip were to be identical open rectangles, like graves cut out of the floor, to frame the few remaining fragments of the barracks. Slightly larger than the perimeter of the barracks, these holes in the granite walkway (around which one had to walk) were to set the foundations and chimneys as if they were precious relics. The architects did not plan to stabilize the ruins framed by the openings in the granite path: with time they would change. When they designed it, almost all of the barracks had already been removed, and only their chimneys remained standing, uneasily. They served as a temporary concession to our need for symbols; the designers anticipated that they would fall into pieces, and grass would cover the rubble. For some time even this ruin grass would be imbued with memory. But eventually nature would regain possession of the site, leaving the layers of history below to be excavated by archaeologists in the distant future. In the end there would be only that strange granite path traversing the former railroad tracks and ending at the foundations of crematorium II. The walkway did not pass over the scenes of greatest evil: while the undressing room was to jot forwards into the path, the gas chamber was to remain outside it. The visitor would leave by another opening in the barbed-wire fence. There was to be no monument, no inscription, nothing.

For the designers, the suffering of the victims and the life that had been within the camp had become a history not to be excavated: *that* history could never be memory. The design did not provide for a place to rest, a spot where

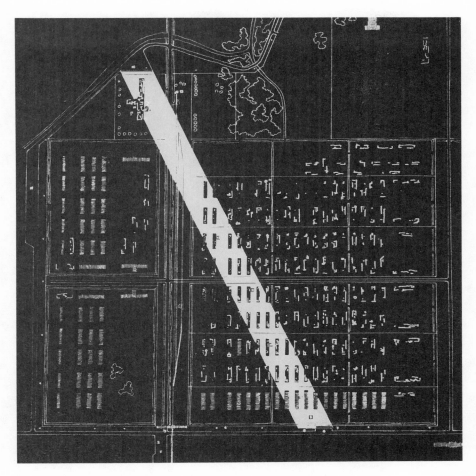

Plan of the design for a monument at Birkenau. Forum (1959).
The granite walkway is indicated by the white band.

a visitor could remain. Only one part of the camp could be memory: the world of the perpetrators. Much easier to represent, that world did not belong to the deep recesses of history, but still aggressively framed the horizon of the living. The architects proposed to preserve and maintain the guard towers and the other structures surrounding the perimeter of the camp. Powerful objects in the geography of our world, they were to remain intact.

The proposal was relentless. It refused to accept the illusion of memory.

There were no stones to touch, no center to stand strongly against the ravages of time, no majesty or dignity, no eerie but beautiful aura. There was to be no inscription commemorating the Six Million. Only silence and the bizarre granite walkway to pose the question for future generations: What happened here?

The proposal received the first prize but was not built. Brilliant in its conception, it had failed to take into account that there were survivors. And they had been omitted from the design. The survivors protested that there was no place for them, and they were right. They would have been locked out from their own experience, or locked in forever.

These objections were articulated fifteen years after liberation and at that time they were correct. It would have been unfitting, inappropriate, and above all inaccurate to have constructed a memorial, a transformation of history into a granite-shaped memory, without acknowledging the survivors. The situation in the near future, however, will not be the same as that of the 1950s. When there are no survivors, there will be no memory to connect the living with Birkenau's past. Soon, perhaps, it will be fitting, appropriate, and accurate to construct the Hansens' vision of a memorial with its message of desolation and separation. Future generations may walk through Birkenau but, not being of it, they will be constrained to walk over it. It will be their lot to pass over that terrain, unable to grasp the events of the killing fields.

ACKNOWLEDGMENTS

ONE OF THE PLEASURES OF FINISHING A BOOK IS THAT IT GIVES WRITERS AN OPPORtunity to thank those who have helped make the project a product. This is especially true in our case. We could not have gathered the information, collected the photographs, or afforded the cost of this type of research without the assistance and aid of others.

Our first and greatest debt is to the survivors, whose oral histories were a vital source of information. We are grateful to them for the many, many hours each and every one spent with us, recalling and recording the events of their lives long ago. It was, they said, an "obligation and responsibility," but it was also an enormous undertaking, and we thank them for it.

In the course of our multinational research, many individuals and families took on the project with enthusiasm and, because they wished to see its successful conclusion, offered us hospitality and aid with the practical problems of everyday life in a foreign location. Our acknowledgments to them are in alphabetical order by city. We are deeply obliged to Saskia and Eitan Mazor in Amsterdam, who year after year provided a "base camp" for our travels on the Continent. We are delighted to thank Klaus Rupprecht in Berlin, who offered his friendship as well as his home. We are deeply beholden to Marian and Wanda Sliwka, Grazyna and Janusz Mincer, and Barbara and Kazimierz Senkowsky in Brzeszcze, who welcomed us in Oswiecim, offered us a room, shared their food, and showed us their country. We thank Maria Ember in Budapest for her generous help with introductions and general support. We are very grateful to Ineke and Wim van Pelt in Doetinchem, who, to her delight, took Debórah ice-skating on the Slangenburg moat and whose home provided a regular and welcome escape from the Federal Archive in Koblenz. We are obliged to Joan and Ben Weinreb, whose house was a second home in London, and we keenly regret the loss of Joan, who did not live to see the end of this project. We thank Beata Koszlowska in Oswiecim for her generous help obtaining copies of historical postcards of her hometown, and Sylwia Tempel, who helped us in Oswiecim. In Paris, the entire Barsky-Bérujeau family, as well as Claude Jean and Martin Bressani, offered us hospitality and help, and we thank them. With the death of Odette Bérujeau we have lost a friend and a clear-sighted witness of the razzias in Paris. She remembered these dragnet operations vividly, and had much insight into the simultaneous collusion and helplessness of bystanders such as she. Wanda and Lech Kadlubowski in Sopot shared their home and their knowledge and showed us the beauty of the Vistula delta. In Vienna, Friedrich Katz offered us hospitality and Lotte Badian made us more meals than we could eat. We especially wish to acknowledge the brothers Sidney and Ralph Rose of Worcester, Massachusetts, who endowed the Rose Professorship at Clark University, which Debórah now holds. We are grateful to them for their commitment to Holocaust education and for their generosity of spirit and pocket.

We would like to express our deepest appreciation to the many individuals who generously shared historical documents and photographs. Niels Gutschow received us in Absteinach as he was leaving for Nepal, and we never thanked him properly for all the material he gave us. Susanne Heim in Berlin shared her research material from Katowice with an open hand, and we are grateful. We thank Slawomir Staszak in Cracow for making available to us photos from his excellent collection of architectural drawings pertaining to the history of Oswiecim. And we salute Jean-Claude Pressac in Ville-du-Bois, who generously shared his time and knowledge in Brzezinka, his company in Oswiecim, Paris, and Ville-du-Bois, and his initial findings for Moscow.

Jane Hersey, Judy Jolly-Bunge, and Robert Wiljer read the manuscript and offered critical suggestions, for which we are extremely grateful.

We have the support of many colleagues at our own universities and elsewhere. Again in alphabetical order, by institution, it is a pleasure to thank Jörn Rüsen of Bielefeld University for his encouragement and Dan Hofman of Cranbrook Academy for providing the first external forum for our ideas. We were greatly enriched by Yehuda Bauer (Hebrew University) and Elana Mayroz's semester at Yale. They were engaged and committed colleagues, and we are delighted to acknowledge their support. We are indebted to Michael Berenbaum of the Unites States Holocaust Research Institute for facilitating our research; Krystyna Gorniak-Kocikowska of Southern Connecticut State University and Mikolaj Kadlubowski of the University of Waterloo for helping us with translations from Polish; Jonathan Webber and Annette Winkelman of Oxford University who took seriously our historical work on Auschwitz in their consideration of the future of the site; and Marianne Gerschel (New York) and Christopher Browning of Pacific-Lutheran University in Tacoma for asking the right questions. It is a special satisfaction to thank Nechama Tec of the University of Connecticut for her keen interest and clear-sighted understanding of the significance of the material, Leo Katz at the University of Pennsylvania for his step-by-step involvement with both project and product from commencement to completion, Michael Marrus of the University of Toronto for his perspicacity and encouragement, and Raul Hilberg of the University of Vermont for his appreciation of the application of this genre of historical material to the history of the Holocaust. From the University of Waterloo, Rick Haldenby, Brian Hunt, and Donald McKay facilitated Robert-Jan's prolonged absences from the university, Thomas Seebohm helped with the computer model, and Richard Sliwka extended the hospitality of his family in Poland. Finally we happily thank Gillian Rose of Warwick University and George Hersey of Yale University for their critical reading and equally critical suggestions.

Some of our research was made into a television documentary called "Blueprints of Genocide" by BBC-Horizon and "Nazi Designers of Death" by PBS-Nova, and we would like to thank the producer Isabel Rosin and director Mike Rossiter for their interest in our work.

We thank Peter Gallagher for his many months of work on the Birkenau computer model, and Paul Bakewich for his skill in giving life and context to the resulting computer drawings. Don Bonner and Jacques Chazaud remained cheerful every time we changed our minds about the way the historical maps should be drawn. We thank Kate Mullin for the wonderful, simple, very legible axonometric representations of key buildings she extracted from the confused blueprints. Harun Rashid quickly responded to a last-minute request to transform fragmented material into a legible plan of the IG Farben Buna plant, and Jason Ha fine-tuned some of the reconstructions. We are very grateful to Philip Doele for his lovely reconstruction of medieval Auschwitz, and to Michael Hanney for his effort to remove digitally the dirt from Stosberg's New Year's greeting card and his final design for the new town of Auschwitz. Mikolaj Kadlubowski patiently and efficiently redrew the original plans of the crematoria, and we share his dismay that including these drawings in his portfolio did not help him get a job in Albert Speer's post-Spandau firm.

The staff from the photographic department of the Auschwitz-Birkenau State Museum, Ryszard Kozlowski (Oswiecim), Robert McNair from the University of Waterloo and Inge Altena, Carl Kaufman, Richard la Plante, Daniel Lopez, and Joseph Szaszfai of Yale University went far out of their way to reproduce the illustrations, and we thank them for their time and their efforts. They were a pleasure to work with, although we were no pleasure to them. Ann Sharpe has transcribed the English language oral histories for over a decade now, and with each passing year it becomes more difficult to express the extent of our gratitude.

A study such as *Auschwitz, 1270 to the Present* requires many support services, and we are beholden to Hilda Hofstetter, Eleanor Kaufman, Heather Murphy, and Ena Wrighton.

We are very appreciative of the many expert librarians and archivists who helped us to identify sources, and who facilitated access to them. We are particularly obliged to Helena Kubica, Barbara Jarosz, Stanislawa Iwaszko, Izabela Smolen, Henryk Swiebocki, Krystyna Olesky, and Franciszek Piper of the Auschwitz-Birkenau State Museum; David Marwell, Erika-Annemarie Ude, and Renate Wolf of the Berlin Document Center; Josef Henke, Rainer Hofman, Gabriele Jakobi, Ellen Kaiser, Meinrad Nilger and Werner Schahrmann of the Bundesarchiv in Koblenz; Rainer Egger and Karl Rossa of the Heeresarchiv in Vienna; Hans Reiter of the Institut für Zeitgeschichte in Munich; Elfriede Kozumplik and Reinhard Hager of the Landesgericht für Strafsachen in Vienna; Dick van Galen

Last of the Rijksinstituut voor Oorlogsdocumentatie in Amsterdam; Elzbieta Skalinska-Dindorf and Pawel Hudzik of the Oswiecim Municipal Archive; William Connelly, Brewster Chamberlain, Elizabeth Koenig, and Carl Modig of the United States Holocaust Research Institute in Washington, D.C.; Richard Pinnell and his colleagues of the University of Waterloo Map Library; and Arthur White and his many patient colleagues of the Sterling Memorial Library of Yale University, New Haven.

A study such as this is very costly, and we are deeply indebted to the Social Sciences and Humanities Research Council of Canada, which supported the research in Europe, and to Paul Ashmore of the Toronto Dominion Bank, who extended credit and increased overdraft limits whenever the need arose. We are delighted to acknowledge the support of the John Simon Guggenheim Memorial Foundation, which awarded us Fellowships. These uninterrupted blocks of time gave us the opportunity to complete our book, and we are infinitely appreciative. Debórah Dwork's ongoing research on the history of Jewish children during and after the Holocaust has been supported by an anonymous donor since 1993. This help allowed her to continue her work in this area while engaged with the Auschwitz project. Debórah hopes the anonymous donor will read these lines and understand the extent of her gratitude.

We thank Ed Barber, our editor at W. W. Norton, for accepting with good grace a manuscript he did not expect but on which he worked with enthusiasm and care. Our literary agent, Anne Borchardt, was equally surprised but did not drop us, for which we are grateful. She remains our true friend. Ed's assistants, Omar Divina and Sean Desmond, made sure that the many bits and pieces of this complicated manuscript remained in order and together. Otto Sonntag was an amazing copyeditor. Our book was designed by Chris Welch, whose professional and personal hospitality we appreciate. Nancy Palmquist, the managing editor, was astonishingly unflappable and extremely capable, and we thank her heartily. We also thank Kate Barry, who proofread the messy galleys. And we are in awe of Andrew Marasia, director of manufacturing, who worked with us on every detail of the book as an art object.

Finally we wish to thank Robert Jan's housemates, Jane Holland and Val Rynnimeri, who put up with Robert Jan's chronic absenteeism and put in the storm windows and shoveled the sidewalks themselves. Debórah's husband Ken Marek, by contrast, put up with Robert-Jan's chronic presence, but in return got someone who helped put in the storm windows and shovel the sidewalks. Debórah's daughters, Hannah and Miriam, unlike other authors' model children, were *not* patient and were *not* supportive. Now aged five and seven respectively, they were cheerful and enchanting, and they made us laugh every day. Theirs was a rare accomplishment.

New Haven
January 1996

NOTES

Note on the Name Auschwitz

In the oldest documents the German name of the town is variously spelled "Auss-wenznis," "Auwswinczen," "Ausswintzin," and so on. At the time the town was founded, scribes probably wrote the digraph *au* to represent the vowel *o*. The original pronounciation, therefore, would have been "Osswenznis," "Owswinc-zen," "Osswintzin," etc. This would explain the modern Polish name Oswiecim, pronounced "Oswientzin," According to one rather absurd theory, the pronounciation of "Oswientzim" changed as a direct result of the discontinuity of German settlement. When a new influx of German weavers came to the neighboring town of Bielitz, there were no Germans left to tell them that they should pronounce the digraph *au* as the vowel *o* and that they should not pronounce the digraph *ss* as the consonantal diphtong *sch*. Of course, this presupposes that the Swabian weavers could read, but could not hear. In any case, the theory is that they erroneously began to pronounce what the Poles called "Oswientzim" as "Auschwintzim," which slowly turned into "Auschwintz" and finally "Auschwitz." Thus the genealogy of the name Auschwitz suggests the very discontinuity of German settlement which, in the 1940s, would lead to Himmler's project to re-Germanize the town. See Rudolf Temple, "Herzog Kasimir von Auschwitz (Oswiecim)," *Zeitschrift des Vereins für Geschichte und Alterthum Schlesiens* 14 (1878):41; Napsal Prasek ("The piglet has written"), *Dejiny knizetstoi Tesinskeho* (Opave: Nakladem Vlastnim, 1894), 112f.

Abbreviations

PMOB   Archive of the State Museum Auschwitz-Birkenau
BAK   Federal Archive, Koblenz
"Farben Case" *Trials of War Criminals before the Nuerenberg Military Tribunals*, vol. 8

("The I. G. Farben Case") (Washington, D.C.: Government Printing Office, 1952)

LO/S   Landesplanung Gau Oberschlesien
OAM   Osobyi Archive, Moscow
PAK   Provincial Archive, Katowice
RK   Reichspropagandaamt Kattowitz
USHRI   United States Holocaust Research Institute, Washington D.C.

Introduction

1. Frieda Menco-Brommet, interview with Debórah Dwork, Amsterdam, Netherlands, 18 June 1986, transcript, 15f.

2. Josef Goebbels, "Der Osten als Erfüllung," in Heinrich Hoffmann and A. R. Marsani, *Deutscher Osten Land der Zukunft* (Munich: Heinrich Hoffmann, 1942), 4.

Chapter One: An Ordinary Town

1. André Neher, *The Exile of the Word: From the Silence of the Bible to the Silence of Auschwitz*, trans. David Maisel (Philadelphia: Jewish Publication Society of America, 1981), 143.

2. Hans Stosberg, "Zum Jahreswechsel 1941–1942," PAK, coll. LO/S, file 467, 148–51. Susanne Heim and Götz Aly discovered the Stosberg greeting card and first published it in their pathbreaking *Vordenker der Vernichtung: Auschwitz und die deutschen Pläne für eine neue europäische Ordnung* (Hamburg: Hoffmann und Campe, 1991). Their focus on the responsibility of mid-level bureaucrats, planners, administrators, and the like has opened a new way of thinking about the evolution of the Final Solution.

3. Franz Lüdtke, *Ein Jahrtausend Krieg zwischen Deutschland und Polen* (Stuttgart: Robert Lutz Nachfolger/Inhaber Rudolf Weisert, 1941), 73.

4. Instruction of the Propaganda Ministry Pro 2110/41/50–4/11, dated 28 January 1941, PAK, coll. RK, file 6, 20.

5. SS-Hauptamt-Schulungsamt, *Der Kampf um die deutsche Ostgrenze* (Berlin: SS-Hauptamt, 1941), 41ff.

6. See, for example, Willy Hoehm, *Wir Brandenburger!* (Berlin: Edwin Runge, 1935), 69f.

7. Rudolf Kötzschke and Wolfgang Ebert, *Geschichte der ostdeutschen Kolonisation* (Leipzig: Bibliographisches Institut, 1937); Wilfried Krallert, Walter Kuhn, and Ernst

Schwartz, *Atlas zur Geschichte der deutschen Ostsiedlung* (Bielefeld, Berlin, and Hannover: Velhagen & Klasing, 1958); Walter Schlesinger, ed., *Die deutsche Ostsiedlung des Mittelalters als Problem der europäischen Geschichte* (Sigmaringen: Jan Thorbecke, 1975); Charles Higounet, *Die deutsche Ostsiedlung im Mittelalter*, trans. Manfred Vasold (Berlin: Siedler, 1986). For an authorative account of the settlement of Upper Silesia, see Walter Kuhn, *Siedlungsgeschichte Oberschlesiens* (Würzburg: Oberschlesischer Heimatverlag, 1954).

8. Ewald Liedecke, "Die Städte des deutschen Ritterordens in der Raumordnung der Gegenwart," *Raumforschung und Raumordnung: Monatschrift der Reichsarbeitsgemeinschaft für Raumforschung* 5 (1941): 159f.

9. Karlheinz Schmidt, "Deutsche Post Osten," *Das Generalgouvernement* 1, no. 4 (1940–41): 30.

10. For information on the history of Auschwitz, see Gottlieb Biermann, "Zur Geschichte der Herzogthümer Zator und Auschwitz," *Sitzungsberichte der kaiserlichen Akademie der Wissenschaften: Philosophisch-Historischen Classe* 40 (1862): 594–631; Rudolf Temple, "Herzog Kasimir von Auschwitz (Oswiecim)," *Zeitschrift des Vereins für Geschichte und Alterthum Schlesiens* 14 (1878): 41–50; Walter Kuhn, "Kastellaneigrenzen und Zehntgrenzen in Schlesien," *Neue Beiträge zur schlesischen Siedlungsgeschichte* (Sigmaringen: Jan Thorbecke, 1984), 12–49, and "Siedlungsgeschichte des Auschwitzer Beskidenvorlandes," ibid., 166–237; Elzbieta Skalinska-Dindorf, *Oswiecim: Zarys dziejow* (Oswiecim: Municipal Office of Oswiecim, 1988); Andrzej Nowakowski, *Dzieje ustrojo i prawa ksietstw Oswiecimskiego i Zatorskiego*, Dissertationes Universitatis Varsoviensis, vol. 363 (Warsaw: University Printers, 1988).

11. Wilhelm Abel, *Die Wüstungen des ausgehenden Mittelalters* (Stuttgart: Gustav Fischer, 1955), 75ff.

12. Temple, "Herzog Kasimir von Auschwitz," 44, 48f., Biermann, "Zur Geschichte der Herzogthümer Zator und Auschwitz," 617ff.; Nowakowski, *Dzieje ustrojo i prawa ksietstw Oswiecimskiego i Zatorskiego*, 53ff.

13. Jan Ptaszkowski, *Opowiesci Spod Zamkowej Gory: Karty z prezeszlosci Oswiecimia*, vol. 1, ed. Jan Raszka (Teschen: Towarzystwo Milosnikow Ziemi Oswiecimskiej/ Cieszynska Drukarnia Wydawnicza, n.d.), 45ff.

14. Lüdtke, *Ein Jahrtausend Krieg*, 128.

15. Heinrich von Treitschke, *Politics*, trans. Blanche Dugdale and Torren de Bille, ed. Arthur James Balfour, 2 vols. (London: Constable, 1916), 2:112.

16. As quoted in Adolf Hitler, *My New Order*, ed. Raoul de Roussy de Sales (New York: Reynel & Hitchcock, 1941), 729.

17. Emil Gassner, ed., *Im Dienste Europas: Fünf Jahre deutscher Arbeit im Generalgouvernement* (Cracow: Zeitungsverlag Krakau-Warschau, 1944), 31.

Chapter Two: The Prussian Connection

1. Emil Ludwig, "Krieg gegen Preussen," *Das Neue Tage-Buch* (10 and 17 February 1940), as quoted in Samuel Dickinson Stirk, *The Prussian Spirit: A Survey of German Literature and Politics, 1914–1940* (London: Faber and Faber, 1941), 23f.

2. Stirk, *The Prussian Spirit*, 7.

3. Julius Schmidhauser, *Der Kampf um das geistige Reich* (Hamburg: Hanseatische Verlagsanstalt, 1933), 249f.

4. Two good English-language introductions to Prussian history are Hannsjoachim W. Koch, *A History of Prussia* (London and New York: Longman, 1978); Sebastian Haffner, *The Rise and Fall of Prussia*, trans. Ewald Osers (London: Weidenfeld and Nicolson, 1982).

5. For a history of the Teutonic Order, see Hartmut Boockmann, *Der Deutsche Orden: Zwölf Kapitel aus seiner Geschichte* (Munich: C. H. Beck, 1981); also Eric Christiansen, *The Northern Crusades: The Baltic and the Catholic Frontier, 1100–1525* (London: Macmillan, 1980).

6. For an astute analysis of the significance of the acquisition of Prussia for the Hohenzollern dynasty, see Heinrich von Treitschke's magistral and extremely partisan *History of Germany in the Nineteenth Century*, trans. Eden and Cedar Paul, 8 vols. (London: Jarrold & Sons, 1915), 1:32.

7. William John Rose, *The Drama of Upper Silesia: A Regional Study* (Brattleboro, Vt.: Stephen Daye Press, 1935), 76ff.

8. As quoted in A. O. Meyer, "The Development of Silesia and Especially of Upper Silesia in Modern Times," *Germany and Poland in Their Historical Relations*, ed. Albert Brackmann, trans. S. Miles Bouton (Munich and Berlin: R. Oldenbourg, 1934), 161.

9. For a concise description see Hans-Georg Aschoff, "Die Kolonisation," in Jürgen Ziechmann, ed., *Panorama der Fridericianischen Zeit: Friedrich der Grosse und seine Epoche—Ein Handbuch* (Bremen: Edition Ziechmann, 1985), 386ff.; also Udo Froese, *Das Kolonisationswerk Friedrichs des Grossen: Wesen und Vermächtnis* (Heidelberg and Berlin: Kurt Vowinckel, 1938).

10. Gustav Freytag, "Bilder aus der deutschen Vergangenheit," *Gesammelte Werke*, 2d ser., 7 vols. (Leipzig and Berlin: S. Hirzel and Hermann Klemm, 1920), 7:279f.

11. Ibid., 280f.

12. See William W. Hagen, *Germans, Poles, and Jews: The Nationality Conflict in the Prussian East, 1772–1914* (Chicago and London: University of Chicago Press, 1980).

13. Klaus Zernack, *Preussen—Deutschland—Polen*, ed. Wolfram Fischer and Michael G. Müller (Berlin: Duncker & Humblot, 1991), 67.

14. Gotthold Rhode, "Staatliche Entwicklungen und Grenzziehungen," in Gotthold Rhode, ed., *Die Ostgebiete des Deutschen Reiches* (Würzburg: Holzner, 1956), 116f.

15. See J. J. Kulczycki, *School Strikes in Prussian Poland, 1901–1907: The Struggle over Bilingual Education*, East European Monographs 82 (New York: Columbia University Press, 1981), 218.

16. Rhode, "Staatliche Entwicklungen," 152.

17. Max Weber, "Capitalism and Rural Society in Germany," in Max Weber, *From Max Weber: Essays in Sociology*, ed. H. H. Gerth and C. Wright Mills (London: Routledge, 1991), 382; see also Max Weber, "Der Nationalstaat und die Volkswirtschaftspolitik," in Max Weber, *Politische Schriften*, ed. Johannes Winckelmann (Tübingen: J. C. B. Mohr [Paul Siebeck], 1971), 6ff.

18. See Jack Wertheimer, *Unwelcome Strangers: East European Jews in Imperial Germany* (New York and Oxford: Oxford University Press, 1987), 11.

19. Ibid., 13.

20. Ibid., 93ff.

21. Mary Antin, *The Promised Land* (Boston and New York: Houghton Mifflin, 1912), 174f.

22. Ibid., 177.

23. Bonnie Mendes Kahn, *Cosmopolitan Culture: The Gilt-Edged Dream of a Tolerant City* (New York: Atheneum, 1987), 95.

24. The official autonomy of the duchy of Oswiecim and Zator was of some importance to the international community after the collapse of the Napoleonic empire. In 1818 the Austrian chancellor Metternich, for very practical reasons, included Oswiecim and Zator within the German Confederation but excluded the rest of Austrian Poland. At the Congress of Vienna, Russia, Prussia, and Austria had agreed to declare the strategically important citadel of Cracow, desired by all three powers, a neutral and nominally independent territory. To make the mini-state economically viable, they granted it 455 square miles of territory along the Vistula. Metternich realized that an independent Cracow could become a hotbed of Polish nationalism. To strengthen his hand if unrest should arise, he created a common border between the Austrian part of the German Confederation and Cracow. This would allow him to interpret any trouble as a threat to the German Confederation and to send in the Austrian army with German backing. As Cracow was separated from the Austrian part of the German Confederation by the duchy of Oswiecim and Zator, Metternich formally incorporated the duchy in the German Confederation, thus establishing a 20-mile-long border with the free city. Metternich's decision to shift the border paid off in 1846–47, when it provided him with the leverage to occupy and dissolve the Republic of Cracow. With Cracow officially incorporated in Galicia there was no need to keep Oswiecim and its surroundings in the German Confederation, and the territory was separated from the Confederation in 1850 and joined with Galicia.

25. For an overview of the economic, social, and political situation in nineteenth-century Galicia, see United Kingdom, Foreign Office, *Austrian Poland* (London: H.

M. Stationery Office, 1920); Francis Bujak et al., "Galicia and Silesia of Cieszyn," in Committee for the Polish Encyclopedic Publications at Fribourg, *Polish Encyclopaedia*, 3 vols. (Geneva: Atar, 1921–22), 3:237ff.; Stefan L. Zaleski, "General Demography of Poland," ibid., 2:75ff.

26. Jan Ptaszkowski, *Opowiesci Spod Zamkowej Gory*: *Karty z przeszlosci Oswiecimia*, vol. 2, ed. Jan Raszka (Teschen: Towarzystwo Milosnikow Ziemi Oswiecimskiej/ Cieszynska Drukarnia Wydawnicza, n.d.), 17f.

27. Andreas Mytkowicz, *Ausländische Wanderarbeiter in der deutschen Landwirtschaft* (diss., University of Munich, 1914, Posen: Verlagsdruckerei "Praca," 1914), 91f.; see also Johannes Nichtweiss, *Die ausländische Saisonarbeiter in der Landwirtschaft der östlichen und mittleren Gebiete des Deutschen Reiches*: *Ein Beitrag zur Geschichte der preussisch-deutschen Politik von 1890 bis 1914* (Berlin: Rütten & Loening, 1959), 88, 193ff.

28. Ptaszkowski, *Opowiesci Spod Zamkowej Gory*, 2: 93ff.; Report of the Oswiecim Industrial Society, 14 January 1918, Oswiecim Municipal Archive.

29. Ludwika Stasiaski, "Oswiecim," *Nowej Reformy* (1920), as quoted in Ptaszkowski, *Opowiesci Spod Zamkowej Gory*, 2:51.

30. Max Nordau, *Degeneration* (Lincoln and London: University of Nebraska Press, 1993), 2, 537; Hans-Walter Schmuhl, *Rassenhygiene, Nationalsozialismus, Euthanasie*: *Von der Verhütung zur Vernichtung "lebensunwerten Lebens," 1890–1945* (Göttingen: Vandenhoeck & Ruprecht, 1987), 76f.

31. Ernst Haeckel, *The History of Creation*: *or, The Development of the Earth and Its Inhabitants by the Action of Natural Causes*, trans. E. Ray Lankester, 2 vols. (New York: D. Appleton, 1876), 1:170f.

32. Ibid., 173.

33. Alfred Ploetz, *Die Tüchtigkeit unserer Rasse und der Schutz der Schwachen* (Berlin: S. Fischer, 1895), 144f.

34. Alfred Hoche, "Ärztliche Bemerkungen," in Karl Binding and Alfred Hoche, *Die Freigabe der Vernichtung lebensunwerten Lebens*: *Ihr Mass und ihre Form* (Leipzig: Felix Meiner, 1920), 55.

35. Ibid., 100f.

36. Adolf Hitler, *Mein Kampf*, trans. Ralph Manheim (Boston: Houghton Mifflin, 1943), 255.

37. Adolf Hitler, *Hitler's Secret Book*, introd. Telford Taylor, trans. Salvator Attanasio (New York: Grove Press, 1961), 18.

Chapter Three: Germany's Turn to the East

1. Erich Ludendorff, *My War Memories, 1914–1918*, 2 vols. (London: Hutchinson, 1919), 1: 57; John W. Wheeler-Bennett claims that Lieutenant Colonel Max Hoff-

mann, who actually planned most of the battle, suggested to Ludendorff to adopt Tannenberg as the symbolic site of the battle. See Wheeler-Bennett, *The Wooden Titan: Hindenburg in Twenty Years of German History, 1914–1934* (London and Hamden: Archon Books, 1963), 28.

2. Walter Flex, "Ostmarkenlied," in Walter Flex, *Gesammelte Werke*, 2 vols. (München: S. H. Beck, 1936), 1:84.

3. "Kriegsziel-Eingabe der sechs grossen Wirtschaftsverbände an den Reichskanzler vom 20. Mai 1915," in Wolfgang Schumann and Ludwig Nestler, eds., *Weltherrschaft im Visier: Dokumente zu den Europa- und Weltherrschaftsplänen des deutschen Imperialismus von der Jahrhundertwende bis Mai 1945* (Berlin: VEB Deutscher Verlag, 1975), 109; "Petition an den Reichskanzler, 20 Juni 1915," as quoted in S. Grumbach, *Das annexionistische Deutschland: Eine Sammlung von Dokumenten, die seit dem 4. August 1914 in Deutschland öffentlich oder geheim verbreitet wurden* (Lausanne: Payot, 1917), 135f.

4. Memorandum written by Ludendorff presented to the commander in chief of the eastern front, dated 9 September 1916, quoted in Robert Stupperich, "Siedlungspläne im Gebiet des Oberbefehlhabers Ost (Militärverwaltung Litauen und Kurland) während des Weltkrieges," *Jomsburg* 5 (1941): 356f.

5. [Paul Nikolaus Cossmann], "Die Ostjuden," *Süddeutsche Monatshefte* 13 (1915–16): 673; see also Julius Berger, "Deutsche Juden und polnische Juden," *Der Jude* 1 (1916–17): 137–49.

6. See Georg Fritz, *Die Ostjudenfrage: Zionismus und Grenzschluss* (Munich: J. F. Lehmanns, 1915); Wolfgang Heinze, "Ostjüdische Einwanderung," *Preussische Jahrbücher* 162 (1916): 98–117; idem, "Internationale jüdische Beziehungen," ibid., 169 (1917): 340–66, and ibid., 170 (1917): 65–81.

7. Wolfgang Siegfried, "Siedlungsgedanken," *Deutschlands Erneuerung* 2 (1918): 33ff.; idem, "Die Notwendigkeit und Möglichkeit eines grossen deutschen Siedlungswerkes im Osten," ibid., 521ff.

8. See G. Jenny, "Der Friede im Osten," *Die Woche* 20 (16 March 1918): 257–60; Rudolf Strass, "Des Baltenlandes deutsche Stunde," ibid., 283–86.

9. Adolf Hitler, *Mein Kampf*, trans. Ralph Manheim (Boston: Houghton Mifflin, 1943), 204f.

10. Paul von Hindenburg, "The Stab in the Back," in Anton Kaes, Martin Jay, and Edward Dimendberg, eds., *The Weimar Republic Sourcebook* (Berkeley, Los Angeles, and New York: University of California Press, 1994), 15f.

11. Ernst Jünger, "Die totale Mobilmachung," in Ernst Jünger, ed., *Krieg und Krieger* (Berlin: Junker und Dünnhaupt, 1930), 28.

12. See Rüdiger Graf von der Goltz, *Als politischer General im Osten (Finnland und Baltikum) 1918 und 1919* (Leipzig: K. F. Koehler, 1936).

13. Gustav Noske, *Von Kiel bis Kapp: Zur Geschichte der deutschen Revolution* (Berlin: Verlag für Politik und Wirtschaft, 1920), 177f.

14. Ernst von Salomon, *The Outlaws*, trans. Ian F. D. Morrow (London: Jonathan Cape, 1931), 99f.

15. Erich Edwin Dwinger, *Der letzte Traum*: *Eine deutsche Tragödie* (Jena: Eugen Diederichs, 1934), 9, 19.

16. Quoted in Josef Ackermann, *Heinrich Himmler als Ideologe* (Göttingen: Musterschmidt, 1970), 198.

17. Institut zum Studium der Judenfrage, ed., *Die Juden in Deutschland* (Munich: Franz Eher, 1939), 111.

18. Ibid., 112.

19. Carl Lange, "Ehre der Nation, deutsches Volkstums und Würde des Menschentums," in Carl Lange and Ernst Adold Dreyer, eds., *Deutscher Geist 1935* (Leipzig: R. Voigtländer, 1934), 273.

20. Hitler, *Mein Kampf*, 687.

21. In the official SS historiography, Himmler's appointment marks the true beginning of the SS; see Gunther d'Alquen, "Die SS: Geschichte, Aufgabe und Organisation der Schutzstaffeln der NSDAP," in Paul Meier-Benneckenstein, ed., *Wehrhaftes Volk*: *Der organisatorische Aufbau Teil II*, vol. 2 of *Das Dritte Reich im Aufbau* (Berlin: Junker und Dünnhaupt, 1939), 204.

22. As quoted in Herbert F. Ziegler, *Nazi Germany's New Aristocracy*: *The SS leadership*, *1925–1939* (Princeton: Princeton University Press, 1989), 38.

23. As quoted in Bernd Wegner, *The Waffen-SS*: *Organization, Ideology and Function*, trans. Ronald Webster (Oxford: Basil Blackwell, 1990), 16.

24. Christopher Browning, "Beyond 'Intentionalism' and 'Functionalism': A Reassessment of Nazi Jewish Policy from 1939 to 1941," in Thomas Childers and Jane Caplan, eds., *Reevaluating the Third Reich* (New York: Holmes & Meier, 1993), 216.

25. D'Alquen, "Die SS," 205.

26. Ibid., 206.

27. A good introduction to the Artaman Society and its ideology can be found in Klaus Bergmann, *Agrarromantik und Grossstadtfeindschaft*, vol. 20 of the *Marburger Abhandlungen zur politischen Wissenschaft* (Meisenheim am Glan: Anton Hain, 1970), 247ff.; also Michael H. Kater, "Die Artamanen—Völkische Jugend in der Weimarer Republik," *Historische Zeitschrift* 213 (1971): 577ff.

28. Rudolf Höss, *Death Dealer*: *The Memoirs of the SS Kommandant at Auschwitz*, ed. Steven Paskuly, trans. Andrew Pollinger (Buffalo: Prometheus Books, 1992), 79.

29. As quoted in Ulrich Linse, ed., *Zurück, o Mensch, zur Mutter Erde*: *Landkommunen in Deutschland, 1890–1933* (Munich: Deutscher Taschenbuch Verlag, 1983), 331.

30. Wilhelm Kotzde, (report on the beginning of practical Artaman work) in *Der Falke* 5 (1924): 107.

31. See Anne Bramwell, *Blood and Soil*: *Walther Darré and Hitler's "Green Party"* (Bourne End, Bucks.: Kensal Press, 1985).

32. Walther R. Darré, "The Peasantry as the Key to Understanding the Nordic Race," in Barbara Miller Lane and Leila J. Rupp, eds., *Nazi Ideology before 1933*: *A Documentation* (Manchester: Manchester University Press, 1978), 105.

33. Walther R. Darré, preface in Heinrich Bauer, *Geburt des Ostens*: *Drei Kämpfer um eine Idee* (Berlin: Frundsberg, 1933), 5.

34. Walther R. Darré, "The Farmers and the State," in Miller Lane and Rupp, eds., *Nazi Ideology before 1933*, 133.

35. A. Hillen-Ziegfeld, "Deutscher Lebensraum," in Lange and Dreyer, eds., *Deutscher Geist 1935*, 71f.

36. Otto Maull, *Das Wesen der Geopolitik* (Leipzig and Berlin: Teubner, 1936), 31.

37. Hans Weigert, *Generals and Geographers*: *The Twilight of Geopolitics* (New York: Oxford University Press, 1942), 95.

38. The standard biography on Haushofer is Hans-Adolf Jacobsen, *Karl Haushofer*: *Leben und Werk*, 2 vols., Schriften des Bundesarchivs 24/I and 24/II (Boppard am Rhein: Harald Boldt, 1979).

39. Hitler, *Mein Kampf*, 139f., 654.

40. Rudolf Kötzschke and Wolfgang Ebert, *Geschichte der ostdeutschen Kolonisation* (Leipzig: Bibliographisches Institut, 1937), 19.

41. Ibid., 10.

42. United States Department of State, *The Treaty of Versailles and After*: *Annotations of the Text of the Treaty*, Conference Series 92, Publication 2724 (Washington, D.C.: Government Printing Office, 1947), 258ff.

43. William Harbutt Dawson, *Germany under the Treaty* (Freeport: Books for Libraries Press, 1972), 175.

44. Ibid., 222f.

45. Fritz Arlt, *Siedlung und Landwirtschaft in den eingegliederten Gebieten Oberschlesiens* (Berlin: Deutsche Landbuchhandlung Sohnrey, 1942), 31ff.; see also Günther Saath, *Die Industrie der eingegliederten oberschlesischen Ostgebiete* (Berlin, Prague, and Vienna: Volk und Reich, 1942), 29ff.; Walter Kuhn, *Siedlungsgechichte Oberschlesiens* (Würzburg: Oberschlesischer Heimatverlag, 1954), 186f.; and William John Rose, *The Drama of Upper Silesia*: *A Regional Study* (Brattleboro, Vt.: Stephen Daye Press, 1935), 96.

46. Arlt, *Siedlung und Landwirtschaft*, 36.

47. See Robert Donald, *The Polish Corridor and the Consequences* (London: Thornton Butterworth, 1929), 186.

48. See J. Weinstein, *Upper Silesia*: *A Country of Contrasts* (Paris: Gebethner & Wolff, 1931).

49. Salomon, *The Outlaws*, 216ff.

50. Walther Rathenau, as quoted ibid., 213f.

51. Statistics are taken from Gotthold Rhode, ed., *Die Ostgebiete des Deutschen Reiches* (Würzburg: Holzner, 1956), 82f., 122ff., 154.

52. As quoted in Wolfgang J. Mommsen, *Max Weber and German Politics, 1890–1920*, trans. Michael S. Steinberg (Chicago and London: University of Chicago Press, 1984), 312f.

53. Dawson, *Germany under the Treaty*, 382ff.

Chapter Four: The Third Reich

1. John W. Wheeler-Bennett, *The Wooden Titan: Hindenburg in Twenty Years of German History, 1914–1934* (London and Hamden: Archon Books, 1963), 311ff.

2. Letter of President Hindenburg to Chancellor Müller-Franken, 18 March 1930, as quoted in Herbert Michaelis and Ernst Schraepler, eds., *Ursachen und Folgen: Vom deutschen Zusammenbruch 1918 bis 1945 bis zur staatlichen Neuordnung Deutschlands in der Gegenwart*, 26 vols. (Berlin: Dokumenten-Verlag Dr. Herbert Wendler, n.d.), 8:488.

3. As quoted in Francis Ludwig Carsten, *A History of the Prussian Junkers* (Aldershot: Scolar Press, 1989), 167.

4. For the text see Michaelis and Schraepler, eds., *Ursachen und Folgen*, 8:505–7.

5. Speech of Chancellor von Schleicher, 15 December 1932, as quoted ibid., 725f.

6. "Verordnung des Reichspräsidenten zum Schutz von Volk und Staat," *Reichsgesetzblatt*, 28 February 1933, 83.

7. Harwood L Childs, ed., *The Nazi Primer: Official Handbook for Schooling the Hitler Youth* (New York and London: Harper, 1938), 69f.

8. Hans-Walter Schmuhl, *Rassenhygiene, Nationalsozialismus, Euthanasie: Von der Verhütung zur Vernichtung "lebensunwerten Lebens," 1890–1945* (Göttingen: Vandenhoeck & Ruprecht, 1987), 175.

9. Karl Ludwig Rost, *Sterilisation und Euthanasie im Film des "Dritten Reiches"* (Husum: Matthiesen, 1987), 67ff.

10. Ibid., 234.

11. Ibid., 237.

12. As quoted in Adolf Hitler, *The New Germany Desires Work and Peace: Collected Speeches by Reichskanzler Adolf Hitler*, ed. Josef Goebbels (Berlin: Liebheit & Thiesen, 1933), 35.

13. Joachim Haupt, *Neuordnung im Schulwesen und Hochschulwesen* (Berlin: C. Heymann, 1933), 94.

14. Will Decker, *Der deutsche Arbeitsdienst: Ziele, Leistungen und Organisation des Reichsarbeitsdienstes* (Berlin: Junker und Dünnhaupt, 1937), 11ff.

15. Fritz Edel, *German Labour Service* (Berlin: Terramare Office, 1937), 18; for another consideration of Frederick the Great's colonization as a precursor of National

Socialist settlement policies, see Udo Froese, *Das Kolonisationswerk Friedrichs des Grossen*: *Wesen und Vermächtnis* (Heidelberg and Berlin: Kurt Vowinckel, 1938), 55ff., 113ff.

16. As quoted in Simon Taylor, *Prelude to Genocide*: *Nazi Ideology and the Struggle for Power* (London: Duckworth, 1983), 90.

17. Werner Schäfer, *Konzentrationslager Oranienburg*: *Das Anti-Braunbuch über das erste deutsche Konzentrationslager* (Berlin: Buch und Tiefdruck-Gesellschaft, 1934), 25.

18. Ibid., 41.

19. Ibid., 229.

20. Ernst Klee, *"Euthanasie" im NS-Staat: Die "Vernichtung lebensunwerten Lebens"* (Frankfurt: S. Fischer, 1983), 38ff.

21. As quoted in Martin Broszat, "The Concentration Camps, 1933–45," in Helmut Krausnick, Hans Buchheim, Martin Broszat, and Hans-Adolf Jacobsen, *Anatomy of the SS State*, trans. Richard Barry, Marian Jackson, and Dorothy Long (New York: Walker, 1968), 455.

22. Speech of Greifelt, January 1939, as quoted in Michael Burleigh and Wolfgang Wippermann, *The Racial State*: *Germany, 1933–1945* (Cambridge: Cambridge University Press, 1991), 175.

23. Heinrich Zillich, "Deutsches Volk und Buch in der Welt," *Das innere Reich* 3 (1936): 1080f.

24. See Hans-Adolf Jacobsen, *Karl Haushofer*: *Leben und Werk*, 2 vols., Schriften des Bundesarchivs 24/I and 24/II (Boppard am Rhein: Harald Boldt, 1979), 1:279ff.

25. See Waldis O. Lumans, *Himmler's Auxiliaries: The Volksdeutsche Mittelstelle and the German National Minorities of Europe, 1933–1945* (Chapel Hill and London: University of North Carolina Press, 1993), 38f.

26. Ibid., 51.

27. Ulrich Greifelt, "Dokument 2," in Dietrich A. Loeber, ed., *Diktierte Option*: *Die Umsiedlung der Deutsch-Balten aus Estland und Lettland* (Neumünster: Karl Wachholtz, 1972), 6.

28. Karl Stuhlpfarrer, *Umsiedlung Südtirol, 1939–1940*, 2 vols. (Vienna and Munich: Löcker, 1985), 2:618.

29. William Shirer, *The Rise and Fall of the Third Reich* (New York: Simon and Schuster, 1960), 453.

30. Jan Karski, *Story of a Secret State* (Boston: Houghton Mifflin, 1944), 3ff.

31. Ibid., 6f.

32. As quoted in Shirer, *The Rise and Fall of the Third Reich*, 589.

33. Karski, *Story of a Secret State*, 7. See also E. Thomas Wood and Stanislaw M. Jankowski, *Karski* (New York: John Wiley, 1994).

34. Franz Lüdtke, *Ein Jahrtausend Krieg zwischen Deutschland und Polen* (Stuttgart: Robert Lutz Nachfolger/Inhaber Rudolf Weisert, 1941), 191.

35. The original agreement of 23 August identified the Vistula as the border

between Germany and the Soviet Union. Lublin, among other cities, would go to the Soviets, while Germany would get Lithuania. In the treaty of 28 September, Germany exchanged its claim on Lithuania for the territory between the Vistula and the Bug, which became the Lublin district and the location of the Nisko project.

36. Hermann Seifert, *Der Jude an der Ostgrenze* (Berlin: Zentralverlag der NSDAP, 1940): 8f.

37. Ibid., 16.

38. Ibid., 29.

39. "Selbsterlebte Geschichte in den Feldpostbriefen des Reichsinstituts für Geschichte des neuen Deutschlands, 1939/40," in *Reich und Reichsfeinde*, vol. 1 (Hamburg: Hanseatische Verlagsanstalt, 1941), 14, 17.

40. "Polnische Juden auf 'Bienen'-Jagd," *Illustrierter Beobachter* 14 (19 October 1939): 1152f.

41. As quoted in Christopher R. Browning, "Genocide and Public Health: German Doctors and Polish Jews, 1939–1941," *Holocaust and Genocide Studies* 3 (1988): 23.

42. "Auswurf der Ghettos," *Das Schwarze Korps* 6 (2 May 1940): 8.

43. Ibid., 8.

44. "Grässliche Zumutung," *Das Schwarze Korps* 6 (16 May 1940): 3.

45. "Die Juden müssen arbeiten!," *Illustrierter Beobachter* 14 (12 October 1939): 1546f.

46. As quoted in Poland, Ministry of Information, *The Black Book of Poland* (New York: G. P. Putnam's Sons, 1942), 232.

47. Ibid., 233.

48. Adolf Hitler, *My New Order*, ed. Raoul de Roussy de Sales. (New York: Reynel & Hitchcock, 1941), 737f.

49. As quoted in Stuhlpfarrer, *Umsiedlung Südtirol*, 2:631.

50. Site plan December 1939, PMOB, box BW 2/1 file 2/1.

51. Eyewitness Testimony 24, "Expulsion from the Town of Auschwitz," in Isaiah Trunk, ed., *Jewish Responses to Nazi Persecution: Collective and Individual Behavior in Extremis* (New York: Stein and Day, 1979), 174.

52. Jochen von Lang, with Claus Sibyll, eds., *Eichmann Interrogated: Transcripts from the Archives of the Israeli Police*, trans. Ralph Manheim (New York: Farrar, Straus & Giroux, 1983), 60.

53. As quoted in Poland, Ministry of Information, *The Black Book of Poland*, 239f.

54. Raul Hilberg, *Die Vernichtung der europäischen Juden*, 3 vols. (Frankfurt: Fischer Taschenbuch, 1990), 2:416f.

55. Browning, "Genocide and Public Health," 24.

56. As quoted in Jeremy Noakes and Geoffrey Pridham, eds., *Nazism, 1919–1945*, 3 vols. (Exeter: Exeter University Publications, 1983–88), 3:1065.

57. Chaim A. Kaplan, *Scroll of Agony*: *The Warsaw Diary of Chaim A. Kaplan*, trans. Abraham I. Katsh (New York: Macmillan/Collier Books, 1973), 223.

58. Ibid., 225.

59. Ibid., 226.

60. Sara Grossman-Weil, interview with Debórah Dwork, Malverne, N.Y., 29 and 30 April 1987, transcript, 22; Debórah Dwork, *Children With A Star*: *Jewish Youth in Nazi Europe* (New Haven and London: Yale University Press, 1991), 197.

61. As quoted in Noakes and Pridham, eds., *Nazism, 1919–1945*, 3:1069.

62. As quoted ibid., 1008.

63. Christopher R. Browning, *Fateful Months*: *Essays on the Emergence of the Final Solution*, rev. ed. (New York and London: Holmes & Meier, 1991), 58ff.

64. As quoted in Noakes and Pridham, eds., *Nazism, 1919–1945*, 1010f.

65. As quoted ibid., 1019.

66. Klee, *"Euthanasie" im NS-Staat*, 207.

67. As quoted in Noakes and Pridham, eds., *Nazism, 1919–1945*, 3:1025f.

68. As quoted ibid., 1028.

69. Browning, *Fateful Months*, 59.

70. As quoted in Noakes and Pridham, eds., *Nazism, 1919–1945*, 3:1040.

71. As quoted ibid., 1042.

Chapter Five: A Paradise of Blood and Soil

1. Hanns Johst, *Ruf des Reiches—Echo des Volkes*: *Eine Ostfahrt* (Munich: Franz Eher Nachfolger, 1940), 21ff.

2. Ibid., 28f.

3. Ibid., 29f.

4. Erhard Kroeger, Dokument 314, in Dietrich A. Loeber, ed., *Diktierte Option*: *Die Umsiedlung der Deutsch-Balten aus Estland und Lettland* (Neumünster: Karl Wachholtz, 1972), 648.

5. Ibid., 649ff.

6. Ibid., 651f.

7. Dokument 41, ibid., 46.

8. See Helmut Krausnick, *Hitlers Einsatzgruppen*: *Die Truppen des Weltanschauungskrieges, 1938–1942* (Frankfurt: Fischer Taschenbuch, 1989), 26ff.

9. As quoted in Hans Buchheim, "The SS—Instrument of Domination," in Helmut Krausnick, Hans Buchheim, Martin Broszat, and Hans-Adolf Jacobsen, *Anatomy of the SS State*, trans. Richard Barry, Marian Jackson, and Dorothy Long (New York: Walker, 1968), 177.

10. As quoted ibid., 178.

11. As quoted in Jeremy Noakes and Geoffrey Pridham, eds., *Nazism, 1919–1945*, 3 vols. (Exeter: Exeter University Publications, 1983–88), 3:929.

12. As quoted ibid., 1051.

13. As quoted ibid., 929f.

14. As quoted ibid., 1053.

15. As quoted ibid., 927.

16. Robert Lewis Koehl, *RKFDV: German Resettlement and Population Policy, 1939–1945: A History of the Reich Commission for the Strengthening of Germandom* (Cambridge: Harvard University Press, 1957), 28, 54.

17. Ibid., 50.

18. "Erlass des Führers und Reichskanzlers zur Festigung deutschen Volkstums vom 7. Oktober 1939," BAK, coll. R 49, file 2, 3ff; translation from Koehl, *RKFDV*, 247.

19. Speech by Himmler to SS leaders in Posen, 24 October 1939, as printed in Rolf-Dieter Müller, *Hitlers Ostkrieg und die deutsche Siedlungspolitik* (Frankfurt: Fischer Taschenbuch, 1991), 119f.

20. Ibid., 120.

21. Ibid., 121.

22. "Erste Anordnung," BAK, coll. R 49, file 4, 11–12; translation from Koehl, *RKFDV*, 249f .

23. "Erlass des Führers und . . . vom 7. Oktober 1939," BAK, coll. R 49, file 2, 3ff; translation from Koehl, *RKFDV*, 248.

24. "Aktenvermerk über die Besprechung zwischen SS-Gruppenführer Pancke . . . und dem Reichsbauernführer Walther Darré," BAK, coll. NS 2, file 138; as printed in Müller, *Hitlers Ostkrieg*, 118.

25. Ibid., 117.

26. "Erlass des Führers . . . vom 7. Oktober 1939," BAK, coll. R 49, file 2, 3ff.; translation from Koehl, *RKFDV*, 247.

27. Planungshauptabteilung, Der RFSS-RKfdFdV, "Planungsgrundlagen für den Aufbau der Ostgebiete," BAK, coll. R. 49, file 157, 3.

28. Ibid., 4f.

29. Ibid., 9.

30. Ibid., 10.

31. Ibid., 13.

32. Ibid., 10, 12, 14.

33. Ibid., 10f., 13f.

34. "Vermerk betr. Umsiedlung," BAK, coll. R 113, file 129.

35. "Erste Anordnung," BAK, coll. R 49, file 4, 11; translation from Koehl, *RKFDV*, 249.

36. As quoted in Noakes and Pridham, eds., *Nazism, 1919–1945*, 3:1056.

37. Koehl, *RKFDV*, 105ff.

38. Reinhard Heydrich, "Ausführungen zu dem Problem der notwendig gewordenen Rückführung der Volksdeutschen aus Estland und Lettland," in Loeber, *Diktierte Option*, 123ff.

39. "Bemerkungen für die Behandlung der Balten-Frage in der deutschen Preses," ibid., 140f.

40. "Aus Baltenbriefen zur Rückkehr ins Reich," *Soldatenblätter für Feier und Freizeit*, July 1940, 155.

41. Otto Engelhardt-Kyffhäuser, "Der Film 'Heimkehr' wird gedreht," *Das General-Gouvernement* 1, (1941): 34ff.

42. Johst, *Ruf des Reiches*, 126f.

43. Walter Geisler, *Der deutsche Osten als Lebensraum für alle Berufstände* (Berlin, Prague, and Vienna: Volk und Reich Verlag, 1942), 12.

44. "Allgemeine Anordnungen und Richtlinien des Reichskommissars für die Festigung deutschen Volkstums," BAK, coll. R 49, file 4, 43.

45. "Anordnung 1/II," BAK, coll. R 49, file 2, 10.

46. As quoted in Poland, Ministry of Information, *The Black Book of Poland* (New York: G. P. Putnam's Sons, 1942), 184.

47. Ibid., 198f.

48. Ibid., 210f.

49. Josef Umlauf, "Die Geplante Verteilung der Bevölkerung in den eingegliederten Ostgebieten," BAK, coll. R 49, file 990, 9f.

50. Ibid., 23.

51. As quoted in Poland, Ministry of Information, *The Black Book of Poland*, 185.

52. M. Klawan, "Ein neues Leben beginnt," *Soldatenblätter für Feier und Freizeit*, July 1940, 158.

53. "Deutscher Bauer aus Wolhynian und Galizien!," BAK, coll. R 49 Anh. I, file 40a, 1.

54. Klawan, "Ein neues Leben beginnt," 159f.

55. Note of Himmler, 24 June 1940, BAK, coll. NS 19, file 3282, 1.

56. Ibid., 6.

57. Reichsführer-SS, Reichskommissar für die Festigung deutschen Volkstums, "Allgemeine Anordnung Nr. 7/II vom 26. November 1940: Grundsätze und Richtlinien für den ländlichen Aufbau in den neuen Ostgebieten," *Gestaltung der neuen Siedlungsgebiete* (Berlin: Verlag deutsche Landbuchhandlung Sohnrey, 1943), 10.

58. Ibid., 10.

59. Ibid., 8f.

60. "Notiz über einen Ideeenwettbewerb für Entwürfe zu neuen Dörfern in den Ostgebieten," 14 February 1941, BAK, coll. R 49, file 711a.

61. Reichskommissar für die Festigung deutschen Volkstums, Stabshauptamt,

Hauptabteilung: Planung und Boden, *Planung und Aufbau im Osten: Erläuterungen und Skizzen zum ländlichen Aufbau in den neuen Ostgebieten* (Berlin: Verlag deutsche Landbuchhandlung Sohnrey, 1941).

62. See correspondence and notes in BAK, coll. R 113, file 7; also Gert Gröning and Joachim Wolschke-Bulmahn, *Die Liebe zur Landschaft*, pt. 3, *Der Drang nach Osten* (Munich: Minerva Publikation, 1987), 163ff.

63. Fritz Todt, "9. Anordnung: Betrifft Neubauverbot," BAK, coll. R 49 Anhang I, file 40a, 23.

64. Johst, *Ruf des Reiches*, 86ff.

Chapter Six: A Concentration Camp

1. Fritz Gerlach, "Bekenntnis zum deutschen Osten," BAK, coll. R 69, file 689.

2. RSHA Statistical Tables, BAK, coll. NS 19, file 3979, 3, 11.

3. Fritz Bracht, "Zur Tätigkeit der Dienststelle," in Upper Silesia, Office of the Gauleiter as Representative of RfSS-RKfdFdV, *Entwicklung, Organisation, Arbeitsleistung der Dienststelle des Gauleiters und Oberpräsidenten als Beauftragter des Reichsführers SS Reichskommissar für die Festigung deutschen Volkstums in Oberschlesien vom Sept. 1939 bis Jan. 1943* (Kattowitz, 1943), 1. Interestingly, for exactly the same practical reasons which made the Germans think twice about deporting Polish industrial workers in 1939, the Poles were unwilling to expel, after 1945, German industrial workers from Upper Silesia. As a result, some 300,000 to 400,000 Germans resided in 1989 in the Polish provinces of Opole and Katowice.

4. Upper Silesia, *Entwicklung, Organisation, Arbeitsleistung*, 59.

5. Ibid., 2.

6. As quoted in Nuernberg Military Tribunals. "The RuSHA Case," *Trials of War Criminals*, 15 vols. (Washington, D.C.: Government Printing Office, 1950), 4:762f.

7. Alfred Konieczny, "Bemerkungen über die Anfänge des KL Auschwitz," *Hefte von Auschwitz* 12 (1971): 5ff.; Danuta Czech, "Konzentrationslager Auschwitz: Abriss der Geschichte," in Jozef Boszko and Wanda Michalak, eds., *Auschwitz: Geschichte und Wirklichkeit des Vernichtungslagers* (Reinbek: Rowohlt, 1980), 15ff.

8. Danuta Czech, *Kalendarium der Ereignisse im Konzentrationslager Auschwitz-Birkenau, 1939–1945*, trans. Jochen August, Nina Kozlowski, Silke Lent, and Jan Parcer (Reinbek: Rowohlt, 1989), 30.

9. "Baubericht über den Stand der Bauarbeiten für Bauvorhaben K.-L. Auschwitz," 10 August 1941, OAM, coll. 502/1, file 219, 2f. (USHRI, microfilm RG 11.001M.03, reel 34).

10. OAM, 502/1, file 214, 91–100 (USHRI, microfilm RG 11.001M.03, reel 34).

11. Letter of Schlachter to Höss, 30 August 1940, OAM, coll. 502/1, file 214, 91f. (USHRI, microfilm RG 11.001M.03, reel 34).

12. OAM, coll. 502/1, file 214, 85 (USHRI, microfilm RG 11.001M.03, reel 34).

13. OAM, coll. 502/1, file 215, 38 (USHRI, microfilm RG 11.001M.03, reel 34).

14. Enno Georg, *Die Wirtschaftliche Unternehmungen der SS* (Stuttgart: Deutsche Verlags-Anstalt, 1963), 51.

15. See Martin Broszat, "The Concentration Camps, 1933–45," in Helmut, Krausnick, Hans Buchheim, Martin Broszat, and Hans-Adolf Jacobsen, *Anatomy of the SS State*, trans. Richard Barry, Marian Jackson, and Dorothy Long (New York: Walker, 1968), 400ff.

16. Hermann Kaienburg, *"Vernichtung durch Arbeit"*: *Der Fall Neuengamme: Die Wirtschaftsbestrebungen der SS und ihre Auswirkungen auf die Existenzbedingungen der KZ-Gefangenen* (Bonn: J. H. W. Dietz Nachf., 1990), 102.

17. See Gordon J. Horwitz, *In the Shadow of Death*: *Living outside the Gates of Mauthausen* (New York: Free Press, 1990), 23ff.

18. Eugen Kogon, *The Theory and Practice of Hell*: *The German Concentration Camps and the System behind Them*, trans. Heinz Norden (New York: Farrar, Straus, 1950), 93.

19. For the budget allocation see "Baubericht über den Stand der Bauarbeiten für Bauvorhaben K.-L. Auschwitz," 10 August 1941, OAM, coll. 502/1, file 219 (USHRI, microfilm RG 11.001M.03, reel 34).

20. Pery Broad, "Reminiscences," in Rudolf Höss, Pery Broad, and Johann Paul Kremer, *KL Auschwitz Seen by the SS*, trans. Krystyna Michalik (Warsaw: Interpress Publishers, 1991), 109, 127f.

21. Wieslaw Kielar, *Anus Mundi*: *Fünf Jahre Auschwitz*, trans. Wera Kapkajew (Frankfurt. S. Fischer, 1979), 204f.

22. Ibid., 110.

23. Ibid.

24. Letter of Topf to SS-Neubauleitung, 20 June 1940, OAM, coll. 502/1, file 326 (USHRI, microfilm RG 11.001M.03, reel 42).

25. Letter of SS-Neubauleitung to Topf, 7 November 1940, OAM, coll. 502/1, file 312 (USHRI, microfilm RG 11.001M.03, reel 41).

26. Letter of SS-Neubauleitung to Hauptamt Haushalt und Bauten, Amt II C.2, 22 November 1940, OAM, coll. 502/1, file 327 (USHRI, microfilm RG 11.001M.03, reel 42).

27. Cable of SS-Neubauleitung to Topf, 11 November 1941, OAM, coll. 502/1, file 312 (USHRI, microfilm RG 11.001M.03, reel 41).

28. Czech, *Kalendarium*, 126ff.

29. Ibid., 137.

30. Ibid., 137f.

31. Broad, "Reminiscences," 119.

32. Letter of Grabner of 7 June 1941, OAM, coll. 502/1, file 312 (USHRI, microfilm RG 11.001M.03, reel 41).

33. Filip Müller, with Helmut Freitag, *Auschwitz Inferno: The Testimony of a Son-derkommando*, trans. Susanne Flatauer (London and Henley: Routledge & Kegan Paul, 1979), 14f.

34. "Bericht 1. Betrifft: Zusammenarbeit zwischen dem Reichskommissar für die Festigung deutschen Volkstums und dem Leiter der Reichstelle für Raumordnung etc." BAK, coll. R 49, file 902.

35. Upper Silesia, *Entwicklung, Organisation, Arbeitsleistung*, 59.

36. Ibid., 56.

37. Letter of Count von der Schulenberg to Himmler, 20 May 1940, BAK, coll. R 49, file 902.

38. Letter of Gerhard Ziegler to Konrad Meyer, 28 June 1940, BAK, coll. R 49, file 902.

39. Letter of Konrad Meyer to Gerhard Ziegler, 5 July 1940, BAK, coll. R 49, file 902.

40. Upper Silesia, *Entwicklung, Organisation, Arbeitsleistung*, 35ff.

41. Ibid., 55f.

42. See Gert Gröning and Joachim Wolschke-Bulmahn, *Die Liebe zur Landschaft*, pt. 3, *Der Drang nach Osten* (Munich: Minerva Publikation, 1987), 58f.

43. Letter of Bach-Zelewski to various provincial authorities, 5 August 1940, PAK, coll. OPK, file 1810, 10f.

44. Ulrich Greifelt, "Vermerk [Siedlungszone I]," 8 August 1940, BAK, R 49, file 902, 2.

45. Ibid., 8–10.

46. Ulrich Greifelt, "Vermerk . . . Besprechung," 11 September 1940, BAK, R 49, file 902.

47. "Vermerk über eine Sitzung am 10.10.40 in Kattowitz," 14 October 1940, BAK, R 49, file 902.

48. Letter of Greifelt to the Oberpräsidenten der Provinz Schlesien, 23 November 1940, BAK, R 49, file 902.

49. "Betrifft: Besprechung über die bevorstehende Evakuierungsaktion in Say-busch," 11 September 1940, PAK, coll. RK, file 4086, 5f.

50. Ibid.

51. "Richtlinien zur Durchführung der Evakuierungsaktion im Kreise Saybusch," 14 September 1940, PAK, coll. RK, file 4086, 7ff.

52. "Erfahrungsbericht über den Einsatz der 2. Kompanie bei der Umsiedlungsak-tion," 17 January 1941, PAK, coll. RK, file 4087, 72ff.

53. "The Tragedy of the Peasants in the Zywiec County," in Poland, Ministry of Information, *The Black Book of Poland* (New York: G. P. Putnam's Sons, 1942), 199f.

54. Ibid.

55. Letter of Arlt to Bracht, 6 June 1941, PAK, coll. OPK, file 1810, 185ff.

56. As reprinted in Poland, Ministry of Information, *The Black Book of Poland*, 211.

57. Fritz Arlt, *Siedlung und Landwirtschaft in den eingegliederten Gebieten Oberschlesiens* (Berlin: Deutsche Landbuchhandlung Sohnrey, 1942), 14ff.

58. As quoted in Rolf-Dieter Müller, *Hitlers Ostkrieg und die deutsche Siedlungspolitik* (Frankfurt: Fischer Taschenbuch, 1991), 120.

59. Planungshauptabteilung der RFSS-RKfdFdV, "Planungsgrundlagen für den Aufbau der Ostgebiete," BAK, coll. R 49, file 157, 19.

60. Arlt, *Siedlung und Landwirtschaft*, 57.

61. Among the many intruiging paths of investigation suggested in Arno Mayer's provocative *Why Did the Heavens Not Darken?*, the short discussion concerning the relation between the development of Auschwitz and Himmler's role as Reich Commissioner for the Consolidation of the German Nation proved particularly valuable. See Arno Mayer, *Why Did the Heavens Not Darken?: The "Final Solution" in History* (New York: Pantheon Books, 1988), 356f.; see also Arlt, *Siedlung und Landwirtschaft*, 58.

62. Rudolf Höss, *Death Dealer: The Memoirs of the SS Kommandant at Auschwitz*, ed. Steven Paskuly, trans. Andrew Pollinger (Buffalo: Prometheus Books, 1992), 283.

63. Ibid., 283f.

64. "Anhang zum Aktenvermerk vom 29. März 1941. Betreff: Arbeitseinsatz für das neuerstehende Buna-Werk Auschwitz," OAM, coll. 502/1, file 280 (USHRI, microfilm RG 11.001M.03, reel 38).

65. "Vermerk. Betr.: Lager Auschwitz," 12 December 1940, PAK, coll. Landesplanungsgemeinschaft Gau Oberschlesien, file 467,308.

66. Letter of Ziegler to Höss, 23 December 1940, PAK, coll. Landesplanungsgemeinschaft Gau Oberschlesien, file 467,304.

67. "Vermerk. Betr.: KZ-Auschwitz. Vortrag beim Gauleiter-Stellvertreter," 7 January 1941, PAK, coll. Landesplanungsgemeinschaft Gau Oberschlesien file 467, 302.

68. "Gutachten betreffende Verbesserung der wasserwirtschaftlichen Verhältnisse des Auschwitzer Siedlungsgebietes," PMOB, box BW 29/2, file 29/11.

69. "Schnellentwurf zur Regelung der Wasserwirtschaft auf dem Interessengebiete des K.L. Auschwitz," PMOB, box BW 29/2, file 29/11.

70. In order to facilitate the working of the estate, the SS established a number of satellite camps around Birkenau in the villages of Rajsko, Harmense, Budy, Plawy, and Babitz. See Anna Zieba, "Wirtschaftshof—Budy," *Hefte von Auschwitz* 10 (1967):

67–85; idem, "Die 'Geflügerfarm Harmense," ibid., 11 (1970): 39–72; idem, " 'Wirtschaftshof Babitz' Nebenlager beim Gut Babice," ibid., 73–87.

71. Kitty Hart, *Return to Auschwitz: The Remarkable Story of a Girl Who Survived the Holocaust* (London: Sidgwick & Jackson, 1981), 70.

72. Magda Somogyi, oral history recorded by Debórah Dwork, Budapest, Hungary, 19 July 1987, transcript, 9.

73. Hart, *Return to Auschwitz*, 73, 76.

74. Hannah Kent-Sztarkman, oral history recorded by Debórah Dwork, Stamford, Conn., 13 December 1985, transcript, 22f., 37, and 15 July 1995, transcript, 15–16.

75. Debórah Dwork and Robert Jan van Pelt, "Women's Work at Auschwitz: History, Gender, and Interpretation," *Contemporary Jewry*, Debra Kaufman, guest editor, 1996.

Chapter Seven: IG Farben

1. Testimony of Ambros, as quoted in Nuernberg Military Tribunals, "The Farben Case," *Trials of War Criminals*, vol. 8 (Washington, D.C.: Government Printing Office, 1952), 734f.

2. IG Farben stands for the Interessgemeinschaft Farbenindustrie Aktiengesellschaft (Interest Community of the Dye Industry, Inc.), a stock corporation established in 1925 that united Germany's six largest chemical corporations (BASF, Bayer, Hoechst, Agfa, Griesheim, and Weiler-terMeer). See Peter Hayes's *Industry and Ideology: IG Farben in the Nazi Era* (Cambridge: Cambridge University Press, 1987) for a comprehensive, insightful analysis of the relationship between IG Farben's upper-echelon management and the National Socialist hierarchy.

3. As quoted in Louis L. Snyder, *Encyclopedia of the Third Reich* (New York: Paragon House, 1989), 96.

4. Letter of Reich Ministry of Economics to IG-Farben, 8, November 1940, as quoted in "Farben Case," 331.

5. For a concise description of IG Farben buna technology, see Frederick Marchionna, *Butalastic Polymers: Their Preparations and Applications: A Treatise on Synthetic Rubbers* (New York: Reinhold, 1946), 66ff.

6. Walter Greiff, "Raumordnung und Wirtschaftsplanung in Oberschlesien," *Deutsche Monatshefte* 8 (1941–42): 428ff.

7. Günther Saath, *Die Industrie der eingegliederten oberschlesischen Ostgebiete* (Berlin, Prague, and Vienna: Volk und Reich Verlag, 1942), 34f.

8. District Cosel: Heydebreck (60,000); District Ratibor: Ratiborhammer (15,000), Buchenau (12,000) Olsau (10,000); District Beuthen-Tarnowitz: Rands-

dorf (35,000); District Tost-Gleiwitz: Haselgrund (15,000), Laband (20,000), Peis-kretscham (30,000); District Tarnowitz: Tarnowitz (55,000); District Bendsburg: Zombkowitz (50,000); District Teschen: Freistadt (40,000), Trzeinietz (20,000), Oderberg (65,000); District Rybnik: Rybnik (60,000), Loslau (20,000); District Bielitz: Auschwitz (50,000); District Pless: Tichau (150,000). See "Grundlagen für Raumordnung und Verkehr," BAK, coll. R 113, file 2394, 8f.

9. Letter from Mineralöl-Baugesellschaft to Ambros, 11 January 1941, as quoted in "Farben Case," 334f.

10. File note on a conference of Ambros and Krauch, 6 February 1941, as quoted ibid., 350.

11. Letter of Mayor Gutsche of Auschwitz to IG-Farben, 9 January 1941, as quoted ibid., 333.

12. Arlt, "Übersicht über die oberschlesische Bevölkerungstruktur," BAK, coll. R 49, file 902, 6.

13. "Vermerk! Betrifft: 3. Nahplan," 10 January 1941, BAK, coll. R 49, Anhang I, file 34, 8.

14. Ibid., 7f.

15. Report of conference between representatives of IG Farben and Schlesien-Benzin, 18 January 1941, as quoted in "Farben Case," 337f.

16. IG Farbenindustrie Aktiengesellschaft Proko Büro, *Erzeugnisse unserer Arbeit* (Frankfurt: IG Farbenindustrie AG, 1938), 208ff.

17. Memorandum concerning investigation of prospective sites for the Buna plant in Silesia, 10 February 1941, as quoted in "Farben Case," 345.

18. File note on a conference between Ambros and Krauch, 6 February 1941, as quoted ibid., 350.

19. Memorandum of Kurt Eisfeldt "Buna-plan project—Auschwitz site," 13 February 1941, as reprinted ibid., 353.

20. Letter of Krauch to IG-Farben, 25 February 1941, as quoted ibid., 359.

21. Letter of Göring to Himmler, 18 February 1941, as reprinted ibid., 354f.

22. "Anhang zum Aktenvermerk vom 29. März 1941. Betreff: Arbeitseinsatz für das neuerstehende Buna-Werk Auschwitz," OAM, coll. 502/1, file 280 (USHRI, microfilm RG 11.001M.03, reel 38).

23. Letter of Krauch to Ambros, 4 March 1941, as quoted in "Farben Case," 357.

24. BAK, Coll. NS 19, file 400.

25. "Zur Gründung des Werkes Auschwitz; Niederschrift über die Gründungssitzung am 7. April 1941 in Kattowitz," OAM, coll. 502/5, file 6, 40 (USHRI, microfilm RG 11.001M.03, reel 71).

26. Rudolf Höss, *Death Dealer: The Memoirs of the SS Kommandant at Auschwitz*, ed. Steven Paskuly, trans. Andrew Pollinger (Buffalo: Prometheus Books, 1992), 284ff.

27. Minutes of construction conference of IG Plant Auschwitz, 24 March 1941, as quoted in "Farben Case," 380.

28. Letter of Kammler to Neubauleitung KL Auschwitz, 27 June 1941, OAM, coll. 502/1, file 215 (USHRI, microfilm RG 11.001M.03, reel 34).

29. Report of visit, as quoted in "Farben Case," 373f.

30. Ibid., 374f.

31. Report of visit, Document NI-15148. These sections were omitted in the translated version printed in "Farben Case," 373; they can be consulted in the typescript version produced for the Office of Chief of Counsel for War Crimes.

32. The minutes of this meeting were partly printed in "Farben Case," 383–88. For the part that was left out, we will refer to a complete set of the minutes preserved in OAM, coll. 502/5, file 6 (USHRI, microfilm RG 11.001M.03, reel 71).

33. Minutes of Founding Meeting of IG Farben-Auschwitz, 7 April 1941, as quoted in "Farben Case," 384.

34. Ibid., 385f.

35. Ibid., 386.

36. Minutes of Founding Meeting of IG Farben-Auschwitz, 7 April 1941, OAM, coll. 502/5, film 6, 11 (USHRI, microfilm RG 11.001M.03, reel, 71).

37. "Skizze Generalbebauungsplan Auschwitz," June 1941, PMOB, box BW 2/1, file 2/11.

38. Letter of Kammler to Höss, 18 June 1941, PMOB, box BW 1/2, file 1/9; also OAM, coll. 502/1, file 215 (USHRI, microfilm RG 11.001M.03, reel 34).

39. Ibid.

40. Letter of Schlachter to Hauptamt Haushalt und Bauten, Amt IIB, 11 August 1941, OAM, coll. 502/1, file 215 (USHRI, microfilm RG 11.001M.03, reel 34).

41. Höss, *Death Dealer*, 293.

42. Ibid., 235.

43. "Kostenüberschlag für das Bauvorhaben: SS-Unterkunft und Konzentrationslager Auschwitz," OAM, coll. 502/1, file 216 (USHRI, microfilm RG 11.001M.03, reel 34).

44. Minutes of 13th construction conference, 19 November 1941, as quoted in "Farben Case," 402.

45. IG-Farben-Auschwitz weekly report no. 30 (15–21 December 1941), as quoted ibid., 403f.

46. See "Erläuterungsbericht zum prov. Ausbau des Konzentrationslagers Auschwitz O/S," OAM, coll. 502/1, file 223 (USHRI, microfilm RG 11.001M.03, reel 34).

47. See "Erläuterungsbericht zum Bauvorhaben Konzentrationslager Auschwitz O/S," OAM, coll. 502/1, file 222 (USHRI, microfilm RG 11.001M.03, reel 34).

48. "K.L. Auschwitz, Lageplanskizze," PMOB, box BW 2/2, file 2/17.

49. Kammler, "Bericht des Amtes II-Bauten des Hauptamtes Haushalt und Bauten über die Arbeiten im Jahre 1941," OAM, coll. 502/1, file 13, 5 (USHRI, microfilm RG 11.001M.03, reel 19).

50. PMOB, box BW 3/3a, 3/5.

51. Kammler, "Bericht des Amtes II-Bauten des Hauptamtes Haushalt und Bauten über die Arbeiten im Jahre 1941," OAM, coll. 502/1, file 13, 4 (USHRI, microfilm RG 11.001M.03, reel 19).

52. Jean-Claude Pressac, Auschwitz: *Technique and Operation of the Gas Chambers*, trans. Peter Moss (New York: Beate Klarsfeld Foundation, 1989), 16ff.

53. Ibid., 20.

54. Weekly report of 12 July 1940, OAM, coll. 502/1, file 214 (USHRI, microfilm RG 11.001M.03, reel 34); Höss, *Death Dealer*, 118.

55. Andrzeje Rablin, deposition made on 2 February 1961, as quoted in Pressac, *Auschwitz*, 25.

56. G. Peters and E. Wüstinger, *Entlausung mit Zyklon-Blausäure in Kreislauf-Begasungskammern* (Berlin: Duncker & Humblot, 1940), 6f.

57. Letter of Heerdt-Linger to SS New Construction Office Auschwitz, 1 July 1941, OAM, coll. 502/1, file 322 (USHRI, microfilm RG 11.001M.03, reel 42); Letter of Kammler to Höss, 18 June 1941, PMOB, box BW 1/2, file 1/9.

58. "Kostenüberschlag für das Bauvorhaben: SS-Unterkunft und Konzentrationslager Auschwitz," OAM, coll. 502/1, file 216, 2 (USHRI, microfilm RG 11.001M.03, reel 34).

59. "Erläuterungsbericht zum Bauvorhaben Konzentrationslager Auschwitz O/S," OAM, coll. 502/1, file 222, 13 (USHRI, microfilm RG 11.001M.03, reel 34).

60. See material in PBMOB, box BW 160/1, file 160/7.

61. Sherry Weiss-Rosenfeld, interview with Debórah Dwork, Southfield, Mich., 26 January 1987, transcript, 20.

62. Hannah Kent-Starkman, interview with Debórah Dwork, Stamford, Conn., 13 December 1985, transcript, 26.

63. Alexander Ehrmann, interview with Debórah Dwork, West Bloomfield, Mich., 15 November and 13 December 1986 and 24 January 1987, transcript, 36.

64. Mania Salinger-Tenenbaum, interview with Debórah Dwork, Bloomfield, Mich., 10 and 21 January 1987, transcript, 33f.

65. "Raumprogramm Kommandantur-Gebäude für ein Grosslager (ca. 30–35000)," PMOB, box BW 173/7, file 173/33, 31.

66. Höss, *Death Dealer*, 216.

67. Rudolf Vrba and Alan Bestic, *I Cannot Forgive* (London: Sidgwick and Jackson, and Anthony Gibbs and Phillips, 1963), 109.

68. Affidavit of Norbert Wollheim, as quoted in "Farben Case," 8:590.

69. Affidavit of Charles J. Coward, as quoted ibid., 607.

70. Paul M. Hebert, "Dissenting Opinion on Count Three of the Indictment," filed 28 December 1948, as quoted ibid., 1321.

71. Primo Levi, *If This Is a Man?*, trans. Stuart Woolf (New York: Orion, 1959), 81, 82.

Chapter Eight: Birkenau

1. Letter of Frick to Göring, Lammers, Himmler et al., 22 July 1941, BAK, Coll. R 113, file 730, 2f.

2. Ibid., 4f.

3. Günter Pahl, "Das grössere Oberschlesien," *Die Woche*, 16 April 1941, 6.

4. Gerhard Ziegler, "Grundlagen des künftigen Städtebaus in Oberschlesien," *Raumforschung und Raumordnung: Monatschrift der Reichsarbeitsgemeinschaft für Raumforschung* 5 (1941): 156.

5. Ibid., 155.

6. "Verordnung zur Ergänzung der Verordnung über Neuordnungsmassnahmen zur Beseitigung von Kriegsfolgen," *Reichsgesetzblatt*, 22 February 1942, 97.

7. See Mechtild Rössler, "*Wissenschaft und Lebensraum*": *Geographische Ostforschung im Nationalsozialismus* (Berlin and Hamburg: Dietrich Reimer, 1990), 146ff.

8. Walter Christaller, "Land und Stadt in der deutschen Volksordnung," *Deutsche Agrarpolitik* 1 (1942–43): 53f.

9. Walter Christaller, "Die Kultur-und Marktbereiche der zentralen Orte im deutschen Ostraum und die Gliederung der Verwaltung," *Raumforschung und Raumordnung* 4 (1940): 500.

10. Adolf Hitler, *Mein Kampf*, trans. Ralph Manheim (Boston: Houghton Mifflin, 1943), 212ff.

11. Gottfried Feder with Fritz Rechenberg, *Die neue Stadt: Versuch der Begründung einer neuen Stadtplanungskunst aus der sozialen Struktur der Bevölkerung* (Berlin: Julius Springer, 1939), 1.

12. Ibid., 73.

13. Ibid., 477.

14. Ibid., 468.

15. Hans Reichow, "Grundsätzliches zum Städtebau im Altreich und im neuen deutschen Osten," *Raumforschung und Raumordnung* 5 (1941): 225–30; Wilhelm, Wortmann. "Der Gedanke der Stadtlandschaft," ibid., 15–17.

16. Carl Culemann, "Die Gestaltung der städtischen Siedlungsmasse," *Raumforschung und Raumordnung* 5 (1941):123.

17. Ibid., 124.

18. Ibid.

19. Ibid., 126.

20. Josef Umlauf, "Zur Stadtplanung in den neuen deutschen Ostgebieten," *Raumforschung und Raumordnung* 5 (1941):107.

21. Ibid., 112ff.

22. Ibid., 108.

23. Karl Neupert, "Die Gestaltung der deutschen Besiedlung," *Raumforschung und Raumordnung* 5 (1941):63.

24. Ibid., 68.

25. Reichsheimstättenamt der Deutschen Arbeitsfront, *Siedlungsgestaltung aus Volk, Raum und Landschaft*, 5. *Planungsheft*: *Das deutsche Siedlungsbild im Osten* (Berlin: Verlag der deutschen Arbeitsfront, 1941), 11.

26. Reichsführer SS, Reichskommissar für die Festigung deutschen Volkstums, "Allgemeine Anordnung Nr. 13/II vom 30. Januar 1942: Richtlinien für die Planung und Gestaltung der Städte in den eingegliederten deutschen Ostgebieten," *Gestaltung der neuen Siedlungsgebiete* (Berlin: Verlag deutsche Landbuchhandlung Sohnrey, 1943), 12.

27. Ibid., 14

28. Ibid., 15.

29. Hans Stosberg, *Brückenkopf Breslau* (Ph.D. diss., Technical University Hannover, 1933; Breslau: Privately published, 1935), 97.

30. Hans Stosberg, "Auschwitz: Erläuterung zur Raumordnungsskizze," PAK, coll. LO/S, file 467, 1f.

31. Ibid., 3.

32. Ibid., 4ff.

33. Hans Stosberg, "Zum Bebauungsplan der Stadt Auschwitz. Eigenbedarf und öffentliche Anlagen in der I.G. Bereitschaftssiedlung," Archive Niels Gutschow, Absteinach. Niels Gutschow has discussed Stosberg's acivities as the municipal architect of Auschwitz in two important publications on German and Polish plans of urban reconstruction during and after the war. See Werner Durth and Niels Gutschow, *Träume in Trümmern*: *Stadtplanung, 1940–1950* (Munich: Deutscher Taschenbuch, 1993); Niels Gutschow and Barbara Klain, *Vernichtung und Utopie*: *Stadtplanung Warschau, 1939–1945* (Hamburg: Junius, 1994), 87ff.

34. Umlauf, "Zur Stadtplanung in den neuen deutschen Ostgebieten," 111.

35. Hans Stosberg, "Erläuterungsbericht um Bebauungsplan für die Stadt Auschwitz O/S," Archive Niels Gutschow, Absteinach, 1.

36. Ibid.

37. Hans Stosberg, "Verteilung der öffentlichen Gebäude (ohne Schulen)" and "Zum Bebauungsplan der Stadt Auschwitz: Verteilung der Schulen im Stadtgebiet," Archive Niels Gutschow, Absteinach.

38. "Konzentrationslager Auschwitz: Generalbebauungsplan—KL und Siedlung im Massstab 1: 20,000," PMOB, box BW 2/3, file 2/26.

39. "Vermerk betr.: KL-Auschwitz, Eisenbahn-, Siedlungs-, Grenz- u. Wasser-fragen," PAK, coll. LO/S, file 467, 96–99.

40. "Konzentrationslager Auschwitz—Generalbebauungsplan," PMOB, box BW 2/3, file 2/25.

41. Danuta Czech, *Kalendarium der Ereignisse im Konzentrationslager Auschwitz-Birkenau, 1939–1945*, trans. Jochen August, Nina Kozlowski, Silke Lent, and Jan Parcer (Reinbek: Rowohlt, 1989), 337ff.

42. Letter of Gerhard Ziegler to Himmler, 18 February 1942, PAK, coll. LO/S, file 467, 130.

43. Rudolf Höss, *Death Dealer*: *The Memoirs of the SS Kommandant at Auschwitz*, ed. Steven Paskuly, trans. Andrew Pollinger (Buffalo: Prometheus Books, 1992), 285.

44. Letter of Regierungsbaurat Derpa to the Mayor of Auschwitz, 3 January 1941," OAM, coll. 502/1, file 76, 53 (USHRI, microfilm RG-11.001M.03, reel 23).

45. "Der Reichsführer-SS vor den Oberabschnittsführern und Hauptamtschefs im Haus der Flieger in Berlin am 9. Juni 1942," BAK, coll. NS 19, file 4009, 18.

46. Report of meeting held between representatives of IG Farben and Schlesien-Benzin in Ludwigshaven, 16 January 1941, and memorandum by Santo, 10 February 1941, as quoted in "Farben Case," 337, 346.

47. See especially the record of interviews with German military leaders involved in Operation Barbarossa in Frans Pieter ten Kate, *De Duitse aanval op de Sovjet-Unie in 1941*: *Een krijgsgeschiedkundige studie*, 2 vols. (Groningen: Wolters-Noordhoff, 1968), 1: 91f.

48. Franz Lüdtke, *Ein Jahrtausend Krieg zwischen Deutschland und Polen* (Stuttgart: Robert Lutz Nachfolger/Inhaber Rudolf Weisert, 1941), 7f.

49. Gerhard Schumann, "Krieg—Bericht und Dichtung," in Rudolf Erckmann, ed., *Dichter und Krieger* (Hamburg: Hanseatische Verlagsanstalt, 1943), 70f.

50. Minutes of the ministerial conference held at the Ministry of Propaganda, Berlin, 27 June 1941, in Willi A. Boelcke, ed., *The Secret Conferences of Dr. Goebbels*: *The Nazi Propaganda War, 1939–43*, trans. Ewald Oser (New York: E. P. Dutton, 1971), 176.

51. Ibid.

52. Reichsführer-SS, SS-Hauptamt, *Der Untermensch* (Berlin: Nordland, 1942), 4f.

53. Christian Streit, "The German Army and the Politics of Genocide," in Gerhard Hirschfeld, ed., *The Policies of Genocide*: *Jews and Soviet Prisoners of War in Nazi Germany* (London, Boston, and Sydney: Allen & Unwin/German Historical Institute, 1986), 4.

54. As quoted in Jürgen Förster, "The German Army and the Ideological War against the Soviet Union," in Hirschfeld, ed., *The Policies of Genocide*, 20.

55. As quoted in Omer Bartov, *Hitler's Army: Soldiers, Nazis and War in the Third Reich* (New York and Oxford: Oxford University Press, 1991), 129.

56. Ibid., 130f.

57. Höss, *Death Dealer*, 132.

58. Stanislaw Ploski, "German Crimes against Soviet Prisoners-of-War in Poland," in Central Commission for the Investigation of German Crimes in Poland, *German Crimes in Poland*, 2 vols. (Warsaw: Central Commission, 1946–47), 1:266.

59. Ibid., 270f.

60. Letter of Ambros and Dürrfeld to Krauch, 25 October 1941, OAM, coll. 502/5, file 6 (USHRI, microfilm RG 11.001M.03, reel 71).

61. Ibid.

62. Christian Streit, *Keine Kamaraden: Die Wehrmacht und die sowjetischen Kriegsgefangenen, 1941–1945* (Stuttgart: Deutsche Verlags-Anstalt, 1978), 217ff.

63. Our discussion of the construction of Birkenau is a summary of Robert Jan van Pelt, "A Site in Search of a Mission," in Yisrael Gutman and Michael Berenbaum, eds., *Anatomy of the Auschwitz Death Camp* (Bloomington and Indianapolis: Indiana University Press, 1994), 93–156.

64. "Erläuterungsbericht zum Vorentwurf für den Neubau des Kriegsgefangenenlagers der Waffen-SS, Auschwitz O/S," OAM, coll. 502/1, file 232 (USHRI, microfilm RG 11.001M.03 reel, 35).

65. PMOB, box BW (B) 3a, file BW 3a/1.

66. Telegram of SS-Hauptstürmführer Sesemann to the Architectural Office of the Waffen SS, Auschwitz, 25 October 1941, OAM, coll. 502/1, file 215. (USHRI, microfilm RG 11.001M.03, reel 34).

67. Höss, *Death Dealer*, 132f.

68. Tadeusz Borowski, *This Way for the Gas, Ladies and Gentlemen*, trans. Barbara Vedder (New York: Viking, 1967), 110f.

69. For the appropriate clauses in the 1899 Hague Convention, see Carnegie Endowment for International Peace, Division of International Law, pamphlet 5, *The Hague Conventions of 1899 (II) and 1907 (IV) Respecting the Laws and Customs of War on Land* (Washington, D.C.: The Endowment, 1915), 10f.; for the appropriate clause in the 1929 Geneva Convention, see United States Congress, Senate, *Treaties, Conventions, International Acts, Protocols and Agreements between the United States of America and Other Powers (1923–1937)*, 75th Cong, 3d sess., 1938, S. Doc. 134, 5231.

70. PMOB, box BW (B) 3/3a, file 3/5.

71. Terrence Des Pres, *The Survivor: An Anatomy of Life in the Death Camps* (New York: Oxford University Press, 1976), 60.

72. Ibid.

73. Gisella Perl, *I Was a Doctor in Auschwitz* (New York: International Universities Press, 1948), 33

74. Telegram of Bauleitung, 11 October 1941, OAM, coll. 502/1, file 313. (USHRI, microfilm RG 11.001M.03 reel 41); Letter of Topf, 14 October 1941, ibid.

75. Plan of the Main Camp at Auschwitz, 19 February 1942, PMOB, box BW 2/2, file 2/17.

76. Kammler, "Bericht des Amtes II-Bauten des Hauptamtes Haushalt und Bauten über die Arbeiten im Jahre 1941," OAM, coll. 502/1, file 13, 4. (USHRI, microfilm RG 11.001M.03, reel 19).

77. OAM, coll. 502/1, file 313. (USHRI, microfilm RG 11.001M.03, reel 41); also Oswiecim, BW (B) 30/27 and BW (B) 30/34.

78. POMB box BW (B) 30/1-7.

79. Letter of Topf, 31 October 1941, OAM, coll. 502/1, file 312. (USHRI, microfilm RG 11.001M.03, reel 41); letter of Topf, 4 November 1941, OAM, coll. 502/1, file 327 (USHRI, microfilm RG 11.001M.03, reel 42).

80. Moreover, calculations of the capacity of the crematorium suggest a non-genocidal intention. See van Pelt, "A Site in Search of a Mission," 140ff.

81. Höss, *Death Dealer*, 133.

82. Letter of Bischoff to Kammler, 4 December 1941, OAM, coll. 502/1, file 219, 26–28. (USHRI, microfilm RG 11.001M.03, reel 34).

83. OAM, coll. 502/1, file 232, 3. (USHRI, microfilm RG 11.001M.03, reel 35).

84. Letter of Kammler to the Auschwitz Zentralbauleitung and other construction offices, 27 November 1941, PMOB, box BW, 1/2, file 1/9.

85. Plan of Auschwitz-Birkenau, 6 January 1942, PMOB, box BW (B) 2/6.

86. Directive of Keitel, 31 October 1941, as quoted in "Farben Case," 399.

87. See Streit, *Keine Kamaraden*, 209.

Chapter Nine: Summer 1941

1. Jan Sehn, "Concentration and Extermination Camp Oswiecim (Auschwitz-Birkenau)," in Central Commission for the Investigation of German Crimes in Poland, *German Crimes in Poland*, 2 vols. (Warsaw: Central Commission, 1946–47), 1:27f.

2. Tadeusz Borowski, *This Way for the Gas, Ladies and Gentlemen*, trans. Barbara Vedder (New York: Viking, 1967), 112f.

3. Jean Paul Sartre discussed this phenomenon at some length in his *Nausea*, trans. Lloyd Alexander (New York: New Directions, 1964), 39f.

4. Robert Musil, *The Man without Qualities*, trans. Eithne Wilkins and Ernst Kaiser, 3 vols. (London: Pan Book, 1979), 2:70.

5. Whitney R. Harris, *Tyranny on Trial: The Evidence at Nuremberg* (Dallas: Southern Methodist University Press, 1954), 334f.

6. As quoted in International Military Tribunal, *Trial of the Major War Criminals*, 46 vols. (Nuremberg: Secretariat of the International Military Tribunal, 1947), 11:415, 416.

7. Gustave M. Gilbert, *Nuremberg Diary* (New York: Farrar, Straus, 1947), 250.

8. International Military Tribunal, *Trial of the Major War Criminals*, 11:398.

9. Ibid., 416.

10. Rudolf Höss, *Death Dealer: The Memoirs of the SS Kommandant at Auschwitz*, ed. Steven Paskuly, trans. Andrew Pollinger (Buffalo: Prometheus Books, 1992), 27.

11. Stanislaw Klodzinski, "Die 'Aktion 14f13': Der Transport von 575 Häftlingen von Auschwitz in das 'Sanatorium Dresden,'" in Götz Aly, ed., *Aktion T4, 1939–1945: Die Euthanasie-Zentrale in der Tiergartenstrasse 4* (Berlin: Edition Hentrich, 1987), 136ff.

12. Adolf Hitler, *Mein Kampf*, trans. Ralph Manheim (Boston: Houghton Mifflin, 1943), 679; see also 169.

13. Adolf Hitler, *Hitler's Table Talk 1941–44: His Private Conversations*, trans. Norman Cameron and R. H. Stevens (London: Weidenfeld and Nicolson, 1973), 29.

14. Ibid., 409.

15. As quoted in Jürgen Förster, "The German Army and the Ideological War against the Soviet Union," in Gerhard Hirschfeld, ed., *The Policies of Genocide: Jews and Soviet Prisoners of War in Nazi Germany* (London, Boston, and Sydney: Allen & Unwin/German Historical Institute, 1986), 20.

16. Höss, *Death Dealer*, 29.

17. Irena Strzelecka, "Hospitals," in Yisrael Gutman and Michael Berenbaum, eds., *Anatomy of the Auschwitz Death Camp* (Bloomington and Indianapolis: Indiana University Press, 1994), 389.

18. Christian Streit, "The German Army and the Politics of Genocide," Hirschfeld, ed., *The Policies of Genocide*, 8.

19. Document 447-PS, in Office of United States Chief Counsel for Prosecution of Axis Criminality, *Nazi Conspiracy and Aggression*, 8 vols. (Washington, D.C.: Government Printing Office, 1946), 3:410.

20. As quoted in Jeremy Noakes and Geoffrey Pridham, eds., *Nazism, 1919–1945*, 3 vols. (Exeter: Exeter University Publications, 1983–88), 3:1088f.

21. As quoted ibid., 1091f.

22. Philippe Burrin, *Hitler and the Jews: The Genesis of the Holocaust*, trans. Patsy Southgate, intro. Saul Friedländer (London, Melbourne, and Auckland: Edward Arnold, 1994), 97.

23. International Military Tribunal, *Trial of the Major War Criminals*, 11:477.

24. Document 1017-PS, in *Nazi Conspiracy and Aggression*, 3:676.

25. Document 1019-PS, ibid., 684.

26. Document 1024-PS, ibid., 685.

27. Document 1028-PS, 690.

28. Document 1024-PS, ibid., 689.

29. Ibid.

30. Letter of Meyer to Himmler, 15 July 1941, BAK, coll. NS 19, file 1739, 2.

31. Erhard Wetzel, "Stellungnahme und Gedanken zum Generalplan Ost des Reichsführers SS," *Vierteljahrshefte für Zeitgeschichte* 6 (1958):297ff.

32. "Kurze Zusammenfassung der Denkschrift Generalplan Ost," BAK, coll. NS 19, file 1739, 5.

33. Burrin, *Hitler and the Jews*, 104.

34. Document L-221, in *Nazi Conspiracy and Aggression*, 7:1087.

35. Ibid., 1093.

36. Albert Speer, *Infiltration: How Heinrich Himmler Schemed to Build an SS Industrial Empire*, trans. Joachim Neugroschel (New York: Macmillan, 1981), 25.

37. See Yitzhak Arad, *Belzec, Sobibor, Treblinka: The Operation Reinhard Death Camps* (Bloomington and Indianapolis: Indiana University Press, 1987), 14f.

38. Document 710-PS, in *Nazi Conspiracy and Aggression*, 3:525f.

39. Streit, "The Army and the Policies of Genocide," 10.

40. Frans Pieter ten Kate, *De Duitse aanval op de Sovjet-Unie in 1941: Een krijgs-geschiedkundige studie*, 2 vols. (Groningen: Wolters-Noordhoff, 1968), 1: 91f.

41. Ibid., 49.

42. Ibid., 70.

43. Höss, *Death Dealer*, 28.

44. Wojciech Barcz, "Die erste Vergasung," in H. G. Adler, H. Langbein, and Ella Lingens-Reiner, eds., *Auschwitz: Zeugnisse und Berichte* (Frankfurt: Athenäum, 1988), 17f.

45. Letter of Grabner of 7 June 1941, OAM, coll. 502/1, file 312 (USHRI, microfilm RG 11.001M.03, reel 41).

46. See Jean-Claude Pressac, with Robert-Jan van Pelt, "The Machinery of Mass Murder at Auschwitz," in Gutman and Berenbaum, eds., *Anatomy of the Auschwitz Death Camp*, 209; also Jean-Claude Pressac, *Auschwitz: Technique and Operation of the Gas Chambers*, trans. Peter Moss (New York: Beate Klarsfeld Foundation, 1989), 131ff. Pressac's dating of the first gassing in December 1941 is not substantiated by the evidence.

47. Danuta Czech, *Kalendarium der Ereignisse im Konzentrationslager Auschwitz-Birkenau, 1939–1945*, trans. Jochen August, Nina Kozlowski, Silke Lent, and Jan Parcer (Reinbek: Rowohlt, 1989), 122.

48. Höss, *Death Dealer*, 156.

49. Ibid., 156f.

50. As quoted in Herbert Michaelis and Ernst Schraepler, eds., *Ursachen und Folgen*: *Vom deutschen Zusammenbruch 1918 bis 1945 bis zur staatlichen Neuordnung Deutschlands in der Gegenwart*, 26 vols. (Berlin: Dokumenten-Verlag Dr. Herbert Wendler, n.d.), 18: 526f.

51. Wladyslaw Bednarz, "Extermination Camp at Chelmno," in *German Crimes in Poland*, 1:112f.

52. Hitler, *Table Talk*, 87.

53. Ibid., 141.

54. As quoted in Noakes and Pridham, eds., *Nazism, 1919–1945*, 3:1125f.

55. Letter of Pohl to Himmler, December 1941, BAK, coll. NS 19, file 2065; also "Vorschlag für die Aufstellung von SS-Baubrigaden für die Ausführung von Bauaufgaben des Reichsführers-SS im Kriege und Frieden," ibid.

56. Letter of Himmler to Pohl, 31 January 1942, BAK, coll. NS 19, file 2065.

57. Kammler, "Vorschlag für die Aufstellung von SS-Baubrigaden für die Ausführung von Bauaufgaben des Reichsführers-SS im Kriege und Frieden," BAK, coll. NS 19, file 2065, 7ff.

58. Minutes of the Wannsee Conference, as quoted in Lucy S. Dawidowicz, ed., *A Holocaust Reader* (New York: Behrman House, 1976), 74.

59. Ibid., 78.

60. Hitler, *Table Talk*, 235f.

61. As quoted in Martin Broszat, "The Concentration Camps, 1933–45," in Helmut Krausnick, Hans Buchheim, Martin Broszat, and Hans-Adolf Jacobsen, *Anatomy of the SS State*, trans. Richard Barry, Marian Jackson, and Dorothy Long (New York: Walker, 1968), 483.

62. State of Israel, Ministry of Justice, *The Trial of Adolf Eichmann*: *Record of Proceedings in the District Court of Jerusalem*, 5 vols. (Jerusalem: Trust for the Publication of the Proceedings of the Eichmann Trial, 1993), 4:1424, 1431.

63. Yehuda Bauer, *Jews for Sale? Nazi-Jewish Negotiations, 1933–1945* (New Haven and London: Yale University Press, 1994), 65.

64. As quoted in State of Israel, *The Trial of Adolf Eichmann*, 4:1508.

65. Helen Tichauer-Spitzer, interview with Debórah Dwork and Robert Jan van Pelt, New York, N.Y., 20 April 1995, transcript, 24f.

66. Ibid., 25.

67. Ibid., 26ff.

68. Ibid., 28.

69. See Alfred Konieczny, "Die Zwangsarbeit der Juden in Schlesien im Rahmen der 'Organisation Schmelt,'" in Götz Aly et al., *Sozialpolitik und Judenvernichtung*: *Gibt es eine Ökonomie der Endlösung?*, Beiträge zur Nationalsozialistischen Gesundheits- und Sozialpolitik, 5 (Berlin: Rotbuch, 1987), 91ff.

70. Pery Broad, "Reminiscences," in Rudolf Höss, Pery Broad, and Johann Paul

Kremer, *KL Auschwitz Seen by the SS*, trans. Krystyna Michalik (Warsaw: Interpress Publishers, 1991), 128f.

71. Letter of Bischoff to Topf, 5 March 1942, PMOB, box BW 30/25, 1; see also letter of Bischoff to Wirtz, 30 March 1942, PMOB box BW (B) 30/34, 37. These letters are published in Pressac, *Auschwitz*, 191, 193.

72. Letter of Bischoff to Topf, 22 October 1941, OAM, coll. 502/1, file 313 (USHRI, microfilm RG 11.001M.03, reel 41).

73. Reworked version of plan of Birkenau of 6 January 1942 (no date, but probably produced just after 27 February 1942), OAM, coll. 502/2, file 95. (USHRI, microfilm RG 11.001M.03, reel 63).

74. Czech, *Kalendarium*, 186.

75. Höss, *Death Dealer*, 31.

76. Bauer, *Jews for Sale?*, 66.

77. As quoted in State of Israel, *The Trial of Adolf Eichmann*, 4:1509.

78. Czech, *Kalendarium*, 206.

79. ''Aktenvermerk Betr.: Anwesenheit von Obering. Prüfer der Fa. Topf u. Söhne Erfurt, bezüglich Ausbau der Einäscherungsanlagen im K.G.L. Auschwitz,'' 21 August 1942, OAM, coll. 502/1, file 313 (USHRI, microfilm RG 11.001M.03, reel 41).

80. Pressac, with van Pelt, ''The Machinery of Mass Murder at Auschwitz,'' 213.

81. Czech, *Kalendarium*, 241ff.

82. As quoted in Noakes and Pridham, eds., *Nazism, 1919–1945*, 3:1180.

Chapter Ten: The Holocaust

1. Felix Kersten, *The Kersten Memoirs, 1940–45* (London: Hutchinson, 1956), 132.

2. For discussions of the General Plan East, see Dietrich Eichholtz, ''Der Generalplan Ost: Über eine Ausgeburt imperialistischer Denkart und Politik (mit Dokumenten),'' *Jahrbuch für Geschichte* 26 (1982):217–74; Rolf-Dieter Müller, *Hitlers Ostkrieg und die deutsche Siedlungspolitik* (Frankfurt: Fischer Taschenbuch, 1991); Bruno Wasser, *Himmlers Raumplanung im Osten: Der Generalplan Ost in Polen, 1940–1944* (Basel, Berlin, and Boston: Birkhäuser, 1993); and the following contributions in Mechtild Rössler and Sabine Schleiermacher, eds., *Der ''Generalplan Ost'': Hauptlinien der nationalsozialistischen Planungs- und Vernichtungspolitik* (Berlin: Akademie, 1993): Czeslaw Madajczyk, ''Vom 'Generalplan Ost' zum 'Generalsiedlungsplan,' '' 12–19; Karl Heinz Roth, '' 'Generalplan Ost'—'Gesamtplan Ost': Forschungsstand, Quellenprobleme, neue Ergebnisse,'' 25–95; Dietrich Eichholtz, ''Der 'Generalplan Ost'

als genozidale Variante der imperialistischen Ostexpansion," 118–24; Bruno Wasser, "Die 'Germanisierung' im Distrikt Lublin als Generalprobe und erste Realisierungsphase des 'Generalplans Ost,' " 271–93.

3. Konrad Meyer, "Generalplan Ost: Rechtliche, wirtschaftliche und räumliche Grundlagen des Ostaufbaues," BAK, coll. R49, file 157c, 29ff.

4. Ibid., 42ff.

5. Ibid., 52f.

6. Ibid., 61ff.

7. Heinrich Himmler, "Der Reichsführer-SS vor den Oberabschnittsführern und Hauptamtschefs im Haus der Flieger in Berlin am 9. Juni 1942," BAK, coll. NS 19, file 4009, 18.

8. The marches were Ingermanland, or Ingria, which occupied the western half of the Russian province of Leningrad (anticipated 350,700 settlers in twenty-five years), the Memel-Narev area, which covered Courland and Lithuania (712,300 settlers), and Goth Province, which was to occupy the Crimea and the Ukrainian province of Kherson (925,100 settlers). The footholds were thirty-six towns with a surrounding *Weichbild* of around 750 square miles and included Pskov (24,800), Riga (105,900), Warsaw (319,400), Lublin (40,400), Zamosc (17,700), Cracow (71,900), Lemberg (90,700), and Rovno (20,000). The town of Jaslo also was to become a foothold of settlement, with 14,400 settlers. The settlers never arrived, but the town got its intended face-lift. See Meyer, "Generalplan Ost," 71ff.

9. Ibid., 19f.

10. Kersten's notes about Himmler's conversation with Hitler are dated 16, 17, 19, 21, 22, and 23 July. Himmler was with Hitler in Zhitomir on 16 July, but on 17 and 18 July in Auschwitz, and from 19 to 22 July in Lublin. Kersten does not mention that he accompanied Himmler on this trip, and the specific mention of a conversation with Hitler's secretary Brandt on 17 July immediately after a conversation with Himmler suggests that Kersten was either confused about dates, embellished the conversation with Himmler about German settlement in Russia, or reduced elements of conversations held over a much longer time to a compact narrative lasting a few days. The entry of 16 July seems remarkably fresh and has a ring of authenticity that the others lack. See Kersten, *The Kersten Memoirs*, 132ff.

11. Yehuda Bauer, *Jews for Sale?: Nazi-Jewish Negotiations, 1933–1945* (New Haven and London: Yale University Press, 1994), 102f.

12. Kersten, *The Kersten Memoirs*, 132.

13. Ibid., 133.

14. Richard Breitman, *The Architect of Genocide: Himmler and the Final Solution* (New York: Alfred A. Knopf, 1991), 237ff.

15. As quoted in Yitzhak Arad, *Belzec, Sobibor, Treblinka: The Operation Reinhard Death Camps* (Bloomington and Indianapolis: Indiana University Press, 1987), 47.

16. Chaim A. Kaplan, *Scroll of Agony: The Warsaw Diary of Chaim A. Kaplan*, trans. Abraham I. Katsh (New York: Collier/Macmillan, 1973), 379.

17. Ibid., 382.

18. Adam Czerniakow, *The Warsaw Diary of Adam Czerniakow*, ed. Raul Hilberg, Stanislaw Staron, and Josef Kermisz (New York: Stein and Day/Scarborough, 1982), 23.

19. Kaplan, *Scroll of Agony*, 385.

20. As quoted in State of Israel, Ministry of Justice, *The Trial of Adolf Eichmann: Record of Proceedings in the District Court of Jerusalem*, 5 vols. (Jerusalem: Trust for the Publication of the Proceedings of the Eichmann Trial, 1993), 4:1563.

21. Ibid.

22. Ibid.

23. See Wasser, *Himmlers Raumplanung im Osten*, 60ff.

24. Rudolf Höss, *Death Dealer: The Memoirs of the SS Kommandant at Auschwitz*, ed. Steven Paskuly, trans. Andrew Pollinger (Buffalo: Prometheus Books, 1992), 255f.

25. Wasser, *Himmler's Raumplanung im Osten*, 109ff., 126ff.

26. State of Israel, *The Trial of Adolf Eichmann*, 4:1474.

27. Rudolf Vrba and Alan Bestic, *I Cannot Forgive* (London: Sidgwick and Jackson, and Anthony Gibbs and Philllips, 1963), 10ff.

28. Ibid., 14.

29. Höss, *Death Dealer*, 286f.

30. PMOB, box BW (B) 30/30, 23; BW (B) 30/26, 22.

31. Höss, *Death Dealer*, 287.

32. Ibid., 32f.

33. Letter of Ziegler to Himmler, 18 February 1942, PAK, coll LO/S, file 467, 132.

34. Höss, *Death Dealer*, 288.

35. Ibid., 290.

36. The construction of the treatment plants generated a lot of paper work; some key documents are the following: ''Richtlinien nr. 35 für vorläufige Massnahmen zur Gewinnung eines hygienisch einwandfreien Trinkwassers und zur hygienisch einwand-freien Abwasserbeseitigung,'' PMOB, box, BW 29/2, file BW 29/13, 27f.; letter of Bischoff to Kammler, 26 July 1943, PMOB, box BW 1/5, file 1/17; ''Aktenver-merk betr.: besuch des Hauptamtschef . . . Pohl in Auschwitz, 17. August 1943,'' OAM, coll. 502/1, file 233; (USHRI, microfilm RG 11.001M.03, reel 35).

37. Vrba, *I Cannot Forgive*, 90.

38. This is important, as it explains why the bunkers and crematoria IV and V did not appear on the master plan of 15 August 1942.

39. PMOB, box BW (B) 30b, file 30c/22.

40. ''Aktenvermerk Betr.: Anwesenheit von Obering. Prüfer der Fa. Topf u.

Söhne Erfurt, bezüglich Ausbau der Einäscherungsanlagen im K.G.L. Auschwitz,'' OAM, coll. 502/1, file 26; (USHRI, microfilm RG 11.001M.03—20.

41. PMOB, box, BW (B) 30b, file 30c/23.

42. As quoted in International Military Tribunal, *Trial of the Major War Criminals*, 46 vols. (Nuremberg: Secretariat of the International Military Tribunal, 1947), 11:417.

43. Andrzej Strzelecki, ''The Plunder of Victims and Their Corpses,'' in Yisrael Gutman and Michael Berenbaum, eds., *Anatomy of the Auschwitz Death Camp* (Bloomington and Indianapolis: Indiana University Press, 1994), 253f.

44. Vrba, *I Cannot Forgive*, 133.

45. Albert Speer, *Infiltration: How Heinrich Himmler Schemed to Build an SS Industrial Empire*, trans. Joachim Neugroschel (New York: Macmillan, 1981), 23.

46. PMOB, file BW (B) 30/34, 96.

47. PMOB, file BW (B) 30/12.

48. Raul Hilberg, *Die Vernichtung der europäischen Juden*, 3 vols. (Frankfurt: Fischer Taschenbuch, 1990), 3:1300; Franciszek Piper, *Die Zahl der Opfer von Auschwitz*, trans. Jochen August (Oswiecim: Panstwowe Muzeum w Oswiecimiu, 1993), table D (between 144 and 145).

49. Joseph Billig, ''The Launching of the 'Final Solution,' '' in Serge Klarsfeld, ed., *The Holocaust and the Neo-Nazi Mythomania*, trans. Barbara Rucci (New York: Beate Klarsfeld Foundation, 1978), 65f.

50. Georges Wellers, ''The Number of Victims and the Korherr Report,'' ibid., 145ff.

51. Ibid., 183, 194.

52. Ibid., 206.

53. Ibid., 173.

54. Hans Stosberg, ''Erläuterungsbericht zum Bebauungsplan für die Stadt Auschwitz O/S,'' Archive Gutschow, Absteinach, 6.

55. PMOB, file BW (B) 30/27, 17.

56. ''Aktenvermerk Betr.: Stromversorgung und Installation des KL und KGL,'' OAM, coll. 502/1, file 26 (USHRI, microfilm RG 11.001M.03, reel 20).

57. See Jean-Claude Pressac, *Auschwitz: Technique and Operation of the Gas Chambers*, trans. Peter Moss (New York: Beate Klarsfeld Foundation, 1989), 481ff.

58. PMOB, file BW (B) 30/41, 28

59. Danuta Czech, *Kalendarium der Ereignisse im Konzentrationslager Auschwitz-Birkenau, 1939–1945*, trans. Jochen August, Nina Kozlowski, Silke Lent, and Jan Parcer (Reinbek: Rowohlt, 1989), 440.

60. Ibid., 445.

61. Transfer agreement of 19 and 22 March 1943, OAM, coll. 502/2, file 54 (USHRI, microfilm RG 11.001M.03, reel 21); letter of WVHA, 24 June 1944, OAM, coll. 502/1, file 281 (USHRI, microfilm RG 11.001M.03, reel 37).

62. Letter of Topf, 10 May 1943, PMOB, file BW (B) 30/34; also Pressac, *Auschwitz*, 386ff.

63. Transfer agreement of 24 June 1943, PMOB, file BW (B) 30/43.

64. Czech, *Kalendarium*, 374.

65. Vrba, *I Cannot Forgive*, 18.

66. Letter of Bischoff to Kammler, 4 June 1943; PMOB, box BW 1/3, 106.

67. Franciszek Piper, ''The System of Prisoner Exploitation,'' in Gutman and Berenbaum, eds., *The Anatomy of the Auschwitz Death Camp*, 34ff.; Shmuel Krakowski, ''The Satellite Camps,'' ibid., 50ff.

68. Hilberg, *Die Vernichtung der europäischen Juden*, 3:1300; Piper, *Die Zahl der Opfer von Auschwitz*, table D (between 144 and 145).

69. Lucy S. Dawidowicz, ed., *A Holocaust Reader* (New York: Behrman House, 1976), 131ff.

70. Speer, *Infiltration*, 289.

71. Filip Müller, *Auschwitz Inferno: The Testimony of a Sonderkommando*, with Helmut Freitag, trans. Susanne Flatauer (London and Henley: Routledge & Kegan Paul, 1979), 124.

72. Ibid., 126.

73. Ibid., 130.

74. Ibid., 132.

75. Ibid., 123f.

76. As quoted in Speer, *Infiltration*, 289.

77. Alexander Ehrmann, interview with Debórah Dwork, West Bloomfield, Mich., 15 November and 13 December 1986 and 24 January 1987, transcript, 34f.

78. Ibid., 37f.

79. Sara Grossman-Weil, interview with Debórah Dwork, Malverne, N.Y., 29 and 30 April 1987, transcript, 22.

80. Josef Zelkowicz, ''Days of Nightmare,'' in Dawidowicz, ed. *A Holocaust Reader*, 301f.

81. Grossman-Weil, transcript, 21; also Dwork, *Children With A Star*, 195f.

82. Grossman-Weil, transcript, 27; also Dwork, *Children With A Star*, 205.

83. Grossman-Weil transcript, 28; Dwork, *Children With A Star*, xixf.

84. Grossman-Weil transcript, 29.

85. Ibid.

86. Ibid., 30.

87. Ibid., 34.

88. Ibid.

89. Ibid., 28; Dwork, *Children With A Star*, xixf.

90. Müller, *Auschwitz Inferno*, 61.

91. Ibid., 60f.

92. Ibid., 115f.

93. Hannah Arendt, *Eichmann in Jerusalem*: *A Report on the Banality of Evil* (New York: Viking, 1963), 255f.

Epilogue

1. Jane Perlez, "Survivors Pray at the Crematories at Auschwitz," *New York Times*, 27 January 1995.

2. See Heinrich Freiherr Senfft von Pilsach, "Expellees in the Federal Republic of Germany," in Goettingen Research Committee, ed., *Eastern Germany*: *A Handbook*, 3 vols. (Würzburg: Holzner Verlag, 1960), 3:107ff.

3. Wolf Jobst Siedler, *Weder Maas noch Memel*: *Ansichten vom beschädigten Deutschland* (Stuttgart: Deutsche Verlags-Anstalt, 1982), 37.

4. Walter Kuhn, "Eine Jugend für die Sprachinselforschung," in *Neue Beiträge zur schlesischen Siedlungsgeschichte* (Sigmaringen: Jan Thorbecke, 1984), 270.

5. Walter Kuhn, "Siedlungsgeschichte des Auschwitzer Beskidenvorlandes," in *Neue Beiträge zur schlesischen Siedlungsgeschichte*, 166.

6. Gordon Craig in interview, *Der Spiegel*, 13 November 1989, 185.

7. David Irving, the godfather of the Holocaust deniers and the ally of German Neo-Nazis, predicts that in the year 2,000 the lost territories will have returned to Germany. See David Irving, *Deutschlands Ostgrenze*: *Weder Oder noch Neisse—Die Rückkehr des deutschen Ostens* (Kiel: Arndt, 1990).

8. Wolf Jobst Siedler et al., *Deutsche Geschichte im Osten Europas*: *Eine Bilanz in 10 Bänden* prospectus (Berlin: Siedler, n.d.), 4.

9. Ibid., 4f.

10. Ibid.

11. Ibid., 14f.

12. Rudolf Augstein, *Preussens Friedrich und die Deutschen* (Nördlingen: Franz Greno, 1986), 8.

13. Norbert Conrads, "Schlussbetrachtung," in Norbert Conrads, ed., *Deutsche Geschichte im Osten Europas*: *Schlesien* (Berlin: Siedler, 1994), 701.

14. Iwona Irwin-Zarecka, "Poland, after the Holocaust," in *Remembering for the Future*: *Working Papers and Addenda*, 3 vols. (Oxford: Pergamon Press, 1989), 1:147.

15. Debórah Dwork, *Children With A Star*: *Jewish Youth in Nazi Europe* (New Haven and London: Yale University Press, 1991), 210.

16. As quoted in S. I. Minerbi, "Pope John Paul II and the Shoah," in *Remembering for the Future*, 3:2976.

17. Irwin-Zarecka, "Poland, after the Holocaust," 147.

18. Wladyslaw T. Bartoszewski, *The Convent at Auschwitz* (New York: George Braziller, 1991), 7.

19. Minerbi, "Pope John Paul II and the Shoah," 2977.

20. Ibid., 2984.

21. Ibid., 2983.

22. Jane Perlez, "Separate Auschwitz Services Highlight Jewish-Polish Dispute," *New York Times*, 26 January 1995.

23. Perlez, "Survivors Pray at the Crematories of Auschwitz."

24. Telephone conversation, Elie Wiesel and Debórah Dwork, 29 March 1995.

25. Jane Perlez, "In Auschwitz, Snow Faintly Falls on the Living and the Dead," *New York Times*, 28 January 1995. N.B.: President Walesa's speeches were printed prior to his discussion with Elie Wiesel. The word "Jew" is nowhere to be found in these printed editions. Telephone conversation, Elie Wiesel and Debórah Dwork, 29 March 1995.

26. Letter of Bischoff to WVHA/C:I, 4 June 1943, PMOB, box, BW 1/3, 106.

27. The jury of the competition was chaired by the English sculptor Henry Moore. After an initial selection seven teams were invited to submit designs in a second round. Three of these revised proposals were considered to be good, yet none was judged to be "entirely adequate." The best of the three was the project under discussion, submitted by Oskar and Zofia Hansen, Jerzy Jarnuszkiewicz, Julian Palka, Lechoslaw Rosinski, Edmund Kupiecki, and Tadeusz Plasota. This team's approach to the problem was considered "exceptionally brilliant," yet the protests of the former inmates and the lack of a plastic element that could provide an emotional focus was seen as problematic. See Henry Moore's comments in *Auschwitz Monument* (Oswiecim: Panstwowe Muzeum, 1959) and Jadwiga Bezwinska et al., *Katalog Wystawy Projektow Nadeslanych Na Miedzynarodowy Konkurs Budowy Pomnika w Oswiecimiu* (Oswiecim: Panstwowe Muzeum, 1959).

FULL TITLES OF
SOURCES REFERRED TO
IN THE CAPTIONS

Gunther d'Alquen, Editorial note to the first installment of Erich Edwin Dwinger, "Die letzten Reiter," *Das Schwarze Korps* 2 (6 February 1936): 18.

Udo Arnold et al., *800 Jahre Deutscher Orden: Ausstellung des Germanischen National-museums Nürnberg in Zusammenarbeit mit der Internationalen Historischen Kommission zur Erforschung des Deutschen Ordens* (Gütersloh and Munich: Bertelsmann Lexikon, 1990).

Vernon Bartlett, *Nazi Germany Explained* (London: Victor Gollancz, 1933).

Petrus Bertius, *P. Bertij Tabularum geographicarum contractarum Libri Septem* (Amsterdam: Jodocus Hondius, 1616).

Carl Culemann, "Die Gestaltung der städtischen Siedlungsmasse," *Raumforschung und Raumordnung: Monatschrift der Reichsarbeitsgemeinschaft für Raumforschung* 5 (1941): 122–34.

"Die Juden müssen arbeiten!," *Illustrierter Beobachter* 14 (12 October 1939): 1546–47.

Sutherland Edwards, *The Polish Captivity: An Account of the Present Position of the Poles in the Kingdom of Poland, and in the Polish Provinces of Austria, Prussia, and Russia*, 2 vols. (London: W. H. Allen, 1863).

Herbert Erb, ed., *Der Arbeitsdienst: Ein Bildberichtbuch* (Berlin: Freiheitsverlag, 1935).

Gottfried Feder, with Fritz Rechenberg, *Die neue Stadt: Versuch der Begründung einer neuen Stadtplanungskunst aus der sozialen Struktur der Bevölkerung* (Berlin: Julius Springer, 1939).

Walther Franz, *Wir Preussen!* (Berlin: Edwin Runge, 1936).

Emil Gassner, ed., *Im Dienste Europas: Fünf Jahre deutscher Arbeit im Generalgouvernement* (Cracow: Zeitungsverlag Krakau-Warschau, 1944).

Paul Gauss, ed., *Das Buch vom deutschen Volkstum: Wesen-Lebensraum-Schicksal* (Leipzig: Brockhaus, 1935).

Helmut Gauweiler, *Deutsches Vorfeld im Osten: Bildbuch über das Generalgouvernement* (Cracow: Buchverlag Ost, 1941).

Wilhelm Grebe, "Wiedergesundung und Neuausrichtung des ländlichen Bauwesen: Zu dem Bauernhof-Wettbewerb, 1941–1942, *Monatshefte für Baukunst und Städtebau* 26 (1942): 213–20.

Karl Gruber, *Die Gestalt der deutschen Stadt: Ihr Wandel aus der geistigen Ordnung der Zeiten* (Munich: Georg D. W. Callwey, 1952).

Karl Haushofer, *Grenzen in ihrer geographischen und politischen Bedeutung* (Berlin-Grunewald: Kurt Vowinckel, 1927).

Karl Haushofer and Gustav Fochler-Haube, eds., *Welt in Gärung: Zeitberichte deutscher Geopolitiker* (Leipzig and Berlin: Breitkopf & Härtel/Deutscher Verlag für Politik und Wirtschaft, 1937).

————, *Weltpolitik von Heute* (Berlin: "Zeitgeschichte" Verlag und Vertriebs-Gesellschaft, 1939).

Friedrich Heiss and A. Hillen-Ziegfeld, eds., *Deutschland und der Korridor* (Berlin: Volk und Reich Verlag, 1933).

Peter Hellman, Lili Meier, and Beate Klarsfeld, *The Auschwitz Album: A Book Based upon an Album Discovered by a Concentration Camp Survivor, Lilie Meier* (New York: Random House, 1981).

Otto Helmut, *Volk in Gefahr: Der Geburtenrückgang und seine Folgen für Deutschlands Zukunft* (Munich: J. F. Lehmanns, 1934).

Hans Joachim Hemigk, *Oberschlesische Landbaukunst um 1800* (Berlin: Verlag für Kunstwissenschaft, 1937).

Jost Hermand, *Der alte Traum vom neuen Reich: Völkische Utopien und Nationalsozialismus* (Frankfurt: Athenäum, 1988).

Heinrich Himmler, "Deutsche Burgen im Osten," *Das Schwarze Korps* 7 (23 January 1941): 4.

Willy Hoehm, *Wir Brandenburger!* (Berlin: Edwin Runge, 1935).

Werner vom Hofe and Peter Seifert, *Die Ewige Strasse: Geschichte unseres Volkes* (Dortmund and Breslau: W. Crüwell, 1943).

Rudolf Höss, *Death Dealer: The Memoirs of the SS Kommandant at Auschwitz*, ed. Steven Paskuly, trans. Andrew Pollinger (Buffalo: Prometheus Books, 1992).

Hanns Johst, *Ruf des Reiches—Echo des Volkes: Eine Ostfahrt* (Munich: Franz Eher Nachfolger, 1940).

Wolfgang Jünger, *Kampf um Kautschuk* (Leipzig: Wilhelm Goldmann, 1942).

Hans Krieg et al., *Deutsches Schicksal: Der Bauer und das Reich* (Stuttgart: Stuttgarter Verlags-Institut, n.d.).

Der Landrat in Saybusch, *Heimatkalender des Beskidenkreis Saybusch*, 1941 (Gleiwitz: Gauverlag NS Schlesien, 1941).

"Nützbringend verwandt," *Das Schwarze Korps* 7 (26 June 1941): 8.

Oberschlesische Heimatbund, *Oberschlesische Heimatkalender für das Jahr 1943* (Breslau: Schlesien, 1943).

Günter Pahl, "Das grössere Oberschlesien," *Die Woche*, 16 April 1941, 6.

Gustav Paul, *Grundzüge der Rassen- und Raumgeschichte des deutschen Volkes* (Munich: Lehmanns, 1935).

Rudolf Proksch, ''Artamanen: Der Beginn einer Bewegung zur Heimkehr der Jugend aufs Land,'' *Wille und Macht* 10, no. 5 (May 1942): 16–28.

Alfred Pudelko, *Wir Schlesier!* (Berlin: Edwin Runge, 1937).

Reichsführer-SS, SS-Hauptamt, *Der Untermensch* (Berlin: Nordland, 1942).

Reichsheimstättenamt der Deutschen Arbeitsfront, Hauptabteilung Städtebau und Wohnungsplanung, *Siedlungsgestaltung aus Volk, Raum und Landschaft, 5. Planungsheft: Das deutsche Siedlungsbild im Osten* (Berlin: Verlag der deutschen Arbeitsfront, 1941).

Reichsheimstättenamt der Deutschen Arbeitsfront, Hauptabteilung Städtebau und Wohnungsplanung, *Siedlungsgestaltung aus Volk, Raum und Landschaft, 7. Planungsheft/1. Teil: Die Gestaltung des Dorfes* (Berlin: Verlag der deutschen Arbeitsfront, 1941).

Reichskommissar für die Festigung deutschen Volkstums, Stabshauptamt, Hauptabteilung: Planung und Boden, *Neue Dorflandschaften: Gedanken und Pläne zum Ländlichen Aufbau in den neuen Ostgebieten und im Altreich* (Berlin: Verlag deutsche Landbuchhandlung Sohnrey, 1943).

E. Reventlow, *Judas Kampf und Niederlage in Deutschland: 150 Jahre Judenfrage* (Berlin: ''Zeitgeschichte'' Verlag und Vertriebs-Gesellschaft, 1937).

Friedrich Wilhelm Runge, ed., *Das Buch des deutschen Bauern* (Berlin: Zentral-Verlag, 1935).

Werner Schäfer, *Konzentrationslager Oranienburg: Das Anti-Braunbuch über das erste deutsche Konzentrationslager* (Berlin: Buch und Tiefdruck-Gesellschaft, 1934).

Gerhard Schultze-Pfaelzer, *Hindenburg und Hitler zur Führung vereint* (Berlin: Verlagsanstalt Otto Stollberg, 1933).

Rudolf Strass, ''Des Baltenlandes deutsche Stunde,'' *Die Woche* 20 (23 March 1918): 283–86.

Alfred Thoss, *Heimkehr der Volksdeutschen* (Berlin: Zentralverlag der NSDAP, Franz Eher Nachf., 1941)

Walther Threde and Peter Nasaski, *Posen und sein preussische Streifen, 1919–1939* (Berlin and Bonn: Westkreuzer 1983).

Kurt Trampler, *Am Volksboden und Grenze* (Heidelberg and Berlin: Kurt Vowinckel, 1935).

Upper Silesia, Office of the Gauleiter as Representative of RfSS-RKfdFdV, *Entwicklung, Organisation, Arbeitsleistung der Dienststelle des Gauleiters und Oberpräsidenten als Beauftragter des Reichsführers SS Reichskommissar für die Festigung deutschen Volkstums in Oberschlesien vom Sept. 1939 bis Jan. 1943* (Kattowitz, 1943).

Gerhard Ziegler, ''Grundlagen des künftigen Städtebaus in Oberschlesien,'' *Raumforschung und Raumordnung: Monatschrift der Reichsarbeitsgemeinschaft für Raumforschung* 5, (1941): 151–159.

INDEX

Page numbers in *italics* refer to maps and illustrations.
Letter page references indicate plate section.

425